D1351442

Items should be returned on or before the last date shown below. Items not already requested by other borrowers may be renewed in person, in writing or by telephone. To renew, please quote the number on the barcode label. To renew on line a PIN is required. This can be requested at your local library.
Renew online @ **www.dublincitypubliclibraries.ie**
Fines charged for overdue items will include postage incurred in recovery. Damage to or loss of items will be charged to the borrower.

IRELAND 1963

A Year of Marvels, Mysteries, Merriment
and Misfortune

The Author

Kevin C. Kearns, Ph.D., is a social historian and Professor Emeritus at the University of Northern Colorado. He has written more than ten books on Dublin, most notably *Dublin Tenement Life*, which was number 1 on the *Irish Times* bestseller list for many weeks. He now resides in Maine.

Also by Kevin C. Kearns

Georgian Dublin: Ireland's Imperilled Architectural Heritage
Dublin's Vanishing Craftsmen
Stoneybatter: Dublin's Inner Urban Village
Dublin Street Life and Lore: An Oral History
Dublin Tenement Life: An Oral History
Dublin Pub Life and Lore: An Oral History
Dublin Voices: An Oral History
Streets Broad and Narrow: Images of Vanishing Dublin
Dublin's Lost Heroines
The Bombing of Dublin's North Strand, 1941
Ireland's Arctic Siege
The Legendary 'Lugs' Branigan

IRELAND 1963

A Year of Marvels, Mysteries, Merriment and Misfortune

KEVIN C. KEARNS ～

Gill Books

Gill Books
Hume Avenue
Park West
Dublin 12
www.gillbooks.ie

Gill Books is an imprint of M.H. Gill & Co.

© Kevin C. Kearns 2018
978 07171 8078 3

Print origination by O'K Graphic Design, Dublin
Copy-edited by Seirbhísí Leabhar
Proofread by Neil Burkey
Printed by CPI Group (UK) Ltd, Croydon CR0 4YY

This book is typeset in 11/15 pt Minion.

The paper used in this book comes from the wood pulp of managed forests. For every tree felled, at least one tree is planted, thereby renewing natural resources.

A CIP catalogue record for this book is available from the British Library.

5 4 3 2 1

*To Cathe, my companion, for steadying life's course
and sharing the journey.*

ACKNOWLEDGEMENTS

I owe much appreciation to all those persons featured in this book who shared with me their personal oral histories. Their words, and emotions, placed me 'on the spot' and 'in the moment' over fifty years ago as events unfolded in 1963. This provided an authenticity and immediacy, which enabled me to write a 'grass roots' social history of that extraordinary year.

Particular gratitude is due to those such as Éamonn Fitzpatrick, who was a young Dublin Fire Brigade member back then and was one of the first men on the tragic scene of the Fenian Street tenements collapse. To him fell the wrenching task of lifting the limp bodies of two cherubic little girls from the rubble. Tony Doran, bus conductor, caught on duty in Dublin's worst 'flash flood' in living memory. Dockers Martin Mitten and Willie Murphy who fought to hold on to a trade that was becoming extinct before their eyes. Maureen Lynch, canal-side cottage dweller who faced a threat by Government to fill in the canals for motorways. Publican Tommy Smith, who as a young barman had to witness the desecration and destruction of lovely old Victorian pubs he loved. Bridie Colgan, who had the joy of getting into the Adelphi Theatre that magical night when The Beatles stormed the stage. Young zoo attendant Gerry Creighton, who struggled to keep the animals safe from the blizzards and deadly cold of January.

Special thanks are extended to those few gardaí who were chosen to serve as President Kennedy's personal motorcycle escort during his historic four-day visit – often only feet away from him, on and off their cycles, and sometimes standing directly beside him to keep the thrusting crowds back. Their first-hand, participatory experiences inject great life into the book.

Sitting with such persons, the small Sony tape recorder whirring softly, oral history does not get any more intimate.

As always, my archival research at the Dublin City Library and Archive on Pearse Street was flawlessly facilitated by Dr Mary Clark and her superb staff. Welcoming and highly professional, they made my research especially enjoyable.

My publisher, Gill Books (formerly Gill & Macmillan), have for the past twenty-two years made me feel 'part of the family', always supportive and deft in shepherding me through the editorial process. Director Nicki Howard, Commissioning Editor Deirdre Nolan and Managing Editor Catherine Gough create a harmony in which revisions and reductions are made in a compatible spirit. While Teresa Daly oversaw the design of the book jacket, blurb and publicity, allowing me generous input.

Inexpressible gratitude goes to my partner, Cathe Brown, who for twenty-two years has encouragingly supported my various book projects – while cheerfully accepting the quirks of my writing life. Sharing life's joys and sorrows, she is an anchor in every storm, providing comfort, tranquility and indefinable happiness.

CONTENTS

PROLOGUE

A year of which the stories will forever remain a part of history ... Outstanding events of this most sensational of years.

Irish Press, 31 DECEMBER 1963

I t was a year like no other. Not for any single monumental or transformative event but for an astonishing sequence of occurrences – triumphs and tragedies, joys and sorrows – stretching from the first day of January to the last of December. As well as having a scattering of bizarre 'happenings' (in the jargon of the sixties), it was an unrelenting roller-coaster ride of dramas, traumas, mysteries and felicities, often inexplicable, and inexpressible. On 31 December the *Irish Press* summed it up: 'The year of sensations'.

It was a dizzying series of events: nature gone awry with blizzards, paralysing cold, torrential rain, a flash flood of biblical proportions and spectacular electrical storms. There was commotion in the streets: hooliganism by GAA supporters, battles for the preservation of Georgian buildings, dockers' marches, demonstrations by angry housewives, eruptions of Beatlemania – protests following protests.

In Dublin there was a cityscape imperilled by tenement collapses and massive evacuations, and by threats to St Stephen's Green, to its canals and to the Olympia Theatre. There was news of a socially transformative bingo craze, a UFO sighting, an Aga Khan Cup victory, a daring heist and kidnapping, the 'Great Walk', a frightening mystery caller and a prehistoric reptile.

There were also the tragedies of record road deaths and drownings, a macabre murder mystery, the unexpected death of a beloved cardinal, and of a Pope, and the shocking deaths of university students in the Dublin Mountains. But these incidents were interspersed with a variety of happy events, which helped to balance people's emotions.

And, of course, there was President John F. Kennedy's triumphant 'homecoming' – followed only months later by his devastating assassination. The year had as its climax the drama of thirty Irish passengers on board the liner *Lakonia*, 'ablaze and sinking' during Christmas week.

All this occurred within the span of but one year. Journalists struggled to try and capture the ethos of this phenomenal year, drawing upon grandiose prose and evocative descriptions. More than half a century later it is no easier a challenge to do justice to the year 1963. In fact, it is all the more improbable. To be sure, countless books have been written about one of the year's events: Kennedy's four-day visit in June. This has tended to leave the impression – a highly inaccurate one – that it was the only newsworthy event of that year.

Unlike those books, this is not a clinical historical book, nor is it a work of political or diplomatic study. Only part of it is devoted to Kennedy's visit – and this is treated in a personal manner, as a homecoming affecting ordinary people.

This book deals primarily with other subjects, many of which were missed or dismissed or have been long forgotten. It is a *biography*, of an unconventional, social-historical and grass-roots sort. Such an inimitable and idiosyncratic year begs for an off-beat approach.

Biographies are not limited to the history of persons. They can be an account of a coin, a building, a painting, a sculpture or a document. It could be of a particular place or period. In 1936 Christine Longford wrote *A Biography of Dublin*, in which she sought to identify aspects of the city's unique character. Eric Burns's book *1920: The Year That Made the Decade Roar* is a biographical examination of a single year during America's Roaring Twenties.[1]

In many respects, the biography of a year parallels the life of a person. Both are normally greeted with hope and promise. They follow the seasons, from youth to middle age, before facing the winter of their lives – eventual decline and demise.

Along life's way, each develops a unique ethos, or character, leaving behind their own biographical record, as well as a reputation, which may be enduring. Left behind are their aspirations, successes and failures, as well as their blunders and moral lapses – their shining moments and mixed legacies. Those who study them, years later, must search for every defining feature, just as a conventional biographer includes every oddity of personality.

Herein lies the challenge of producing a biography of the year 1963. For it was a bewildering, paradoxical and emotionally conflicting year – one of stunning contradictions and contrasts, of surprises and whimsical doings, and *never* dull or uneventful.

My objective has been to weave a coherent and colourful tapestry of this wondrous year, excavating for hidden or unchronicled features and events, and to capture the life-ways of ordinary people, who gave the year its fascinating character. Sometimes the smallest things can tell us much about the human condition. All this is part of a year's composite 'being'.

This required the discovery of information and personal testimony not found in previous books or writings. To accomplish this, I relied on oral history to create an authenticity and immediacy for the year 1963 – to *humanise* it through words and emotions shared more than fifty years later.

Drawing on forty-two years of oral history research in Ireland, and on a dense social network throughout Dublin, I tracked down observers of, and participants in, some of the most riveting events of that year. Their testimony allows the reader to feel the very pulse of the historic moment. For instance, the firefighter Éamonn Fitzpatrick was one of the first brigade men on the scene of the horrifying Fenian Street tenement collapse, and to him fell the dreadful task of lifting out the limp bodies of the two little girls crushed in the ruins. His story has never before been told. His words are still vivid, and emotions raw.

The gardaí Paddy Farrell, Bill Herlihy and Séamus McPhillips, now well into their eighties, were assigned to the Garda security team that was to remain close to President Kennedy in order to keep him safe while on Irish soil. Their recollections include verbal exchanges with him, as well as unexpected problems and the need for spontaneous reactions. They convey surprising candour and feeling, so many years later.

At year's end, every Irish newspaper justifiably described 1963 in exalted, grandiose language. On New Year's Eve the *Sunday Independent* chose to quote Dickens, calling it 'the best of times, the worst of times'.

Or, as the 83-year-old Una Shaw, of Rutland Street, recalled fifty-two years later, '1963 … Well, an awful lot happened in that year.'

Chapter 1 ~

1962's CHURLISH FAREWELL

December 1962

No-one, it seemed, had spotted his missing leprechaun.

The respectable middle-aged man, attired in suit and tie, had just left the Olympia Theatre in Dublin after the evening's performance. Walking hurriedly along Dame Street, wearing a distressed expression, he politely, and earnestly, asked people in his path, 'Pardon me, but have you seen my leprechaun?'

Puzzled by the odd question from a refined stranger, they kindly replied, 'No, I'm afraid I haven't.'

Then the man was off again down the street, looking left and right. Befuddled by the brief encounter, most people glanced back over their shoulders, wondering what in the world he was talking about.

The merry month of December was off to a good start with a spell of fine weather and excellent offerings at Dublin's cinemas and theatres. The Meteorological Office described the comfortable winter conditions as 'quiet and relatively mild with moderate winds from the southwest or west' – perfect weather for the throngs of Christmas shoppers jamming the streets in high spirits. And the weather was projected to last all the way to New Year's Eve. Meteorologists seemed confident that the year 1962 would depart benignly and with dignity.

Throughout the first two weeks of the month the weather indeed remained mild and calm, with patches of fog at times. Shoppers didn't have to worry about getting soaked, frozen or wind-whipped, as so often happened in December. This allowed adults and children to linger outside, enjoying the dazzling decorations as streets were festooned with red, green and gold garlands, and with bells, wreaths and holly. Seeing the elaborate window displays at Clery's, Switzer's, Arnott's and Brown Thomas, children pressed their noses against the panes to see Santa's workshop busy with elves and reindeer. Carol singers, comfortable for a change, sang with unusual verve. During the sunny spells many people strolled through St Stephen's Green, coveting benches on which to rest their weary legs.

First-rate films and stage shows were always an attraction at Christmastime, competing for audiences. The management of the Olympia proudly put on an extraordinary stage performance that was awing patrons as well as the press. It had succeeded in booking Paul Goldin's famous hypnotism show, which was the rage of Europe, astonishing and transfixing audiences, and leaving them incredulous at what they had seen. As the theatre critic for the *Irish Press* wrote:

> the French telepathist was quite amazing, giving a fantastic demonstration of his gift which he calls a mastery of the sixth sense – thought.[2]

Enrapt audiences had never seen such inexplicable feats of the mind. Drawing upon verified, impartial volunteers from the audience, who he referred to as his 'subjects', he quickly addressed any sceptics in the house. To anyone doubting the authenticity of his performance he offered £1,000, if he 'could be proved a "hoaxer"'. Debunkers could have a try if they wished.

The audience, which happened to include psychologists and garda superintendents as well as theatre critics, watched him bring his subjects 'under his spell'. One demonstration was a favourite of the patrons: he could command a person, who would then be under his mental control, to carry out the most absurd, hilarious deeds. Dignified volunteers might be reduced to performing puerile acts – without realising it. In one case a shy woman from the audience began 'howling like a six-month-old baby'. In another a man commenced seriously playing non-existent musical instruments. People laughed uproariously.

And another man ended up on his hands and knees, searching frantically for his missing (invisible) leprechaun.

One esteemed theatre critic wrote that he marvelled at Goldin's ability as a telepathist, absolutely convinced of the authenticity of the performance. He noted that the audience was 'tickled pink by the absurd antics' of his courageous volunteers, who had been forewarned that his spell might not wear off until some time after the show.

———

By 15 December there was the usual flood of Irish people returning from Britain and elsewhere to spend the holidays at home with family and friends. They were delighted to find such pleasant weather. Shops were bustling, with many reporting business to be up by as much as a quarter on the previous year. Although some women were complaining about turkey prices being high, it didn't deter most from plucking a fat one to take home.

One week before Christmas, weather forecasters described conditions for Dublin as 'fresh and breezy with light showers' and mild temperatures more like spring than winter. Their indications were still that the enjoyable weather would continue through Christmas and beyond. People were counting on it.

However, 'unbeknownst to the nation, a dramatic change' began taking place on 18 December 'over the cold plains of western Russia as an arctic ridge of high pressure extended down into northeastern Europe.'[3] As Ireland was enjoying Atlantic weather, an Arctic system was slowly churning towards continental Europe. Yet Ireland's meteorologists did not issue any warnings or describe dramatic changes on the way. This left many people wistfully hoping for one of those rare white Christmases. The last one was seen in the 1940s. It looked like they would have to be satisfied with the artificial snow in Grafton Street shop windows.

Some happy news arrived from New York. *Time* had chosen Pope John XXIII as its 'man of the year' for 1962. He was the first religious leader to be given the accolade, bestowed for 'what neither science nor diplomacy can provide: a sense of unity as a human family.' His encyclical *Pacem in Terris* condemned racism and endorsed the rights of the world's workers. He was especially revered by the Irish people for having 'humanised' the Catholic Church. People felt a close, loving bond with him. Irish newspapers carried *Time's* announcement for all to read.

By 23 December, with Christmas just around the corner, the arctic invader had marched deeper into Europe as cold air from Russia was being fed westward by an intense anti-cyclone. Snow and freezing temperatures crept across the continent. Ice was already forming in some coastal inlets around the Danish coast – a worrying sign.

On Christmas Eve in Ireland the weather proved fickle, displaying 'many moods'. During the day, as people scurried about doing last-minute tasks, some 'brilliant sunshine' prevailed for a while. By evening this gave way to 'chilly grey overcast' conditions in Dublin. Overnight it would change again, leaving a 'sparkling white frost', hazardous to drivers and pedestrians heading to Mass.

But it was on Christmas Day that the *real* change set in. An unwanted present arrived: as a 'cold, polar airstream was bearing down on Ireland', the temperature tumbled down towards the freezing mark. People indoors, enjoying good conversation before a warm hearth, would not have realised what lay ahead.

Then the first snowflakes, fat and fluffy, drifted down from the grey clouds. Gradually the few became a gentle flurry, first along the east coast, then moving westwards. Some people rushed to their windows to exclaim, 'Snow! Oh, isn't it wonderful!' As the flakes stuck to surfaces, a white coating was being created on the cityscape. In Dublin, by 10 p.m. the streets were layered with a slight frosting – barely enough for the meteorologists to declare it 'officially a "white Christmas"'.

It was just enough for the *Irish Times* to state, 'Snow was visitor on Christmas Day', for the first time in nearly two decades. Now wouldn't it be grand, many thought, if only there could be *more* snow before New Year's Eve so that the children could go sledging? Meteorologists tried to comply with their wishes, predicting that, along with falling temperatures, 'we may see more snow'.

In Dublin, snow at Christmastime not only beautified the city but helped to silence its cacophony, creating an unusual atmosphere of urban tranquillity. That year, however, the traditional calmness of St Stephen's Day was disrupted by a harsh intrusion that assaulted people's eardrums. As the *Irish Times* put it, 'the customary quiet of Anna Liffey was shattered' when speedboats raced in the Castrol Cup for the first time. Their piercing high-powered engines in the heart of the city – right after Christmas – offended the sensibilities of Dubliners. It was an event with 16 speedboats racing back and forth between Butt Bridge and Capel Street – for fifty-five laps! Complaints would flow in for weeks.

By contrast, the Christmas holiday in Limerick was 'one of the quietest on record'. This was with the notable exception of the docks, where the ship *Zapadnaya Dvina* had arrived. The Russian seamen 'provided some excitement', it was reported. Because they did not celebrate Christmas, they faced inactivity and boredom when everything in Limerick shut down. Soon they fell into arguing, which deteriorated into a real row. The shouting drew some local people, who went down to watch, making it one of the liveliest Christmas pageants in town.

The ship's captain decided to settle the dispute in the traditional manner: a duel out on the dockside. With fists. A referee was appointed from among the crew as the ringleaders of the two factions fought it out. For the spectators the entertainment was brief, as the younger and stronger of the two duellists was quickly declared the winner. But it gave Limerick folk something to talk about for a few days.

_____

By 27 December the polar freezing had reached the western coast of Europe. Word was received that ten people had died in France on Christmas Day alone. Some snow was now falling along Ireland's east coast, in some places up to six inches. Many Dubliners gleefully took advantage of the snow on the slopes at Stepaside to enjoy tobogganing. It was the type of falling snow – as opposed to a wind-driven snowstorm – that people had hoped for.

During that night 'most of the country shivered under snow, sleet or hail as the cold spell continued.' In some places the temperature plummeted perilously below freezing. Most counties were now coated with some snow and ice. Motorists were warned by the Automobile Association of driving dangers and told not to go out unless absolutely necessary. Already motorists were reported as being trapped in heavy snowdrifts near the Sally Gap in the Wicklow Mountains, the passengers marooned. Some stranded occupants saw the lights at the Kippure television transmission station and headed towards them for shelter.

On Sunday, the 30th, the weather changed dramatically. By midday a blizzard was raging through parts of counties Wicklow, Dublin, Wexford, Meath, Kildare, Louth and Cork. The landscape was being buried in drifting snow; vehicles were stuck and passengers trapped, and villages were smothered and isolated. One Co. Wicklow farmer, facing twenty-foot drifts on his land, said it was the worst he had seen in his seventy years.

Normal life was becoming paralysed. No-one was prepared. The Government stood mute, unresponsive to the sudden crisis.

Without warning, people were caught in dire circumstances, left to their own initiative. At Kippure, one of the technicians had to go outside to check on equipment only a short distance away. But the gale-force winds held him captive outside. When staff members missed his return, they went in search and rescued him. But the Telefís Éireann crew stationed there were now cut off, as the road to their 2,400-foot mast was made impassable by snowdrifts. No food or water could now reach them.

In Dublin early on Sunday morning, before the blizzard had arrived, Brendan Leathem and Emmet Bergin, van-drivers for Independent Newspapers, were preparing for their regular delivery in the area around Tallaght. It was a trip they'd made umpteen times before. Without forewarning, they had neither heavy clothing nor digging tools. They weren't long out on the lonely road in the dark before the wind kicked up and snow started blowing and drifting. Then their windscreen began freezing over. When they were confronted with near gale-force winds and blinding snow they realised they were in the teeth of a raging blizzard. About thirty miles from Dublin they became bogged down in a snowdrift.

They climbed out and began trekking with heads down, trying to follow a fast-disappearing road. Hours later, and nearly frozen, they reached Baltinglass, Co. Wicklow, where they found shelter at the Garda station. Here they were given tea, bedding – and safety. Unknown to them, Bergin's father, the former senator Patrick Bergin, and a friend, Michael Fleming, had set out by car from Dublin in the swirling snow to find them. But they quickly became snowbound as well.

By Sunday afternoon the winds were reaching seventy miles an hour, whipping up twenty-foot snowdrifts. Buses were becoming stranded on rural roads, some with dozens of frightened passengers. The drivers and conductors were left helpless to assist them. Some twenty-five hikers of An Óige had set out that weekend for a pleasant hike through the Wicklow Mountains, ill-clothed and ill-prepared. Concern for their welfare was mounting.

People living along the east coast stood by their windows in awe of nature's force as monstrous waves of up to thirty feet roared in, smashing sea walls. Among them was Una Malone, a native of Nenagh, Co. Tipperary. She had just returned home to Ireland for the holidays to be with family and friends.

On Sunday 30 December she was staying with friends in Dalkey, Co. Dublin, where the blizzard was particularly vicious. But what a spectacle it was to watch from the window! One crashing wave followed another. By the afternoon she was so intrigued that she decided to go outside to get a closer look and feel its fury. She bundled herself up and headed down to the harbour. Reaching the slipway, she crept a few feet further down. Meanwhile, another resident of the house, Donal Murphy, was watching her with curiosity from his window. And with growing concern.

With an awful suddenness, an enormous wave from what the *Irish Independent* called the 'mountainous seas' rolled in, lifting her like a mannequin and sucking her out into the roiling grey abyss. Shocked, Murphy ran frantically to notify the emergency services, who raised the alarm. But it was far too dangerous for the lifeboat crews to put out at sea.

Everyone knew there was little hope for her survival. She would be among the first to be claimed by the brutal winter of 1962/3.

On Sunday night another harrowing drama was unfolding. On the Hill of Howth, Pat Carthy was returning home when he slipped on an icy, disused railway track and broke his leg. He shouted for help at the top of his lungs, but, with the howling wind, no-one heard him. Here he lay, helpless, near 10 p.m., a hundred yards from the nearest house. He could still see flickering lights in windows, adding frustration to his pain. All he was wearing was a suit and a lightweight mac. A bachelor, he knew there was no-one to immediately miss him. He strained to think clearly:

My leg was in terrible agony. My hands and face lost their feeling. Desperately I tried to keep my mind active. Then suddenly the lights started to go out one by one.[4]

He knew he would now face the night alone.

The following morning, New Year's Eve, people ordinarily awoke with thoughts of welcoming in the new year. But this was no ordinary year. Much of the country was in crisis, with people enduring hardship, marooned or missing. Throughout those counties struck the hardest, 'heavy and persistent snow continued', with winds screaming at sixty miles an hour and higher. Drifts of up to twenty feet were now being widely reported.

On the Hill of Howth, Pat Carthy had to use the full force of his mental discipline to make it through the night. He had dozed in and out of sleep, and perhaps consciousness, through the night's dragging hours. When his spirits were lowest, hopes of seeing the light of dawn kept him going.

When the faint morning light was finally perceptible, he began calling out once more, the strong wind still carrying his voice away. Close to

7:30 visibility was good enough for him to make out moving figures in the distance, but they were still out of contact. Just before 9 a.m., by good fortune he spotted a friend passing by. His emboldened cry for help was heard. An ambulance was summoned, and he was wrapped up in blankets and rushed to hospital. If he could recover sufficiently by New Year's Day, he promised to meet reporters and tell his story.

The Spanish sailor Ricardo Valera was not so fortunate. The trawler *Rosario López* was taking Valera, who had fallen ill, to Bantry Hospital when the rough seas ran the vessel aground on the rocks near Adrigole, Co. Cork, in a thick fog. Eleven crew members scrambled to safety, but by the time Valera could be removed for rescue he had died in the hospital on New Year's Eve.

On the morning of the 31st, the drivers Leathem and Bergin, glad to have survived the previous day, arose and had a hearty breakfast. Then, for some foolish reason, they decided to set out again on foot in the high snow and wind to reach Tallaght. Within a few hours their folly became all too apparent to them. Now they *had* to keep moving for fear of freezing. At one point they had to climb over a twenty-five-foot mound of buried cars. Leathem, with more strength, had to forge ahead, eventually stumbling into Tallaght exhausted almost to the point of unconsciousness. He told the *Irish Times* that it had been a 'nightmare march' for survival.

Late in the day, Peter Yates, of Sandymount, along with a number of other An Óige hikers, reached Blessington after plodding eighteen miles through the blizzard. 'Very bad' all along the route, he said. By evening, most of the other intrepid but utterly naïve hikers would straggle in, some with minor injuries and frostbite. None of the young trekkers expressed any interest in New Year's dancing that night.

Nor did three Dublin women, Elizabeth Mulligan, Marcella Doyle and Elizabeth Delaney. As dusk settled, the three women, who were all pregnant, were counting the hours – and minutes – till midnight on New Year's Eve. Not for the purpose of celebration, however: all were in bed and due to give birth at any moment. Each was left to wonder if their baby would be the last of 1962 – or possibly the *first* of the new year. They all knew what a fuss was made by Dublin's newspapers over the first baby of the new year! A reporter and photographer would show up for an article, often featured on the front page. It was a nice honour – and bit of celebrity for both mother and infant. By 7 p.m., as the minutes ticked away, each woman saw her chances improving.

New Year's Eve in Dublin was as usual alive with throngs of revellers heading to entertainment spots, and then on to Christ Church Cathedral by midnight for the bells ringing in the new year. There was enticing entertainment for those who dared to go out. Some blockbuster films were showing at the cinemas, including a version of Jules Verne's *Five Weeks in a Balloon* at the Capitol, and *Pollyanna,* with Hayley Mills, at the Astoria. At the Gaiety Theatre the ever-popular Jimmy O'Dea was appearing in *Goody Two-Shoes,* always a favourite.

Many would-be celebrants were stuck at home by the storm. Accidents were sending a steady stream of injured people to the city's hospitals.

Mrs Mulligan gave birth to her first child 'a few hours before midnight' at Holles Street Hospital.

Dublin's gardaí and firefighters were on special duty on New Year's Eve, owing to the heavy drinking and wild behaviour that usually occurred. Small bonfires were a feature of many celebrations. That night, with the intense cold, the bonfires roared higher than usual, flames sometimes blazing twenty or thirty feet and becoming uncontrolled in the wind.

Between 8 and 9 p.m. the calls began flooding in to the fire brigade throughout the city. As the night went on, the calls increased, especially at Irishtown, Corporation Street (now James Joyce Street) and Gloucester Place. At Corporation Street an unrestrained crowd were 'throwing tables, chairs, anything they could get their hands on' to fuel the blazes ever higher. More than a hundred belligerent teenagers and men, many of them drunk, began combating the gardaí and firefighters when they showed up. Police dogs had to be called in to break them up. Wild winds whipped some bonfires into raging infernos as dedicated firefighters risked their lives, amidst curses and flying stones and bottles. Before the night was over there would be more than twenty major fires to fight. On New Year's Day fire authorities would declare it the 'worst New Year's *ever*'.

As midnight approached on New Year's Eve, the Russian crew members in Limerick genially raised their glasses and drank to a peaceful New Year. In Russia, Nikita Khrushchev, the Premier, toasted the New Year with what he called a 'realistic warning' to the West that if it unleashed a war it would be utterly smashed within hours – heating up the Cold War.

Across the Atlantic, in the United States, President John F. Kennedy was accustomed to Khrushchev's bombast. This New Year's Eve he and his wife, Jacqueline, were attending a midnight champagne party with friends in Florida. Towards the end of the year there had been some speculation, from reliable sources, that he might visit Ireland in 1963. In Ireland it remained wonderfully wishful thinking.

By 11:50 p.m. the crowd outside Christ Church was estimated at only about a thousand – a fraction of the usual number. One newspaper called it very small but a 'traditional, orderly celebration'. Gardaí huddled in doorways out of the wind.

At 11:52 Mrs Delaney gave birth to a baby girl. This left Mrs Doyle, who was at home in labour, expecting to give birth at any moment. It now looked certain to be recorded as the last baby of 1962 – or heralded as the first of 1963.

When midnight struck, the air rang with the tooting of horns, the sirens of twenty-eight ships in Dublin Harbour and the cheering of crowds. As the mighty bells began to peal, the *Irish Times* covered the scene below:

> Dubliners scorned the bitterly cold winds to give a rousing welcome to 1963 … At Christ Church the arctic weather had little effect on the gaiety … as the crowd was dancing and there was an air of goodwill.[5]

People sang, shouted and shook hands, wishing one another a happy and peaceful new year. They hoped it would be one of tranquillity, free from tumult and harsh weather.

One thing *was* already known: the last hours of 1962 had set in motion a series of events creating havoc and peril throughout the country, fatefully setting the stage for the birth of the new year, 1963.

Chapter 2 ∿

'A GRIM START TO THE NEW YEAR'

It was the soberest start to a New Year that anyone could remember.

TURTLE BUNBURY

New Year's Day, 1963

Surely no new year in Ireland was ever rung in under more dire and dramatic circumstances. At least not in living memory.

The waning hours of 1962 had assured a distressful beginning of the new year – one in which people throughout the country were more concerned with surviving than celebrating. Blizzards, polar cold and fierce winds had buried and paralysed normal life in many counties. 'It was a grim start to the new year all over the country', wrote the *Evening Herald* – the tortured beginning of what would become one of the most extraordinary and fantastical years in Irish history.

With ferocious winds whistling and rattling doors and shutters, many people had slept restlessly, wrought with worry over the threatening storm. At midnight Marcella Doyle of Carna Road in Dublin was awake for a different reason: she was expecting to give birth at any moment. Her husband sat nervously in the next room.

At 12:14 a.m. their new baby, Sarah, entered the world, heralded in the press as the first baby of the new year. When reporters knocked at the door they found the parents beaming and gracious. Though she welcomed a bit of attention, Mrs Doyle candidly confessed that the wonderful experience of childbirth wasn't exactly new to her: Sarah made it an even dozen!

———

With the first light of New Year's Day, people throughout the country wondered how those in other parts had fared. Early radio broadcasts told of people missing, with some feared dead. Those fortunate enough to get their hands on a newspaper, mostly in Dublin, saw from the headlines the extent of the storm:

Irish Times: 'Villages isolated by snowdrifts'.
Irish Independent: 'Food and fuel may be running short'.
Irish Press: 'Army convoy stands by to aid snowbound areas'.
Evening Herald: 'Wicklow still an isolated "snow-man's land"'.

Brendan Leathem and Emmet Bergin, the stranded van-drivers, were now rested and ready to talk. Sitting down with a reporter from the *Irish Times*, they described their ordeal. Leathem called it 'the worst experience of my life … Conditions were unimaginable, but I was determined to make it!' He recalled that, when they stumbled in to Tallaght, looking like two ghosts returning from the Arctic Circle, one observer assessed their haggard forms and called their survival 'an amazing feat of endurance'.

Later on New Year's morning, Pat Carthy, who had his own near-death experience after breaking his leg on the Hill of Howth, was recovering at Jervis Street Hospital and eager to chat to a few reporters:

For me, it was the longest night of my life … I never want to have another like it! I was certainly glad to see the warmth of even a hospital bed.[6]

He attributed his survival to his ability not to fall into a deep sleep during the seemingly endless night alone on the track – and to his faith in his discovery. Was it a 'miracle' that in the early-morning hours a friend had heard his cries? That wasn't for him to say. The *Irish Press* simply titled their article 'Night-long ordeal'.

Elsewhere on the first morning of the new year, Thomas Guy, a farmer from Ballyconneely in Connemara, ventured out to harvest some seaweed washed up by the strong winds. His part of the country had not experienced the heavy snow of Co. Wicklow and the south-east. However, fierce and incessant wind had blown the snow and sand into a newly sculpted landscape, with camouflaged forms hiding perils. Bog holes, ponds and streams were disguised.

But, on this morning, he had no such thoughts on his mind. No-one knew the local terrain better. So he set out across the strand with his horse and cart to gather the seaweed, as he had done countless times in the past. Along the way, he always liked to daydream, since his four-year-old mare knew every step and led him along.

With an awful suddenness, everything changed. His feet first sank to his ankles. Then it was up to his calves. And he kept sinking slowly. He knew he was caught in quicksand – a death trap. Either by instinct or by quick thinking, he acted:

Trapped in quicksand, he saved himself by climbing on to the back of his mare. As the horse struggled, he shouted for help.

The still-brisk wind apparently carried his voice in the right direction, as his cries were heard by two neighbours, Tom McDonagh and John Conneely:

They managed to rescue him with a rope only seconds before the horse and cart disappeared beneath the sand.[7]

The *Irish Press* reporter to whom he later told his chilling story featured it on the front page as a warning to readers to be wary of how the powerful storm had transformed the landscape.

Residents of Co. Wicklow, struck especially hard by the blizzard, needed to be particularly cautious, and were already suffering:

Wicklow was isolated today as hundreds of homes were marooned by 10 and 15-foot-high snowdrifts. Stories of hardship and want are trickling in from marooned homes on the slopes of the mountains where families are cut off.

Supplies of essential foodstuffs were reaching danger level … Roads were virtually blotted out by a treacherous white carpet. The few who ventured out followed routes indicated by electric cables.[8]

That is, if the cables could still be seen. Around Blessington it was verified that the snow had 'drifted as high as the telephone wires'.

Without forewarning, neither shopkeepers nor householders had stocked up on supplies of fuel and food. Families with many members, especially children, were growing desperate. One woman in Donard noted:

> We have no bread, flour or meat … and a candle is worth its weight in gold. We are so badly off for light that families all over the place are dividing half and quarter candles between them.[9]

They also worried about their dwindling supplies of turf and briquettes. Everyone was trying to assess how long they could hold out. It would not be long before some would grow panicky.

At about midday on New Year's Day there was an abatement in the snow and wind in some areas. This provided an opportunity for individuals and gangs of men to launch into action with every digging tool they could get their hands on. Most fortunate were those county councils possessing such heavy equipment as bulldozers, tractors and excavators. In Co. Wicklow every strong back was needed as the engineer Joseph T. O'Byrne organised 250 men 'armed with shovels and spades' to try and break through some of the worst snow-blocked roads, in hopes that food and milk vans might be able to get through. In the Brittas area more than a hundred men, all volunteers, set about trying to reach motorists and their passengers marooned on roads and to get to isolated farms, where they knew children would be in need of food.

Meanwhile, Teilifís Éireann's crews stationed at Kippure, Co. Wicklow, and Mullaghanish, Co. Cork, were barricaded by twenty-foot drifts. Their Land Rovers were useless, since the roads had been buried. When the electricity failed, the transmitter was kept going on a diesel generator. But that could last only so long. Food was rationed and was now cooked on a blow lamp. Kevin O'Connell, the technician in charge at Kippure, described their plight:

> I have never seen anything like it … We did manage to get outside the building for a while today, through a window. To dig away snow piled up against the front door and roof level. Morale is high but we have run out of milk … We are hoping that the roadway to the mountain might be cleared today.[10]

At Mullaghanish, the crew already faced a serious food shortage and decided to take a chance during the lessening of the storm. It called for creativity and courage:

One member of the staff, S. Harvey, a rigger-driver, improvised skis from planks of wood to get down to Ballyvourney – carrying another man on his back.

The two men managed to reach the neighbouring village, secure essential supplies and somehow make it back to the stranded crew.

In Dublin, at the administrative offices of Teilifís Éireann, the story was rather different. Kevin McCourt, the new director-general of RTÉ, had arrived from London on the first day of the new year to assume his duties. His intention had probably been to meet his new colleagues in a congenial atmosphere and ease into his position.

His contract hadn't said anything about managing Teilifís Éireann during a blizzard only shortly after the ink on his contract had dried. Before the day was out he would find himself discussing the proposal of dropping supplies by helicopter to the isolated crews. A TV drama being played out, not on the screen, but in real life.

As dusk fell in Dublin on New Year's Day, just as people were hoping the storm was over, the blizzard started again. And this time meteorologists got their forecast right: 'fresh falls of snow and low temperatures will continue.' By this time, people were reading their copy of the *Evening Herald*, which extended to them a most prophetic New Year's wish:

> We wish all our readers a happy and prosperous 1963. This is a year that should see many significant changes in our ancient land.

With the newspapers dominated by coverage of the storm, many people would have missed a small item tucked away in the *Irish Press*:

> The State Pathologist, Dr Maurice Hickey, will carry out a *post mortem* examination on the body of Mr George Clougher of Four Roads, Roscommon, whose mysterious death is being investigated by the gardaí.[11]

Under the circumstances it could have been passed over, yet the term 'mysterious' might have aroused some readers' curiosity.

Clougher, a man in his fifties, lived with his sister on what was called 'a lonely farm' about eleven miles from Roscommon. It was thought that he had died of food poisoning on 28 December 1962. However, for the previous three days Inspector F. P. Laycock had been carrying out what the Gardaí said was a 'routine investigation'. But some neighbours were suspicious. When asked about it, the Gardaí 'would not say whether they suspected foul play'. Foul play?

In the coming weeks this mysterious case would become bizarre as well, until it eventually made the headlines.

_____

On 2 January all thoughts turned to rescue efforts. An unknown number of people were marooned on roads, trapped or isolated in their homes, or missing. By afternoon the storm had dissipated sufficiently to allow road-clearance gangs to begin their gargantuan task of digging through snowdrifts of up to twenty feet. Some country people found the snow piled up against their doors, windows and even roofs. The *Irish Independent* drew an analogy to their plight:

> Farming people in isolated parts are now in the same peril that often faces sailors on a sinking ship; they cannot be reached because the weather prevents assistance from reaching them.[12]

In higher areas of Co. Wicklow the roads had vanished beneath the deep carpet of snow. They seemed out of reach for rescuers, even those with bulldozers and snowploughs. By late in the day, plans were under way for air-relief efforts. But this was not to be organised by the Government, as it had been in Britain, which had been struck by the same storm system and was using fleets of military helicopters to carry out relief efforts. The Government in Ireland was utterly inert, prompting one newspaper to demand, 'What of official efforts?'

Throughout stricken Ireland, relief would have to be carried out by volunteer citizens and private organisations. The *Evening Herald* led the way with their 'Operation Herald' airlift. The plan was for Captain J. G. O'Donoghue to pilot an eight-seater aircraft from Dublin Airport, loaded with parcels of food, paraffin, matches and medical supplies. These would have to come from generous shopkeepers and private donors. Several of the newspaper's senior reporters were assigned to participate, accompanying the pilot and writing stories for the front page.

One reporter, Barbara Page, grasped the opportunity with zeal, rounding up food supplies for the airlift. 'I did the quickest bit of shopping I have ever done in my life!' Before long, she had hundreds of pounds of sausages, flake meal, soup powder, sugar, biscuits and tea, as well as candles and matches.

Another reporter, John Healy, and the photographer Tony McGrath were anxious to fly what they called their 'mercy missions'. It would be a dazzling but dangerous assignment, sweeping low over the rugged slopes and spotting half-buried villages and houses in great need, and then trying to drop a parcel within reach. Not having any military training in this, the pilot and the reporters faced a challenge in pushing the parcels out at the right moment, as Healy described:

> This 'mercy mission' took us to the hills above Blessington where
> families have been cut off since the blizzard. There did not even seem to
> be a fire in some houses. I saw one cottage with snow as high as the roof.
> It was a vast snowman's land of ice, cold, hunger and hardship.
> Pinpointed against the vast, cruel carpet of white, people waved excitedly
> to us, running toward the parcels we dropped nearby … whole families
> waving their gratitude.[13]

For Captain O'Donoghue and his 'bombardiers', trying to help the television crew marooned atop Kippure was like tossing darts at a small target. As Healy found, 'dropping the parcels was a tricky business because they could have tumbled down the mountainside' if they missed by too much. But after 'two tiny figures came out to wave to us', they gave it a try. They were elated to receive the supplies.

The need for relief in what newspapers were now calling 'Siberian Wicklow' was so great that a second airlift was organised. This one was carried out by the Association for Emergency Relief Operations. They began making two relief runs each day, carrying mostly essential food items. After several days, there was still 'no indication of any Government moves to alleviate the distress' of the suffering thousands.

––––––

Newspapers carried many accounts of the 'heroics' now emerging in what was dubbed the 'land battle' to clear roads in order to reach the needy. Whenever the weather permitted, helpers poured out to volunteer with shovels or picks in hand. County council workers cranked up bulldozers and snow-removal machines, working into the night.

Every newspaper had stories of 'breakthrough victories, small and large'. The *Irish Press* told of Jimmy Craul, a Brittas shopkeeper who, after running out of food for his customers, set out on foot through miles of heavy snowdrift to secure more. Using a large baker's tray, he piled on bread, sausages, butter and sugar, which had to be 'relentlessly dragged after him through drifts of 20 feet … as he fought on bitterly'. He later told a reporter that it was 'the thought of these people that kept me going'.

Séamus Boylan of Valleymount, Co. Wicklow, 'against warnings from gardaí', trekked sixteen miles through blizzard conditions to find food for his ten-month-old baby. 'I *must* get through! I have a baby who must be dying for food … I am *going* and no-one can stop me!'

The Leavy family drew special attention. Mrs Leavy lived in a small dwelling two miles from Brittas with her thirteen-year-old son and three younger daughters. No-one had heard anything from them for more than a week. It was known that they had no electricity, and it was feared that their food and paraffin supplies were running dangerously low. All efforts to reach them had been repelled by drifts of up to fifteen feet. Even a tractor proved to be of no use over the terrain. A neighbour, Larry Healy, who knew the terrain intimately, was warning rescuers that it was 'dangerous to try and walk to the farmhouse … as there were concealed streams under the snow.'

Just when things seemed hopeless, Dick Martin, a skier from Dublin, had an idea. With several other strong skiers, he would set out on a rescue mission *atop* the snow, carrying sacks of food and two gallons of paraffin. Along the way they encountered snowdrifts 'as high as the telephone wires in places'. Finally reaching the Leavy home, they found the family trying to burn green wood for a fire. The mother and children were weakened, but they had been saved in time.

What made the Leavy rescue so astonishing, the *Irish Independent* wrote, was that their drama was taking place 'only 15 miles from the heart of Dublin'. It might as well have been on the Arctic frontier.

By 3 January the Government was under intense pressure from the public and the press, because of its blatant failure to mount a rescue operation. Newspapers demanded to know why there were no rescue helicopters. For years the public had been clamouring for them. The answer had always been the same: the Government had 'not yet finished the report on helicopters'. As the papers printed more graphic accounts of mounting hunger, heatless houses and harrowing suffering, the public's outrage grew. Editors felt a civic duty to express their positions, as did the *Evening Herald* under the heading 'This is the time of crisis':

> The desperate situation of families marooned in snowed-up areas cannot be ignored. Food and fuel supplies are running critically short. Yet there has been no step by authorities to relieve the dire situation.
>
> The Government MUST act without further dillydallying. Surely we have an Air Corps! There has been too much talk and too little action![14]

An army spokesperson said the army was ready to deal with the request for aid – but it had not received an official order.

This meant that the private relief efforts would need to be expanded, as some planes were now flown from morning till dusk, when low-flying missions became dangerous. People on higher ground in south-eastern areas, in effect cut off, had become accustomed to the whirring sound of the propellers overhead. Some waved sheets and coloured blankets, and others tried to stamp out a large x or sos in the snow.

After several days of drops the pilots and reporters became far more accurate. The wind was always a critical factor: in some cases, where people were elderly or infirm, a parcel dropped only twenty yards away could be too far for retrieval. But when the wind died down, a woman living near Blessington had her parcel landed 'only four yards from her front door', as if delivered by hand.

Dedicated Red Cross officials were especially frustrated at their inability to reach people in dire need. T. Lucas, an area director, had two ambulances and crews ready to go – but they couldn't possibly reach people until the roads had been cleared. In one case, a Mrs Keogh had walked through two miles of deep snow in order to reach a telephone to report to the Red Cross that her husband and two children were in immediate need of a doctor, only to be told that they were unreachable.

———

On 5 January the outlook, as reported in the *Irish Independent*, remained bleak: 'the general picture is one of sleet and snow ... deep snowdrifts persisting, lonely farms still cut off.' While pilots could fly over the treacherous landscape, those fighting the land battle had to shovel, hack, chip and curse their way forward a yard at a time. Farmers continued to warn rescuers of the hidden streams and ponds beneath the white blanket. Some rescuers noted that when 'plodding through snowdrifts every step had to be tested with long poles'.

Newspapers were increasingly filled with 'many pathetic stories of want', of families who had 'survived on only the barest necessities'. Such was the case of Gladys Westrop and her two sons, who had been cut off for nearly two weeks and 'lived on porridge and mare's milk'.

Another notable case was that of Joseph O'Loughlin, the popular gamekeeper at Kippure Lodge, who had not been heard from for more than twelve days. The Irish Mountaineering Club eventually formed a volunteer emergency rescue effort:

> In darkness they made their hazardous way up the vast slope to Mr O'Loughlin's house … spotting a dim light in the distance. They saw no human tracks, only prints of deer. They shouted a greeting and the door was opened by a man in weak condition. There was *no* food in the house except turnips and flour mixed with water. Fuel was almost exhausted … The man's voice was failing from exhaustion and hunger.[15]

In the light of a tiny oil lamp they prepared him a meal. His rescuers stayed with him for about two hours, learning of his ordeal. He had not seen a human for fourteen days. He told them he had given up hope of getting anything to sustain him. Upon departing, they left him a supply of bread, sausages and tea. And probably saved his life.

When the gamekeeper had recovered enough strength he would talk of his worry about his beloved animals on higher ground, of how their natural habitat was buried beneath snow or ice. Throughout the country there were now many reports of the piteous suffering of animals, especially sheep and cattle caught out in the open, stranded by the blizzard and drifts, then gradually buried, partially or entirely. One newspaper wrote that 'hungry cattle all over the country are lowing for fodder which the farmers cannot take to them.' Nor their water. Some farmers daringly headed out to dig all day, trying to free a few animals, usually with little luck. Sheep in flocks were reported as dying by the hundreds and even thousands.

The airlift pilots and reporters saw the tragic scene in vivid detail: cattle and sheep below them, entrapped in snowdrifts, unable to move. The animals were steadily growing weaker – and more helpless. Some of the stories written by the reporters were distressing for people to read: animals dead and dying being picked apart by predators. Some were picked upon by hungry birds, and many were buried alive, *in situ*, and then feasted upon by starving foxes, themselves only trying to survive. Entire herds were lost.

Some newspapers began publishing articles depicting foxes as 'killers', preying upon sheep, cattle, goats, pigs and hens – even upon house pets. The *Irish Press* ran an evocative front-page article, 'Killer foxes', that drew wide attention:

> Hungry foxes attacked and killed a number of sheep and cattle ... Late last night farmers were out guarding their flocks.

Such coverage bred a widespread aversion to foxes. Some farmers began shooting them whenever possible.

A short break in the weather over the weekend of 5–6 January allowed rescuers to again make some difficult attempts. The three stranded technicians at Kippure's transmission station were still so fogged in that food drops were not possible. At this point the stranded men – Anthony McColgan, Joe Dillon and John Kelly – felt so isolated that they became seriously worried about their dwindling provisions. Kelly especially felt anxiety, because he was the father of a newborn baby he had not yet seen. Since their road remained buried, someone needed reach them some way.

On Sunday another Teilifís Éireann technician from Dublin, Brendan Lande, drove several expert skiers as far as he could in a Land Rover. When the road became impassable they climbed out, strapped on their skis and headed up the slopes, carrying supplies. Even for experienced skiers it was an arduous ascent. When they finally reached the station, the three men inside were thrilled to see them and gratefully accepted the supplies.

A quite different case was highlighted by the press, because of its unusual nature. An expectant mother in Co. Wicklow's most rugged country desperately needed to get to a hospital. A doctor and ambulance below were ready to take her, but she was unreachable.

Something had to be done. Acting with haste and ingenuity, local men devised a contraption to get her down to safety. A team of six volunteers and two gardaí 'braved 15-foot snowdrifts to drag the expectant mother down to safety on a crudely improvised "sledge" made from a corrugated iron sheet.' With great caution, she was eased down the treacherous slopes.

The next day, when the story made the newspapers, citizens again lambasted the Government for not yet having a civil rescue force and a helicopter ready to fly into action. This was 1963! Plans were under way elsewhere in the world to launch spacecraft and land men on the moon – and the Government *still* had no rescue helicopter.

Some reporters wrote of the gulf between the comfortable city-dwellers and the country people, isolated and suffering. One, returning from what he called the 'unknown world' beyond Dublin, reflected upon the startling juxtaposition:

Coming back through the snow at Crooksling [Co. Dublin] to reach the city and the theatre-bound evening crowds was like crossing the frontier into another country. So great is the contrast between city conditions and snowline that begins *only seven miles* from the Pillar, and gets worse with every mile on the road.[16]

Did the crowds in Dublin's streets even know that only a few miles away were fellow-countrymen and women who were imperilled and often suffering?

On the afternoon of Sunday 6 January this juxtaposition was accentuated. The sun burst forth brightly, exhilarating spirits and prompting pent-up Dubliners to get outside and bask in the luxury. Children and adults headed for the snow-carpeted Phoenix Park and frozen ponds throughout the city. As Jim Fitzpatrick, a young firefighter at the time, recalls half a century later:

the slopes of the Phoenix Park resembled Switzerland and were scenes of happy adults and children … Anything that could be used to slide down the slopes, including car mats, spare tyres, you name it!

However, some of Dublin's more affluent winter sportspeople who owned a car preferred to drive a few miles out of the city for some skiing and tobogganing on Co. Wicklow's *real* slopes. They went as far as a cleared road would allow.

It was later in the afternoon that the real problem began. Throngs of foolhardy Sunday sightseers decided to take a jaunt south of the city to see if the 'dramatic and tragic' conditions, as described by the newspapers, were authentic or exaggerated. This warmer Sunday also provided relief vehicles with their best chance yet for reaching those in need. Before long, a snaking stream of 'gawkers' were on the roads leading to Co. Wicklow. They began holding up rescue convoys. With the favourable weather, everyone had expected to make great progress in relief efforts. Tempers flared as the crews were held up. Reporters trying to do their job were no less frustrated, as described by one in the *Irish Independent*:

> Hundreds of sightseers drove up the mountains to see conditions for themselves. And this caused big traffic jams on the road to Blessington where only one-way traffic was possible. Many cars became stuck, unable to turn around and come back. Motorists found themselves further afield than they intended.[17]

And, naturally, many of the stranded Sunday pleasure-seekers expected those driving snowploughs and relief lorries to halt and help them. Many quickly realised how foolish they had been. Perhaps deservedly, when they got stuck in the snow or could not turn around, they got a taste of isolation and helplessness: some had to spend the night in their cars. Others tried hiking back to the city.

———

On Tuesday morning, 8 January, when readers picked up their copy of the *Irish Times* they were greeted with a cheerful and paradoxical proclamation: 'Spring is promising to "bust out" all over this year'.

Despite the break in the harsh weather, with its glimpse of bright sunshine, the mere mention of spring blooming seemed oddly premature only eight days into January. Was it based on a new weather prediction or simply an attempt to give a psychological boost to gloomy readers suffering from winter depression?

Readers soon realised that the article was written by the fashion editor, who was actually referring to 1963's elegant new spring designs, already being displayed in some of Dublin's chic shops. That year, the venerable House of Dior featured a spring look with an 'accent on the bust'. The fashion editor wrote enthusiastically about the 'return of the bosom' in Irish society – so expect 'very deep necklines', she wrote.

To window-gazers along O'Connell Street and Grafton Street, bundled up in heavy coats, hats and scarves, the mannequins displaying the new spring fashions must have seemed an anachronism. Yet the windows at the department stores drew plenty of admirers – women and men.

But the *Irish Independent's* witty columnist John D. Sheridan was having no part of it. He immediately retorted with what he called his 'contrarian view' – and it did not allow for talk in January of 'spring busting out' with exposed bosoms. He haughtily declared that 'in the matter of clothing, I choose warmth rather than elegance.' In his case, this meant bed clothing with pyjamas, a 'hefty cardigan', socks of thick báinín wool and a hot-water bottle. His favourite item was a 'decrepit woollen headpiece' that his aunt had knitted back in the 1920s, which he wore at night. He unabashedly called it his 'granny cap'. Now he was outfitted from top to bottom. His loyal readership doubtless appreciated his honest, practical view.

To get in on the discussion, the *Irish Press* ran an article giving tips on 'how to keep those feet warm' at night: wear bed socks, do not put a hot-water bottle *on* your feet but behind your knees, and rub iodine ointment into your feet at night. In the morning 'paint them with iodine solution and Friar's Balsam, then dust them over with some talcum powder.' Oh, yes, and a 'brisk five minute walk to get the circulation going'. It was not explained how this walk was to be done on the slick, icy streets. Perhaps up and down hospital corridors.

———

The short reprieve from winter's cold and snow had buoyed people's spirits. But, alas, it was fleeting.

Dubliners had fared much better than their isolated country cousins. Nonetheless, residents of Dublin had felt confined during the freezing weather, deprived of their normal socialising, shopping and entertainment. By the second week of the new year many people were feeling claustrophobic. By Saturday 12 January they were anxious to get out and about to the theatres, pubs and restaurants, and certainly to the rollicking dance halls. There were a few tempting films showing: Frank Sinatra and Kim Novak in *Pal Joey*, Elvis Presley as Kid Galahad, and the more serious *The Longest Day*, playing at the Ambassador to smashing reviews. Publicans and shopkeepers were anticipating a busy and profitable weekend for a change. Things looked promising for an exciting weekend.

And indeed it would be – but not for the reasons anticipated. Early on Saturday morning parts of the east coast, particularly Co. Dublin, were unexpectedly struck full force with what newspapers would dub a fierce 'snow blitz'. In both city and suburbs a wet snow fell as temperatures began plummeting well below freezing. Every surface began receiving a coating of ice, which thickened by the hour. As people awoke and glanced out their windows they assumed that the glistening coating would melt quickly. Then, when the freezing snowfall ceased and the sun broke out, a fast melt seemed certain.

Nature, however, was once again deceptive, as the *Evening Herald's* headline revealed: 'The sun shone to-day – yet it was Dublin's worst Saturday in years.'

Encased in ice, Dublin glistened in the sun. It was stunningly beautiful. And deadly dangerous, to both pedestrians and motorists. Its hazards were not appreciated at first. Many people had to leave home early for their Saturday-morning work, without realising that the city was a calamity zone. Icy footpaths were as slick as greased glass. Immediately, people began falling; cars slid and crashed. Ambulances struggled to reach them as roads became clogged with abandoned vehicles. By the middle of the morning Dublin was thrown into chaos, as one newspaper described:

> Traffic piled up as skidding cars crashed or became immobile on the plate-glass roads. Huge traffic jams built up as there were blocked bridges and junctions. Even the slightest hills were impassable to negotiate. Buses were caught in the traffic jams and passengers marooned. Passengers in vehicles and buses got out to walk and slipped and fell all over the place.[18]

The *Sunday Independent* christened it perfectly: 'Skid Saturday'.

As the temperature remained below freezing, accidents and injuries mounted. At one location there were sixty cars, three buses and several heavy lorries all strewn across the roads, blocking traffic as far as the eye could see. Tony Doran, then a conductor on the no. 19 bus, remembers it fifty years later as 'nightmarish':

Snow and ice! I remember on the Finglas Road buses would come down the hill *sideways*! *And* cars! You couldn't use your brakes: you had to try and steer it. Buses didn't have gripping. CIE sent out trucks with a bit of sand, but it wasn't adequate.

Hospital staff couldn't keep up with injuries of every type: not only sprains and broken bones but serious head injuries. Because of the shortage of staff and rooms, the injured had to be 'stockpiled' in hallways and corridors. Medical personnel were in a frenzy. It was little use for hospital administrators to try and call in extra doctors and nurses, since they could hardly make their way there.

Dublin Airport was closed, all sports fixtures were cancelled and the AA warned people not to drive unless it was an emergency. Some drivers still felt they had to try and get out on the road. One was John Burke, who had to deliver food to his pig farm in Blanchardstown. Before getting far, he skidded into a collision with a heavy lorry and found himself seriously injured and trapped in his van. By good fortune, a motorist, Dr Frank Friselle, was creeping by. He stopped, administered a sedative and waited with him until the fire brigade arrived to cut him free. The firefighters found that 'we could not keep our feet on the ground', as they kept slipping on the icy surface. Only by patiently using hacksaws were they able to extricate Burke, who was by then semi-conscious. He was finally removed and taken away by ambulance.

For forty-eight hours the cold spell continued. 'Dublin was the hardest hit', reported the *Irish Independent*, 'as people shivered under a blanket of fresh snowfall.' To make matters more treacherous, there set in a freezing fog that caused windscreens to ice up, resulting in more accidents and a further impeding of ambulance-drivers and firefighters. A bus conductor, Hugh Maguire, recalled that thick and freezing fogs could virtually blind the bus-driver. 'When the fog got very bad we were handicapped. I'd walk in *front* of the bus ... waving my handkerchief!'

The night of the 13th was declared the 'coldest night of the cold spell' throughout the country. Shannon Airport recorded temperatures of 4°F (−15°C), or 18 degrees frost. Meteorologists scanning their records found only nine nights colder since 1863. Rivers and lakes were frozen: the lakes of Killarney, Loughrea, the River Corrib, and the River Liffey in Co. Kildare. At Limerick parts of the Shannon and the Abbey River were frozen. Even in Dublin the Liffey was freezing up, as were the streams and ponds in St Stephen's Green.

Pubs in Dublin were reporting that stout kept in cellars or back rooms was freezing in the bottles – as were bottles of milk delivered outside houses.

Meanwhile, more animals were being trapped and frozen. In the Nire Valley in Co. Waterford a desperate operation was under way to 'use shovels to hack away the snow from more than 4,000 sheep which lay frozen under the snow.' Volunteers struggled to climb the hillsides to try and save them.

In Dublin a similar rescue was being carried out. CIE workers were called to St James's Walk, where two swans had been frozen in the sudden ice. Grappling irons had to be used to smash the ice that held them prisoner. It was an emotional sight for onlookers; cheers went up when they were freed.

Since the onset of the 'Siberian weather', as journalists were now commonly calling it, there had been a resurgence of sure-footed cart horses on Dublin's streets. Suddenly, real 'horse power' was needed to deliver carts of milk, bread and coal in slippery streets and narrow alleys. Fortunately, there were still enough carters and cart horses available for emergency service.

The problem was that these horses had to be fitted with frost nails on their hooves for maximum grip. This called for farriers capable of carrying out the task. Following the Second World War and the rise in motorisation, Dublin's farriers had dwindled to but a few. There were just enough still around to care for racing horses, show horses and the RDS crowd. Now they were called into action to meet the immediate demand for cart horses.

It was a brief period during which the city's last farriers made great profits but got little sleep. James Harding, born in 1917, began 'striking at the anvil', as he puts it, at twelve years of age, serving his seven-year apprenticeship back when the 'horse was still king of the roads'. His small forge, tucked down Pleasants Lane, off Camden Street, was barely doing enough business in 1963 to keep him going. But he had enjoyed working at a leisurely pace while chatting to old customers.

Then the January boom struck. He had to arrive at 3 a.m. to meet a dozen or more carters with their horses already queued up outside, and then work till ten at night.

Across town another farrier, John Boyne, kept similar hours at his small forge hidden off Pearse Street. He knew that a hard frost or ice could throw

Dublin into paralysis and that horses with frost nails were still the best solution. He didn't mind the frenzy – or the profits:

> It was a kind of harvest time for farriers. In the middle of the night we'd be *out* of bed – a very panicky time for us. No time for dillydallying! You'd get sleep the best way you can.

What was most important to the hard-pressed farriers was knowing that they were helping their city function in time of crisis.

Then there were those who had to help keep Dublin going by continuing their work in the worst of weather conditions: postmen, dockers, street dealers, zookeepers, firefighters, gardaí, newspaper sellers, stonemasons, street cleaners – even gravediggers. While others in the city might have arisen to go to work in a heated office, factory or shop, they had to face the freezing elements, often without being properly outfitted for the arctic conditions.

The postman Davy Sheridan had begun his duties in 1928. In 1963, when the big storm hit, he was fifty-three, still having to carry his bag of post weighing more than thirty pounds. 'And we weren't supplied with gloves! Ah, the tips of your fingers would be terrible sore.' Seeing him straggling from house to house in a blizzard, people would feel great sympathy. 'People would invite me in (quickly) for tea. Now the rules said, No … but you'd go in!'

Dublin's storied street dealers exhibited a stoicism in standing their ground, whatever the discomfort. Explaining that they *needed* each day's money for their large families, the legendary Moore Street dealer Lizzy Byrne never let a blizzard or freezing temperatures deter her:

> Ah, we *never* gave up … Came out in hail and snow. Oh, God, it was cold! And we'd put on plenty of clothing – *three* coats maybe. We always got by … don't you worry!

No-one in all Dublin faced a more demanding job than the gravediggers. Burials couldn't cease just because of snow-packed, frozen ground. In fact, the death rate always increased in winter, when conditions were the harshest. At Glasnevin Cemetery, Jack Mitchell had to carve out his graves and get the coffins into the earth – somehow. The ground that January was as solid as granite on the surface and had to be hacked open like a quarry pit. The gravedigger's hands and feet were numb. Mitchell remembers it as a grey world of pickaxe and shovel sounds:

> The graves were nine feet deep, and everything still dug by hand. Eight o'clock till five, six days a week. It was slavery.

Even the mourners showed sympathy for Mitchell and his workmates.

During the record cold spell, people inside their homes had to combat the freezing temperatures. Many dwellings still had no central heating. Dependent upon burning coal and turf in their hearths, they stoked the fire day and night. Nonetheless, they might still find the water in their toilet freezing over.

Tenement-dwellers were the most desperate for heat, stuffing their small hearths with turf, leading to a rash of fires in the city. Every fire station was kept busy day and night. Firefighters often had great difficulty on the icy streets in simply reaching the blaze. Éamonn Fitzpatrick was stationed at the Tara Street station:

> Ah, a very bad winter – the snow and *ice*! Crews had to be careful of the road conditions. They introduced chains, but they weren't a great success … They were more of a hindrance.

Upon reaching a burning tenement house, a firefighter's risks soared. But he realised that lives were always at stake, especially with so many children usually in occupation:

> Tenement fires were very, *very* dangerous. You were never sure of the stability of the buildings … and old rickety stairs. The hearths would split and ash went down in the cracks between the floors and ceilings. And it would smoulder for weeks!

Even after he and his colleagues had extinguished the blaze and departed, cinders could still be alive hidden behind walls.

The frigid winter of 1963 was also particularly bad for gas fires and gas accidents. Gas leaks could result from frozen and fractured mains. On 14 January a woman died and four other residents required hospital treatment following a gas accident at Courtney Place in Ballybough. Firefighters found that escaping gas from the broken line had filtered into five adjacent houses as well. This could have taken a far greater toll. When people went to bed they had no way of knowing whether a gas line might fracture during the night. It was becoming a widespread fear. The winter of 1963 was taking lives in many different forms.

———

Reliable reports of animal deaths on an appalling scale were now filtering in to animal-protection agencies in Dublin. Entire herds of cattle and sheep, as well as vast flocks of birds, had become entombed in snow and ice. An alarmed public sympathetically sent in donations to 'save the animals' associations.

From the hillsides and mountains of Connemara and Co. Wicklow came the most distressing stories. In some parts of Co. Wicklow, farmers predicted that they would lose 90 per cent of their sheep herd. Farmers in Co. Meath told of having to be on their full guard against foxes ranging the fields where lambs were falling. Journalists were now calling it 'nature's slaughter' of Ireland's herds. Even deer, driven by hunger, were coming down into the lowlands of Co. Wicklow. One resident of Glenealy had two deer come virtually up to her house to feed on greens she had left out for them.

Ireland's multitude of bird-lovers had cause for great distress. With the temperature falling as low as −10, the trees – leaves, bark and berries – were encased in layers of ice, and the earth was buried in feet of snow. With rivers and ponds freezing over, birds had trouble even finding water. First they became weak, then they died, some simply toppling from branches into the jaws of hungry foxes.

Farmers saw birds pathetically trying to forage for food, their bodies later littering the snowy surface. They commonly came upon thrushes, redwings, chaffinches and wagtails. The Dublin suburbs attracted thrushes and starlings searching for food and shelter. Blackbirds were faring the best, as they had a great capacity for hard work in foraging where there were breaks in the snow exposing small patches of ground.

By contrast, seabirds were surviving the frigid conditions relatively well. The east wind was littering the shores with food, including razor shells, starfish and whelks. Along the beach from Portmarnock to Rush in Co. Dublin the seagulls amassed in tens of thousands, screaming over the luscious scraps. In the Malahide Estuary it was reckoned that at least 30,000 seabirds were gathered at one time, feeding in the incoming tide.

However, geese and swans were struggling to survive. Geese flocked to the island at Malahide but were 'heavily shot at' by unscrupulous hunters, despite an official order protecting them. There were many complaints to the police about this abuse – or 'gunning slaughter' – but they could do little about it under the difficult conditions.

Dubliners found the plight of swans especially heart-breaking. F. M. Ardagh of the Dublin Society for the Prevention of Cruelty to Animals took a personal interest in this sad struggle. As she explained to reporters, it was a time of travail for the swans. 'This is the way of nature ... and nature can be cruel.' It was an effort to try and put people's minds more at ease. Swan-lovers were heartened when several suffering swans were rescued and turned over to compassionate nuns at two convents, where they found sanctuary.

Behind the scenes at Dublin Zoo another drama was occurring in the effort to cope with the weather crisis. The unpredicted blizzard had not allowed the staff members to prepare for such an emergency. Consequently, the superintendent, Dr Terry Murphy, and his dedicated staff suddenly faced some almost insurmountable problems. Dr Murphy took charge, asking his staff to work night and day to save as many endangered animals as possible. Their most urgent efforts were directed at boiler problems, frozen and bursting pipes, iced cages and locks, snowdrifts impeding the movement of large wheelbarrows with food, and the low temperature threatening the lives of some delicate animals. All these problems were striking at once.

Gerry Creighton, who started work at the zoo in 1958 at the age of fourteen, walking the children's ponies, remembers his role in the crisis. By that time he was an assistant helper to the staff. Eventually, he would work his way all the way up to the position of head animal-keeper. He has since recounted the scene at the zoo in January 1963:

The winter of '63 – I remember the icy wind that would cut you in two! The zoo got frozen up. The boilers were really old, almost every pipe in the zoo was frozen. All the animal houses were heated by coal furnace, and every three hours or so the furnaces had to be raked and cinders and clinkers removed, and new coal put in. This was a 24-hour job! And trees that fell [in the storm] were cut up by us staff, for the boilers.

Everything was manual, with a shovel and big wheelbarrows – through the ice and snow. Oh, my job was twice as hard! Almost all the animals had water troughs, so you had to break up the ice every day and then go around with the wheelbarrows loaded with food. And we weren't supplied with gloves in those days! There was even a problem with the locks to the cages when they'd freeze and you weren't able to get the keys into the locks … to go into your animals. So, we would have a cigarette-lighter or matches to hold under the lock to melt the ice.

The animals most affected by the cold were our tropical birds, like toucans and hornbills. And we had to take in the flamingos and penguins and sea lions, because ice was forming around them and they were caught in the ice. And the monkeys, because of their long fingers … which can get frostbite.

While the plight of farmers' herds, wild animals and zoo animals received coverage in the newspapers, it was a single, frightened fox that came to command the most sympathetic attention as it captured the hearts of Dubliners.

It all began back in August 1962 without much interest, when it was noted that 'a small fox had been living quietly in St Stephen's Green'. She was spotted now and then by visitors, who usually smiled and pointed as she slunk away into the bushes and disappeared. Occasionally, a few feathers were found around the Green, a clue that she was up to her foxy ways. But the park constables John McEvoy and James Lynch did not regard it as a significant problem.

Until January 1963, that is.

With the onset of the brutal winter came those *Irish Press* articles about 'killer foxes' ravaging herds of sheep and raiding farms. As sport, some young hunters began trying to track down this little fox. The animal retreated to the safety of a tiny island in one of the ponds in the Green. Then came the hard freeze:

Thick ice covering the pond meant that small and not-so-small boys disturbed her hitherto retreat on the island in the centre of the pond.[19]

Now, in terror, the fox had to find a last refuge on the branch of a tree, as tormentors below shouted and threw objects to try and knock her off.

Crowds began to gather daily to watch the spectacle, some cheering as others protested against the cruelty. When reporters got wind of it the subject became a controversial and emotive one for animal-lovers. There were all sorts of ideas about how it should be handled. There were even some awkward attempts by 'well-meaning citizens to knock the fox down into a coat held below':

> Eyes flashing, pink tongue flickering in and out, it clung terrified to the tip of the branch.[20]

Finally the crowds had to be dispersed by park constables. Why they or the staff of Dublin Zoo had not made a concerted effort earlier to save the trapped fox is not known.

Owing to the growing public interest, the saga became known simply as the 'fox in the Green'. For some it was merely an amusing story, but there were those to whom the incident was a socially significant symbol, revealing the worst in human nature. Impassioned followers of the drama vented their feelings in letters to the papers. One concerned citizen, signing themselves 'Disillusioned', wrote to the *Evening Herald*:

> The episode of the poor trapped fox is an amazing exhibition of hysteria and sadism – the urge to kill. Obviously, we are not in England, Denmark or Holland where they are noted for kindness to animals. What, may reasonably be asked, is being taught in our schools?[21]

Rosemary O'Callaghan-Westrop had visited the scene several times, horrified by the cruelty she witnessed when young people tried laughingly to injure or kill the terrified creature:

> The behaviour of the mob who gathered to terrify a helpless little fox in the Green is a serious and alarming sign of our times. He lives in terror and hunger.
>
> Mob law will come out on top if decent people do nothing about it. The primary responsibility rests with parents and schools.[22]

For weeks to come, such letters would continue to appear, making it a hot topic in conversation and debates. Was it a sign of deteriorating morals? some wondered.

During the first two weeks of January, relief workers and rescue crews had forged ahead with pick and shovel to reach the most outlying homes. Volunteers and county council workers had worked till near-exhaustion to find those down to their last morsels of food and fuel.

On 14 January one of the winter's saddest discoveries was made: the double death of an elderly couple in Co. Waterford. James and Elizabeth Murphy were found in their isolated house. There was no fire in the grate, and two dogs were whining in the kitchen. When last seen, Mrs Murphy was trying to keep warm in front of the small fire of sticks. News of their deaths shocked the nation, provoking harsh condemnation of the inert Government – and of Irish society as well. As one newspaper wrote:

> shame on us, all of us! An elderly couple was found dead in their cottage at Kilbarry caused by the extreme cold. No step had been taken by authorities – nothing was done. They stood by idly. A tragedy that strikes at the smug complacency of many of us. Two people died of neglect … [We were] indifferent to their plight. *Shame!*[23]

The Government had been well aware of the widespread, often desperate, shortages of food and fuel. And yet it had never called upon a ready army to provide life-saving assistance. It seemed beyond all reason and compassion.

On 15–17 January there was hopeful news: some meteorologists expressed their belief that the 'Siberian cold' was finally subsiding. Life should soon be safer.

CIE announced that week that it was doing its part to make life more comfortable for Dubliners. A spokesperson told reporters the good news that more than half of Dublin's 700 buses had now been fitted with heaters. For regular passengers on these routes it was pure luxury. It was promised that another hundred buses were to be fitted during February.

Meanwhile, buoyed by some warmer weather, people began strolling the city's streets again. Some paused at the entrances of record shops to listen to some of the top ten: Elvis Presley's 'Return to Sender', Cliff Richard's 'The

Next Time', Chubby Checker's 'Limbo Rock'. All had a good beat, suggestive of warm spring weather … and fantasies of summer. Even some oldsters seemed to feel the tempo.

The *Irish Independent* made it official on 17 January with its welcome headline 'The crisis is over'. The article featured a 'tribute to the heroes of the freeze-up', citing an array of those who had given so much: bulldozer and snowplough-drivers, council road-clearance crews, volunteer shovellers, airlifters and 'mercy mission' parcel-deliverers, van-drivers, ambulance crews, Red Cross workers, doctors and gardaí. A special mention was given to the 'splendid reporters and photographers' who had 'daringly brought back their stories from dangerous scenes'. They had all contributed to the 'memories of human endurance, suffering and sacrifice under the worst imaginable conditions'.

The following day Aer Lingus pilots were wondering where the 'calm winds' the meteorologists had predicted were. Captain W. G. Black was on a routine flight from London to Dublin when he encountered what he called the 'fairest wind' he had ever had from the east. It caught his plane and zipped it to Dublin at a record speed of 59 minutes, much to everyone's surprise.

Did the powerful east wind carry any greater meaning?

On 20 January the *Irish Independent* had to publish a startling retraction, needing only a three-word headline: 'Blizzards are back!' As if it were a returning nightmare, it continued:

> Blizzards swept across the country … Five foot drifts blocked roads …
> It was freezing again last night and weather experts said they could not
> foresee when the cold spell would end.[24]

It was dispiriting news throughout the country, just as morale had been on the rise.

But it bred new types of heroism. On Inchiquin, the largest of Lough Corrib's islands, six families had suffered a long spell of freezing weather and isolation. Now they were desperate for food, water and fuel. They were beyond the reach of mainlanders, but on 23 January several courageous islanders stepped forward to go for provisions. They cautiously managed to hack their way forward in a boat through four-inch ice. But the effort seemed interminable. They decided to risk walking the rest of the distance on top of the uncertain ice layer. They succeeded in their precarious journey but probably with some good luck.

The next day, readers were discouraged when they saw the *Irish Press* headline, 'Freeze-up goes on', and further disheartened when it was noted that Icelanders were already enjoying some 'mild spring weather', with temperatures up to 6 degrees. In fact, 'early spring flowers were already in bloom' there.

At least the few technicians stranded at Kippure were cheered up that afternoon. When the new blizzard struck they put in an immediate request for additional water supplies. It was decided that the metal casks used by Guinness would be the ideal container for the airdrop. Guinness gladly supplied eight, and when there was a break in the weather they were dropped successfully. At the last minute Guinness had decided to contribute a ninth cask – this one full of stout.

Some rescues were taking place in Dublin as well. The following night, Neil Kennedy of Drumcondra was returning home from a dance. Walking along Aston Quay, he heard someone shout that there was a woman in the Liffey. At first he thought he was joking, but then he saw the commotion and ran towards it. The woman was lying on her back as gardaí were trying unsuccessfully to get her out with a grappling hook.

A strong swimmer, Kennedy quickly divested himself of coat and trousers and was about to dive in. At the last moment, however, he realised that the *tide was out*. There was only about four feet of water.

Gardaí lowered a rope, which he climbed down, wading out to the exhausted woman. He pulled her to safety and helped hoist her up. Both were rushed to Jervis Street Hospital, where he was treated for minor cuts.

The next day's newspapers wrote of the 'hero of the rescue who pluckily snatched' the woman from the river, adding that she 'probably would have died' without his actions. Kennedy was modest about his 'heroic' title, saying little more than that he was 'lucky I did not dive – I probably would have broken my neck.'

Surprisingly, no-one had yet rescued the little 'fox in the Green'. The torment had continued, as had the avalanche of letters on editors' desks. Most writers expressed condemnation:

What of the people who clamoured for the death of the dumb animal in the capital of Catholic Ireland? The chant of 'kill it, kill it!' in St Stephen's Green is a terrible reflection on our city by the people responsible for it.

Another wrote:

> May I protest against the brutal treatment and vicious attitude of the majority of the mob towards a helpless and frightened animal. In today's state of 'civilization' over two hundred people let their desire to destroy run riot … A hostile crowd of 'human' beings.
>
> They should hang their heads in shame for their cruelty. That these people are Irish is most disturbing.[25]

Finally, on 26 January, the fox was rescued – or 'captured', depending upon one's perception of the episode. It was quickly determined that she was indeed quite tame and apparently very happy to be in safe arms.

The next day a new weather report was issued:

> Sunshine and rising temperatures … easement of the cold spell throughout the country … as slow thaw continues.

But how accurate was this latest forecast? The credibility of meteorologists had been tarnished by their dismal performance over the previous five weeks.

In any case, at the end of what would go down as one of the most brutal Irish winters of the century, people could at least pray for warmer, happier days ahead – for some bright sunshine, climbing temperatures and a hint of a few spring flowers, like their neighbours the Icelanders.

Chapter 3 ～

TEARS FOR THE DEARLY DEPARTED

O n the first day of February 1963 headlines brought unexpected sad news to the nation: 'Cardinal D'Alton dies in Dublin'.

His sudden loss was deeply felt throughout the country. Though eighty years of age, he had been fit and active. Only a few days earlier he had attended the funeral of his close friend Cardinal Godfrey, Archbishop of Westminster. Upon his return from London, Cardinal D'Alton had casually mentioned that he 'felt unwell', but his condition 'did not give cause for anxiety'. However, late that night his condition suddenly worsened. Early on the morning of Friday 1 February he 'died peacefully in his sleep'. Word of his death spread far and wide.

When Pope John was given the news he immediately went to his private chapel to pray. Vatican sources said the Pontiff felt a 'deep sadness', since it was known that he too loved the cardinal for his great humanity, humility and natural empathy. It was often said that D'Alton was no ordinary cardinal.

Born in Claremorris, Co. Mayo, in 1882, he was ordained in 1908. Shortly thereafter he began his long association with St Patrick's College, Maynooth. In June 1942 he was consecrated bishop. It was his 'qualities of kindness, sympathy and humility', wrote the *Irish Independent*, that 'won him a particularly warm place in the hearts' of the people. His warm, gentle manner endeared him to everyone immediately. As one journalist wrote:

> no personal problem of one of his flock was too small to merit his concern and assistance … It was his warm humanity. As a truly Irish priest he identified himself with his neighbours.[26]

Yet he was also a man of great intellect and insight, as well as profound wisdom. It was often said that he 'grasped the nettle of partition', and he was quoted as referring to 'this island of ours which God intended to be one and undivided'. This personal statement was recognised as an 'act of particular courage'. Furthermore, he often expressed his opinion that the Irish language is a 'primary factor in preserving our national identity'. For a figure of his stature to speak with such conviction on complex political and cultural matters was a rarity.

Dr Cornelius Lucey, Bishop of Cork, recalled that D'Alton was 'in complete touch with the people … a great man'. President de Valera, who had known him for sixty-five years, called him 'kindly, forbearing, gentle … To know him was to admire and, indeed, to love him.'

In the last two decades of his life, no-one knew D'Alton more personally than his valet, John Ward, from Co. Westmeath. For some seventeen years he had served him faithfully, becoming his close friend. As he told an *Irish Press* reporter, D'Alton was unfailingly 'kindly, considerate, fatherly', with an emphasis on the last trait. Ward stressed how very 'human' he was, 'fond of flowers and rockeries', loving children and speaking often of his own nieces. And, Ward revealed, it was his 'secret ambition to be a parish priest … to have a parish of his own.' A most humble ambition. To Ward, the news of his death was a blow. 'He was a most lovable man and will be a loss to all – and I should know.'

By Friday afternoon Cardinal D'Alton's body lay on a simple wooden bed in St Vincent's Hospital (then at St Stephen's Green) as people filed in and out to pray at his bedside. He was laid out in ceremonial violet Mass vestments. On a table at his bedside was the red biretta of his high office.

As mourners streamed past D'Alton's body, not far away at Spencer Dock, on the Royal Canal, two young boys were happily – and dangerously – playing on the ice. They heard a terrible crack and the 'ice gave way under them', plunging both into the frigid water. They drowned before any rescue could be made.

With all the newspaper space devoted to Cardinal D'Alton's death, little attention was given to this tragic accident. Their drownings would be added to the number of the many lost in previous years in Dublin's canals. This would renew the debate over what should be done with the hazardous, often polluted, canals in the city. In the coming months the issue would receive plenty of attention in the news.

On Saturday the cardinal's remains were removed to St Patrick's Cathedral in Armagh, where they were to lie in state until his funeral on

Wednesday. At noon multitudes of Dubliners defied the weather to pay their respects. With snowflakes tumbling, 'hushed thousands lined the principal streets, silent but for the tramp of marching feet and the muffled notes of the Dead March' played by the army band. People had stood ten-deep along O'Connell Street as the bells tolled when the cortege passed towards Parnell Square on the journey to the North:

> The Dead March caught up the emotions of the crowd thronging the streets – the emotions of a city and of a nation.[27]

The cortege was led by a guard of honour; shops were closed and all traffic came to a halt. Papal and national flags fluttered at half-mast, 'whipped by a bitter east wind'.

Then the hearse turned, headed north, and slowly vanished from sight.

For all those unable to attend Cardinal D'Alton's funeral, the new medium of television brought the dramatic coverage into their homes. On the day of the funeral there was a newspaper editorial on the 'uses of television'. In Ireland it was in its infancy, and most people did not yet own their own set. They shared television viewing with relatives and neighbours. The effect of the medium on the public was a frequently debated subject. Most early programmes had to be imported from Britain or America, and only the most wholesome programmes were allowed. But there was immense potential for expanding both foreign and Irish programming.

In 1963 many people believed that television should be primarily used for learning and serious news. An emphasis on 'entertainment' could be a threat to Irish culture and to morals. Perhaps it was better to concentrate on teaching the Irish language and instructing farmers on how better to use their land, with occasional concerts of classical music, art programmes and political events.

But during the first week of February, Irish television took a quantum leap with its live coverage of parts of Cardinal D'Alton's funeral. Sitting before their small, flickering black-and-white televisions, people had a sense of participation in these dramatic events. It was a new experience.

All of a sudden, television seemed indispensable to the people. By the end of 1963 it would be even more so.

———

The nation's attention was drawn in 1963 to the saving of lives. This was the year in which a road safety campaign was finally launched. The statistics on road deaths and injuries for the previous year had just been released, and they were even more distressful than anticipated. This compelled A. Kelly, secretary of the Safety First Association, to ask:

> Can Ireland continue to have its population reduced and maimed by the rising number of accidents? It is appalling that we have the present toll on the roads in a country of less than three million – with 332 people killed and over 5,000 injured (1962).[28]

The *Evening Herald* in its New Year's message, entitled 'Year of changes ahead', had mentioned the national shame of the increasing road accidents, declaring, 'This year a special effort must be made to reduce the toll of the roads.' Everyone agreed: the time had come.

In response, the Irish Hospital Trust initiated the Road Safety Campaign by contributing £10,000 to the cause. The goal was to 'awake the public conscience' and stop what was being called the 'slaughter' on Ireland's roads. The Government would need to do its part. The 'great deficiency', asserted the *Irish Independent*, 'is the lack of a *test* for drivers, and vehicles', as implemented by sensible countries. As a spokesperson for the Road Safety Campaign candidly put it:

> it is ridiculous that a person can get a driving licence just by paying £1 and *no* questions asked about his ability to sit behind a wheel.[29]

Without *any* formal instruction, many – and possibly most – Irish drivers did not really know how to properly handle a vehicle in all situations. Nor were many of their vehicles fit for the road. Old rattle-traps and cars poorly maintained, with faulty brakes, tyres and steering mechanisms, put everyone on the road at risk. And the mounting accident statistics proved it.

The year had come for reform on Ireland's roads.

———

In early February a less heralded campaign was showing positive results. It was in relation to the 'indiscriminate shooting of wild fowl' during the harsh winter months, when the birds were weak and helpless. This laudable effort had been championed by conservation groups, hunters' organisations and various newspapers. There was already evidence that it had paid a dividend: in many areas there had been a cease-fire, as gun clubs and game associations in every county had worked vigorously to protect endangered birds, as well as educate hunters about conservation. Violators were spotted, identified and issued warnings. Results were increasingly gratifying.

Not everyone was sensitive to the need for protecting wildlife. On 13 February the three-day National Coursing Meeting was held at Clonmel, proudly called the 'biggest in the world'. Visitors from England, Scotland, Wales and Northern Ireland showed up enthusiastically for the grand event.

National Coursing Week included the annual coursing dance, the social highlight of the event. There was no talk of cancelling the coursing activity just because the foxes, rabbits, birds and other game were weak and suffering from cold and hunger. Traditions were to be upheld; the chase was on.

In the middle of February winter's wrath struck yet another unexpected blow, as the 'Siberian cold returned with a phenomenal snowstorm that smothered the West' and again buried parts of Co. Wicklow. As before, people were not prepared.

Country people in what some journalists were now calling the 'unreachable' hills and mountains of Co. Wicklow were again quickly cut off by deep drifts. The *Herald's* rescue teams flew into action with their mercy missions to provide villages and farmers with provisions before it got any worse. Some of the mountain roads had only recently been cleared; now they were buried again.

This did not deter the reporter Michael Ryan and the photographer Seán Horgan as they loaded their car with food parcels and headed into remote Co. Wicklow. Having been on these missions before, they knew what they faced. For quite a distance they were plodding along, 'steadily climbing icy roads', when their car 'suddenly skidded and slid into a great wall of snow'. Armed with shovels, they began digging for hours until semi-darkness caught up with them. Then came the realisation that they might face spending the night in their car.

But they finally freed their car and set out again for Ballyknocken. Here they got out and trudged to the house of Mrs K. Weston-Byrne, an eighty-year-old woman they knew would be in great need. With an armful of food and other provisions they knocked on her door. 'God bless you,' she said. 'My prayers have been answered!' She welcomed them in, saying that people in her predicament could only 'pray for help'.

Throughout the country, people were trying to get out of harm's way. Among them were the Travellers, who suffered the cold and winds when the worst of weather struck. No-one was more at the mercy of nature out on the open roads. In 1963 they were still regarded as pariahs in many areas, forced to move on. Only in some communities were they accepted during bad winter spells.

As people on land once again struggled against the cold and snow, furious gale-force winds roiled the seas, putting ships and sailors in peril. They too had been blindsided by the unpredicted fury of the storm.

On 14 February a sea drama was unfolding as 'a grim battle in mountainous seas was being tenaciously fought' off Mizen Head, Co. Wicklow. At 5:30 a.m. the German ship *Milos* had radioed a distress signal saying its steering was out of order, placing the vessel at the mercy of the sea. The Arklow lifeboat and the *Irish Holly*, taking their own chances, made a dash to try and save the stricken ship and its eight crew members. When the *Irish Holly* reached the *Milos* it was being battered in a force-seven gale, in grave danger of drifting into the Arklow Bank or the Horse Shoe Bank. When the lifeboat arrived on the scene, under its cox, Michael O'Brien, the two rescue boats began working together.

Shortly before noon the German vessel was finally being taken in tow, making for Wicklow, much to the relief of its crew. But then the line snapped. Another was attached, but it soon snapped as well, leaving the seamen helpless again in the churning seas.

With great determination 'a frantic effort' was again made to reconnect the tow line with the *Irish Holly*. Meanwhile, according to the news accounts, the 'sea drama was closely followed in Arklow' by the crews of ten 'storm-bound trawlers' that were powerless to assist the rescue, because of the extreme danger.

By the afternoon Captain Neil Gillespie of the *Irish Holly* adroitly towed the *Milos* to safety. He and his crew were praised for their 'magnificent work' and profusely thanked by the eight German crewmen.

At about the same time, another water rescue was under way in Dublin. Ellen Chaffey had been drawn to the South Wall to watch the Liffey being churned up by the gale. However, a gust of wind caught her, and she was blown into the river.

Christy Cummins, a Dublin ferryman, was just moving away from the North Wall when he noticed the figure of a woman and saw 'a splash, as if she had been thrown into the water … and I saw a woman's head in the water.' Hurriedly, he reached her and threw a rope, which she held tightly. Two men passing by rushed over, and 'we pulled her out of the water'. She was taken to a café to wait for an ambulance.

Unfortunately, no-one was in a position to help Howth's fishermen. The freezing weather and resultant changes in the sea had imposed great hardship on them and their families. To greater Irish society, it was not headline news. But to those involved it was a crisis.

For two months the fishermen had been deprived of their livelihood by bad weather. It was reported that the majority of the sixty fishermen had earned no money since before Christmas. One of them lamented that 'it's the longest spell of bad fishing we've *ever* experienced at Howth.' Their families were now barely making ends meet.

Owing to the violent seas, the fish had disappeared from their usual grounds. There were twelve boats in the Howth fishing fleet, and when one of them went out on 14 February for twelve hours it returned with half a basket of fish. Several others reported that they had caught nothing. The fishermen explained that the fish were plentiful about twelve miles off the coast, but they couldn't go out that far because of storm danger and the cost of fuel. In past years, during a spell of poor fishing, the fishermen could temporarily earn some money in the building trades. That year, however, cold and snow had virtually brought that to a halt as well.

————

Foul weather once again played havoc with the country's sports venues. So in frigid February, Christie McCormack and a few friends decided to try and revive a moribund sport that had once been quite popular: roller hockey. To their thinking, the time was right. The Irish Roller Hockey Association was founded in 1948 and had prospered during the fifties, its teams making several appearances in Spain and Switzerland. Its popularity gradually faded and the sport fizzled out, possibly because of poor management.

McCormack and his backers were convinced that the lively sport now had a future in Dublin. It was five a side and fifteen minutes each way. All McCormack needed was a patch of ground on which to play. He made a request to the Dublin Corporation, which granted them a parcel of ground at South Dock Road. But this acquisition would require money and work to make it suitable for play. They decided to hold their first fund-raiser in March, at the Adelaide Ballroom. In the meantime they would energetically promote the resurgence of roller hockey, seeking the help of the press.

By the end of February they had recruited sixty playing members, to represent six teams in the city. To project an image of an action-packed sport, they chose such team names as Dynamos, Spoilers and Wolves. While it would be a challenge to revive the sport, promoters were promising reporters that fans would support it enthusiastically. With financial backing and good management the Dynamos and Spoilers would be drawing crowds once again.

─────

With the return of hazardous weather from 13 February, the AA again warned motorists to stay off the roads. Most motorists heeded the good advice. On 15 February a general thaw spread across the country, as temperatures nudged a few degrees above the freezing mark. By late afternoon, however, they began slipping down again. Then a light snow and sleet began falling.

For some people it was an absolute necessity to drive. Among them were five members of the Cremin family of Co. Cork. Their mission was to drive from their farm, near Tullylease, to Cork Airport to collect the remains of a family member who had died in England.

The Cremins, with twelve children, were like a small tribe. They were widely known and much liked. The children were close not only in age but in devotion to one another, and to their parents. The parents selected five children to make the car journey together, since it was not an easy or pleasant duty: Michael, Daniel, David, Mary and Hannah. They were not able to leave for Cork until later that afternoon. As dusk approached, conditions grew worse, with slick surfaces, patches of fog and poor visibility.

Weather conditions made their trip longer than anticipated. By 10 p.m. they were doubtless tired from the journey. Along the River Lee, at the quay at Parnell Place, the road became slicker than ever. Suddenly the tyres lost grip and began a free-slide out of control. At 10:25 the 'car went under a guard rail' and made what one newspaper called its 'death plunge' into the frigid waters. Because it was a Friday night some people were still out and witnessed the tragedy.

The car floated on the surface for about two minutes before slowly slipping away. According to a reporter for the *Cork Examiner*, a bus-driver, Seán Boyle, heard the crash and rushed to the water's edge, only 'to see the front of the car disappearing with the face of a girl looking out at him.' At that same moment a motorist who stopped and ran to the spot saw 'a man in the back waving through the window – and then the car sank.' Garda John Morrissey made a brave attempt at a rescue by entering the water with a 'rope tied around his body', but he had to be quickly pulled out and carried to an ambulance.

As reality gripped them, hundreds watched in silence along the quays, the *Cork Examiner* noting that, 'even to pressmen toughened through familiarity with tragedy and disaster, this was a heart-breaking scene.'

The Gardaí and fire brigade were immediately summoned, but the futility of any rescue work was apparent. The car had disappeared in the black current, tilted and begun settling out of sight, as if it had never existed. Once more, the dark surface looked placid.

Only a skilled diver with a wetsuit and equipment could conduct a recovery operation. A request was promptly put in to Dublin to send such a diver.

———

A crowd remained shivering in the sleet, its gaze fixed on the damaged guard rail and the river below in expectation, as if awaiting a miracle. Within twenty minutes, the Rev. Michael Lucey of SS. Peter and Paul Church arrived on the scene. After imparting conditional absolution five times on the spot where the vehicle had plunged in, he led the crowd in reciting the Rosary.

At midnight there was still a small crowd, staring, murmuring. No towing vehicle with cable had yet arrived. Onlookers wondered if the car had been carried downstream by the current. As the hours slipped away, without any trace of the car being raised, the spectators slowly drifted home.

Shortly after 3 a.m. there was a stirring. Several vehicles arrived and a few men climbed out. Searchlights were switched on. One man, Donal McCarthy, who had arrived from Dublin, was clearly the centre of attention. He was a professional diver. The men surveyed the scene as they talked, pointing now and then. The searchlights illuminated the river surface at the accident spot. Now, five hours later, McCarthy had no way of knowing whether the car had drifted away. But he would start here.

He knew the risks he faced. Many rivers were cluttered with rubbish below the surface, as well as with fallen trees. And there were no other divers standing by to rescue him. At about 4 a.m. he entered the numbing water and slipped out of sight. Gardaí and firefighters stood by as suspense grew.

Five minutes later his figure reappeared as he gasped, 'I *found* it! It's on its nose!' Slings were quickly passed to him as he descended once again to secure the line. A small crowd had again gathered. Tensions rose. Were there any passengers still inside? The crane began slowly raising the heavy load.

Lights were fixed on the cable at the water level. Reporters who had arrived from Dublin stood silently. In an age when the news media was still discreet, they could put no morbid details into print. Protecting a victim's dignity was a matter of integrity, both their own and that of their paper. When the car was lifted it was drained and then lowered. One by one all five bodies were removed with great care, as Father Lucey anointed each of them. A hush fell over the scene.

By the middle of the morning, word of the Cremin family disaster had spread throughout the country. As the *Evening Herald* would write in its afternoon edition, 'never, perhaps, has an Irish family been so severely stricken by tragedy.'

It was perceived as a national tragedy. Everyone felt a sense of loss and grief. Ireland was a country in mourning. In every church, prayers were offered for the victims and their family.

On Sunday hundreds of people visited the village church to pray beside the five coffins, laid out side by side. All brothers and sisters. 'Sympathy for the Cremin family has been widespread,' wrote one newspaper, 'with many letters and phone calls expressing shock and sorrow.'

People crowded into the church on Monday for the Requiem Mass, celebrated by the Rev. Michael Twohig. Then they walked behind the coffins as they were borne to the family burial ground. Mourners discreetly caught glances of the parents and surviving siblings – a family reduced from twelve to seven. The three brothers and two sisters were buried in three graves. President de Valera, who had sent a message of sympathy to the Cremins, was represented by Lieutenant-Colonel P. Barry.

Only six weeks into the new year of 1963, winter had claimed five more lives.

———

On the evening of 17 February, at the Shelbourne Hotel in Dublin, the Franciscan friars held an open forum called 'Panel on Your Problems'. Guests could freely ask questions and make comments.

On this night the Franciscans noticed that the attendance was considerably larger than usual. And there were questions quite out of the ordinary. A number of them were probing, even accusatory, about a certain 'Father Malachy', who was becoming a controversial figure in the city. Indeed, many women were not only suspicious but fearful of this mysterious Franciscan. People were now demanding answers.

The Gardaí and newspaper reporters were even more curious, as they had been for several years. Investigative reporters for the *Evening Herald* now referred to it as a 'mysterious case'. The Gardaí had already compiled a bulging file on the matter. But it contained testimonies and questions, not the answers they sought.

The episode of Father Malachy began in 1958 and over nearly six years had grown more complex and worrying. Ostensibly he was a Franciscan friar who was doing research for a book about family life in the parish. To document his work he would telephone women and conduct interviews. His contacts followed no identifiable pattern, and the interviews occurred sporadically. At first they drew little public attention, but as his 'interviews' became more invasive the Gardaí's interest grew.

In January 1963, when the harsh weather began to confine people more and more in their homes, Father Malachy made a bold 'reappearance', as it was called. He began phoning women at an unprecedented rate, asking new questions. His approach was simple, polite and reassuring: he first identified himself, explaining about his book, then said the bad weather was preventing him from going house to house for interviews. Would the women be kind enough to give him a few minutes to answer some questions over the phone? Since this was the only way he could conduct his research, it all sounded perfectly logical.

His was a soft, warm voice – that of a kind and caring priest. Most women were happy to comply, some even finding that it broke the monotony of dreary winter days. His casual manner put them quite at ease, convincing them of the legitimacy of his research. He told the women he was working on a chapter about marriage. Oh, many laughed, they knew plenty about marriage!

His *modus operandi* was polished. His first questions about domestic life were innocuous: how long had they been married? How many children had they? What work did their husband do? He was establishing trust. Then, slyly, his queries became slightly more personal. He was carefully monitoring how far he might go. If he felt the woman was hooked, he proceeded.

————

The Cremin family accident emboldened proponents of the Road Safety Campaign. Mandatory training in order to receive a licence would teach motorists how better to control their vehicles in slippery conditions. It might possibly have made a difference between life and death in the Cremin case and those like it.

Imposing enforceable speed limits was the first act in reducing road accidents, and in February the Gardaí announced that they would soon be using 'a device to detect speed defaulters'. It was high-tech radar technology, and its evidence could be used in court. The 'electrometers' were the same modern type used in the United States and Britain.[30] Reporters were given a demonstration at the Motor Driving School at the Garda Depot in the Phoenix Park. As one reporter from the *Irish Press* wrote, 'speedy motorists beware! By April 1 when the speed limits come into operation' every one of the thirty Garda divisions will be equipped with at least one patrol car with the 'latest apparatus for ascertaining' the speed of cars.

But it would take more than new technology to force motorists to slow down: it needed the greater authority of the courts behind it, and this was a glaring gap in the system of controlling driving abuses. In the courtroom most justices were infamously lenient when it came to handling road violations. In 1963 the press decided that it was time to cast a spotlight on the judicial problems. As one newspaper noted, even in cases where the driver was clearly guilty of a serious accident, too often 'the fines imposed in such cases are laughable'. Whether it was speeding drivers or drink-drivers, a scolding or a paltry fine seemed adequate to many justices. Gardaí knew that if justices didn't support them in court it undercut their authority out on the road.

On 13 February there occurred a most unusual accident in Dublin. It ended up in court, as usual. At noon, when the city was packed with people, an Englishman drove down O'Connell Street at 'a good clip' – going the *wrong way* and scattering other drivers and pedestrians along his path. Standing by Nelson's Pillar was Edward O'Flynn, who was legally blind. He was standing by the kerb waiting to make his way across the street when the driver 'completely caught the blind pensioner off-guard and knocked him down in the street.' It was only by luck that he had not been injured, or that people had not been killed.

Standing in court before Justice Reddin, the driver casually confessed to his multiple driving violations, His punishment? A bit of a lecture – and a £10 fine.

Advocates of the Road Safety Campaign argued for a combined system of the new radar technology, speed limits, tougher judges, driver training and certified licensing. They demanded a more enlightened attitude towards safe, sane driving, along with more discretion and power given to gardaí in enforcing public safety on the roads. The *Irish Independent*, favouring the expansion of Garda powers, despatched one of its journalists to the United States to observe its more liberal police regulations. He observed that American police have the authority to 'stop a driver on the public highway and ask him to produce a certificate showing when his car was last tested [for safety]'. In the process, the police could validate the driving licence, check on any previous violations and determine whether the vehicle was roadworthy. There was also a check of the driver's breath for alcohol to establish whether or not they were fit to drive.

By 1963 these were common-sense policing practices in most countries and indisputably made the roadways safer for everyone. But to many in Ireland they sounded audacious. Some saw them as a violation of their rights and privacy. The very idea that a garda could stop them on the open road and 'interrogate' them! Public attitudes were split between those who welcomed the idea and those who saw it as imposing intrusive regulations.

Ireland's road safety problem was clearly becoming a highly controversial issue.

———

Owing to the press coverage of the Franciscan panel at the Shelbourne Hotel, the 'mystery caller', as he had now been dubbed by the papers, was now alarming women readers. His prime areas were identified by the Gardaí as Raheny, Donnycarney, Kilmainham, Tallaght and Templeogue. But complaints were coming in to other Garda stations as well.

Based on the testimonies of these women, gardaí were developing a profile of the caller. He was believed to be between nineteen and twenty-six and well educated, and he was articulate and skilled at gaining a woman's confidence. Gardaí regarded him as a predator on the prowl. Young Dublin women now saw him as frightening and dangerous. In a Garda analysis of recent testimonies, women most commonly used the terms 'scary', 'disgusting', 'obnoxious' and 'immoral'. His queries were becoming increasingly invasive and explicit. One newspaper described them as 'most intimate' and definitely sexually suggestive. He was now asking women about relations with their husband – in bed. What did she 'like best'?

In late February the Franciscans verified that no such 'Father Malachy' existed in their order. No-one was surprised.

———

There was other news that women throughout Ireland dreaded. On 22 February the issue captured newspaper headlines: 'Purchase tax is coming'.

For months, households had feared the official announcement. Lower-income families especially fretted over its effect on their budgets. They had hoped the Government would not be so heartless as to impose the new tax upon them. Now it seemed inevitable:

> A Purchase Tax is now a certainty. And there is nothing the public can do to ward off the extra burden. For a family any new tax on purchases could be a crippling blow.[31]

Suddenly being taxed on such essential items as food, clothing and medicine seemed unjust, even immoral, to most people.

Dublin's pioneering women reformers were savvy about organisation and protests. However, it was recognised that opposition to the new tax would be most effectively led by housewives themselves.

———

Meanwhile, the *Irish Press* published an article about the prospect of quietening Dublin's noisy streets. This was also intended to contribute to the Road Safety Campaign. Entitled 'The use of the horn', it was a well-reasoned argument on the improper use of horns.

An article devoted to 'honking' and 'tooting' might have struck some readers as more frivolous than serious. But it was quite instructive. The premise was that in Ireland, and especially in Dublin, use of the horn was much abused. As car ownership was rapidly rising, too many drivers were 'inclined to become impatient' with slow traffic and 'show their disgust by blowing their horn'. However, this was '*not* the purpose of the horn'.

According to the article, a horn was 'potentially a lethal weapon'. Its high-pitched sound can alarm and upset elderly people. And, at night, people's sleep. Horns honked at the wrong time can distract and startle other drivers, causing them to brake suddenly or swerve dangerously.

Used properly, the horn is 'a *warning* instrument to others of our approach, or position on the road, or at a blind junction.' These are the only times in which it is justifiable and courteous to use a horn: to avoid a collision and possible injury or death. Drivers needed to learn the rules of the road and show patience and plain courtesy. All Ireland could then be safer – and quieter.

———

During the last week of February the mystery caller was on the prowl again, seeking gullible women in new parts of the suburbs. Newspapers called it a 'new spate' of calls, extending his activity into Churchtown and Artane. The Gardaí and the Franciscans were now in regular communication as the complaints mounted. It was learnt that one priest, the Rev. Lucius McClean, actually *was* in the process of writing a book on marriage, and he had been working on the manuscript for more than two years. Word was clearly put out that he was not the impostor.

After one paper reported that the 'soft-spoken confidence trickster has struck again', one woman called the Gardaí to say that he had contacted her twice in the same day, in the morning and late afternoon. The Gardaí concluded that he was becoming more aggressive. It was further learnt that 'savvy women now rang off' on him. A frequency pattern was detected in which he was quite active in phoning for a week or two, but then there was a let-up. After a while it would erupt again. From reading the papers, the scoundrel surely knew that the Gardaí were intensifying their efforts to catch him.

The mounting fear of some women was that the caller might become a stalker. Several told gardaí that they suspected the man had observed them in person and knew what they looked like, and perhaps even where they lived. It was a fact that his subjects were younger women. Possibly he even knew them already. While all the women filing complaints wanted to assist the Gardaí in apprehending the impostor, quite a few confessed that they were 'afraid of any publicity' they might suffer from co-operating too much.

Gardaí tried to convince them that their assistance was critical in the apprehension of the culprit and that their privacy would be protected. At this point, the Gardaí were devising a scheme for trapping the caller by luring him into calling some women back the same day. For this to work they had to have at least a few co-operative women. It was simply a matter of using some cunning, against him for a change. Gardaí told the women to be relaxed on the phone, to talk to him for a few minutes in an obliging manner, then politely ask if he could phone back in about an hour. The women were then to instantly notify the Gardaí so that they could tap the line and trace the caller. It had now become a cat-and-mouse contest.

By the last few days of February they had a few volunteers, and the Gardaí were confident that they were now closing their net on him. It was only a matter of time before he could be trapped and identified. However, 'Father Malachy' might become suspicious, sending him underground once again.

———

Some of the best news of the winter months came at the end of February and did wonders for the spirits of concert devotees. They were thrilled to learn that one of the world's most famous performers would be coming in a few months:

> Igor Stravinsky, the famed Russian composer, is coming to Dublin in June. He will conduct the Radio Éireann Symphony Orchestra in a concert of his own works.

In something of an understatement, one newspaper wrote that 'his visit will be the highlight of the season of opera and concerts.' His admirers were more inclined to regard it as perhaps the highlight of their musical *life*. One reporter saw the occasion in a more profound light:

Stravinsky is a legendary figure in music and his visit will be an historic event in the annals of Dublin.

Only a few days later, another musical coup was announced. Soon to appear on stage in Dublin would be Van Cliburn, the American pianist who had earned enormous reputation. His superb performances had enthralled audiences around the world.

The 1963 concert season would be a truly unique one, long remembered and cherished. With the glorious news, February indeed ended on a high note.

Chapter 4 ~

THE 'GREAT WALK' AND THE UCD HIKERS' TRAGEDY

March, ordinarily a fickle month, began with warmer temperatures, spells of glorious sunshine and a genuine whiff of spring. There was a sense of liberation from winter's grip. People were venturing forth, taking strolls in the park. After the harsh months of January and February there was a feeling of optimism in the air, better luck ahead. John Molloy, the *Irish Independent's* theatre critic, detected it. After seeing the play *There Y'Are* at the Gate, he found himself mulling over the Irishman's resilience:

> No one has a keener sense of humour … He looks life straight in the face and, even in adversity, he can see something of the silver lining behind the cloud. [32]

For Sheila Daly, a farmer's wife from Co. Cavan, 1 March already marked a lucky year. In fact, a most memorable one: she gave birth to twins – for the *third consecutive* time. Doctors were astounded. In something of an understatement, one said, 'In Dublin gynaecological circles it was agreed to be a most unusual occurrence.' The baby boy and girl were born in Holles Street, where they were, of course, the talk of the staff. It didn't take long for the remarkable story to reach the attention of reporters.

While Ireland's pop music fans might not have felt as lucky as the admirers of Stravinsky and Van Cliburn, they were excited to learn in the first week of March of the year's concert schedule. Chubby Checker, the 'king of the twist', would be arriving in early summer for a twelve-day tour. His song 'Let's Twist Again' was topping the American and European charts. Jim Reeves, extremely popular in Ireland, was booked for a two-week tour in June. He was to be followed by Bill Haley and His Comets, whose sensation 'Rock Around the Clock' had ignited the rock-and-roll craze in the fifties. A terrific summer was ahead.

There were even rumours, admittedly unconfirmed, that the Fab Four were considering an appearance in Dublin some time in the autumn. For Ireland's multitude of Beatlemaniacs it would be a fantasy come true.

——

The improved weather was welcomed by no-one more enthusiastically than Dublin's builders and their allies the demolitionists. They were champing at the bit to return to rebuilding the city – after first tearing down the historic buildings, many of which were eighteenth and nineteenth-century structures that had only needed restoration in order to regain their original splendour.

By March 1963 the battle lines between developers and builders and the impassioned preservationists were clearly drawn. The craze for eradicating old Dublin had already led to the irretrievable loss of scores of architectural treasures. Historic dwellings and shops had been ravaged for the purpose of 'modernising'. To preservationists, it was criminal.

Entire historic areas had been wiped off the map to make space for glass-and-steel office buildings. The inhabitants, many third and fourth generation, had been transplanted to new, soulless housing estates.

On 4 March the fears of preservationists were heightened when James Deegan, an auctioneer, addressed a meeting at the Dublin Junior Chamber of Commerce. Speaking candidly, he told his audience that Dublin 'would be a skyscraper city today if it were not for the restrictions on development and building.' He regretted that builders were 'straight-jacketed', as he put it, by protective preservation orders. Many developers were trying their best to have them abolished so that they could erect at will their monstrosities rising into the clouds. And become fabulously rich in the process.

That same afternoon, preservationists were blindsided by a threat previously unimaginable to them: an assault on St Stephen's Green.

With the economic boom of the early sixties, and an expanding, affluent middle class, came a great increase in car ownership. This created exasperating traffic problems and a Darwinian struggle for parking spaces. On the streets around the Green the problem had become especially acute. As well as the Shelbourne Hotel, there were many elite clubs and

organisations whose members demanded convenient parking. By 1963 they
were complaining loudly to the Government.

At about the time that Deegan was finishing his 'skyscraper' speech,
a member of the City Council offered his suggestion for a solution to the
parking problem: the railings around the Green could simply be moved back
about twenty feet, creating much additional space for the Mercedes cars.

When word of his idea leaked out, the public was horrified. All for the
sake of the almighty car! The Green was the 'lungs' of the city, an aesthetic
and social haven where people could retreat for fresh air and relaxation.
Often considered the jewel of Dublin, it was sacred and irreplaceable.

A storm of protest erupted. Letters buried editors' desks. Apart from
the outrage, many letters expressed valid reasoning about why such an act
would be contrary to the intentions of the founders of the Green. They felt
they had history on their side. The letters ranged from raw emotion to the
rationally stated:

> We are told never to write when we feel angry, but I am writing to express
> my horror at the suggestion made by someone in the City Council that
> the railings of the Park be moved back 20 feet – to accommodate that
> pest of modern society, the motorist.[33]

One writer explained that 'from time immemorial' the Green was
a commonage where 'citizens strayed at will'. Then, in the seventeenth
century, wealthy city aldermen usurped the citizens' rights and sold the
city's property to their friends, who enclosed it. Then, 'about eighty years
ago, liberal and public-spirited men' demanded that the citizens be restored
their rights to the Green. Arthur Edward Guinness, Lord Ardilaun, spent
large sums to make it one of the most beautiful parks in Europe, for the
'health and recreation' of the citizens:

> Now, the reactionaries want to take 20 feet all round and pump the
> fumes of petrol and motor oil into the teeth of the men, women and
> children … Aye, the little children from Cuffe Street and York Street to
> whom fresh air means a lot.[34]

The writer further warned readers not to be deceived by the culprits of
the diabolical proposal; their ravenousness would reach far beyond a mere

twenty feet, as long as they got away with it. It would result in an insidious scheme of chiselling away at the periphery of the Green.

One building worker wrote:

> They say it is *only 20 feet* – but give them this and these Philistines will want the whole lot for parking! They must not touch our St Stephen's Green. Not an inch!

'Not an inch!' became the clarion cry of citizens and preservationists. They appealed to newspapers for support and immediately received it. Editors were commended for exposing the threat and vigorously opposing it. One reader wrote that 'it rests on the newspapers to arouse the people's interests before it is too late – and the harm is done.' How many times had Dubliners dallied passively, grumbling without acting as the city's historic architecture and amenities were destroyed before their eyes? It had been scarcely a year since the venerable Theatre Royal had been smashed to smithereens as teary-eyed crowds watched, wondering, *How* could this happen!

And now St Stephen's Green?

———

On the morning of the 5th a sudden drama gripped the city. Johnny Clarke of Marino, a labourer engaged in demolition, showed up for work in Townsend Street. A hard-working Co. Mayo man, he knew the risks of tearing down decrepit tenements. But the money was decent and he had a young family to support. Most of his work was done by hand, pulling and pushing on ropes and rafters, and he was always ready to retreat on a second's warning. His wife worried every day when he left for work.

Just after 8 a.m. he climbed to the first floor of a half-demolished house. Trying to manoeuvre some dangling ropes he made the smallest mistake. According to his workmate William Gallagher:

> a foot was misplaced ... Suddenly he was entangled in the rope and pitching through a gap in the floor, into a 15-foot shaft which crumbled over him. One moment he was beside me, then he was suddenly *gone* – through the floor. I just stood still, and prayed. I was sure he was dead.[35]

Workmen could not attempt a rescue, because 'tons of crumbling masonry hung poised over the trapped figure.' Gardaí and the fire brigade were called.

As a crowd gathered, Father Aiden Burke showed up and began praying. A young doctor from Jervis Street Hospital happened by, halting to remain on the scene. Reporters were already describing it as a 'life and death drama' on their notepads.

By 8:45 it was determined that Johnny was still alive but 'stuck fast in waist-high debris'. Extricating him meant risking bringing down the 'brick mountain and burying him alive', and this could be triggered merely by moving a single wrong brick. The firefighters had no choice but to try. Shortly after nine, several probed their way inch by inch towards him. When they found him he was conscious and able to help and direct them. A reporter captured the scene:

> Everyone about the shaft froze to immobility as a pile of masonry tumbled with a roar in an adjoining section of the building. 'I can't move my leg!' Johnny shouted up![36]

After ninety minutes of the most painstaking effort, a firefighter called out, 'I've reached him!' Every chunk of brick, mortar and wood that was holding him tightly was lifted with great skill. He was then 'expertly hauled up through the floor gap' to a waiting stretcher. A mighty cheer went up as doctors carried out a quick examination before he was whisked off in an ambulance. Johnny seemed 'quite calm', wrote a reporter standing close by, 'as he drew gratefully on a cigarette'.

A short while later, at the demolition site, Johnny's workmates were given orders to pull on three ropes that had 'bridged the gap between life and death', as one newspaper wrote. Within seconds, the spot where he had been trapped became a 'smoking mountain of rubble'.

Similar demolition sites dotted much of the inner city.

——

During the first week of March, newspapers reported on a new movement growing in popularity in the United States – one that might have possibilities in Ireland. As part of his 'new frontier' philosophy, President Kennedy was vigorously promoting a national fitness programme. People needed to get outdoors, exercise, play sports – and simply *walk*. To publicise the project, Robert Kennedy, the US Attorney-General, organised a fifty-mile walk that captured media attention. Walking, jogging and hiking were really coming into vogue in America during 1963, and in city streets and suburban roads it was now a common sight. America was finally getting fit.

Kennedy's 'walkathon', as American papers called it, had been a great success in spurring people towards better health. This prompted the *Evening Herald* to ask, 'If Americans can do it, why not the Irish?'

And so it began.

The *Herald's* idea was to jointly sponsor a similar walk to inspire people to arise from their couches, step out into the fresh air and begin walking. The original goal was a forty-mile walk to be held on St Patrick's Day, inviting men, women and children to come out and do their best. With luck, a few hundred participants would show up for the first effort. If successful it could become an expanded event the following year. It seemed at least worth a try. On 5 March the *Herald* proclaimed its plan: 'It's on! Fitness walk date is set'.

———

The following morning a seemingly unlikely topic made the front page of the *Irish Independent*. It was hardly a dramatic topic on first notice, but it was one with profound implications for Ireland's economy and society. The headline was 'Big supermarket plan'.

It certainly caught the attention of the country's legion of small grocers, and of its farmers as well. No editor needed to explain to them its importance.

It was not news of a single supermarket but rather of a chain of twenty-four to be built in Ireland at a cost of £2 million. When the president of the National Farmers' Association, Rickard Deasy, announced the news, he noted that the plan was that of an 'international combine'. What, exactly, did that mean? readers might have wondered. At first, Deasy was evasive about the ownership and potential effect of the giant supermarkets. That was until he decided to be more candid, when addressing a group in Malahide:

> Farmers must prepare now for the supermarket era. Pre-packaging and self-service could give farmers outlets for their produce. This has for too long been delayed in Ireland.[37]

For both the country's small farmers and its grocers the 'writing was on the wall'. It was unmistakably a serious threat to the traditional economy and to their role in society. Like the old craftsmen and tradesmen – the coopers, farriers, saddle-makers, stone-carvers and the like – they were vulnerable. They feared being rendered obsolete in the modern age by supermarket behemoths, and fading into oblivion.

————

In the second week of March the *Irish Independent* published an alarming exposé of another extremely serious threat to St Stephen's Green. This one was perhaps even more radical and rapacious than the scheme to gobble up twenty feet of its peripheral grounds.

The concept had been alluded to some months previously. Now, however, investigative reporters had uncovered substantive information behind the plan. As the *Independent* revealed, there had in fact been clandestine 'discussions on the possibility of the Dublin Corporation providing an underground car park' beneath St Stephen's Green. It was to be an expansive one that would involve massive excavation projects.

As citizens were trying to comprehend such a drastic proposal, Donogh O'Malley, Parliamentary Secretary to the Minister for Finance, bolted forward with sharp words of opposition, backed by sound reasoning. While conceding that such a plan 'might be feasible', he felt it would 'only be at tremendous' cost in its damage to the Green. Such excavation, he explained, would have to be deep enough to avoid tree roots, water and drainage pipes, and electric cables. Furthermore, the reinforcement of the roof of such a structure would have to be sufficient to bear the weight of all the soil, trees and buildings, as well as of the water in the lake and its concrete bottom. And, realistically, *all* the existing trees might have to be removed. During the years-long project it would be 'unlikely' that the Green could be used by the public at all.

It was difficult to envisage the delicate Green being ravaged in such a manner. An army of opponents to the scheme immediately sided with O'Malley. To support his case, O'Malley quoted from the St Stephen's Green (Dublin) Act (1877), which stipulates the following:

The Commissioner shall maintain the Green and shall allow the same to be used and enjoyed as a public park for the recreation and enjoyment of the public – and not for any other purpose.

O'Malley hastened to point out that there were plenty of derelict and waste sites in the inner city that could be used for multi-storey car parks. Yet he knew that devious developers could influence Government officials to circumvent building codes if the stakes were high enough. And this project would be hugely profitable.

To O'Malley and the multitude of environmentalists and citizens who agreed with him the thought of sacrificing the character of St Stephen's Green for the almighty car was abhorrent. O'Malley wanted to make his attitude clear:

> Under no circumstances would he be prepared to recommend to the Commission of Public Works that *anything* be done affecting St Stephen's Green whereby 'even *one tree* might be lost, or the present area changed in any way'.[38]

In its headline the *Irish Independent* threw its weight behind absolute protection of the park: 'St. Stephen's Green "must remain unchanged".'

———

Every day it seemed that new information about the fitness walk was coming out in the newspapers, stirring the public's enthusiasm. Its name had already been changed to the 'Great Walk'. There was no doubt that it was off to a smashing start, with people signing up at a steady rate. The concept even seemed to be resonating with the sedentary population. Those who were not ready to participate in that first year still expressed their admiration for all those who were plunging in to the event.

Further good news was that the Great Walk was to be open not only to individuals but to teams from offices, schools, shops, clubs, factories – groups of any type. After all, its purpose was fun as well as fitness. The team concept had great appeal, and enrolment jumped quickly. And to make it more festive, even whimsical, it was announced that a prize would be awarded to those participants wearing the 'most original costumes' based on the *Evening Herald* cartoon characters. So walkers should not be surprised to find themselves strutting alongside Mutt and Jeff or some of their pals.

There were, however, rules to be followed. The event would begin at 10 a.m. from Independent House in Middle Abbey Street and go to the Eagle's

Nest in Bray. It was twenty miles each way, for those who chose the return leg. Participants needed to know that there would be 'secret check points' along the route to ensure that no walkers accepted lifts. And 'judges will patrol the route in cars', having the power to disqualify any person breaking the rules. Therefore, it was good to state some of the rules:

1. Running will not be permitted, but trotting is permissible.
2. No short cuts will be allowed.
3. Accepting a lift will incur disqualification.
4. Any type of clothing may be worn.

The more information that was released, the more confusion it created. At first, it had sounded like a true fitness event; then, with the cartoon costumes, it felt more like a lark; but the serious rules made it seem like a competitive race. So what exactly *was* it now: a fitness walk, a comical romp, a trot or a real foot race? Apparently, the organisers themselves were not certain. But did it really matter? To those few competitive runners who had signed up, it did indeed.

———

A few days after the news broke about the supermarket chain planned for Ireland, the *Irish Press* followed it with its own 'inside' story. It revealed that the 'secretive' ownership of the 'international concern' was actually British. This only confirmed many people's suspicions.

Reportedly, a 'major English chain' aimed at an 'invasion' of the Irish provinces as well as Dublin. It was predicted that this would be met with 'mixed feelings'. In an editorial, the newspaper assessed its probable effect on shoppers and the national economy:

Let it be admitted that the notion of supermarkets has come to stay. The advantages are immense. They buy in bulk, employ less staff and can generally sell at a lower price. It is natural that the housewife should rally to them – oblivious to the fact that thousands of small shopkeepers throughout the country will lose their livelihood as a consequence. This is part of the price that must be paid.

We may regret it, but the tide cannot be turned back.[39]

The admission was painful but indisputable. What was especially regretted – indeed, resented – was that British investors were behind the supermarket scheme. As the editorial asked, 'since we must have supermarkets, is it not better that we should have our *own*?' The paper called it 'an English foreign invasion' that would surely sound the death knell for scores of helpless small grocers throughout the country.

———

On 8 March the *Herald* released another bulletin. 'Entries pour in … The Walk has aroused intense interest'. Many hundreds were already signed up. Letters about the Great Walk drew wide readership, as many were amusing, even personal:

> Why not invite the Lord Mayor to take part in the Great Walk? It would help keep his weight down and would also add colour to the event.

Not that the event needed added colour, for 'walking fever' seemed to be sweeping the country, before the first step had even been taken. One group wrote in to announce that at some later date they intended to 'organise a 50-mile walk to Dundalk'. Not to be outdone, another letter boasted of plans being made for a cross-country walk, from Dublin to Galway. And *back*.

No doubt about it, some Irish people were determined to out-perform the Americans.

———

J. Horgan was more concerned about road safety than about all the hoopla over some 'great' walk. Particularly concerning him were the bad drivers responsible for the startling accident rate. Considering himself something of an expert on the subject, he submitted a letter to the 'Your View' column of the *Evening Herald*. He had devised his own 'driver typology' for bad drivers:

> The 'Sunday Driver', the 'Lady Driver' and the 'Road Hog' have all come in for criticism and revile. There are, however, other psycho-pathological types more subtle, more sinister, and less easy to recognise.[40]

Sounding like an automotive psychoanalyst, he proceeded to define his typology: the impatient, the reckless, the aggressive, the exhibitionists and the simple incompetents. Oh, yes, and especially the 'female flunkeys'. His advice: get women off the road and half the problem would be solved.

He hoped the organisers of the Road Safety Campaign would find his contribution helpful in dealing with the problem.

————

It was now only six days until Dublin's big 'happening', in sixties parlance, and the Great Walk monopolised people's conversation. The excitement had become contagious. Journalists joined in with their opinions, serious and silly. On 11 March, Douglas Coupar of the *Evening Herald* wrote an article titled 'Don't sneer at the long-distance runners: it's we layabouts who are crackpots'. He confessed to being surprised at the astounding response as the mantra became 'Get out and walk!' His observation was that it had 'become almost a matter of national pride to participate and match the Americans':

> Everyone from the aged, the affluent, and the athletic to the corpulent and the sedentary have been urged and exhorted to get out and walk. Thus, the hardy and optimistic have 'taken up the challenge' to stump perspiring and with anguished, protesting muscles on long, weary marches.

After writing admirably of walkers with strong character and willpower – plain guts and gumption – he saved his journalistic honesty till last:

> The rest of us apathetic victims of our modern environment are smugly content to sit at home with our feet up … and dismiss the 'crackpots' on the long march.[41]

————

As Coupar's article went to press, 1,350 people were already marching through the streets of Dublin, but with high purpose – walking not for the sake of fitness but for a home for their family. All young women, and recent brides, they were heading for the Mansion House to participate in the fourteenth draw for houses by the Dublin Corporation. Each woman must have been married in the previous two years. Only two hundred lucky winners would be offered a house within twelve months. As they packed into the Round Room some held their babies, and councillors were interrupted by 'an occasional wail or gurgle'.

When the Lord Mayor, J. J. O'Keeffe, was ready to draw the first name, the tension was palpable. Each winner was asked to stand. The first name called was that of Lena Harris. She held her six-month-old daughter, Yvonne, in her arms as she jumped out of her chair. Like all the other women in the room, she had dreamed of having her own home one day – and now she suddenly had it.

The other 199 names were called, to gasps and cries of happiness. When all the winning names were read, the remaining 1,150 women seemed resigned. After all, they knew the odds hadn't been in their favour. What *did* disappoint them was the announcement at the end that this was to be the last new brides' housing draw. No wishing for better luck next year: 1963 marked their last chance for the grand prize.

―――

On 14 March the organisers of the Great Walk had a big announcement to make: there were now more than 1,500 entrants! As the numbers kept ballooning it was looking more like the Great Crusade. Organisers scrambled to meet the growing needs of the crowd. CIE had to put on special buses for the return journey from Bray to Dublin. More gardaí had to be stretched along the route.

After signing up, some of the entrants felt a bit like celebrities as family and friends expressed their admiration for their determined spirit. Participants exhorted others to 'come on … sign up … join in – *walk!*' The most common question now going around Dublin was a simple 'Are you in?' A sheepish look of shame on some faces gave it away.

―――

If 1,500 entrants were eagerly anticipating their walking challenge, some 30,000 children were no less excited about their big contest day. These were the boys and girls who had already signed up for the Yo-Yo Championship heats. It was a huge event for youngsters all over the country who were practising whirling, twirling, whipping and spinning their yo-yos with dazzling dexterity. And, unlike most walking competitors, they had been in serious training for months. They took the competition seriously and dreamt of making it to the national finals.

There was no advantage for more affluent families in the yo-yo contest. A child from the poorest area, or most remote farm, had as good a chance of winning as anyone else. For what was called the 'monster final', the world yo-yo champion, Billy Panama, would be in attendance to give his stupendous demonstration.

———

Ordinarily, as 17 March approached, national attention would be concentrated on the coming St Patrick's Day parade and festivities. But this year St Patrick had to share the spotlight with the horde of Great Walkers. Parade organisers told the press that this year would be the biggest and best in scale and variety. There would be more than seventy-five companies and several voluntary organisations participating. One company alone intended to spend £250 on flowers. The year's theme was 'Dublin of yesteryear', featuring an elaborate scale model of an 1898 Dublin tram.

There was one hope shared by organisers of the parade and of the Great Walk: for good weather!

On the eve of the Great Walk there was a last bulletin. In the final forty-eight hours the number of entrants had gone ballistic: 'a tremendous response … 4,000 will now take part'. Organisers were flabbergasted. The last-minute surge, from 1,500, was unexpected. Nonetheless, the Great Walk was on! Come what may.

———

In the days leading up to the two big events, many citizens must have paid scant attention to other news items. It was being reported that there were rumblings of a possible *national* bus strike – one that could conceivably cripple the country's transport system. However, rumours of bus strikes had become so common that many people tended to dismiss them.

Yet when all the excitement of March had ended and people got back to the humdrum of daily life, the bus strike would claim the headlines. Some feared that it could lead to what might be called the 'Greater Walk', comprising throngs of involuntary participants.

———

On the morning of Sunday, the 17th, thousands of people climbed out of bed and went to their windows to see what the sky might foretell. It was grey and dismal, the clouds hanging just above the city's chimney stacks. They selected the right food items to bring for the race: bananas, apples, biscuits, sandwiches. They were promised piping hot soup at checkpoints along the way, courtesy of Brown and Polson. More than 170 gallons of soup was being prepared, perfect for a day like that. Especially if rain should set in.

Apart from the paraders and walkers, many other events were to take place that day, among them the Railway Cup finals in football and hurling, and the Irish Kennel Club's 42nd Annual Show, held on the RDS grounds in Ballsbridge. In the evening there was an array of dances for St Patrick's Day. Some walkers might have had some hesitation about dancing the night away.

By 8:30 that morning a crowd had begun gathering at the starting-point for the Great Walk. Apart from the 4,000 participants there would be countless friends and spectators. Since everyone seemed energised and anxious, it was difficult to tell one from the other. One of the significant aspects of the Great Walk was its egalitarian composition, a mixture of all social and economic types: housewives, businessmen, factory workers, students, shop clerks, labourers, nurses, dockers, soldiers, solicitors, office workers, postal staff, civil servants. Outfits were fascinating: apart from the predictable Mutt and Jeff outfits and other cartoon characters from the *Evening Herald,* there were cowboys, pirates, film stars, clowns and innumerable get-ups that were simply indescribable. Even Abraham Lincoln showed up in his stovepipe hat.

Many people were wearing their ordinary shoes, boots, house slippers and even high heels. Others milled about carrying banners and placards. One proclaimed, *If Uncle Sam can do it, so can we!*

There were men, women and children of every age and degree of fitness. Among the walkers was Annie Fox of Crumlin, a 63-year-old widow who was delighted, telling reporters that it would be child's play for her, since she regularly made the five-mile walk from Crumlin into the city. A British army pensioner, J. P. Brabazon, 77, was a distinguished senior walker. Ten years earlier he had walked from Dublin to Cork. He was a safe bet to reach Bray. Frank Cahill, 63, had joined the Donore Harriers athletics club in 1923 and remained an avid road-racer. He considered the Bray walk routine exercise. Meanwhile, Patrick Sloan, 49, laughingly told everyone around him that he was walking for a bet: a glass of sherry.

There were some serious garda and army participants out to prove their fitness. For them there was a definite competitive spirit. A few were elite runners. Pat Shea was a cross-country runner with the Phoenix Harriers. His race companion, Kevin Gormley, held the all-Ireland mile and two-mile records. Garda Con Hearty was a champion walker who had competed in Britain and done very well.

Plenty of admiration was heaped upon the children who had entered the walk. The youngest competitor was Hugh O'Donnell, 11, who was accompanied by his mother. Diarmuid Kerrisk was 12. Fiona O'Sullivan, also 12, was accompanied by her brother Colin. While the children would elicit cheers all along the way, there were those who wondered if they should be entered into such a gruelling event. Could they possibly finish?

For reporters it was a field day. Among them was Tom Hennigan of the *Evening Herald*, sponsor of the big event. He admitted to his readers that he would be travelling in a luxury car, supplied with food and drink along the way. He wrote candidly of his early expectations:

> We looked pityingly at them … the test of endurance that lay before them. 'Walk twenty miles?' we found ourselves thinking – 'three-quarters of them won't make Donnybrook!'

———

A few streets away the organisers of the St Patrick's Day parade were feverishly at work on their biggest event yet. The logistics of getting everything in place, on time, was challenging. That year some twenty bands were participating. There was a huge array of floats, one with a group of girls dancing the twist.

Experienced walkers at the Great Walk distanced themselves from the clownish crowd. The Lord Mayor, J. J. O'Keeffe, was on the scene to act as starter. He had unabashedly decided not to join in: apparently, he didn't regard himself as an Irish Robert Kennedy. Meanwhile, organisers were doing their best to separate the walking participants, all 4,000 of them, from the gawkers. Clearly many participants were more interested in socialising than in actually walking the twenty miles.

Some had come prepared with rain gear; others had no protection. By the time the Lord Mayor made his way to the starting-post the drizzle was turning to rain. At ten he gave the signal for the Great Walk to begin.

Within the first few strides it was clear that this was to be a classic 'hare and tortoise' event. For many, delusions of Olympian grandeur would be fleeting: the early show-offs would soon ignominiously fall behind. Hennigan recorded what he saw:

> The motley army moved off briskly singing and laughing, pushing gaily into the teeth of a rain storm that, as the hours passed, got worse. We saw it all from a staff car, in our rather corpulent condition … We didn't feel like joining in.[42]

Though the St Patrick's Day parade organisers were discouraged, it was not to begin until 11:30, and they could hope that the weather would pass over. But it worsened into a rainstorm with strong winds. Before long, the unprotected walkers at the race were soaked to the skin. Hennigan's jocular attitude began changing. Much to his surprise, walkers were *not* dropping out:

> Our car purred through the forest of plastic macs, sodden jeans. Before the start, we had the idea that the crowd would be sobbing … but to their credit there was no wailing. This was a lark on an epic scale.
> On and on they slogged, up one hill and down the next. We watched in mounting admiration. Undismayed by signposts which coldly proclaimed that Bray was (still) fifteen miles away.

He noted that 'one young lady did give up' somewhere near Kilternan when 'a city bus pulled up just beside her …"78

It was too much to resist.' She sheepishly climbed aboard. Certainly he didn't fault her.

Within the first few miles the mass of walkers had begun to spread-eagle conspicuously along the route. Eventually they would stretch over a distance of nearly twelve miles. By the half-way point they faced a lashing rainstorm with torrential downpours. Yet it seemed to imbue most walkers with a new determination and collective spirit. With the terrible weather there were now few spectators along the route to cheer them on. But the break for hot soup was heavenly. For nearly everyone it had now become a matter of pride.

Meanwhile, the St Patrick's Day parade moved off slowly from St Stephen's Green. The *Irish Press* described the conditions as 'torrential rain, driven by an almost gale-force south-easterly wind'. Participants appeared more resolute than cheerful. The crowds along O'Connell Street were discouragingly smaller than usual, despite the big build-up in the newspapers.

Parade performers dutifully carried out their acts. The bands blared their lively numbers. Several floats were for admirable causes, including the Red Cross float seeking 'Freedom from hunger'. Another was that of the Water Safety Campaign, hoping to encourage people to learn how to swim and to be cautious in the water. In 1962 some 120 people had drowned, most unnecessarily.

Despite the drenching, everything seemed to be going according to plan. Until, that is, one unplanned 'outlaw exhibit', as reporters dubbed it, burst into the parade, causing quite a furore. For spectators it was a few minutes of unscripted, exciting action. For organisers and gardaí it was an embarrassment and a challenge. The outlaw car had cleverly weaselled its way into the procession at just the right moment, carrying placards calling for the release of Joseph Doyle, who was in prison in England in connection with the IRA raid on the Hazebrouck Barracks, near Arborfield, Berkshire. After the car went directly past the reviewing stand, gardaí halted it and 'manhandled' it out of the parade. However, its mission had been accomplished.

The lengthy parade took forty minutes to pass the reviewing stand. Despite the gloomy Sunday, the *Irish Independent* would rave that it was the 'most colourful, impressive and imaginative' parade in the city's history, 'definitely the best one ever seen'. Unfortunately, there were far too few spectators. One soggy reporter called it the 'foulest weather that ever washed out a St Patrick's Day'.

Meanwhile, the walkers had got beyond the half-way point, and it had become a test of endurance. It was now mostly a silent march. But no-one seemed to be complaining, even when the soup provisions grew low. With every mile, Hennigan's admiration grew. He was simply astonished at their resilience. 'The hours passed and the weather got worse and worse – but nobody thought of giving up!'

As the walkers sloshed along in their marathon of misery, over at the RDS grounds pampered pooches were strutting their stuff before admirers at the Irish Kennel Club's annual show. That year there was a particularly strong performance from Britain and the Six Counties. Cocker spaniels were the largest entry, with 163. Poodles came next, with 130. Great Danes made their first appearance in twenty-two years. There were 109 registered breeds with the club. As usual, the obedience tests drew the most admiring audience.

In Bray a sparse crowd had gathered by late afternoon to welcome the Great Walk finishers. The first man in sight was the 28-year-old garda Con Hearty. One reporter recorded that Hearty went through the field like a hot knife through butter, finishing well ahead of his nearest rival, John Doyle. When the 63-year-old Annie Fox walked briskly across the finishing line she said, 'It didn't take a feather out of me – I'd take the twenty-mile walk back but for a blistered heel!' No-one seemed to doubt her.

The oldest competitor, J. P. Brabazon, showed that he still had a sprightly step, completing the course in a little over seven hours. The youngest walker, 11-year-old Hugh O'Donnell, came into the Bray promenade at 4:30 with his mother – to great cheers for both. And, of course, Patrick Sloan earned his glass of sherry.

Remarkably, there had been no accidents among the four thousand walkers. There was no cheating, no complaining, no cursing the weather. One newspaper summed it up: 'joviality was the keynote throughout'.

Ten men announced that they were going to complete the forty-mile walk back to Dublin. And so they did. Among them was the 63-year-old Frank Cahill, who arrived back at Independent House a few minutes after 9 p.m. He completed the entire Great Walk in slightly under ten hours. He was ready to take on Bobby Kennedy.

Everyone received their certificates of accomplishment. Fifty years later, some still proudly show it off.

The next day Hennigan was effusive in his praise and admiration in his column. And humble in his admissions. '*How wrong!*' he had been to have had such doubts about their tenacity and spirit. Along with other reporters he declared the Great Walk to have 'been a great success – and national inspiration'.

Students at Trinity College, Dublin, were not to be outdone. They announced their third annual Belfast to Dublin walk, to be held on the morning of 4 May. This herculean challenge was only for participants in top form. Last year there were nearly fifty starters for the 103-mile race. While the majority reached the border, only eight crossed the finishing line at Trinity. Dick Harvey endured to become the much-admired winner. This year's race was expected to be even more exciting.

And what was the grand award for such an Olympian victory? Organisers would again be 'offering a barrel of stout to the winner'.

———

On 18 March, as thousands of people were resting their feet, an *Irish Times* headline brought bad news: 'National bus strike almost certain'.

This was not to be another localised strike in Dublin: it would affect the entire country. Furthermore, it was 'likely to be prolonged'. In 1963 the majority of citizens didn't own a car. Bus transport was indispensable.

As people waited anxiously, hoping for an eleventh-hour settlement, a new potential crisis in Dublin came to light. On the 21st, Dubliners learnt that another natural amenity was under threat. The placid canals were being eyed by the Corporation and developers, once again for the sake of the almighty automobile. Word got out that the Corporation was considering 'a decision to fill in the Grand Canal'. Citizens found the news incredible. It was further learnt that the Engineering Department at City Hall was already 'considering whether the former waterways may be converted into a link road.' *Former* waterways? Their assumption was clear: both the Grand Canal and the Royal Canal would be filled in and made open to new uses.

A confident spokesperson for the Corporation stated that the 'numerous bridges' in the city 'spanning the canal may be used as traffic fly-overs'. When the public outcry was immediately heard, the Corporation trotted out some engineers to convince people that it was a practical idea. One engineer stood firm, contending that it 'was worth converting the former canals into fast motorways', because it would 'speed up Dublin's traffic flow and ease congestion'.

To Dubliners, the canals were an irreplaceable aesthetic and social amenity, without which the city would not be the same. From childhood, they could trace their affection for the canals – swimming, fishing, boating, playing along the banks. For years the city's preservationists and environmentalists had been hoping for just the opposite news, that the Corporation would fund a reclamation project to *restore* the canals to their original cleanliness and beauty. Any scheme for draining and burying their canals could not go unchallenged. Some causes were worth fighting for. *Save the canals* posters immediately went into print.

In the year 1963 it seemed that the Corporation and city officials were on a rampage of desecration and destruction throughout the city. Often they were pawns of influential developers. 'Tear down!' was their strategy for modernisation, resulting in rubble heaps galore. It was not unusual for visitors to comment that it reminded them of parts of bombed-out post-war cities.

Preservationists pleaded for the protection and restoration of the city's treasured historic architecture and streetscapes. Year after year, nothing was done as O'Connell Street was transformed from a once-elegant street, one of the finest in Europe, into a shocking state of neglect. Why had the Corporation not aggressively protected it and funded reclamation? so many people wondered. By March 1963 O'Connell Street had deteriorated into a national embarrassment. No-one could deny this. The abuses were blatant: people were habituated to littering both along the pavement and from car windows, without concern for being penalised.

Visitors from other countries, where environmental preservation laws were enforced, could hardly conceal their horror. Some wrote in to newspapers to say they actually had to 'wade through' some trashy parts of the street where newspaper heaps had blown into knee-high mounds of litter.

Exacerbating the street's decline, shops in the early sixties had become more sleazy, with gaudy signs and façades, especially those advertising food and gaming. The so-called casinos were the worst offenders. To preservationists it was a vile infestation, and they argued that it needed to be stamped out.

The joint honorary secretaries of the Irish Housewives' Association had watched it deteriorate for years, with great sadness. In March they felt compelled to write a letter to the papers in which they expressed their feeling that the 'fair face' of the street had been tragically 'despoiled by the garish shopfronts'. They especially disdained the *Bingo played here!* signs proliferating along the street.

To the most respectable merchants and business people along O'Connell Street it had become a sordid sight. In March the owners of the Gresham Hotel and Clery's department store, together with fine jewellery shops and other reputable shop-owners, protested vehemently to the Corporation about the desecration of the street, particularly the plague of gaming establishments. Some councillors expressed the view that gaming should never have been allowed, and others contended that it should now be banned. Of course, this would be a struggle, since powerful financial backers were involved.

———

As the last week of March neared, a national bus strike appeared almost inevitable. 'Big bus strike looming', warned the *Irish Independent*. The newspaper's advice – prepare:

> This time the country is to suffer, and the provincial cities ... [must prepare] for foot-slogging, traffic jams, dependence on motorists' charity.

This would be no ordinary bus strike: it could cripple the economy and inflict hardship on people in every county.

Newspapers endeavoured to explain the cause of the strike. In essence, it was CIE's shift from a two-man to a one-man bus system. On many routes conductors were simply no longer needed. Drivers had been equipped with a new device for collecting money and issuing tickets. And CIE needed to cut costs. 'Conductorless' buses were financially logical.

There would be no redundancy, since CIE would train the conductors for new positions, and some could even become drivers if they wished. But in some cases it could mean being transferred. Many conductors opposed this, since it would be disruptive to their home life. The strike was also more complex, as it involved a better pension system and other concessions. The dispute was a tangled affair not easily or quickly settled. Both sides felt they were in the right and sought the moral high ground. As the *Irish Times* put it:

> public sympathy, if it exists, will not favour either party ... It will quickly turn into simple resentment against management and labour force. CIE has had enough shilly-shallying and is ready for a fight.[43]

Everything pointed to a long and bitter strike. Brace yourself, warned the *Irish Times* editorial: 'Here we go again!'

———

When the UCD student Elizabeth Walsh became the first woman to cross the finishing line in Bray on the Great Walk it created quite a buzz at the university. Some students began forming their own small groups for walks and hiking expeditions south of Dublin.

On Sunday 24 March fourteen students from UCD decided to embark upon an outing. Several called it a 'hike', others a 'climb', into the mountains.

There would be no reporters covering their great walk – at least, not at the beginning.

By late March those living at lower elevations regarded the brutal winter merely as a bad memory. But for some country people, especially in mountain terrain, winter's relics were still quite evident. Shadowed slopes were still buried beneath deep snowdrifts, and there were icy patches camouflaging dangerous crevices and hidden streams.

Although the higher slopes of Co. Wicklow were still dangerous, their beauty was alluring to photographers and hikers, including to young, vigorous students. To their parents it sounded perfectly normal when the fourteen students announced their plans for a Sunday-afternoon outing. Their destination was Lugnaquilla Mountain, 3,031 feet high, towering over the bogs.

To one reporter, however, it was 'a snow-capped peak ... with treacherous crevasses'. It was not to be so casually climbed, so long as it was still blanketed in winter's snow.

The party of fourteen students drove to Co. Wicklow on Sunday afternoon. Arriving at 1:15, they discussed their plan over lunch. How cold would it be up on the higher trails? Was their clothing sufficient? How about their footwear? They had no designated leader or set plan for everyone. One thing they agreed upon was that they would all be down well before dark and back in Dublin for dinner.

One of the students, Ross Geoghegan, was an experienced mountaineer and had brought along a map and compass. The others were eager adventurers but apparently novices at climbing even the foothills. In what was described as a 'rather loose group', they began their climb up Camera Mountain, one of the foothills of Lugnaquilla.

The higher they climbed, the poorer the visibility became, and a light mist was felt on their faces. Before long it turned to a misty rain, and visibility became very poor. Bad weather was obviously moving in on them, but no-one wanted to talk of turning back.

By 3:15 it was raining and windy on Camera Mountain. The group halted to discuss their strategy. While some members expressed concern, others were game for going on. One or two stated their belief that conditions had deteriorated to a risky level and that it might be wise to turn back. Six students decided to head down, wishing the others well.

Among the remaining group of eight hikers was Miriam O'Callaghan (not the broadcaster), correspondence secretary of the UCD Literary and Historical Society. Her hiking partner was John Toomey, an economics student.

They had not gone far before the eight were halted once again. They now realised that the rain and mist had become so thick that they were virtually stepping forward blindly. What should they do?

Perhaps it would blow over. Several voted to move forward, others to descend the slopes, which were now slippery. Four students bid the others good luck as they headed down.

This now left only four climbers on Camera Mountain. Two of the remaining students were O'Callaghan and Toomey. With them were Moore McDowell and Rose Bresnihan, both of Dublin. Both twosomes faced the predicament of heavy rain, thick mist, high winds and slick footing. Visibility was reduced to only a few feet. McDowell and Bresnihan soon decided to turn and head down. O'Callaghan and Toomey would make their own way. But within ten to fifteen minutes of parting, both pairs realised they were lost. Being marooned on a mountain with nightfall coming was a daunting prospect:

> They realised they were lost and could not get to the roadway which was nearly two miles away. They decided to stay on the mountain and take shelter.[44]

By about midnight, when none of the four missing students had showed up, it was assumed that they had wisely found shelter together for the night and would hike down next morning.

At first light on Monday morning the parents of the four students were gathered at the base of Camera Mountain, along with gardaí. They waited anxiously, scanning the landscape, fully expecting to see the four figures emerge at any moment. However, as morning dawned they 'were surprised that in the early hours of sunlight' they did not see them come into view.

No-one was yet thinking it was a life-or-death situation. At worst, 'they feared that one of the students may have sprained or injured a leg on the tricky mountainside.'

At about 5 a.m. McDowell and Bresnihan had begun their cautious descent, as the weather had improved. Having found decent shelter overnight, the two were unharmed. They assumed that their friends, O'Callaghan and Toomey, were doing the same not far behind them. Part of the way down they encountered Seán Toomey, father of John, climbing up the mountain with two gardaí and a few searchers. They explained that the four had split up into pairs, one heading down immediately and the other lingering behind. Seeing McDowell and Bresnihan hiking down encouraged Seán Toomey to hope that his son and O'Callaghan would be following not far behind.

By mid-morning, when the two still hadn't appeared, worry increased. A full search was now organised. A large search party from local garda stations was joined by a contingent of soldiers from McKee Barracks in Dublin. Not long after noon a mist again blanketed the slopes as the rescue squads 'with tracker dogs continued the search through the treacherous crevasses.'

In the early afternoon a decision was made to solicit the expertise of Johann Gottfried Thieme, a geologist at UCD. He had made a detailed survey of Lugnaquilla and knew its pitfalls better than anyone. Right away he made reference to an area called the North Prison – highly dangerous cliff terrain. Be wary of its hidden hazards, he warned.

At about 3 p.m. about a hundred soldiers, equipped with walkie-talkies, joined the search. An army plane was called in as well. By now, newspapers were closely following the story. It was thought that one of them might have suffered a serious injury that could be impeding or preventing their descent. On the other hand, they could still just be lost and wandering.

Those who knew Lugnaquilla best did not describe it benignly. In summer its trails were relatively safe, if followed properly. In winter, snow and ice hid its many dangers. Captain Thomas Healy of the Eastern Command said he and his soldiers were searching terrain 'very rugged and dangerous, even in daytime, covered with deep holes' that had been hidden. Even they were finding the cliff areas especially hazardous.

During the late afternoon, soldiers were scouring the terrain suggested by Thieme, using dogs. A few minutes past five, a Private Murray spotted something on the banks of the River Slaney. It was Toomey's body, facing upwards near a boulder 'in an area that is particularly treacherous with water-filled holes and streams.' It was believed that he had died about 2 a.m. on Monday, and so he had been dead for some time. His body was retrieved and taken down the mountainside to an army ambulance and to Baltinglass District Hospital.

This was now headline news. And Lugnaquilla was no longer being described as merely 'tricky' but as 'deadly'.

It was now assumed that, in the light of Tuesday morning, Miriam O'Callaghan would be found in the vicinity. In what condition, no-one knew.

One front-page headline read 'Plane joins big search', yet there was still no sight of O'Callaghan. Surely the two would have been close together, it was reasoned. With the full search now resumed, it had to be just a matter of time.

At 1:45 p.m. on Tuesday, a full mile from where the body of Toomey had been found, a member of the Irish Mountaineering Club was searching the North Prison, the area Thieme had suggested as the most likely spot. And there he discovered the body of O'Callaghan 'lying face down about half way down the Prison'. She appeared to have fallen a considerable distance. Early reports stated that 'it appears as if Miss O'Callaghan sustained serious injuries in the fall … and that Toomey had set off to find help.' This suggested that they were together when she fell. Probably he had set off at an incautious pace. He got about a mile away before he had his accident.

O'Callaghan's body was brought down the mountain on a stretcher dropped from a British army helicopter, which had come from Belfast to aid in the search. She had a broken leg. There was a lot of snow on the cliff, and marks about thirty yards from the body indicated that she had slipped and plunged to her death. Her father, mother and sister were waiting at the base of the mountain, where they had hoped to see her materialise from the mist. Her body was also taken to Baltinglass.

On Wednesday, the 27th, the headlines heralded the news: 'Tragic story of climbers' deaths'.

As readers followed the details of the discovery, they had a hard time understanding how it could have happened. After all, Ireland was hardly known as a mountain-climbing country.

Had John Toomey died a hero's death going for help for his climbing partner?

The inquest was held that day by the coroner for west Co. Wicklow, Dr Joseph M. Clerkin, with a sitting jury. It drew great interest from the public. One of the students, Moore McDonnell, was composed in giving his description the deteriorating weather. He too had assumed that the missing students had survived the night unharmed.

The coroner stated that all the evidence pointed to misadventure.

The funerals were held on Thursday morning. Many thousands of their fellow-students, along with teachers and university staff members, were among those in attendance, including Professor Michael Tierney, president of UCD.

The deadly winter of 1963 had claimed its last two victims. Surely April would bring spring sunshine, warm weather and the blossoming of flowers. And outings with happy endings.

Chapter 5

COMMOTION IN THE STREETS AND ON THE DOCKS

On 1 April the *Irish Independent* ran a snippet of news from the *Chicago Tribune*. Some readers in Ireland might have taken it as an April Fool's joke, except that it was written by the respected journalist Walter Trohan, chief of the *Tribune's* Washington bureau. He had access to inside information from the White House:

> Although it has not been announced, or even whispered yet, President Kennedy will make a sentimental journey to the land of his ancestors this summer.[45]

Furthermore, Trohan stated, 'unnamed sources' said there were already 'arrangements being made quietly' for such a visit. It all sounded deliciously secretive.

Thus began a period of speculation. There had, of course, been talk of it, and hopes had been expressed since Kennedy's election day, in 1960. Now, with Trohan's information, rumours flew up and down the country. And especially to Co. Wexford, the home of his ancestors. Trohan predicted that 'there will be a great stir and commotion' when the evidence behind the rumours slowly leaked out.

Even if the rumours proved to be wishful thinking, it all raised people's spirits as spring arrived.

Unfortunately, some worrying news on 1 April was no joke. A headline, 'Bus stoppage imminent', was verified by the press. And new speed limits and parking regulations really were coming into effect that same day. Plans to fill in the canals of Dublin were also apparently proceeding.

Motorists held varying views of the new speed limits. Neil Blaney, Minister for Local Government, sounded almost apologetic about it. As one journalist put it, Blaney 'made a plea for a fair trial for speed limits … appealing to drivers' in order to give them a chance. Asking motorists to 'accept the new laws with generosity … to respect the law' was intended to reduce the number of accidents and save lives. It seemed more like a social experiment than the declaration of a new law.

———

The first day of April heralds the arrival of spring, when people are drawn to Dublin's canals on pleasant days. It was a delightful amenity for people of all ages. One newspaper editorial, 'Filling in the canal', contended that such an act 'would be a very serious thing'. Apart from depriving people of the canal's pleasures, it would 'cut off forever the only link between the Irish Sea and the Shannon'.

Public sentiment strongly supported the cry 'Hands off the canal!' In preservationist and environmentalist circles the anger was volcanic. Letters streamed in to the papers. Tom Flynn sent his 'Plea to keep the canal open' to the *Evening Herald*, making special note that the canals had been 'compulsorily acquired with public funds':

> For the Dublin Corporation to fill in the Grand Canal would be a shocking act of vandalism. It is an amenity offering enjoyable walks along the banks, providing life-giving country breezes, and helps counteract the fumes of motor traffic and belching chimneys. And the canal is suitable for canoes and houseboats.
>
> What sins are committed in the name of commerce and progress! There has even been a proposal to diminish that beloved haven, St Stephen's Green.
>
> I sincerely hope they keep their eyes off our Phoenix Park![46]

———

Some 5,500 busmen, meanwhile, were on the verge of going on strike. As negotiations went on, people hoped for a last-minute reprieve. They knew that chances were slim. Then, on the morning of 2 April, there was a surprising headline: 'Strike averted'.

Sighs of relief swept across the land. The Minister for Industry, Jack Lynch, was credited with being the saviour, providing the 'right kind of intervention at the right moment'.

The reprieve allowed for a few more days of sensible discussion between the busmen and CIE. The ballot would now be handed to the busmen on Thursday, with the votes to be tallied the following day. The result, however, would be announced some time on Sunday. If the majority of busmen voted to strike, it would begin the following day.

A great suspense hung in the air.

———

One man, John Long, was more concerned about what many young women were wearing in Dublin's streets. On warm days they were attired in what he regarded as indecent clothing. And he was by no means alone in this opinion. In America and England the 'swinging sixties' were well under way. Long was among those who condemned such liberated behaviour. He wrote to the papers to ask:

> what has gone wrong with our young ladies? To wear clothes as short as draws attention to the backs of their knees. Young women seem to hit the headlines in activities in skirts – and slacks – it's hard to distinguish male and female.
>
> In this age … humanity is slowly lowering itself into the gutter.[47]

He was among the many 'decent' adults who disapproved of the drift of Irish youth away from the Church and traditional family values. It was not only their dress but their music, language, dancing, manners, public behaviour and lack of respect for their parents and elders. All this accentuated the growing generation gap in Ireland.

———

On Saturday the nation held its breath as the last of the busmen's votes was being counted. Everyone expected the vote to be close.

On Sunday afternoon the result was announced: some 2,312 busmen voted to strike until the issue of the conductors and all other matters relating to 'sick pay, improved pensions and free travel' were settled; 1,161 did not want to go on strike; the rest abstained. To many people the outcome was jolting. It was hardly a close call, as predicted. And it was sure to lead to disputes among the busmen.

On Sunday night people climbed into bed uncertain about how they would cope in the days and weeks ahead.

———

Many of the country's island-dwellers were barely affected by the bus strike. They could simply travel to the mainland by boat for most of their needs. On Sunday groups of excited islanders from Valencia Island, Co. Kerry, were heading to Cahersiveen to watch their team in a big football match.

That evening, after watching their team win, a group of young men went to the pub before returning home in their small boat. They had enjoyed what was described as a 'gay party'. According to Maura O'Neill, the proprietor, they each had 'about three drinks and were all sober' when they left her premises at about 10 p.m. As it was getting dark, the men scrambled down to their boat, joking all the way. They might not have noticed that a strong wind had kicked up.

Their boat, which had an outboard motor, was loaded to capacity. Two of the men were brothers. About fifty yards from Cahersiveen, 'at the height of a strong south-easterly wind during ebb tide', one of the men stood up or leaned too heavily to one side. The boat suddenly flipped over, dumping the men into the dark, choppy sea.

Seven of the men could swim. Three could not.

It was only about seven minutes after the men had walked out of her pub, Mrs O'Neill estimated, that the 'front door got a fierce pounding'. It was Timmy Murphy telling her, nearly hysterically, that the boat had turned over, and 'he supposed they were all lost'. After ringing for the lifeboat station, she ran down to the pier and cried out to them in the wind, 'Hang on! Help is coming!'

The men who knew how to swim headed for the shore. The three non-swimmers clung to the upturned boat, helpless. By the time the lifeboat arrived they were missing. A night-long search began. The missing men were James Lynch and his younger brother, Jerry, only nineteen, and Tom Murphy. The lifeboat, assisted by a help fleet of neighbours and friends, began 'grimly scouring the sea'. Before long, the bodies of James Lynch and Tom Murphy were spotted. In the early morning light the body of Jerry Lynch was sighted.

The inquest called it an accidental drowning. Proponents of the Water Safety Campaign called it more *unnecessary* accidental drownings. The seven swimmers all made it safely to shore. It was an all-too-familiar case of people losing their lives merely because they had not learnt how to swim. It was astonishing that many islanders remained non-swimmers their entire lives – even many who were regularly out in boats.

––––

On Monday morning the public was hit by a double whammy. Not only did the bus strike begin but an unexpected dock strike was called. As one newspaper described the crisis:

> the country is now faced with two crippling disputes – one affecting road passenger transport and the other paralysing the deep sea end of the Dublin port. Although only 39 cranesmen are directly involved in the port dispute, more than 2,000 other employees refused to pass the pickets.[48]

Besides crane-drivers and dockers, other workers also refused to work. The port pilots also remained out. It was declared a '100 per cent stoppage'.

This also affected hundreds of lorry-drivers, carters and warehouse workers. Meanwhile, more than twenty ships lay unattended in Alexandra Basin with their cargoes. Most critical were the perishable fruit, vegetable and meat. Merchants were losing large sums of money by the hour. Street dealers couldn't get their stock, and grocery shelves were emptying.

––––

The weather was kind to walkers on Monday, the first day of the bus strike. Traffic lights were switched off as gardaí took over point duty to try and sort out the army of cars, cyclists, walkers and hitchhiking pedestrians flowing through the city. Between 8:30 and 9:30 a.m. thousands of cars were bumper to bumper in massive traffic jams. Some walkers were making better progress than motorists.

One newspaper, in oxymoronic phrasing, wrote that taxi-drivers were 'run off their feet'. One driver wrote that 'we never had it so good!'

Many people hauled their bicycles out from storage. It was a curious sight to see so many well-attired men and women astride rusty, tottering bikes, weaving through traffic. Bicycles were piled up outside factories and office buildings.

Pedestrians hoping to hitch a ride simply had to take their chances. During the first few days, drivers tended to be generous. Some sympathetic motorists even affixed signs to their windscreens indicating their destination.

With the passing of each day, reality set in as it became doubly difficult to find a lift, as many drivers no longer wanted to be bothered. Trying to get back home at the end of the day was especially challenging. Everyone was growing weary and impatient. The *Evening Herald* captured the mood in its two-word headline, 'Footsore Dublin':

> A nation on the march – that was Ireland to-day without its massive fleet of buses, immobilized because of the complete strike. As thousands walked, cycled or were driven to work by private cars or taxis there was no ray of hope for an early settlement.
>
> For footsore Dubliners faced with the long journeys home for many more evenings, it was a depressing prospect.[49]

On the third day of strikes the newspapers offered what appeared to be a glimmer of hope, with articles on 'Busmen's new vote' and 'Peace move on the port strike'. But such hopes evaporated quickly when it was learnt that there was nothing substantial behind the articles. A port settlement was growing more urgent by the day, as there were now 'fears that perishable goods totalling up to £1,000,000 might be lost'.

There was a gesture of good will on the part of unions in allowing Squibb's Ltd, the pharmaceutical manufacturers, to remove six cases of antibiotics that had been stored at the docks.

———

With all the attention on the strikes, readers might have skipped over the reminder in a newspaper about the looming turnover tax:

> A public meeting to protest against the proposed purchase tax will be held in the Dublin Trade Union Council. Mr P. Donegan, Chairman of the Council, stated that it was of the gravest importance.[50]

It was an issue that would affect every household in Ireland and long outlive the strikes then commanding attention. Before long, it would be grabbing the headlines. The battle was just beginning.

In the first week of the bus strike, when hopes of a quick settlement fizzled out, people dug in their heels for a prolonged ordeal. Dublin rail services were packed to standing-room only. To alleviate the problem, the army put eighty lorries into operation in Dublin and another ten in Cork. Each lorry carried about thirty commuters, and soldiers and gardaí served as conductors. Guard Tony Ruane, now 78, smiles, recalling his role:

> I was twenty years old at the time and there was lots of fun and shrieks of laughter as mini-skirted girls in stiletto heels were helped up the steep ladder by young guards like myself.

During the traffic-jam hours Garda spokespersons reported that the new 'speed limits were being observed' by motorists in Dublin, Cork and Limerick. They added that drivers were now 'keeping their eye on the speedometer', but they failed to explain that it was because vehicles were held to a crawl, and drivers were actually glancing at their speedometers in disgust.

Once people made it into the city during the strike they were stuck there for the day until it was time to try and get back home. With restaurants full, people began bringing packed lunches. This left them with time on their hands about midday, resulting in a conspicuous increase in window-shopping. Shops made special efforts to lure them inside.

Clery's and Arnott's ran enticing special offers. During the first week of the strike, Arnott's declared it Morny Perfume Week, with a lavish display for the lily of the valley fragrance. A gift soap of this fragrance was given to everyone who purchased any of the Morny products. Though few women could afford to buy the luxury perfume, they did receive a complimentary spray.

A few days into the strike, particularly when foul weather prevailed, pedestrians were desperate to travel with any motorist who would take them. Reports began trickling in to Garda stations of drivers with bad intentions. Young women told of male drivers who used suggestive language or touched them improperly. Some even made sexual advances. Gardaí put out warnings for women to be vigilant when accepting lifts.

On 10 April a sixteen-year-old girl going to her domestic job in Rathgar accepted a lift from a man who pulled over and violently attacked her. She 'struggled free and reached her employers in a state of collapse.' Such a brazen attack put real fear in other women about accepting lifts from single male motorists. After the incident a Garda spokesperson told the newspapers, 'I cannot emphasise too strongly the danger when women and girls accept a lift.' While acknowledging that most motorists were well intentioned, he added that there 'will always be the blackguard who will take advantage.'

With workers unable to reach their offices, shops and factories on time, managers found their schedules in disarray. As the bus strike continued, one world event captured people's attention. For a few days it would provide a distraction from Ireland's woes.

Pope John's historic encyclical *Pacem in Terris* disclosed his peace appeal to 'all men of good will' – Catholics and non-Catholics alike. A great visionary for peace in the nuclear age, he was now reaching out to people of all religions. For the Irish people, and many others, he was the most beloved Pope in living memory. They saw him as compassionate and saintly, and he was known to have a special affection for Ireland. People prayed that his encyclical would make the world saner and safer.

Everyone had hoped that the bus strike would have ended by the Easter weekend. In desperation, a small army of civil servants, office workers and others squashed themselves into trains. To exacerbate matters, thousands of travellers making the cross-channel trip from Britain arrived on Irish soil only to learn that a national bus strike was on. In what the *Sunday Independent* called a 'busless Easter Sunday', people were left to their own modes of travel:

> In Dublin chaos reigned in the streets and thousands of cars, motorcycles, buzz-bikes and cyclists jammed the roads in one long apparently endless traffic 'snarl'.[51]

Even the army lorries did not operate during Easter. As one journalist wrote, thousands who had planned a trip to the 'sea or countryside had to be content with a stay-at-home Sunday' on Easter.

Dubliners had hoped that good weather would allow them to attend outings and sporting events. After the washout on St Patrick's Day they deserved a pleasant Easter weekend. However, the Meteorological Office forecast weather that was 'chilly with widespread falls of snow' and even hail in regions, along with strong winds. Parts of the country were reported as 'extremely cold ... with severe frost' in the higher areas. Wintry conditions once again – in *spring*!

Newspapers were blunt, the *Irish Independent* calling it plain 'depressing'. The *Evening Herald* complained with a bit more flare: 'Heartbreak holiday weekend'. One fashion writer was annoyed that the usual bright Easter outfits and colours gave way to 'brollies and macs' as it rained steadily most of the day.

Not even the Easter parade could cheer people up. About twenty minutes before the parade began, O'Connell Street was almost deserted, one reporter noting that the rope barriers 'seemed incongruous'. Gradually a small crowd trickled in. There wasn't much to enjoy: it was mostly a military show of armaments. At least a brass band and two pipe bands marched by.

The parade included three companies of soldiers bound for the Congo, and there were eight armoured cars, artillery and anti-aircraft weapons. Jets made the greatest impression as they swooped low over the street. Suddenly there occurred what one newspaper called an 'awesome moment' as the jet on the right flank seemed nearly to 'sweep Nelson off his base, which aroused enthusiasm'.

The small crowd was less than enthralled with it all, the *Irish Times* candidly calling it 'one of the most dismal Easter week-ends for years'. It seemed that 1963's weather was intent upon socking every holiday right in the eye.

————

Throughout Co. Galway there was a stir of excitement over the Easter weekend, despite the weather. Mary Margaret Revell, a famous American swimmer, had arrived, the *Irish Press* calling her 'a strawberry blonde from Detroit'. She was there for a few days to prepare for her bold plan to swim across Galway Bay in September. She had successfully conquered the Strait of Gibraltar and the dangerous swirling waters of the Strait of Messina, from Sicily to Calabria and back.

Now she was in Galway to inspect by boat the twelve-mile crossing from Black Head, Co. Clare, to the Salthill promenade in Galway. She made notes on water temperature, currents, wind systems – and sharks.

On her swim from Sicily to Calabria she had suffered severe cramps, and three frogmen armed with 'knives and harpoon guns kept watch for sharks' from one of the accompanying boats. But she would have no such protection in Irish waters. She was a daring woman and her 'Galway Bay challenge', as it was being publicised, was igniting excited conversation.

Local fishermen knew of the dangerous currents and sharks. Opinions of her chances of success differed, but all agreed that it was sure to be a courageous and dramatic event, come September.

———

For those who don't know how to swim, even the smallest bodies of water hold risks. Only a few days after Revell's preparations for her swimming challenge, Helen Pearsons, a fourteen-year-old from Castlebar, was happily boating on a placid lake with two pals. When a mild breeze caught their little boat and caused it to begin drifting, the girls panicked and lost one of the oars. One girl, a non-swimmer, jumped out immediately and waded ashore. As the boat drifted further out, another girl, a strong swimmer, plunged into the water and easily swam to shore for help.

Pearsons, who had never learnt to swim, was left alone and frightened, and she apparently fainted and fell into about twelve feet of water. Her body was later recovered by the gardaí – one more tragic drowning statistic.

———

Just after Easter, conflicting speculation about a visit by President Kennedy again grabbed the headlines. This was spurred by a statement in the *Christian Science Monitor* that 'he is almost certain to include a quick stop at Ireland en route homeward' on his summer European trip.

However, that same day the *Irish Independent* reported that an Irish embassy spokesperson discounted the story, asserting that there was 'no basis' for it. Then, later that same day, the *Evening Herald* wrote a conflicting headline: 'The Kennedys *are* coming'.

The next morning, 17 April, the *Irish Independent* responded that there was still 'no definite news from the White House'.

———

At Easter Sunday Mass in St Nicholas' Pro-Cathedral the Bishop of Galway, Dr Michael Browne, had expressed hope that the 'bus strike would be settled soon'. By the tenth day of the strike there was still 'no progress ... as the bus strike seems set to be a long one'. Both sides remained entrenched in their positions. What was an inconvenience for some was a financial crisis for others who were unable to get to their jobs. Domestic workers were among the hardest hit, as one compassionate letter-writer explained:

> Because of the bus strike many poor women who worked in private houses are now unable to reach their place of employment and are in sore need of help. Could their employers send them a little present at this time to tide them over to help them have a decent meal or pay their rent?

For the disabled and the elderly, the bus was often their lifeline to help and to health services. Writers appealed to motorists to stop and give them a lift. One girl wrote in on her own behalf:

> Would any driver going from North Circular Road to Pleasants Street be kind enough to offer a lift to an invalid girl?

However, by the third week of the strike there was growing intolerance, even anger, in the streets between hitch-hiking pedestrians and 'selfish' motorists, as they were being called. Their generosity was fading, and many drivers claimed that the army of walkers were becoming unappreciative and rude. Motorists now whizzed past hitch-hikers, as one writer documented:

> What a different picture this time! Dozens of cars with one occupant drive by. I saw elderly ladies standing out in the road near a bus stop – and no one looked at them. The older you are, the less chance you have for a lift.
>
> Every man for himself!

Dublin was not a cheerful city. People trudged along defiantly from one day to the next. The chipper spirits seen in the first few days had vanished. Joseph Donnelly was inspired to share a bit of poetry in his letter, entitled 'Ode to the Bus Strike':

> My feet are sore and burning,
> My boots, they weigh like lead;

My heart inside is a-churning,
As the weary streets I tread.

By the thirteenth day of the dock strike, 19 April, the strikers buckled under the pressure and settled the dispute. Immediately, the docks sprang back to life. The scene became chaotic as everyone – dockers, crane-drivers, carters, lorry-drivers, warehouse workers – competed in making up for lost time. They worked around the clock to clear the backlog.

By contrast, the bus strike was now having a domino effect on the country, the *Irish Times* reporting that the 'decline in trade was getting very serious'. Much of it was due to a 'desperate lack of spending by suburban housewives', who were unable to reach their usual shopping centres. Many men were unable to get to their pubs, and one publican noted that his business had dropped by fully half since the strike began. In the evenings, restaurants, cinemas and shops saw their business grow sluggish. Normally the Savoy and Adelphi cinemas would have packed houses for their two hit films, the thriller *Cape Fear,* starring Gregory Peck and Robert Mitchum, and the Elvis Presley film *Girls, Girls, Girls.* The scant evening audience had no difficulty getting tickets now. On some evenings O'Connell Street looked like a ghost town.

The bus strike created some surprising problems, one of the most serious being its adverse effect on the telephone system. Complaints were flowing in about long delays in service in general phone usage. People making long-distance calls found the system jammed. Officials explained that the heavy usage on the service was causing the delays. This was especially due to the increased number of calls from Dublin by commercial travellers and others who depended on bus services to reach their businesses. Now they could reach associates and clients only by phone, and many calls were necessarily lengthy.

The phone-jamming problem was compounded by the non-stop calls for taxis and other driving services. Customers unable to reach their shopping destinations were now having to use telephone-shopping services, with free delivery offered during the strike.

Among the busmen there was growing anger at the management. Tony Doran, born in 1937, spent his working days as both conductor and driver. His father had been a bus-driver before him. At the age of fifteen he began with CIE as an office boy in Kingsbridge Station (now Heuston Station), becoming a bus conductor in 1958 and driver in 1966, on the no. 19 bus. The contentious strike of '63 stands out in his mind, as he recalled in an interview with the author in 2013:

> I got strike pay from the Transport Union – but it wasn't very much! And some of the men had to go out and get labouring jobs on building sites. Oh, there was *anger*! Anger at management. And there was hardship for passengers … and people who worked in jobs … It affected *everyone*. It was the fact that *all* the busmen went out. There was no way for most people to get to work … in and out of the city centre. The public was very frustrated. And the strike was so long!

It seemed as if the strike could hardly get worse. Then, in late April, there was a new threat that would make the affair even uglier. Rumours began flying that some busmen were proposing to unleash a new strategy – one that might give them more leverage against CIE. The *Evening Herald* wrote in its editorial that the public:

> has been seriously disturbed that busmen are to introduce a policy of increasing the hardship already imposed. There is talk of placing pickets outside the railway stations – causing further hardship.
> It is very wrong to use the innocent as a weapon in any dispute.[52]

This further split the feelings among the busmen, many of whom disapproved. The newspapers warned that if the busmen resorted to such an act it could cost them the public's good will for a long time to come.

———

On the morning of 22 April the headline in the *Irish Independent* was an injection of optimism: 'Plans to greet Kennedy in June'.

It was a reality, confirmed in both Washington and Dublin. An official announcement was made simultaneously by Áras an Uachtaráin and the White House. President Kennedy would visit Ireland following his trip to Germany and Italy in June. In fact, 'preparations were already under way'. The newspapers enticingly promised 'full details' as they became known.

'Yes, it's *official!*' was heard throughout the country. A thrilling historic event. Newspapers were already leaking news of the 'tremendous excitement' erupting in Dunganstown, Co. Wexford, near New Ross, as Kennedy's cousins were learning that it was true. All around New Ross, wrote one newspaper, there was already 'great rejoicing'.

———

Towards the end of the month there was a perplexing despatch from the Vatican. The much-beloved Pope John was speaking to a group of students in the Vatican courtyard when he made a surprising and most troubling statement:

> Death comes for all of us, even the Pope now speaking … and perhaps even soon.

Though the Pope might have been weary from his busy Easter Holy Days schedule, the Vatican at once confirmed that the Holy Father appeared to be in excellent health. In fact, that evening he planned to attend a symphony concert. Why, then, would he have made what sounded like a prescient statement about his own death?

Even those Vatican officials who were closest to him were left to ponder the meaning of his words.

Chapter 6

MYSTERIES AND MARVELS

T he 'merry month of May' was much anticipated for the Spring Show at the RDS, and for joyful parties, outings and sporting events – a pleasant prelude to summer and the August holidays. The news of Kennedy's visit increased the excitement of the season.

The month got off to a smashing start when the Punchestown Races extended into the first week. As both a sporting and a social event it drew a happy mixture of social classes. That year the traces of snow still lodged in the Wicklow Mountains formed a picturesque view from the grandstand.

With the bus strike still in effect, the attendance was lower than usual. However, the crowd was exuberant, with one *Irish Independent* reporter describing the event as 'gay and informal'. Talk of Kennedy's visit dominated many conversations. There was unrestrained speculation about which social functions he might attend and who might be able to meet him.

Women flaunting their fashionable spring outfits was one of the highlights of every year's race meeting. One fashion reporter wrote that 'marvellous hats stole the show' and that 'confections of tulle and flowers were everywhere' to be admired. And, of course, there was the grand Guinness luncheon and reception for some five hundred select guests.

All would have gone flawlessly had it not been for the angry clouds. Unfortunately, especially for those women who 'sported exotic headgear', dark, sodden clouds moved in. As one newspaper concluded, 'rain was the real spoil sport' for many, though it didn't seem to damp the enthusiasm of genuine racing fans.

What *did* ruffle the feathers of many people on the first day of May was the news that the British Prime Minister, Harold Macmillan, had invited President Kennedy to spend a few days of his visit in Northern Ireland. Real resentment was felt. There was much speculation over what Kennedy would do. To accept Macmillan's invitation to visit the North, even for one day, would inevitably raise the contentious issue of the border, which could taint the very spirit of his 'homecoming'. Kennedy didn't want to offend the British people, especially his friend Sir Winston Churchill. Nonetheless, Kennedy acted decisively. With tact, he offered his polite regrets to Macmillan.

The Lord Mayor of Dublin, J. J. O'Keeffe, was meanwhile in Washington with President Kennedy at the White House. As one Irish journalist put it, they were 'chatting amiably … all smiles and good will'.

The month of May seemed off to a splendid start, except for the bus strike and the looming turnover tax, both of which were causing great distress.

Though the 'tax', as it was now simply known, would squeeze multitudes, the Government was determined to force it through. Bitter opponents were just as determined to fight it. Retail traders and housewives joined forces to organise an active, vocal campaign. Food retailers planned a meeting of the Retail Grocery Dairy and Allied Trades Association, to be held on 14 May at the Mansion House. It was sure to draw public and press attention. Organisers called the tax a 'harsh and unjust imposition on the retail trade', which would ultimately place financial stress on the country's already burdened families:

> Though it is called a state tax, it is, without question, an *extra tax* on food and other items which will increase by 2½ percent.

It was argued that many ordinary people actually feared the tax, since they simply didn't have the amount they would be charged. It was time for housewives, grocers and retailers to unite and fight the injustice tooth and nail.

———

Shortly after midnight on Saturday 4 May, when most people in Dublin were sleeping and the roads were largely empty, A. V. McCormack was driving his Posts and Telegraphs van from Dublin Airport into the city – his routine run. Each night he collected the post from the last London flight, which arrived at 12:30. His orders were to follow a back road through Ballymun so as not to attract undue attention: some of the mail bags were valuable. It was a peaceful job, rambling along in the dark of night with little traffic.

On that night McCormack was a little more than half a mile down the road towards the city when he was flagged down by a man wearing what looked like a garda uniform. When McCormack stopped the van he was immediately jumped on by two others who quickly tied him up and gagged him. The men were masked and silent. In the light of one of their torches he was able to make out the features of one of the gang members – and 'gazed incredulously upon the face of British Prime Minister Harold Macmillan.'[53]

The van was quickly driven off by one of the men as the others shoved McCormack into their car and followed. After what McCormack would later recall as a 'nightmare ride' through four miles of back roads, the two vehicles pulled in to a deserted farmhouse. Here another van and a black car were awaiting their getaway. With wire cutters they broke into the mail van and began transferring eighty bags of mail into their own van. The bags contained American and British mail, the majority of it registered. They flung aside unwanted bags. Still silent, they furiously cut open certain sacks and took exactly what they were seeking. By the light of torches, the entire process was handled deftly, with not a second wasted.

Through it all, McCormack, expertly tied, watched in semi-darkness, awaiting his fate. As the men were completing their task one of them walked over and stared down at him. Then he reached into his pocket. To McCormack's surprise, the man casually pulled out a packet of cigarettes, lit one, removed McCormack's gag and placed it between his trembling lips. A small act of kindness? Or of finality?

Their job completed, they hopped into their vehicles and made their getaway, taking McCormack with them again. After only a few minutes they pulled over to the roadside and McCormack was dragged out. Still not a word was said. There he lay, bound and gagged, and motionless. Then they turned and sped away, leaving him unharmed.

At first, he didn't know whether to try and free himself or simply wait until morning and hope that a passing motorist spotted him. Deciding upon the former, he twisted himself free sufficiently to attract the attention of a motorist at dawn's light. A man pulled over, stepped out and walked towards him. A uniformed man.

By sheer good fortune, his rescuer was an army captain. He freed McCormack, and the two sped towards the airport as McCormack babbled his incredible story. The airport's night staff stood in wonder as the captain and the captive ran madly to notify gardaí and postal authorities. It didn't take long for the Dublin press to get wind of what had happened. Everyone was surprised to learn that the van had been held up so boldly only a few hundred yards from the airport terminal.

Reporters were showing up at the airport hoping to conduct interviews with McCormack, but he had already been whisked away by the Gardaí to their station in Santry. From airport staff and postal authorities they gathered bits and pieces of what had happened. The *Irish Times* printed an uncharacteristically dramatic front-page headline: 'Masked gang rob Dublin mail van: Daring hold-up near airport'.

Every newspaper had the big story. All were anxious for the chance to interview McCormack, as there were many questions to be answered. What exactly was in those bags? Did he fear for his life if he 'talked'? There was already great public interest in the brazen crime. One newspaper called it 'one of the most dramatic robberies ever to take place in this country'.[54]

Though reporters hounded gardaí for facts, they were very tight-lipped at first, saying it would take 'some time to establish the full value of the mails' stolen. Superintendent P. Mullany did concede that it was 'certainly a professional piece of work'. He called it 'a perfect setting for a hold-up, one of the loneliest roads' in that part of Co. Dublin. There were no witnesses, and it was carried out efficiently and silently. This prompted reporters to ask Mullany the obvious question: was it a 'cross-channel gang's job?' He couldn't say yet.

Early on Sunday morning, detectives were hard at work, and over the next forty-eight hours they would yield results. Before long, Superintendent Mullany was proud to tell reporters that the getaway car had been found abandoned in Kilbarrack Avenue in Raheny. Three opened mail pouches were still inside. The van used in the robbery was soon discovered at North King Street. Both vehicles had false number plates and were believed to have been stolen.

On Sunday morning one of the most intriguing mysteries of the case was solved. When detectives were carefully picking through the heaps of discarded mail bags, one garda suddenly froze. Looking up at him was a cheap rubber mask of Harold Macmillan. The press snatched up this bizarre piece of evidence with great delight.

——

On Sunday, over at the RDS grounds in Ballsbridge, workers were putting the finishing touches on the Spring Show for the week ahead. Organisers took great pride in having the showgrounds refined to perfection for visitors. That year they were boasting 'one of the greatest exhibitions of Irish Industry ever assembled'. They assured the few reporters poking around that the last-minute rush they saw was a regular feature; it gave everyone an injection of excitement. Everything would be in tip-top shape come opening day.

If anyone had good reason to feel stress on Sunday morning it was the forty-two students from Trinity College, Dublin, who were preparing for their 103-mile marathon from Belfast to Dublin. The contestants were not in quest of prestigious trophies but were competing for a more useful award – a barrel of stout. And, of course, a touch of fame and a place in the annals of TCD folklore.

Competitors went through a few simple exercises. Some looked more fit than others. If some were anxious for the race to begin, others were conspicuously reluctant. The weather was dry, for which all were appreciative. It was to be a gruelling endurance competition that would be made far worse by slick roads.

But by starting-time ominous clouds hovered overhead. They sagged lower as light showers began. Only a few miles into the race, participants found themselves contending with heavy showers and high wind. They were doomed to a stormy day.

One by one, soaked, fatigued runners dropped out. Ushered into warm, dry cars, they were doubtless brought to a welcoming pub for well-deserved refreshment and rest. By the time they reached Drogheda, thirty-five racers had succumbed to the elements. It was now pruned down to a hardy and determined seven students. From this point on, their progress and positions were 'noted at hourly intervals' on the board in the university hallway as students and supporters strained to see how they were doing. The closer the runners drew to Dublin, the more excited their followers became.

As with Olympians, they tried to set the right pace for themselves, so as not to fall too far behind. As the racers approached Dublin, people began cheering them along the way. And when they hit the last stretch, nearing Trinity, 'scores of students cheered them on', whatever their position. However, it was hardly a photo finish. Ian Angus won spectacularly, finishing far ahead of his nearest rival, John Spence. When he came into sight, Ian was 'escorted through the city to the College Gates by a wildly cheering throng.'

After a cascade of congratulations he was 'immediately whisked off to bed'. Comfortably ensconced and wearing pyjamas, he accepted a stream of well-wishers and gave a few brief interviews. Then he was brought the good news: he had broken the existing record. This especially was a marvel, considering that he had accomplished the feat in wet, windy weather all the way.

He took it all quite modestly. 'It is something one does just once in a lifetime', he said, 'and now it's plenty of rest for me for a few days.' The best news for his friends, however, was his promise that when he recovered 'he plans to organise a party – to dispose of the barrel of stout he won.'

'Hip-hip, hooray!'

―――

On Monday morning Dublin's streets were filled not with well-wishing students but with demonstrators. Busmen strikers were marching from Parnell Square to the head office of the ITGWU in Merrion Square. Along the way they sang songs and carried placards with slogans like *No one-man buses!* When they reached their destination they handed over a letter declaring that they wouldn't 'accept or ballot on' any proposals that would implement one-man buses. Then they marched on to Kingsbridge Station.

Their demonstration drew widespread attention, but there were few signs of public sympathy along their way. CIE had made a good case for one-man buses being logical and financially necessary.

―――

Meanwhile, a murder trial was getting under way in Dublin. It was one that would increasingly draw the public's attention during the week. It all began on 28 December 1962 with a mere snippet of news from Co. Roscommon. Because it was during the mounting winter storm, few readers probably even noticed it.

Now, five months later, it would evolve into a compelling murder mystery in the classic whodunnit tradition. It might have been from the pen of Agatha Christie, for it had unexpected and bizarre twists and turns.

At the outset of the trial, on 6 May, in Mr Justice McLoughlin's court, it seemed like an unusual case but hardly a sensational one. The central figure was Kathleen Clougher, a 57-year-old woman from Mount Talbot who was charged with murder. It was alleged that she killed her brother George, 49, a farmer with whom she lived. She pleaded not guilty. The charge itself aroused people's curiosity. If she was guilty, what could her motive possibly have been?

The prosecutor, J. A. D'Arcy, contended that Kathleen had poisoned her brother by putting strychnine into the fish she had prepared for his meal, for which their neighbour Paddy Kelly had joined them. By 5:15 p.m. George had begun to complain of acute pains in his chest, back and legs. As the pain worsened, he stretched out on the floor and began writhing in agony. A doctor was sent for. When Dr Kilmartin arrived from Roscommon, eleven miles away, he found George dead. He examined the body and concluded that death had been due to natural causes.

As funeral arrangements were being made, a friend who was at the wake asked Kathleen if there would be an inquest. She replied tartly that it was not needed. However, several detectives had been sent out to her farm to have a look around, much to her displeasure.

Shortly before George was to be lowered into the earth a discovery was made. Two dogs on the farm were also found suspiciously dead. The funeral was halted and George's body taken to Roscommon for examination. The following day, New Year's Day, while the blizzard was raging, Dr Maurice Hickey, the state pathologist, conducted a *post mortem* examination. He found traces of strychnine in the brain, kidneys, intestines, liver and stomach. He quickly concluded that George had been poisoned by a fatal dose of strychnine.

Friends and neighbours didn't know what to make of the news. But some minds began spinning.

———

As D'Arcy was laying out his case in court on Monday, the *Evening Herald* reporter Seán Duignan set out to search for more information about what the papers were now calling Ireland's 'great mail van robbery', even though the value of the mail bags still wasn't known. The daring heist remained headline news.

Duignan, known for his ingenuity, sought to gain an original perspective. He managed to interview the van-driver, McCormack, at great length about his experience. Exactly how did he twist free of his bonds, and what were some of his thoughts during the 'nightmare' ride with his captors? Then, Duignan told his readers, 'I retraced the intricate get-away route taken by the hijackers, providing an "on-the-scene" perspective'.

All of Dublin's reporters had plenty of speculation about who the gang behind the robbery were, but they were short on hard facts. Most were convinced that there was a British connection to the robbery. They could only await garda evidence.

———

Back in the court in Dublin, evidence was also D'Arcy's problem. The prosecutor and his assistants had circumstantial evidence but not yet the solid evidence they needed to construct a motive. He conceded before the jury that 'the prosecution must *prove*' that it was Kathleen Clougher who had administered the poison – and done so *intentionally*. However, Dr Hickey testified that this might be a difficult challenge:

> Poisoning is happily very rare in this country. In general poisoners work secretly and therefore the crime can only be proved by piecing together bits of evidence and trying to form a complete picture of what happened.[55]

For months D'Arcy and his team had worked diligently, seeking their vital burden of proof. The Clougher farm had been kept under close surveillance, though this made Kathleen tense and irritable. The prosecution had at first hoped to have the neighbour Paddy Kelly, who had observed George's death, as a prime witness. But shortly afterwards he had departed for Birmingham – where he died on 17 January. D'Arcy received verification that this was the result of a heart attack. But he didn't know what had *caused* it.

On the day of Paddy's death, Detective-Superintendent McLoughlin went to inform Kathleen of it. 'She expressed sorrow … but her reaction did not seem normal.' That night, Garda O'Reilly was in the kitchen with Kathleen when she emotionally blurted out, 'Paddy Kelly has died in England – I will surely *hang* now!' A few seconds later she added that 'I will be in Mountjoy … so I think I'll go and say my rosary now … to get me out of all this.'[56]

Garda O'Reilly remained silent, sensing that Kathleen might have more to say. Fidgeting nervously, Kathleen added, 'I could have put a little

Enuptum in the fish ... but if I did, it was a mistake.' As O'Reilly would later testify in court, it certainly sounded incriminating. But it was also confusing.

Dublin's newspapers now had *two* fascinating cases to cover. During 6–10 May, readers followed the news of the robbery and the Clougher murder court proceedings with keen interest. By the middle of the week gardaí revealed that one of the stolen vehicles used in the robbery had a number plate from Croydon in England. A watch was now placed on all ports and air terminals. Furthermore, it was now thought that a crime committed only a few days previously might have had some connection to the van robbery. Two Englishmen, who had given their names as David Smith and Denis Sissons, had been charged with larceny of a motor car. Superintendent V. Halloran had some suspicions: he ordered the two men brought to Santry Garda Station. He had a few questions for them.

For many people, excitement about the RDS Spring Show overshadowed the big crime cases in the capital city. Exuberant people from all counties streamed into Dublin. The journalist Monica Carr, who wrote a weekly 'Country Diary' feature in the *Irish Independent*, was always fascinated to witness the cultural collision that occurred once a year at show time. During the rest of the year, Carr explained, most country people came to Dublin for shopping, medical treatment or sports matches. They found it a 'teeming, bubbling cauldron of noise and hurry' – not 'their world'. But the week of the Spring Show was the one grand exception.

In the spring of 1963, however, Carr found that the frenetic pace of change in Dublin overwhelmed many country people. Familiar landmarks, buildings and even entire streets had been drastically changed or demolished. Everywhere they looked, the city was booming with demolition and the construction of high-rise buildings. As the *Irish Independent* described it:

> Dublin's skyline is rapidly changing, and the city is having an expansive modern face-lift ... Gaunt steel skeletons stretch crazily for the clouds, giant cranes and massive bulldozers eat their way through old familiar landmarks.[57]

Old Dublin was fast vanishing, replaced with steel-and-glass monstrosities. It was unnerving. By the end of the week, most visitors would be ready to scurry back home.

That year, however, there was one new attraction not to be missed. Showing at the Ambassador was a film causing quite a stir in Dublin. While some reviewers gave it high acclaim, others condemned it as immoral, doing so even from the pulpit. This, of course, raised curiosity and made it all the more alluring for the curious. Stanley Kubrick's adaptation of the novel *Lolita* was so titillating, wrote one Irish reviewer, that the theatre was 'steamed up'. Country men knew this was their one chance to see it, as it would not be shown on the screen of their village picture house.

_____

Each day in court, gardaí who had stayed in the farmhouse with Kathleen Clougher came forward to testify about her statements uttered in the kitchen of her free will. When the prosecutor, D'Arcy, began questioning Kathleen she could be either reticent or surprisingly talkative. It was never known what her mood would be. On Wednesday she revealed a real bombshell that made the headlines: 'Brother had affair – accused'.

Kathleen proceeded to support her revelation. At first, she simply referred to her as the 'girl', giving no age or personal information. After some prodding, she named her as Peg, who lived in Cloonagh. Exposure of George's romantic interest put an entirely new slant on the case. When Kathleen said quite nonchalantly that 'George had an affair with a girl', one could almost feel the reverberations throughout the courtroom, especially among the jury and press. It seemed so out of character for the farmer who had apparently lived with his elder sister for nearly fifty years.

Oh, yes, added Kathleen, and he *drank*!

D'Arcy jumped in. What exactly did she mean?

Well, she explained, on various occasions George would come home drunk and sit by the fire, talking to himself about 'a certain girl ... and that if he did not marry her he would do away with himself'. Kathleen claimed that her brother had an obsession with having to 'get married soon' to Peg. Furthermore, he told Kathleen to go ahead and 'paper the room' – but she didn't do it. Had he intended to marry Peg and bring her into his sister's house?

By gentle coaxing, D'Arcy found that he could lead Kathleen into being reflective, though her testimony seemed to be making the case more convoluted by the day:

> One Saturday night before Christmas, George was very drunk and he was talking to himself about Peg. And he said that if he could not get her, life was no good to him ... that he would poison himself. What good was life without her? He used the word 'poison' very often.[58]

In most of her testimony, however, she would allude to herself as having made a 'mistake'. Detective-Sergeant J. Flood was called as a witness to verify that the accused had made a written statement in her kitchen. It stated that she was preparing the dinner when she brought over a tray with pepper, Chef Sauce and Enuptum – 'which I took over *instead* of salt, by mistake ... I shook some of the Enuptum powder on the fish, by mistake.'[59] She added, 'I know Enuptum powder is poisonous.'

Gardaí who had been keeping close watch on Kathleen in her home presented their testimony. Garda Teresa Feeney recalled that she was returning with her from Mass when Kathleen said it was possible 'she shook the wrong stuff on the fish ... by mistake.' Then Kathleen had started to cry and asked Feeney to pray for her.

————

Over at the Spring Show, all was going splendidly. People had looked forward to it since the snows of winter. Dublin's newspapers gave it colourful coverage. The centre of attention was the legendary Tommy Wade and his famed horse Dundrum, a duo that never failed to captivate an RDS crowd with their spectacular performances. Their perfect pairing had been the highlight of RDS shows since the spring of 1957, when they first appeared. And 1963 was to be no exception.

'Loyal spectators', wrote the *Irish Independent*, 'endured the biting, rain-laden wind which swept across the jumping enclosure' to see Wade and Dundrum surpass all competition in superb form. Once again they delighted spectators, becoming the talk of the show. One reporter gushed that 'the magnificence of the Tommy Wade-Dundrum partnership has captured the hearts of horse-jumping enthusiasts all over the world.' Their performance always added to everyone's excitement at the Spring Show.

As the week wore on there was an injection of fresh news for journalists. President John F. Kennedy's flamboyant, cigar-chomping press secretary, Pierre Salinger, flew in to Dublin with his White House advance party. Establishing his room at the Gresham Hotel as his head office, the witty Salinger entertained the press with his stories and off-the-cuff remarks. And often off the record as well. He daily provided at least a few delicious items for the front pages. Salinger confirmed that President Kennedy would 'definitely visit Wexford and New Ross', but he couldn't yet give the exact dates. And he wasn't sure whether the journey south from Dublin would be by car or helicopter. Stay tuned!

On Thursday 9 May the *Irish Independent* had a bulletin: 'Buses may run on Sunday'.

The word was that a new proposal, this one called a 'formula', was to be presented to the busmen, and it was hoped that it would resolve the issues of sick benefits and pensions. They might be handed the new ballot on Saturday. This one was thought to have a good chance.

Once again, the waiting game commenced. What a lovely sound it would be to have the springtime filled with the hissing, roaring and grinding of buses all over the country.

That afternoon D'Arcy began wrapping up his case against Kathleen Clougher. But he wanted to clarify what Kathleen had told Garda O'Reilly about 'going to Mountjoy' and 'being hanged'. Without appearing to badger Kathleen, he asked gently what she had meant.

'It was just a comment,' she answered. 'I was a suspect then … for something I didn't do.' Which hardly provided the answer he was seeking.

The defence had waited until towards the end of the trial to call Kathleen's brother James Clougher as a witness. He lived quite a distance from her farm but had a few words to say. From all he had observed over the years, Kathleen and George 'got on very well together' – at least when James was around. He knew nothing of any 'Peg' that George had allegedly professed to want to marry, or of drunkenness and mutterings about poison. That was about all he could say.

As both sides drew their cases to a close, the mystery seemed more murky than ever.

At the outset of the trial, D'Arcy had made it clear to the jury that if a person 'deliberately gives poison to another' it is murder. It doesn't matter whether or not a motive is established. He knew that circumstantial evidence was seldom enough to prove a case beyond all doubt. Kathleen Clougher had become a contradictory and confusing defendant.

On Friday morning, the 10th, Mr Justice McLoughlin handed the convoluted case over to the jury. There was little hard evidence to examine and debate, and much of the circumstantial evidence was vague and conflicting. And there were no living witnesses to the alleged crime.

The jury went into deliberation, and everyone else waited on the verdict.

––––––

On Friday morning the White House press secretary, Pierre Salinger, had a few more morsels for the hungry press at the Gresham Hotel. 'I had a long talk with the President before I left Washington and he is looking forward to his Irish visit with the keenest possible interest.' Unlike obligatory diplomatic visits, said Salinger, this trip to Ireland will 'be a *sentimental journey*' for Kennedy.

Furthermore, he will be accompanied by 'a party of 30 to 40 White House officials – and 125 to 140 newsmen.' Ending his 'news chat' – as opposed to a formal news conference – he told journalists that Kennedy's visit was 'arousing more interest among the American press corps' than any other engagement since he took office. They savoured Salinger's personal insights and comments, which enlivened their articles the next day.

––––––

With the jury out, Mr Justice McLoughlin's courtroom had largely emptied. Some court reporters hung around chatting with one another, speculating on when a decision might be reached. Outside, the day was chilly and blustery. To some, Kathleen Clougher had become a sympathetic figure, a simple farm woman who seemed more confused than conniving. To them she was hardly capable of intentionally poisoning her own brother. Others might have found her deviously clever in covering up her crime.

Everyone apparently expected the jury's deliberation to stretch into the following week. So it was a great surprise when, on Friday afternoon, word came in that the jury was returning after an absence of an hour and a half. Reporters scrambled to return, and the suspense inside was palpable.

Wasting no time, Mr Justice McLoughlin saw that all was in order in his courtroom before asking for the verdict.

'Not guilty.'

Silence, then gasps. Slowly it occurred to observers that perhaps it was an inevitable decision, considering the difficulty of proving an intentional act. And a difficulty in imagining Kathleen, nearing sixty, taken from her farmhouse and placed behind bars.

Outside the court, Kathleen Clougher paused to say a very few words to the flock of reporters. With composure, and no evident emotion, she said:

> I felt all along that I would go free. I knew that I had nothing to worry about. What will I do now? I will go back to the farm. That's all I want to say.[60]

And off she went.

———

At about that same time, word came in from the Vatican of Pope John's health. It had been a topic of international interest in the previous three weeks. With conflicting reports, people were left wondering and worrying. By the end of the week the Vatican felt the need to clarify the matter.

To discount the stories that the Pope was seriously ill, even facing death, the Vatican newspaper *L'Osservatore Romano* wrote that the Pope was, in fact, in a 'vivacious' mood when he greeted several thousand pilgrims at week's end. He was described as 'smiling and relaxed' during the Vatican ceremonies. At the age of eighty-one, he might occasionally appear a 'little drawn' at the end of a busy day, but that was certainly normal for a man of his age.

There was no need for undue worry.

———

In Dublin there was need for worry over quite a different matter. Pierre Salinger's revelation that 140 press and media reporters would be converging upon the city in only eight weeks threw authorities into a dither. Their demand for telecommunications would be immense, exceeding anything previously experienced in Ireland. The telephone system was by then archaic and dysfunctional, especially with the strain of the bus strike. Reporters from the United States and other countries would demand modern, reliable communication. Action to correct the system was demanded without delay.

Back in April it had been a heatedly debated issue in the Dáil. Whose fault was it? How could it be fixed in time? The Minister for Posts and Telegraphs, Michael Hilliard, barked that it was not his staff to blame: it was the poor equipment. One angry critic charged that the 'telephone service is so chaotic' because of disorganisation and insufficient equipment, and that 'if saboteurs dropped from the sky intent on causing disruptions of the phone service they could do no better!' Hilliard didn't dispute his claim. He promised to have it working smoothly, in a modern mode, by the time President Kennedy arrived.

With international attention soon to be on Dublin, another member of the Dáil saw it as the perfect time to offer a different criticism – one that had been nagging him for some time now. Irish postal uniforms, he charged, were the 'worst kind in the entire public service, made of a shoddy dust-gathering type of material.' They were unsightly and a national embarrassment. New, smart uniforms were desperately needed – and now was the perfect time. Though there was no wave of support for his proposal, he had at least had his say, as this seemed to satisfy him – for the moment.

———

On Saturday 11 May people throughout Ireland once again waited for the results of the busmen's balloting, due to be announced the following day. But by Saturday night word slipped out that this one was to be a real squeaker.

The final tally showed that it had passed by 315 votes. The *Irish Independent* called it a surprisingly narrow margin. It was uncomfortably close for many. But passengers didn't dwell on statistics: the buses were back!

The *Irish Times* called it 'one of the country's most serious strikes' in many years, regretting the 'great public inconvenience' it had caused. The newspaper calculated that most stranded passengers had 'probably walked more in the last five weeks than they do in an average six months'.

On Sunday, when the news was announced, there was a sort of holiday spirit throughout the country – one of relief. That afternoon CIE tested its first one-man bus between Busáras in Dublin and Longford. Fourteen passengers were on board the bus, driven by Charles Moloney. They found the changes immediately apparent. Climbing into the bus, they read the new notice, *Pay as you enter. Fares ready, please.* To the driver's left was a ticket dispenser, and change was returned with the touch of a button. The driver controlled the automatic door. 'Modernisation', the passengers called it.

Yet they missed their conductor and his warm greeting. To many, he had been a real friend. He had made the trip chatty and enjoyable. Now it was automated – all business. Transforming CIE's fleet of buses would take years, starting with the rural routes. City buses in Dublin, Cork and Limerick would still have their conductors for a while longer.

Some conductors in Dublin, facing their inevitable termination, decided to seek other employment, which meant that CIE would face a shortage of conductors for several years. This prompted one veteran passenger to write to the *Irish Press* with a suggestion:

> This is an opportunity to employ girls in their place. What a blessing it would be to have girl conductors with their smiling faces, cleanliness and friendly manners.

_____

With the strike over, the combined bus and car traffic in Dublin led to packed streets once again. However, during the five-week strike gardaí had been very lenient in enforcing parking regulations. For the most part, drivers could park wherever they liked, so long as they didn't block traffic. Now, with parking laws actually enforced, motorists complained that it was nearly impossible to find a spot to park in.

For country people visiting the city, the problem was even more daunting. One day a motorist from Co. Kilkenny arrived in Dublin to do some shopping. He always found it stressful and especially dreaded finding a parking space. This time he had an idea: driving slowly through a suburban area, he stopped at a house to ask if he might park in their garage for a few hours. The man generously agreed. Happily, the visitor strolled off into town.

Later that afternoon, lugging his packages, he went to retrieve his car. It didn't take long for him to realise that he was lost. He had failed to note the address of his private car park. All the streets and houses looked alike. Gardaí were called in, but he could give them no directions. Feeling defeated, he finally had to take the bus home – to sheepishly tell his family and friends of his misadventure.

Days later, the man with the garage reported the car as left behind. For the motorist, the mystery was solved. The gardaí probably assured him that he was not the first visitor to the city to have made such a blunder.

————

On Sunday 12 May the celebratory mood of Dubliners happy to have the buses back was conspicuous. The city was packed with people excited to attend the National Football League final that afternoon at Croke Park. It was a chance to watch the all-Ireland champions, Kerry, face a tough Down team.

The match had no reserved seats. The gates would be open to one and all, but many spectators had been lulled into taking their time. About an hour before the match, throngs of people were suddenly flooding the streets all around Croke Park, all confident that they would find a seat. However, they made a startling discovery: only six of the thirty turnstiles were working. Enormous snaking queues began forming, but soon people grew impatient, then panicky, as they began running off to find an open gate. Then there was a general realisation of what was happening.

An *Irish Independent* reporter witnessed the 'amazing scenes' that ensued. The Hogan Stand was full half an hour before the start of the match as others raced and pushed their way towards the Cusack Stand. In the desperation to gain admittance and find a seat, violence erupted both inside and outside the stadium. People were pushed aside, knocked down and trampled. Men came to blows. Mass hysteria arose at some gates, and 'women screamed as they were caught in the surging throng'. At one point a reporter watched as 'three main gates were *forced* open', allowing a sudden flood of people to flow through. One man caught in the fury described it. 'I was caught like a cork in the incoming tide.' Park attendants were at a loss to control the madness, for fear of being injured themselves.

People were injured and bloodied by the fighting. Ambulances were called to care first for women and children who had been victims. Extra gardaí were called in to try and halt the bedlam. Some men began 'scrambling over the walls', and one reporter noted that the gardaí, led by an inspector, 'tried to check the rush but were powerless to halt the "human flood"!'

Then shouts erupted to 'burst down the gates'. Two Kerry supporters told of how they saved an eleven-year-old boy from being trampled. 'We lifted him up on our shoulders as he went down in the stampede.'

Even when the match finally got under way it was marred by some regrettable incidents and 'bouts of fisticuffs'. Players 'swapped swipes' and were fortunate not to find themselves taken off. In the opinion of many, the referee, P. McArdle, was far too lenient. Unsporting conduct on the field was deplorable to purists. In a tense finish the champions, Kerry, 'resisted strong pressure' to defeat Down 0-9 to 1-5. While most sports writers agreed that, as a sporting spectacle, it was exciting, it was socially and morally a disgraceful exhibition.

GAA authorities were angry and embarrassed about their having non-functioning gates. While the attendance was more than 57,000, it was estimated that at least 7,000 had smashed down gates and climbed in without paying. It was a black day for Irish sports. In the days following the debacle there was much reflection and fault-finding.

——

The ugly incident at Croke Park, involving so many thousands of people, provided more evidence for the Rev. J. Mercer, who was due to give a speech in the following days. The topic was 'Ireland's declining morals'. He had given the subject much thought since the swinging sixties had arrived in Irish society, and now he was ready to speak out. He was armed with plenty of evidence.

On 17 May, at the session of the General Synod of the Church of Ireland in Dublin, he gave a stirring and quite provocative address. The *Irish Independent* regarded it as important enough to cover expansively. Mercer's language was eloquent, his message simple: in Ireland morals had 'become topsy-turvy'.

In Mercer's opinion, 1963 was a salient year in Ireland's evolving moral character. There was a time in the not too distant past, he said, when 'moral lapses created a sense of shame'. Now they were not only accepted but likely to be a source of 'elation' and a 'feeling of bravado'. The juvenile delinquent had become a hero to his pals; divorce no longer carried a stigma and was accepted as the private concern of two people; marriage vows were becoming meaningless; infidelity was accepted – if not expected; pre-marital sex was regarded as natural; and children conceived out of wedlock were becoming so frequent that it was hardly noticed any more. And films with sexual themes – like *Lolita* – packed cinemas.

The public's behaviour was lacking in what he regarded as common decency, courtesy and consideration for others. Civility seemed to have vanished from vogue. Vulgarities and obscenities flew around the streets like litter, without notice. Gangs of teenagers carried knives and even beat up and stabbed bus conductors on some late-night routes. People felt terrorised. Motorists drank till they were drunk, drove recklessly and injured or killed people at a record rate.

Furthermore, he stressed, 'it was not only in the lower stratum of society that this "jungle morality" was found, but also in the so-called "respectable circles".' In other words, in Ireland the morals of Catholics and Protestants, wealthy and poor, young and old, were in an appalling state of decline.

That same week, in Dublin District Court, Judge Lanigan-O'Keeffe seemed in full agreement with the Rev. Mercer about the immorality of unsafe driving caused by recklessness and drink. He was one of the few judges who took the new safety campaign seriously enough to begin applying tough laws.

An article in the *Evening Herald* reflected his view on the 'deplorable' driving in the country:

> The behaviour on the roads is nothing short of a menace … It is appalling. And the law is not being enforced.

The article expressed amazement at the indifference shown by the gardaí to infringements committed by unlawful drivers. And the courts were culpable for not enforcing the laws and penalising the offenders.

But this was not the case with Judge Lanigan-O'Keeffe. He intended to carry out his duty aggressively. In court he asserted that 'either the new speed limit is a joke, or it is not. As far as I am concerned, it is *not*!' Then he proceeded to fine twelve motorists stiffly for speeding and recorded the conviction on their licences. It was hoped that other judges would get his message.

Many drivers were prone to speeding through the Phoenix Park as if its roads were a racecourse. Every year there were numerous accidents and often deaths. It was especially dangerous at night, when roads were dimly lit by gas lamps. To many Dubliners, especially preservationists, these lamps were a cherished feature of the city's history.

Unfortunately, sometimes progress means losing traditional life-ways and artefacts. By 1963 the rationale for replacing the gas lamps had gained favour among Dublin authorities. There were still more than five hundred cattle roaming free in the park – and on the roads. They were especially hard to see in the mist and fog at night. Some of the black cattle were almost invisible. From the summer of 1962 to 1963 two people had even been killed in the Park.

When the order was given to begin replacing the Park's gas lamps, no-one was affected more personally than Tom Flanagan, the last of Dublin's old lamplighters. Born in 1907, he began tending the lamps in 1924 with his father, still using the pole and torch. In his eighties he reflected on his role in an interview with the author. When he was taken on as his father's helper he was:

> the proudest man in the world! I got one pound fifteen a week … Responsible for 195 lamps in the Park. I had no uniform, but I wore a coat and a tie. The old lamps were great! Oh, they had a warm little glow … This was the last stronghold of gas, here in the Park.

He was kept on to look after a few remaining gas lamps, finally retiring in 1975. 'Fifty-one years at it – *never bored*!'

———

The last week of May ended with gaiety and fun. And, for children, a real whirl. On Sunday, the 26th, the biggest event of the year took place in the National Stadium – that is, if you were an Irish youngster. At last it was the finals. The *Evening Herald's* national yo-yo contest was to be decided; an enormous number of competitors were being pared down. Some hopefuls had been practising day and night for months, trying to master the tricky spins, twirls and around-the-worlds. When the children were called on to perform, their parents stood by watching hopefully and nervously. All were under the expert eye of the world yo-yo champion, Billy Panama, who children idolised as the greatest marvel on the planet.

When it was pruned down to the finalists, there was great tension. All were very talented, but the junior champion was Francis Becker of Foxrock, who was applauded loudly. Then he stepped forward to receive his award. 'I am so thrilled. I never thought I could have won a bike!'

The senior competition was won by Eugene Griffin of Rathgar, who received a moped and was equally delighted with his prize. Both winners gave their new bikes a try before a crowd of admirers, feeling that their countless hours of practice had all been worth it.

Then everyone marvelled at Billy Panama's dazzling demonstration, doing tricks they couldn't have imagined possible. This left everyone heading home happily.

––––

Over at Trinity College, the Trinity Week spectacle would end the month in grand style. As always, there was the Boat Club regatta and competitions in tennis, swimming and cricket. There was also a fashion show in which an 'Elegance Queen' would be selected. More than a thousand people would attend the Elizabethan Society's garden party.

The highlight of the week that year was the whimsical Penny Farthing Parade, an attraction celebrating the Centenary College Races. The week culminated in the Trinity Week Ball, at which some two thousand guests danced to the music of six bands in four halls on the college grounds.

Ending May with such merriment seemed a perfect prelude to what was hoped would be a perfect summer.

Chapter 7 ∽

A WOEFUL WHIT WEEKEND

No month ever held more promise.

Marvellous summer weather was predicted for June. Temperatures were expected to climb high, with abundant sunshine. Plans were being made for outings to the country and seaside. Everyone was anxious to enjoy picnics, biking and boating. Exciting concerts and sporting events were also on tap.

Throughout the country, people were already ecstatic in their anticipation of President John F. Kennedy's visit late in the month.

The month began even better than one could have imagined, with glorious Whit weekend weather. Older people claimed that it was the best in their memory. As the *Irish Independent* noted:

> blue skies, brilliant sunshine and temperatures touching the seventies made it a record-breaking Whit Weekend. Thousands flocked to the seaside and into the country to enjoy the first real spell of summer weather. If ever there was an out-of-doors Whitsuntide, this was it.[61]

With throngs enjoying nature's gift, the AA reported 'extremely heavy traffic' on the roads and warned drivers to exercise great caution. Pleas were also made by water-safety proponents for swimmers and boaters to be careful.

Tenement-dwellers sat in front of their buildings, chatting away cheerfully while sewing or knitting. They enjoyed soaking up the rays of sunshine as they watched children frolic up and down the street.

Spirits were dimmed, however, by the *Irish Independent's* headline: 'Pontiff slowly dying'. Pope John's health had been in an uncertain state for weeks, but he always rallied and returned to his duties. But the new reports sounded far more serious. Many Irish people were now closely following despatches from Vatican Radio, which were being translated all over the world.

It was particularly distressing to hear that the Pope was conscious but 'suffering terribly'. But at his bedside were his three brothers, Giuseppe, Alfredo and Zavario, as well as his sister, Assunta. His sister tenderly wiped his forehead with a handkerchief. Irish listeners followed every detail of his condition.

Over the weekend, with the first spell of dry weather, some of Dublin's tenement-dwellers noticed fragments of mortar loosening and falling out, freeing bricks from their binding. They were also hearing new sounds of creaking and cracking. Occupants in some buildings became alarmed.

Throughout March, April and May, Dublin Corporation had been bombarded with complaints from frightened residents who reported not only sounds but cracks and holes. But since the Corporation could not yet provide most of them with alternative, safe housing, they had nowhere to go. Rather than be rendered homeless, they stayed. And lived in a hellish fear.

The unusually harsh winter had brought penetrating snow and ice, with periodic thawing and refreezing. This was accompanied by gale-force winds that shook and further cracked the structures. This all hastened wood rot and brick-and-mortar disintegration, and the brittle tenements groaned and split, some leaving holes so large that one could poke one's hand through and see the sky above. In early summer J. A. Culliton, head of the Defective and Dangerous Buildings Department of the Dublin Corporation, candidly assessed the crisis:

> The brickwork of the old buildings absorbed moisture like a sponge ...
> Walls which were eighteen inches thick in some cases were saturated to
> the core, from the outer facing to the inner facing. When the heat wave
> came, all the moisture evaporated – leaving nothing to hold the bricks
> in place, no adhesive between them. The timbers of the houses became
> swollen and they pushed the walls out as they expanded.[62]

It was little wonder that occupants could hear that the buildings were in their death throes. Thunderclaps and heavy lorries rumbling past furthered the process of destabilisation. Residents commonly complained that merely trying to hang a picture on the wall with a small nail or tack could bring the whole wall down.

Over the Whit holiday, as others were enjoying the heatwave, the weather was leaving some tenement mortar crumbling like sand.

_____

When it became apparent that the Pope's death was impending, some of those Irish who knew him personally expressed their affection for him. Monsignor Thomas Ryan revealed that when the Pope was a youth in his native Bergamo he had heard about Daniel O'Connell. Thus began his study of, and admiration for, the national struggle of common Irish people. He often expressed this sentiment when he met Irish priests and pilgrims. Ryan verified that 'His Holy Father held the Irish people in great affection.'

When he received Cardinal D'Alton in audience after his coronation, the Pope 'spoke with marked love of Ireland'. It was a feeling warmly and widely reciprocated throughout the country.

In recognition of this, the *Irish Independent* printed an article entitled 'His love for Ireland'. One trait that especially endeared the Pope to the Irish people was his empathy for working-class people and the downtrodden of society.

Every Irish newspaper gave intense attention to the Pope's last few days and hours. The *Irish Independent* sent its Vatican correspondent, Liam Shine, to St Peter's Square. His accounts were vivid and often emotional. The Holy Father, he wrote, was 'slowly going out like a candle', retaining 'full lucidity of the mind', but 'he suffers much … he suffers.' Shine encountered there a large number of Irish priests, nuns, brothers and pilgrims:

> Sorrowing thousands keep watch … as a sliver of moon arose. We all feel sad here tonight … many are in tears, but they kept their vigil.[63]

The Irish faithful followed as closely as they could on the Vatican Radio.

_____

On Saturday night, 1 June, the weather in Dublin was warm and windows were flung open. By midnight most people in Bolton Street had settled into bed. Some were listening to sounds that kept them awake – from within their walls.

To the ears of the occupants of number 20 the sounds were all too familiar. They were more audible at night, when things became quiet outside. Usually there was a faint creaking and cracking, as if the ancient building were groaning in its misery. Everyone knew what the sounds were. After all, the house was more than 150 years old, and it had been neglected generation after generation. But the occupants had nowhere else to go, other than the open streets.

They could tell that the winter weather had taken a toll on the stability of the dwelling. To exacerbate matters, the houses adjacent had recently been demolished after being condemned by the Corporation. Just as their own building had been condemned. Without the adjoining buildings for support, the gable wall was now unsupported. Pedestrians and motorists passing by often gazed up in amazement at the disaster waiting to happen. Yet, inside, people still tramped up and down the rotten stairs and held on to rickety bannisters.

When a strong wind struck or a heavy lorry rumbled past just a few feet from the front door, the entire structure shuddered. Some of the residents called it 'trembling'. Other condemned tenements throughout the city experienced the same thing.

On this particularly stuffy night there was a whole chorus of distressing sounds, unnerving the occupants from top to bottom.

The top floor of the three-storey tenement was occupied by the Smyth family. Patrick and his wife, Esther, had three children, Christine, Ellen and Patrick, the youngest, who was eleven. Everyone loved having younger residents in the house, as it made it more lively. Many tenements had only older occupants.

The middle storey was home to the 84-year-old Leo Maples and his wife, Mary, 82. She had recently broken her leg and used a crutch, and she had left hospital only the previous week to rejoin her husband. The Maples were the parents of Esther Smyth, just above them. People said how wonderful it was that three generations lived under the same roof.

Mrs Ryan, an invalid and the owner of the house, had the ground floor, where she had a shop, herself living at the rear. However, she often had her niece Joan Ryan stay overnight with her, especially on weekends.

This was one of those weekends.

Joan was handy, always glad to give Mrs Ryan a helping hand around the shop. In fact, it had been only the previous Saturday when Mrs Ryan had asked Joan to 'take everything off the shelves', because 'the wall seemed to be moving ... and the crumbling masonry was damaging the goods.'

Fit and strong, Patrick Smyth was in charge of all matters of maintenance and supervision. He was especially attuned to the risks of living there, because of their three children. With the recent demolition of the two supporting structures, he was now more worried than ever. He had filed forceful complaints to the Corporation – to no avail. He and his wife both now considered their house highly dangerous.

At about 4 a.m. on Sunday, Patrick was sleeping. Yet he was half-consciously aware of unusual noises of structural stress. With an awful suddenness, he was jolted into full consciousness:

Just after 5 a.m. I was awakened by a loud crash, a crack from the floor below, followed by a roar like thunder. Suddenly, I found myself still in bed as the floor gave way, falling down into the ground floor. It seemed like an endless drop, and I was terrified.

The house caved in all around me ... and bricks and slates and rafters and furniture tumbled down in a crazy mess. I was thrown from the bed as it hit the rubble. Miraculously, I was not buried and managed to stumble out ... in a cloud of dust, cries all around me.[64]

He began searching frantically for his family, as he 'could hear my children screaming for me, crying, "Daddy, daddy, daddy!"' As he began digging furiously with his hands to try and reach them he also 'heard other people screaming for help'.

The middle storey, home to the elderly Maples, had collapsed first, on top of Mrs Ryan's, below. Then the Smyth floor collapsed. The structure simply crumbled upon itself, with everyone trapped inside – in the dark of night. Falling through space, they were catapulted out of their beds when they hit the rubble. Within seconds number 20 Bolton Street was reduced to a mountain of bricks, timber and mortar, barely visible at first through the dense cloud of dust. Inside, the occupants were struggling to get free.

By incredible good fortune, Garda Blessing – his name symbolic of his presence – on motorcycle patrol, happened to be passing the tenement at the moment when it crumbled to the ground. 'I could hardly believe what I saw! *Stunned!*' Then he spotted 'a woman's legs in the rubble'. He called for help on his radio telephone and then dashed into the wreckage to try and rescue the victims.

When he saw Patrick Smyth doing the same, the two men began working together in lifting heavy objects. They first found his son, Patrick, whose legs were pinned down in the rubble. He was dug out quickly. 'My wife was not far away but had been hit by an iron gas cooker ... Then I went to free my two daughters.' They listened for other cries for help. Before long they found Leo and Mary Maples, still and silent, described by one reporter as having been 'hurled to their deaths, buried beneath tons of rubble'.

Though Patrick, senior, had suffered a blow to the head, he carried out the rescue work vigorously. But he and Garda Blessing could have used more help. A few minutes later, when Blessing had to take a quick break to gasp for air, he spotted four men who had stopped their car to gawk at the horror before them. At first, Blessing thought he was in luck. But when he tried to enlist their help in the rescue the 'four men *refused* to help the victims – and drove off!'

Meanwhile, neighbours who had been awakened by the thundering crash and screaming voices rushed to the scene to help in any way they could. To James O'Neill, of number 37, who was one of the first neighbours on the scene, it sounded like 'a bomb exploding ... It was terrible with people groaning and screaming.' Denis O'Connell, a mechanic who lived across the road, was 'confronted by a young girl who staggered out in her night attire, covered with dust and crying.' Another neighbour, George Nason, arrived at the scene just in time to find Joan Ryan 'buried up to her chest in debris', telling rescuers to 'search for her invalid aunt'.

As all this was occurring, the gardaí and fire brigade were rushing to Bolton Street. A crowd was already gathering, some indiscreetly calling out, 'How many killed?'

Arriving at the scene, the gardaí went to work keeping the crowd back and blocking off the road. Firefighters entered the wreckage with their hand tools in order to dig people free and carry them out on stretchers. Mrs Ryan was soon found covered in debris not far from her niece, and only slightly injured. The firefighter Joe Riordan was twenty-nine in 1963; some fifty years later he recalled that one of his brigade mates, Jim Robinson, went beyond the call of duty to help Mrs Ryan when she was extricated from the ruins:

One old lady, she was very upset about her budgie. Oh, *very* upset! So, Jim, he went in – and it wasn't very safe. He was a huge, big man, an

Irish boxing champion. But he could see this budgie, in a cage, and he went in and got it for her. And she was so happy!

Mrs Ryan was determined to retrieve valuable belongings from her shop on the ground floor. Jim Fitzpatrick, another firefighter, recalls that as soon as Mrs Ryan was released from hospital she hurried back to the site and insisted that she be allowed to rummage for something specific she *had* to find. Fitzpatrick remembers that 'she returned to her shop to collect a considerable sum of money from the wreckage' – and, sure enough, she soon found it.

Considering that they were inside a three-storey house that had collapsed upon them, the Smyth family and the Ryans survived with remarkably little harm. Esther Smyth was suffering from shock, Christine had an eye injury, Ellen had a fractured shoulder, and young Patrick suffered a leg injury. The Ryans below, upon whom it had all fallen, incredibly had only minor injuries. As Patrick Smyth told reporters, it was 'only by the grace of God' that all except the elderly Maples had survived. What struck reporters profoundly was a statement by Patrick at the end of his interview. He told them that, having lived in the tenement for twenty-two years, he had 'always expected the house to fall some day'.

The *Irish Press* heaped praise upon Garda Blessing, calling him a hero who had 'risked his life to go to the aid of people trapped among tottering walls'. His dented helmet was evidence of the 'narrow escapes' he had had.

Within a few hours of the Bolton Street collapse, fears of the dreaded domino effect arose. As J. A. Culliton, head of the Defective and Dangerous Buildings Department, explained it, a collapse like the Bolton Street one 'can cause earth shock … This can result in damage to houses in the vicinity', further destabilising them, to the point of collapse. This was especially true of 'tooth gap' tenements left standing on their own after the adjacent houses had been demolished.

When the Bolton Street building fell with a thunderous crash, it sent earthquake-like reverberations along nearby Dominick Street, which was already mostly decrepit. This prompted housing authorities to race over in hopes of averting another tragedy. The firefighter Jim Fitzpatrick recalls that on:

that *same* night sixteen people were advised to vacate their three-storey tenement house at Upper Dominick Street. But some of them *refused*, as they wished for more suitable accommodations … although large cracks were seen to appear.

Three families lived in the dilapidated dwelling that had further cracked and now looked ready to split open. However, they had 'earlier ignored the advice' of Corporation authorities and gardaí and refused to evacuate – unless it was on *their* terms. This time, though, most occupants were frightened enough to flee on their own. Michael Keogh, his wife and their seven children, aged three to sixteen, quickly fled down the rickety stairs when their building trembled. When keys to a three-bedroom Corporation house in Cabra were handed to them, Mrs Keogh cried, 'It is a dream come true … We could jump for joy!' Shortly thereafter, Anne Lanigan, who was expecting her first baby, happily agreed to take a flat in Dolphin's Barn.

However, Elizabeth McGuinness, a widow, vehemently refused to take the offer of a flat in Gardiner Place, at £2 per week – a generous offer. She told reporters, 'I would not live in a flat under *any* circumstances – I want to go to Cabra!' She was typical of many elderly tenement-dwellers who had lived all their lives in a tenement house and had an entrenched bias against flats, which 'encaged' them. Some declared, 'I'd rather *die* here before I'll live *there*!' And, indeed, some did.

The Bolton Street tragedy sent fear throughout inner-city tenement districts. As the firefighter Riordan recalls, 'many people identified with those people – and now they saw themselves as possible victims.'

On Monday there was news that the Pope was now slipping away. It was his last day – everyone knew it. The Vatican did not try to conceal his great suffering during his final hours, though it was said to be wrenching to watch. The reporter Liam Shine wrote in the *Irish Independent* that:

> death is not far away … As the Holy Father endures his agony … he understands his suffering … [but] his stout heart still resists.[65]

On Monday evening, as multitudes were listening to the Vatican Radio broadcast describing his last moments, there was a special announcement, at 7:49:

Here is Vatican Radio. Praise be Jesus Christ. We are about to read an important communiqué. The Supreme Pontiff, John XXIII, is dead.

His agony was over. The *Irish Times* noted that his had been 'the shortest reign since that of Pius VIII,' who died in 1830, 'but for intensity it had no rival'.

Ireland experienced widespread mourning and a sense of personal loss. Messages of commiseration were sent by President de Valera and the Taoiseach, Seán Lemass. Some Irish priests were already calling Pope John 'saintly', as testimonies to his virtues flooded in. Dr Michael Browne, Bishop of Galway, spoke of the Pope's 'personal goodness, kindness ... his human approach and passion for peace'. Dr William Philbin, Bishop of Down and Connor, shared his sentiments. 'No one, I believe, *ever* established himself in the affection and the esteem of the whole world to the extent that he has done.'[66]

As the Pope lay in state it was all covered by the Irish media. During his burial in St Peter's, Irish business was suspended 'and normal life came to a standstill'. Offices, shops and schools closed. More than a thousand CIE workers marched in file to a church in Inchicore to attend a Requiem Mass. The ceremonies were watched on television and listened to on radio with great reverence, reflecting the 'depth of feeling which exemplified the affection of the Irish people' for the departed Pontiff. In summing up the nation's emotions, the *Irish Independent* wrote that the Holy Father was 'a Pope who is perhaps the best loved and most popular in modern history'.

———

On 3 June, when his close friend Pope John XXIII had been on his deathbed, the great composer Igor Stravinsky arrived in Dublin for his concert. He told a reporter for the *Irish Press* that he was 'in great distress' over the Pope's condition but that he was delighted to finally be in Ireland. 'I have never been in Ireland – *never*! Can you believe that? I want to see Ireland ... and show them my music.'

Though his week-long visit would be marred by the death of the Pope, it did not diminish his great enthusiasm for everything he would experience in the country. Beginning with a visit with his wife, Vera, to Áras an Uachtaráin to meet President de Valera, he travelled to the James Joyce Tower in Sandycove and then to the monastery of Clonmacnoise in

Co. Offaly. He raved to Brian Fallon of the *Irish Times* that 'your landscape is magnificent – green and stones!'

To the 2,300 patrons at the sold-out Adelphi Cinema he was a legendary figure. As the music critic Charles Acton, of the *Irish Times*, wrote, his very appearance 'made a huge impression on aficionados', who held the elderly genius in reverence. Mary MacGoris of the *Irish Independent* described his effect on the audience:

> On his entrance, the audience rose to applaud. He is stooped and slight and walks with a stick and was helped on to the rostrum. But in his direction of the music there was no sign of frailty.

His works were performed by the Radio Éireann Symphony Orchestra and Choral Society. The audience found his *Symphony of Psalms* to be absolutely 'heavenly'. Acton gave Stravinsky the highest praise imaginable:

> To hear it alive under its creator was a thrilling experience. How grateful I am for a historical event not too far away from Mr Handel's appearance in Fishamble Street in 1742!

The thunderous applause of the audience sent tremors throughout the theatre. No-one was happier than Stravinsky himself, who fell in love with Ireland and his admiring audience.

Upon his departure he said, with great conviction, that 'I will come back to Ireland – if not to make music, then to make a holiday.'

Sadly, he never would.

————

Ireland's legion of small grocers had been living in fear of extinction. In 1963 this threat had become quite real.

The country's ubiquitous small grocers had been seriously worried for some time about the massive take-over of their trade by huge British companies. The bad news struck them head-on in a provocative front-page article in the *Evening Herald* entitled 'The battle of supermarkets'.

It documented the intentions of British chains to quash small Irish grocers throughout the country, with alarming rapidity. Journalists began using the terms 'war' and 'battle' when covering the issue:

The war for the privilege of filling the housewives' basket has taken a new turn in Ireland with the news that the £83 million Garfield Weston empire is moving into the Republic in a big way.[67]

This news sent reverberations throughout the small-grocery trade in Ireland.

At first, their instincts were to somehow fight against the foreign threat. After all, it was not only their livelihood but their very way of life, with centuries of tradition behind them. Like the local publican, small grocers had been a central figure in the daily life of communities, whether urban or rural. They were a genuine friend, in good times and bad. In 1963 some even still extended credit to neighbours in hard times.

During the first few days of June, Carl Oppermann, director-general of RGDATA, tried to strike back at the powerful British 'invaders', a term used by Irish journalists. 'We have spent *years* agitating against' this outside threat to Ireland, he told the press. However, the economic realities of the modern grocery trade militated against the survival of the 'small man':

Outside chains with vast resources come into this country and operate below costs, to the detriment of native traders. We think it terribly unfair that the Government has done nothing to help.[68]

It was hoped that terminology pitting 'invaders' against 'native traders' would appeal to the consumers' patriotic loyalty when it came to supporting their local shop. To housewives struggling with the weekly budget, however, it had to be a matter of pocketbook over patriotism. Lower costs were undeniable, as were the alluring selection of goods and better counter services. Mammoth new supermarkets were simply irresistible to most shoppers.

By the first week of June, with confirmation of the invasion of British chains, the future was determined. One British company boldly declared its intention to attain 'penetration of all Irish towns of considerable size, as well as the suburbs and city centres'. To realistic small grocers, the writing was on the wall.

In fact, a large British supermarket was already under construction in South George's Street in June. It was promised to be the first of many. Such supermarkets were already planned for Talbot Street, Thomas Street, Dolphin's Barn and Dún Laoghaire. Some British companies liked to enhance their image by using the term 'power supermarkets', as if to crush those in their way.

Family grocers were forced out of business, one after the other. Their boarded-up shops – once so welcoming – began to dot towns and villages throughout the country. There were those, mostly elderly, loyal customers who recognised the heartbreak of what was happening. The shelves grew bare; the door was closed and bolted; windows were shuttered or covered with paper; fumes and dust covered windowpanes with a grey film, and children scribbled on the glass. Surely the once-beloved little shop deserved a better fate. When the small shopkeeper fell on hard times there was no-one there to help him.

The demise of Ireland's countless small grocer's shops is more than a sad tale: it is a transformative event in Irish social and cultural history, yet it has never received its due in Irish history books.

———

With the favourable weekend weather, motorists were fighting for space on the roads, many speeding and swerving to reach their destinations, seemingly oblivious to the warnings of the Road Safety Campaign. It would result in a rash of accidents and serious injuries, with three more deaths in the coming week.

That summer the motoring hordes would be bringing with them another troubling problem, in a higher proportion than ever before: they were littering roads and roadsides in an alarming manner. All sorts of litter were thoughtlessly tossed out car windows and blown about by the wind. Environmentalists and tourists were now regularly commenting on the shame of Ireland's natural beauty being despoiled so carelessly.

This prompted the magazine *Autocar* to publish an editorial about reducing holiday traffic, speeding and littering. The editors introduced a novel, and surely controversial, idea. It was so intriguing that the *Irish Independent* decided to share it with their wider readership under a catchy title: 'Abolition of bank holidays urged'.

As hoped, it drew wide attention. It argued that public holidays cause 'chaos and casualties on the roads and overrun the countryside with people, machines and rubbish'. Few could deny this. Therefore, it continued, would it not be better if 'everyone had an official extra *week* of holidays instead of these disruptive long weekends!' The extra week could be taken any time between May and October – but separate from the main summer holiday.

A simple concept but a highly debatable one. While it might have appealed to some, it was surely rejected by many. At least it stirred some fresh thought on the subject.

———

In the weeks following the Bolton Street tragedy, the Dublin Corporation frantically sought to increase its number of building inspectors. An epidemic of fear was spreading in the city. It was impossible to keep up with the phone calls from frightened tenement-dwellers reporting cracking and crevices in their walls and ceilings. In its haste to meet demand the Corporation gave minimal training to many certified 'inspectors', placing people's lives in their hands. Speaking of the Summerhill area, Una Shaw, who lived nearby in Rutland Street, remembered that:

> after the building collapse there was a panic! The inspectors had to really start looking through *all* the old houses – one even came *here*!

They were swarming around the tenement districts, knocking on doors, asking a few questions, glancing around. They either slapped a *Condemned* notice on the building or moved on to the next house. It wasn't up to them to worry about those occupants who would be rendered homeless by their actions.

Sometimes inspectors didn't get there in time. Only a few days after the Bolton Street collapse a passer-by in Upper Bolton Street noticed dust falling from a deep crack running down the gable of a house. It was clearly on the verge of collapsing. Inspectors and gardaí were rushed to the scene, where they ordered the twenty-nine occupants out. Within minutes, eight terrified families, including nine children, clambered down the rickety stairs into the daylight. They were ordered not to enter the building again, even to retrieve possessions, as the house was marked as condemned. Inspectors stood outside looking up at the gaping thirty-foot crack in the gable wall, wondering how the four-storey building was still standing.

Before long, reporters showed up to get the stories of the evacuated families, who were now out on the street bewildered, some crying, at so suddenly being made homeless. James Clausen told an *Irish Press* journalist that he lived on the top floor with his wife and fifteen-month-old daughter. 'My wife is sick with fear every time we close the door and plaster falls from the walls.' He said he could 'see out through a hole in the roof'.

His neighbour on the lower floor was quick to match that. 'I can look through a hole in the gable from my room and see the sky.' Thomas Davenport said he had lived in the tenement for forty-four years, but after the winter weather he feared that its 'day of doom' was near. Yet all had remained, because they had nowhere else to go.

When darkness fell and the Corporation officials and reporters had left the scene, the evacuated families were left sitting on the footpath. Later that night some of them disobeyed orders and sneaked back in to get blankets and retrieve a few possessions. When the Corporation got wind of it the next day they posted a nightwatchman to keep them out. They wanted no more bad publicity of deaths from tumbling tenements.

One ejected occupant, Mary Navagh, a seventy-year-old invalid, looked especially lost and piteous. Callously ordered out by an inspector, she had made it down the stairway and now stood forlornly in the street. Her photograph in the papers elicited great sympathy. For many she would come to symbolise the drama and shame of the thousands of evacuations yet to come.

It was at this time, on the eve of the summer holidays, that people began realising how abnormal – indeed, extraordinary – the year 1963 had been during its first five months. The sequence of incidents, tragedies and dramas had taken everyone by surprise. It felt like being on an emotional roller-coaster.

However, with President Kennedy's visit not two weeks away, a fresh excitement and positivity infused the population. There was a hope that the coming seven months would bring happy events and revive the national spirit.

Chapter 8 ∿

FLASH FLOOD!

Oh, that was a *real* flash flood! I was on duty that day, when it came down in buckets ... We had never experienced anything like it before. The *amount* of water. Oh, it was unbelievable!

TONY DORAN, BUS CONDUCTOR

Thursday 11 June, 8 a.m.

A summer morning in all its glory. It was what people had fantasised about in the blizzard months of January and February: the promise of a resplendent day.

Dubliners were upbeat. The city was already humming with preparations for President Kennedy's visit. By late morning it was in full swing, the streets and footpaths jammed. At the *Evening Herald* office, the reporter Stanley Paisley was most likely at his desk, facing a day with no particularly interesting news to write about. Charles Mitchel, RTÉ's premier news presenter, was probably still at home thinking much the same. It looked like one of those dull news days hardly worth reporting on. An alluring day to be outdoors.

At about 11:50 in the morning the sky began to change.

A weather front pulled a curtain of dark clouds overhead. The sun vanished. Then rainfall, with wind, began, which people took for a passing summer squall. They checked to see if they had brought their umbrellas.

Just after noon it struck with a typhoon-like force. Large raindrops pelted people and blurred windscreens. People rushed for cover, their umbrellas of little use. They sheltered in shops, under awnings – any cover they could find. Thousands of office workers stood at their windows watching in awe. It was no ordinary rainstorm.

Meteorologists were suddenly tracking an unexpected major weather event. The rising temperature, which had already reached above 23 degrees in Dublin by noon, played a role. Weather experts would explain it in the simplest terms as a sudden natural phenomenon:

> The *cause* of the violent thunderstorm was a rather weak trough of low pressure coupled with extreme heat … a front passing over the western areas before it got too warm there, then 'hit' the east coast and triggered off the thunderstorm with great intensity.[69]

It bore down on Dublin and the central east coast with ferocity, an extraordinarily powerful collision of weather systems. Such explanations would be inadequate to explain everything that was about to take place. As the *Irish Times* would write, 'There were incredible happenings during the height of the storm.'[70]

The city and surrounding areas were unable to handle the onslaught. Sewers and drains were incapable of coping with the riverine flows, clogging up quickly. This caused the water to overflow and rise at an astonishing rate before unbelieving eyes. Pools, then ponds, then *lakes* began forming. Within the first hour, motorists were brought to a crawl, some to a dead halt, in a foot or two of water. Pedestrians had to roll up skirts and trouser legs and wade through the water. Children had to be carried; the elderly and infirm dared not even try. Buses moved at a snail's pace, if at all, and emptied distressed passengers into swamped streets.

What would become the 'worst traffic jam in Dublin's history' was now under way – and only in its first hour.

———

People still expected it to end as suddenly as it began. But it didn't.

In parts of south Co. Dublin, parents at first allowed children to romp happily outside, splashing in low spots where water was collecting. That was until they noticed that their streets were becoming streams and strong water flows were invading their houses, washing out gardens and loosening stone walls. Then their children were hurriedly ordered indoors. In their homes, at least, they felt safe. For the moment.

Then the spectacular aerial show began: a cacophony of crashing peals of thunder, blinding lightning bolts, torrential rain and pounding hail. There were thunderous explosions that caused tremors. Residents at Mount Merrion, one of the hardest-hit spots, described it as a 'violent tropical storm … with bad thunder and lightning raps and flashes every five seconds.' Dogs cowered beneath furniture as frightened children cried. Out in Dún Laoghaire, where there were holiday crowds, the town 'reverberated to crashing peals of thunder, accompanied by vivid flashes of lightning.'

In the tenement districts of the city the quaking explosions were causing the 150-year-old buildings to tremble, further loosening bricks and mortar. Many were showing huge new crevices in walls and ceilings. Roof slates shook loose and slid off as the rain poured in and down through three and four storeys.

Many people were most fearful of the fierce lightning bolts. Along the east coast they had never seen anything like it. As the *Irish Press* described it, 'lightning forked over the city in menacing flashes', threatening to strike anyone, anywhere. In Rathmines a bolt struck the chimney stack of a house, 'sending bricks flying in all directions'.

In Collins Avenue a pub had lightning strike its aerial, destroying the television set in the lounge. Then the flash shot through the bar downstairs, along the stainless steel fittings on the shelves, where it hit a member of staff, Michael O'Dowd, giving him a severe shock.

At about that same time, in Cabinteely, sixty girls ran in panic from the Linen Replacement Services Company when 'a lightning bolt struck the premises'. Reports of similar lightning strikes were coming in from all over Dublin and environs.

Lightning would actually strike several people, fortunately not killing anyone. One of the luckiest was Kevin Baker, a young man from Fairview, who was rushing along Pearse Street in the storm when 'a flash of forked lightning struck him and hurled him several yards into the air'. He was treated for burns at Sir Patrick Dun's Hospital.

Those inside their homes felt safe – yet they were not. Gertrude Goodhue of Sandyford was talking to her husband, Derek, on the phone, seeking his comfort, when lightning hit the wires. Derek 'heard a loud bang, and a moan'. He immediately phoned a neighbour, who rushed over to check on Gertrude. She was found unconscious. It took two hours for her to recover, and she was treated for burns.

Another feature of the violent storm, wrote the *Irish Independent*, was the fall of hailstones around Mount Merrion and elsewhere. Umbrellas and awnings were torn to tatters and windows smashed. To those in vehicles it sounded as if they were being machine-gunned.

By 1:30 people were in disbelief that the storm was still raging, its ferocity undiminished.

All the while, the water rose biblically.

In Dublin and Kilkenny the rain was measured at a rate of at least one inch per hour, the equivalent of about 22,000 gallons of water per acre. The average rainfall for most of the country during the entire month of June was about three inches. In some of the worst-hit areas, including Goatstown, Dundrum, Sandyford, Ballsbridge and Merrion Road, it was falling at a considerably greater rate, in places pooling up to a depth of nearly five feet.

Near 2 p.m. the crisis stage was reached: a flash flood. Many streets had become streams and torrents, which were washing away much in their path. In some places there were cataracts of fast-falling water, even waves threatening houses.

Throughout the southern areas of the county, walls were being weakened, and many toppled. It was reported that smaller walls 'crumbled like matchwood', and higher stone walls became 'one of the big dangers, undercut by the flood … and suddenly falling'. At the same time, 'sewers burst as heavy drain coverings were thrown from their anchorage' by the force of the water. Trees, some huge, their roots saturated, were blown by the strong wind and loosened, and they tipped and fell onto roads, vehicles and houses.

By the early afternoon, the *Irish Times* confirmed, 'floodwaters rampaged through the city suburbs causing untold damage to property and threatening life.' Areas south of the city took the 'full brunt' of the water, which roared down the Dublin Mountains:

> At Blackrock rain poured down like a waterfall as frantic wives evacuated their kitchen and moved upstairs as the flood waters moved in. A thunderbolt shook every building in Drogheda and sent people running into churches and shops … in havoc and fright.[71]

Hundreds of businesses, shops and factories suffered flooding, loss of electricity and leaking roofs; frightened staff members didn't know how to get home.

RTÉ faced an emergency. During such a crisis its responsibility was to keep the public informed. But at about 2:30 in the afternoon water began seeping through the emergency overflow grid and into the ground floor of the studios; stage hands worked furiously to try and sweep it out. Then the power failed. The station began operating on emergency power. However, when some electric lighting failed it looked as if the news would have to be read by natural light.

Whatever the conditions, RTÉ had somehow to get the news out. This meant that Charles Mitchel – a reassuring figure to viewers throughout the country – needed to be in the presenter's chair for the evening news. But he was still at home.

By about 3 p.m. streets, roads and arteries were flooded. In Co. Dublin, especially, lakes had formed. Traffic extended for miles, as drivers sat with engines turned off, or flooded, water creeping well above their tyres, seeping into the car. A reporter from the *Irish Press* who had apparently been caught in the flood was able to provide a description:

> Stillorgan Road from Donnybrook outwards for several miles was like a lake ... Cars were abandoned by their drivers ... as motorists were seen wading in waist-deep water. Double-deck buses and heavy lorries were also abandoned.[72]

Dundrum was described by local residents as an 'Irish Venice', but without the charming, romantic aura. At first, many frustrated motorists thought they could unclog the traffic by incessant honking. Throughout the city, drivers lost their patience and tried to drive up onto the pavement and even across people's gardens. By midday, hotels and guesthouses in the city would be nearly filled. Some sympathetic people began taking in stranded motorists.

Buses had their own problems. Though they had larger tyres and better clearance, they still became stuck in traffic. Many people stayed on board in hopes that the storm would cease and the traffic begin moving again. The bus crews rose to the occasion by reassuring distressed passengers, especially the elderly.

On that fateful day the conductor Tony Doran was on duty. Although he had also been a bus-driver, he was most fond of his days as a conductor, because of the special relationship he enjoyed with regular passengers:

> It was a *friendship*. You knew everyone. Oh, the conductors were the witty ones; they had all the sayings, all the proverbs. And a conductor

could chat and listen ... all the little stories about their troubles and woes. We were like the psychiatrist!

Doran knew how to calm people's worries and fears. He was always calm and confident. But, in his long career, no day was so memorable as 11 June 1963. He had to keep his composure while contending with an unprecedented crisis, as he shared with this author some fifty years later:

I remember that we didn't really realise what we were witnessing. I was on duty that afternoon when it came down in buckets ... serious flooding around Ballsbridge and the RDS and the Coombe. And with the double-decker bus the driver had to drive the bus up onto the path – and opened the emergency door *upstairs* – a window – and people actually had to crawl out the window. And let people come out on the first floor windows and in ... then brought them down the stairs and into safety. And then people had to crawl *into* the bus.

Oh, it was a dangerous situation, really – if they fell! Oh, it was unbelievable. But they'd crawl in and out of the window of the bus!

He shakes his head when describing the experience.

In their desperation, frantic people phoned 999. But in a crisis of flooded streets their saviours could be helpless as well. The fire brigade reported having received more than a thousand calls, but they could deal with only the worst cases. A spokesperson reported that 'we would need nearly 500 pumps to take care of every area' calling for help. And that's if they had been able to reach them.

Then in his early twenties, Tom Geraghty had just joined the fire brigade. He had performed excellently in every aspect of his training, yet he recalls the frustrating feeling of inadequacy among his fellow-firefighters at not being able to handle all their calls:

There was no other emergency service in the city, so the fire brigade were called up for *everything*: drownings, collapsed buildings. Any emergency. But we hadn't got boats at the time!

On Kilmacud Road a terrifying drama was under way. Dr McNeany was at home with his wife, Vera. Like many others, they had watched the storm out their windows with fascination. Then a slight concern came over them as they saw the water rising so quickly. Fear gripped them when the swirling waters smashed down three walls and 'swept five feet deep, like a tidal wave, and crashed into his home.' As he would later tell a reporter, he immediately 'shepherded his family to safety upstairs':

> I have seen films of tidal waves and this is what it looked like. It was frightening, the sight of the walls crumbling … so incredible that I was mesmerized. I rushed to open all doors to give the waves a chance to sweep through the house. The lower rooms were strewn with furniture … a *fantastic* sight.[73]

He and his wife admitted that 'we were terror-stricken'. In fact, in the aftermath of the storm, Vera said her husband was 'so upset that he could not speak to me … he lost his voice from the shock'.

Parts of the city centre were largely spared serious flooding and damage. In the early afternoon those in the Dáil were having a mostly humdrum day. But at the height of the storm 'the lights flickered frequently and were extinguished' on several occasions. Then 'water cascaded down from the windows in the dome of the chamber and caused a hurried exit' from the Fine Gael front bench. Soon thereafter all phone communication at Leinster House was disrupted.

At Dublin Zoo there were unique problems to be dealt with. The incessant thunder and lightning terrified many animals, driving them to seek a hiding place or become frantic. Their handlers struggled to calm them. Meanwhile, parts of the grounds were flooding and electricity was threatening to go out. Gerry Creighton had worked at the zoo for only a few years, but he was among the strongest and most agile of the staff. One of his jobs was to find a missing lion cub:

> Suddenly all the electricity turned off. The lions had a litter of cubs who were about eight months old. I remember running over to the father and mother of the three cubs – and one was missing! The panes of glass in the lion house had been shattered and were falling down. The lions didn't seem as upset as the tigers were.
> I found the lion cub scared for his life on the top of the fence. I had to run and get a ladder and climb up it and tried to push him down, but

his claws were so hard to move from his grip he had on the wire. Then I tried pushing him off with a sweeping brush. Meanwhile, I was getting drenched to the skin and scared, because I was touching the fence and standing on a steel ladder! It took me nearly an hour to move him.

Next he had to check on the primates, which were terrified. They took refuge in the Guinness barrels and in the treetops. Everything at the zoo seemed out of whack and needed attending to. Even the polar bear pool was rising above the safety limit.

It would take some days, Creighton, now in his seventies, recalls, to get everything at the zoo back to a state of calm after the storm.

Shortly after three in the afternoon, as the storm raged on, people continued to be caught by surprise. Kathleen Kavanagh, of Irvine Cottages, East Wall, was cleaning up when she looked out to see if the rain had stopped, but instead she saw water lapping at her window. She grabbed her baby and escaped to higher ground in the nick of time.

In Donnybrook residents faced an unexpected crisis. Fourteen families living in a row of one-storey houses were suddenly confronted by a 'wall of water that bore down on them, bursting their doors open and destroying their houses.' Their low-lying terrace took the brunt of a huge wave that surged down the road from nearby Beech Hill. Within only minutes their houses were flooded to a depth of three feet – and rising. People screamed when their front doors were ripped off and an ocean of water invaded.

By luck, busmen from the nearby garage heard their cries and realised what was happening. They were able to drive a bus through and rescue the trapped people.

————

The storm seemed to be hanging *in situ* over the central east coast, neither moving away nor dissipating. This was unnatural – indeed phenomenal. Reporters needed on-the-scene coverage, interviews, photographs. But from their offices they could drive only so far into the heavily flooded areas before they were halted. Some decided to wade into the abyss as far as they could go in search of interviews.

In the afternoon the reporter Stanley Paisley left his *Evening Herald* desk with a different scheme in mind. He reasoned that in the worst-hit areas there would surely be some people paddling in small boats. Maybe this was his solution. He managed by wading to reach St Alban's Park in Sandymount, where the water deepened to five feet. Here he saw distressed residents 'marooned upstairs'. Then, as hoped, he spotted Good Samaritans in boats assisting them. Bread and milk were placed in baskets and pulled up to their bedroom windows. Before long, he sighted a boy alone in a canoe easily moving through the water. He called out and motioned for the boy to come over:

> I had to wade through the water before getting into the canoe which was paddled by a 14-year-old boy, to make a tour of the area.[74]

Paisley easily struck up a deal with the lad to take him wherever he wished. His mobility now allowed him to interview marooned residents from their windows, and motorists in their stranded cars. He gave real meaning to the term 'roving reporter'. From their windows the occupants told him of furniture floating around in the rooms below them. Personal belongings bobbed up and down in what was described as 'five feet of filthy, muddy water'. Many were pleading for some 'food to be brought to them by canoes and boats', especially for the children and elderly.

In the afternoon the RTÉ presenter Charles Mitchel set out in his car for the studio. With each street he passed, the water deepened. Eventually he was forced to abandon his car at Woodbine Avenue when the water was high enough to start flowing inside. Suddenly he was stuck, like thousands of other motorists. By that time, the *Irish Times* would write:

> traffic jams were more than five miles in length … Thousands of vehicles of every description, cars, lorries, buses – bumper to bumper. Passengers trapped.[75]

Vast areas of Co. Dublin had been transformed into sprawling lakes. Abandoned cars left looking like contented hippopotami in the muddy water.

Mitchel was not about to concede defeat: he was determined to reach his studio – and *on time*. After managing to force his door open against the force of the water, he began to wade waist deep through the floodwaters to the studios. His progress was slow but steady. Unfortunately for him, 'The storm was at its height shortly before 4 p.m.'

At 4:55 a crew of demolitionists continuing their work on a dilapidated tenement house in Buckingham Street had largely been ignoring the storm. Their foreman, Frank Carolan, never let even the worst weather interfere with their work. But they could hardly overlook the loud growl as a 'huge part of the gable wall, weakened by the soaking, came crashing down.' Thinking quickly, they smashed a window and jumped out before the entire structure collapsed upon them. But, suddenly, they saw that they were too high. 'So we rushed down and got out the front door, hardly able to see through the clouds of dust', barely escaping before the rotten dwelling crumbled further. Nature had done part of their work for them.

What had the forces of nature done to all the other decrepit tenement houses strewn across the city?

It is not recorded what the staff at RTÉ said when Charles Mitchel scrambled up to the studio doors. He rushed to the wardrobe department for a change of clothes before collecting himself and preparing to go on camera. With no time to spare he headed for his desk, arriving in time to announce the six o'clock news, having been part of the big story he was reporting.

All the while, newspapers were trying to piece together whatever information their reporters had managed to gather. There would be many stories of heroism and lucky escapes to hold their readers' interest for days to come.

Yet, as editors worked late into the evening, the storm was still not over. It was, however, mercifully weakening. In its latter stages it decided to take a swipe at north Co. Dublin, which had escaped the main force of the onslaught. There was violent thunder and lightning and torrential rain at about 10 p.m. Swords and Balbriggan were the worst affected. Throughout the evening and into the night, what the *Irish Press* called 'rogue late night occurrences' continued to roam menacingly and strike in 'sporadic outbursts'. These caused people to leap up in their beds.

Into the night, motorists continued to experience what the *Irish Times* reporter aptly termed a 'nightmare'. By 8 p.m. every hotel in Dublin had been booked out, leaving thousands stranded without shelter for the night. One reporter for the *Irish Independent* remained on duty through the night as the waters slowly began to recede. He wrote of seeing the streams of bedraggled, muddy motorists 'still walking with their trousers rolled up' well past midnight, some looking like dazed zombies.

By then, a blessed calm had settled on most of Dublin and the central east coast.

_____

Wednesday morning, 12 June

The next morning people rushed to look outside. In most places the water had receded significantly, leaving in its wake a muddy landscape littered with debris. Some areas had survived far better than others.

Everyone, of course, was mad to get their hands on a paper, perhaps forgetting that reporters had faced the same constraints as themselves. This was immediately apparent when *Irish Times* readers sought the weather chart. In its place they found an apology:

> We are unable to present our daily weather chart this morning. The artist who draws the map could not make the journey to the *Irish Times* office last night because of the floods.

Throughout the day, meteorologists analysed what had occurred and wondered how to explain it to the public. They faced a problem, however, for they too were largely perplexed by what exactly had happened and by the storm's astonishing duration. One newspaper simply wrote that 'Mother Nature played a mean trick' – hardly a satisfying explanation. A meteorologist for the *Evening Herald* termed it a 'freak storm' that had come 'out of nowhere'. The Meteorological Office resorted to stating that it was 'fantastically abnormal'.

On Wednesday morning a stunning fact about the storm was revealed:

> Many areas of the suburbs did not have *any rain* at all. Indeed, some were bathed in brilliant sunshine.

Dalkey had only a slight shower, and 'most of the day was sunny'. Freakish indeed.

Everyone clamoured for a forecast of the coming days. Had the storm been part of a larger weather system that might strike again? Wanting to play it safe, meteorologists were cautious. Newspaper forecasters did the same, one saying that 'the long-distance forecast remains cheerful, with no immediate break expected.'

Cheerful weather?

Storm-ravaged Dublin was a sight to behold: a doleful scene in places. Some newspapers wrote about the mopping-up effort that was necessary. The 'normally quiet little cul-de-sac' in Donnybrook that was so badly affected was described by one newspaper as a 'scene of desolation and havoc ... a pitiful scene.' Many residents could not even bear to look upon the devastation. Others went away weeping.

Reporters aptly christened it 'Heartbreak Terrace'. There were many other similarly pitiful scenes throughout the city.

————

Thursday 13 June

It was only to be expected that in the aftermath of the calamity journalists sought to place the sensational event in a larger context. There was a consensus that the flash flood was the worst in living memory.

Beyond all doubt, it was a unique storm. As the *Evening Herald* put it in its editorial, unsuspecting people were understandably shocked by its wrath:

> Who could have believed it? One minute Dubliners were basking in Heatwave sunshine – and only a few minutes later thousands of citizens were stranded by floods or trying to protect their homes from the rising waters.
>
> Seldom has the life of the capital been so badly disrupted.[76]

One newspaper verified that it was 'one of the most devastating electrical storms of the century'. The *Irish Times* stated that the 'traffic jams were the greatest ever experienced in Dublin'.

But people had precious little time to dwell upon the storm. They needed to focus on the future: the President of the United States would be stepping off his plane in two weeks. Dublin would be in the global spotlight for several days. The city would have to be more than 'mopped up'.

Chapter 9 ∾

'TWO ANGELS'

Two angels, God bless them ... *innocent*! Tons and tons of rubble ... the children buried there. And *I had* to lift up the bodies! I'll tell you, it's *heart-wrenching* ... men broke down and cried.'

ÉAMONN FITZPATRICK, firefighter

Wednesday morning, 12 June

The morning after the flash flood, Dublin was struggling to recover. Thousands of people were stripping away ruined linoleum and carpets, peeling off soaked wallpaper, examining damaged furniture. By dawn, phones were ringing at insurance companies as victims sought to file claims. Ultimately, claims from householders and car-owners would total £1 million or more (1963 figures). Meanwhile, firefighters and Corporation employees were pumping millions of gallons of flood water, still up to four feet deep, from thousands of houses.

Children who had been cooped up during the storm were itching to get outside. Parents told them to stay away from damaged stone walls and trees. Among the horde of children let loose were Linda Byrne and Marie Vardy, both eight. As toddlers they had become best friends and were now inseparable. Always happy, laughing and singing. Along Holles Street, no-one was more popular.

After school, whenever they had a few pence, they liked to trek around the corner to Fenian Street to visit Mr Maher's sweetshop. It was an area where people enjoyed a quiet life. However, some of its 150-year-old tenements were on the Corporation's list of dangerous dwellings. Many should have been demolished years before, but the Corporation hadn't got around to it yet.

Mr Maher's shop occupied the ground floor of number 3 Fenian Street. John Hanlon (54) and his wife lived on the top floor with their three children. He was well attuned to the sounds of the creaky tenement house.

At about eleven on Wednesday morning he heard some unfamiliar cracking noises, followed by rumbles. Alarmed, he got his family out immediately, then 'spread the word throughout the building'. Shortly after noon he rang the Corporation to tell them that his tenement was in *immediate* danger of falling. When no-one showed up he rang again. He felt absolutely certain that the building was about to collapse.

Another occupant, a docker, Paddy Richardson, and his wife, Irene, agreed:

> We sensed that it was about to happen … Since yesterday's storm we could see some fresh cracks; we could *feel* the old place going.

He too phoned the Corporation to warn them but was told their inspectors had been overworked since the storm the day before.

Next-door, in number 4, Andy Dent and his wife had noticed a large new slit in the building. He immediately pointed it out to the landlord, George Perry, who had a barber's on the ground floor, adjacent to Maher's sweetshop.

By early afternoon all the tenants in numbers 3 and 4 had been warned of the danger. Some remained inside gathering up possessions, while others stayed clear of the building. Both buildings were three-storey tenements fragilely bracing one another. Like two tipsy, tottering drunks might lean against one another, shoulder to shoulder, barely upright – till one gave away.

At 3:40 on Wednesday afternoon Linda Byrne and Marie Vardy began their familiar trek around the corner to the sweetshop, where they loved taking their time looking over Mr Maher's alluring display. Liking their company, he never rushed them. Both children were known to be very cautious about crossing streets, as their parents had warned them.

Meanwhile, the firefighter Éamonn Fitzpatrick was in Tara Street Fire Station. Having proudly been 'born and reared in a tenement … where people were the "salt of the earth"', he knew plenty about the dilapidation and dangers of buildings. His father had been a firefighter before him. Éamonn joined the force in 1955 and loved his job. Now in his eighties, he remembers 12 June 1963 above all other days:

> Funny thing about that day: I had just completed a heavy pump driving course, and that particular morning was my first time as a driver. And I

was anxious, waiting for the alarm to go off, wondering what was going to happen ... where I would be going. Probably some routine fire.

Suddenly, at 3:55, Paddy Richardson, inside the house in Fenian Street, felt the building crumbling apart. He 'found himself gazing out on to the roadway' as the 'front of the house gave way without warning'.[77] Acting instinctively, 'my wife grabbed one of the children and the other two under my arms', and they clambered down the shaking stairs.

In number 4 Andrew Dent and his wife 'heard a crack and a terrific crash and this house next-door fell asunder.' They too managed a close escape as he 'jumped for his life as the building toppled'.

Survivors of the two-building collapse would have slightly different accounts of the sequence of events. According to the most accepted account, 'one of the houses collapsed internally first, and then the front wall of the other collapsed on the top of two cars and a van.' Both buildings crumbled in unison, one largely upon itself, the other spilling outwards onto the street.

At that moment the landlord had been in his barber's chatting with a friend. To get out he had to crawl through a rear window. Others escaped by clinging on to drainpipes and descending slowly. James Murphy, a passing motorist, would be anxious to tell reporters his story:

I had to *accelerate* through flying bricks and clouds of dust ... I saw bricks come apart and a woman rushing into the street screaming ... I just barely made it!

Valerie Burke and her aunt Noreen Barrett were standing just across the street by a shop when they heard a 'tremendous noise' and thought 'lightning must have struck the petrol tank at the garage next-door.' A garage attendant, Tommy Murray, coughing and choking in a 'cloud of dust ... just stood stunned'. Another shaken observer said that 'it hit as if by a *bomb!*'

With the front wall stripped away the buildings looked like a doll's house, and 'a television set stood balanced 40 feet above'.

Immediately, alarms went out to gardaí and firefighters. At Tara Street Fire
Station, Éamonn Fitzpatrick was called to duty as pump-driver for the first
time. His anxious wait was over:

> The alarms went, we got our gear, we responded and got on board …
> and *I* was the driver. An officer, Mr O'Gorman, he came down and got
> into the cab – and he just said, 'Fenian Street!' He didn't give you any
> information – just gave me 'Fenian Street!'

As gardaí and firefighters from several stations were responding to the
calls, local people were rushing to the scene. Occupants trapped in the
rubble were struggling to free themselves, assisted by neighbours. One by
one they were found and extricated.

Meanwhile, fearful inhabitants of adjacent tenements were vacating
their buildings with great haste. A cloud of choking dust had settled over
the site as ominous cracking and falling bricks could be heard here and
there. It was obvious to all that the thunderous crash of numbers 3 and 4
had shaken surrounding buildings, further destabilising them and raising
fears that they too would now topple.

All the while, a large crowd continued to gather along Fenian Street,
straining to see what had happened.

When Éamonn Fitzpatrick swung his fire engine into Fenian Street and
raced to the scene, the crowd had been cleared back by a few gardaí who
had just arrived. Until this moment, Fitzpatrick and his crew had assumed
they were attending just another routine fire:

> When we turned into Fenian Street there were large crowds – and then
> suddenly it hit us! A building – *devastated*. Two buildings … like an
> earthquake! Tons and tons of rubble and clouds of dust. We pulled in
> not knowing what to expect … We didn't know or not if there were
> lives involved. To me, it was a new experience, because I hadn't seen the
> collapse of buildings.

All was chaos and confusion. At that point, the rescuers didn't know
how many lives might be at risk. Residents themselves began trying to make
a count of those who had survived. Since it was afternoon, all might not

have been in their homes at the time of the collapse. Occupants tried to recall who they had seen, and when.

Firefighters and gardaí were in consultation about their plan of action. They repeatedly asked survivors how many were still trapped inside. No-one knew. Firefighters needed to know whether they were on a rescue mission to save people buried beneath the rubble or on a recovery mission to remove the bodies. If all occupants were out and accounted for there was no need to send firefighters into the ruins and place them at risk. Demolitionists could do the job.

While listening intently for any cries for help or sounds of suffering, O'Gorman and his fire crew waited anxiously for another count of inhabitants. To everyone's great relief, within a few minutes a full count was reached, and no-one had been seriously injured. For the time being, firefighters could relax.

——

But, unknown to them, another local count was being made. In the surrounding streets, parents were rounding up their children to warn them to stay away from the zone of dangerous tenements. They first needed a count to make certain all were safe.

Meanwhile, at the collapse site, some uncertainty was arising about the possibility of victims who had not been tenants. Considering that the building had toppled outwards onto the pavement and part of the street, the question was raised of passers-by who might have been caught at the wrong moment and buried by the mountain of bricks, beams and slates. There was no way to know this, unless someone had witnessed it.

With this possibility now in mind, O'Gorman grew uneasy. His orders were for all the fire crew to remain on the site. Neighbours were asked if they had seen anyone walking near numbers 3 and 4. They weren't sure. Because a horde of children had roamed about in the area on that afternoon, the count of children went on with growing anxiety.

Fitzpatrick and the other firefighters, as well as other back-up fire crews, stood by awaiting orders to return to their stations. Then came the news, Fitzpatrick recalls.

> Then word started to percolate around that there were two or three children missing. That they had been seen playing outside the shop,

on the pavement. And *then* the realisation started in – that there are
children buried there

Women were crying … people very upset, because they didn't know
who the children were! There were neighbours, all running around
trying to locate their own children … and see where Johnny was and
where Mary was … We were absolutely *horrified*. We were so shocked
… We weren't sure who was in there.

The crowd, which had dwindled, began to grow again with the news of
missing children. Parents came to report that all their children had been
accounted for. But there was no way to keep a tally on all the children in
the area. Gardaí and firefighters only needed to know if any children were
definitely unaccounted for.

Word came soon. Two children from nearby Holles Street were missing.
Their parents and friends had searched everywhere for them. They never
roamed beyond the immediate area – except around the corner to Mr
Maher's sweetshop.

Linda's and Marie's parents notified gardaí of their missing children. Mr
Byrne confirmed that the children had been given a few coins to head over
to the shop – at about the time of the collapse. He told gardaí that 'they
would never leave the footpath … because they were very good children.'

There were now twenty firefighters and a dozen Corporation workers
ready to fly into action. However, O'Gorman and his fellow-officers decided
otherwise, as Fitzpatrick explains.

There was absolutely mountains of rubble. Tons and tons! So the
decision was made that it was too dangerous to move in machinery,
because of the unstable nature of the remaining buildings … There
were still vibrations that could bring it all down … remnants of bricks
and slates still falling down.

So all this was going to have to be removed by hand. And the terrible
fear was that, with every brick you moved, it was causing vibration …
pulling out window frames and floorboards, or moving beams. And
causing a lot of dust.

The parents of the missing children were now on the scene, speaking
quietly to gardaí and firefighters. Excavation was proceeding entirely by

hand, cautiously, as each fragment of brick and mortar was removed with the precision of a surgeon. They halted periodically to listen for sounds of life. An ambulance stood close by.

Onlookers watched silently, some praying or crying. And, as Fitzpatrick puts it, 'there were always the "ghouls"'. These were gawkers drawn by the horror. They were strongly resented by gardaí and firefighters, who learnt to spot them and push them back.

O'Gorman had ordered Fitzpatrick and his crew in first. Even though he had never seen a disaster of this kind, Fitzpatrick was suddenly in the front line searching for victims:

> Your adrenaline was very high. Talk was kept to a minimum amongst the crew: we'd all be focused on what you were doing, and looking out for each other. Oh, there was a lot of danger. Absolutely! And our helmets in those days were made out of cork. Everything was by hand – so confined. If you saw anything moving … an odd slate or bits of brick, you'd get into a crouch. And you'd wait … until an 'all clear'.

An hour went by. No sounds of life beneath the rubble. But the steady excavation did not slow down. By the end of the second hour, after considerable debris had been cleared, most firefighters had reached their own conclusion, without mentioning it to their colleagues. Most 'knew', as Fitzpatrick recalls:

> It was now a recovery effort, because anybody that was under there … particularly children … There wasn't much hope.

Their deliberate pace continued, into the third hour. Firefighters were now covered with filth, dust coating their clothing and faces, eyes stinging. Their hands were raw and bloody, because bare hands were required for much of the most delicate work. Then, at 6:50 p.m., Fitzpatrick and his colleagues froze for a second:

> Somebody said, 'Stop!' and a hand appeared in front of us. So, gingerly we started to move things, and we exposed limbs … exposed the bodies. There were two children, around nine years of age. Very close together … right beside one another.

Now in that instant we sat back ... and there was a silence with the crew. And, you know, a silent prayer was said, a Hail Mary or Our Father. And the enormity of the thing – to see two young children playing innocently, and all of the sudden there's a *crack* ... and they're gone.

He and his crew called for O'Gorman and the other fire officers to come over. Muttering rippled through the crowd. Fitzpatrick's most difficult duty commenced:

I *had* to lift up the bodies ... and that's not something you would ever wish on anybody ... because the bodies, God bless them, were badly crushed, as you can well imagine. Under tons of rubble ... badly crushed. Their life was gone, in a matter of seconds. And innocently playing!

It took some time to get the stretcher-bearers in, because we had to clear it for them to have a reasonable passage in. Carrying out the children ... People were very upset and everything had gone quiet, and women were saying prayers. I'll tell you, it's heart-wrenching! It really is. Men broke down and cried ...

Nothing was hurried. Stretcher-bearers entered the ruins and slowly removed the bodies. Gardaí kept newspaper photographers pushed back, though the indiscreet ones snapped away anyway. One aggressive photographer managed to jockey himself into a position for a close shot of the bodies before they had been properly covered – much to the disapproval of Fitzpatrick and the other firefighters:

Everybody was kind of staring in, and there was this photographer who wanted to take a photograph – and I resented this. You know, intruding on the privacy of these children. So we used to wear heavy old black slickers, as they called them, and I took off my slicker and covered these children – to give them some dignity. And then another fireman took off his and we covered them up, waiting for the stretcher-bearers to come in.

A reporter for the *Irish Press* had been jotting down notes since his arrival, shortly after four o'clock. In his article he would depict the scene:

Old ladies and little girls recited the rosary, amid their cries, as mud-splattered firemen removed the body of Linda Byrne, and then minutes later that of her friend Marie Vardy. Two priests, Fr Sean Byrne and Fr John McCarthy, knelt amid the shattered beams and clouds of dust to administer the Last Rites ... as Gardaí and firemen stood hatless with sweat and dirt flowing from their brow.

A great quiet fell over the jostling crowd as the little bodies were taken away in ambulance to Sir Patrick Dun's Hospital for identification.[78]

Another reporter from the *Irish Independent* sought a few words from the distraught parents. He was sensitive in approaching them, asking only if they cared to share a few words. Mr Vardy replied, 'The two girls loved one another ... They have been together since they were old enough to walk.' Linda's father, Matthew, was composed enough to add that it was:

three hours of torment ... We hoped against hope. When we saw that one of the girls had been found, my wife and I turned away ... We knew the other would be right beside her ... they were so inseparable.[79]

As people drifted away from the scene, Éamonn Fitzpatrick and the crew remained. 'We *still* searched among the rubble ... We didn't stop.' Just to make certain.

———

In the aftermath of the tragedy, the Dublin Corporation and housing authorities were in crisis mode, under a barrage of criticism from the public and press. With more evacuations mounting by the day, charges were flying in the Dáil. Declan Costello stated angrily that the crisis has existed for years past, but it:

has taken four deaths to bring it to the notice of the proper authorities, and it is most tragic that it required such extreme results to bring about ... a public interest in a situation ... which I believe to be a scandal and a shame in a community that calls itself Christian.

Every newspaper was condemning the situation, publishing editorials that hit hard. The *Irish Times* wrote that, once again:

the public conscience has been shocked by the loss of life caused by the collapse of two more worn-out tenements. When a child or adult can walk to his doom unwarranted, no one is safe.[80]

The *Evening Herald* emphasised the terrible fright now felt by thousands of tenement-dwellers. It was depriving them of sleep at night and causing anxiety during the day:

> Fear, which could amount to terror, is spreading among tenants of the old houses. Something must be done to allay these fears – and it must be done quickly.[81]

In response, the Corporation despatched another flock of housing inspectors, many ill-trained. They slapped more *Condemned* notices on tenements and ordered tenants to evacuate, then marched off to the next building. Some especially dangerous streets were Coleraine Street, North Great George's Street, Aungier Street, Wolfe Tone Street, Gardiner Street and Dominick Street. As one person evacuated from Coleraine Street put it, 'how could we go to sleep, not knowing what might happen!'

One man wrote to the *Evening Herald* noting that:

> an English visitor said to me some years ago, 'Central Dublin is a heap of junk!' He was not far off the mark. Drastic action must be taken.[82]

In the absence of real action by the Government, people took to the streets with their own form of action. On Thursday morning, as rubble was being cleared in Fenian Street, more than fifty women and three hundred children marched through the streets of Dublin. The *Irish Independent* called it a 'slum peril protest walk' – the first of many.

Banners read *Clear the slums!* and *Don't wait for the houses to fall!* They marched through the fashionable streets, contrasting their impoverished world of fright. They congregated at City Hall to carry their protest directly to the city manager's office.

He didn't bother to see them.

Refused admission, they marched off through George's Street, College Green, Nassau Street and Dawson Street. At the Mansion House they were sympathetically welcomed by the Lord Mayor. He spent half an hour with them discussing their grievances. He promised them that those who had been evacuated would be rehoused as safely and quickly as possible.

On Friday morning, 14 June, the *Irish Press* headline was 'Fifty houses in danger'. So many condemnation notices had been plastered around the city that it looked as if it were pockmarked by a plague. As demolition gangs were working from dawn till dark, new panic swept through families in Summerhill and North Great Charles Street after huge cracks were detected.

A Corporation spokesperson stated that there were now more than 590 families on their waiting lists for safe housing, the number increasing each day.

Raymond Smith, a resourceful reporter for the *Evening Herald*, decided to do an inside story on the tenement crisis. He trekked through the most dangerous, dilapidated streets in order to interview the occupants. He was invited in for some blunt talk. He would title his article 'I walk through streets of fear':

The two house collapses have cast a shadow of fear over Dublin's slumland. I have been down among the decaying houses and I have seen the fear across the threshold … in tenements where there may be 16 families in 10 rooms, with fissures and cracks, openings in walls and ceilings.

I saw terror in the eyes of a woman who is expecting a baby this month, fear that the ceiling would cave in on her.[83]

The term 'slumland' would catch on.

On Saturday, Marie Vardy and Linda Byrne were buried. Owing to the newspaper coverage, people felt they almost knew the children. Nothing so wrenched their emotions as the photos of the two girls in their First Communion dresses.

The funerals took place following a Requiem Mass at St Andrew's Church in Westland Row, celebrated by the Rev. C. F. Lee. Children from the girls' school formed a guard of honour outside the church. The coffins were borne from the crowded church by the men of the confraternity, and children carrying wreaths and floral tributes walked behind. 'Women and companions of the dead girls wept and prayed' as the cortege passed by.

At Deansgrange Cemetery, the Taoiseach was represented by Commandant J. O'Brien. Before family and friends, the 'two little friends were laid side by side in their graves'.

Inseparable in death as in life.

In 2014 the firefighter Éamonn Fitzpatrick, at eighty-one years of age, reflected on the tragedy:

> I was thirty-seven years in service … but Fenian Street is *always* there … Oh, that's one thing that sits in my mind. It was so tragic, the death of those two children … And the tenement people back then were 'family', and they were there in the hundreds for the funeral, to see those children buried.
>
> Two angels, God bless them … What else can you say about them … *Innocent!* And I had to lift up the bodies … Oh, it pulls at your heartstrings.

Despite the tragedies of the first two weeks of June, life had to go on. In Dublin, cinemas and theatres were filled with crowds drawn by special attractions. At the Olympia Theatre the *Champagne Follies on Ice* delighted audiences, as did the festival of Italian opera at the Gaiety. The lively, colourful film *Can-Can* was showing at the Capitol Cinema.

Dublin's pop music scene was really swinging, and there was a new feeling of teenage rebellion. Young people were now out till all hours singing and dancing to their favourite tunes. That month the big hits were by Buddy Holly, Gerry and the Pacemakers, Elvis, Bobby Rydell and Roy Orbison. Jim Reeves was on tour, drawing large crowds wherever he appeared. And there was talk of the Fab Four appearing on a Dublin stage later in the year. The hopes of Beatlemaniacs were never higher.

More certain was an appearance on the Adelphi's stage on 16 June. It was not a pop star but a musician who thrilled classical music aficionados. Months earlier it had been announced that the celebrated American pianist Van Cliburn was scheduled for a Dublin concert. Tickets vanished almost immediately. Music critics and reviewers were no less ecstatic. One enthused that:

for some time we have heard of Van Cliburn ... His triumph in Moscow is a modern legend, and his regal progress through the nations has made his name a household word.[84]

Now he would be appearing before the Irish nation with the Radio Éireann Symphony Orchestra.

Journalists would not be able to contain their praise for his performance. As one would write, 'we are all aware of what a remarkable musical genius he is – but what we *did not* know was the tremendous impact he makes in a personal appearance.' He electrified the audience. From the moment he set foot on stage he enthralled everyone in the house.

One critic deemed it one of those rare 'performances for the ages'. Another critic had more flare for description:

He cast a mighty spell and his playing was followed with breathless admiration – no wonder he conquered Moscow. His mastery of colour and tone ... Who could resist such dynamic playing.

One can only talk in superlatives. The passion, fire and beauty of his playing transported us all to Elysium.[85]

Another reviewer said that 'the pity is that we may have to wait many a day before hearing him again.'

———

Sports enthusiasts were not to be denied their own rapture in the summer of 1963. There were major contests in horse-racing, showjumping, football, boxing, rugby, cycling, sailing and golf. Some events featured international as well as national competitors.

One event in particular engaged the imaginations of sports fans. It was to be one of the greatest horse races ever seen on an Irish racecourse. For weeks, sports writers had been stirring the pot of high excitement with their articles about the spectacular race it was sure to be. One prominent writer declared that the Irish Sweeps Derby was 'attracting world-wide interest'.

There was great interest in the race throughout Europe and North America, thanks to Ireland's entry into the television age. Viewers in France, Britain and other countries could watch the race live.

And what magnificent horse was to make the Irish Derby so special? It was the French sensation Relko, the talk of the European horse-racing world. Even people who normally had little or no interest in horse-racing were being caught up in 'Relko fever' in June. Followers were counting the days till the Irish Derby was run, on the 29th.

On 14 June, John F. Kennedy's press secretary, Pierre Salinger, arrived in Dublin to check every detail of the coming visit. Reporters showed up to cover the rehearsal. The Americans could not have missed the stories of collapsing tenements still on the front pages of newspapers. But the presidential motorcade would be directed well away from Dublin's 'slumlands'. These were at odds with the idealised American vision of Ireland. It was hoped that no curious visiting reporters would poke around in the tenement streets, tempted to do a side story on the city.

Salinger and his staff set about the task of establishing the Gresham Hotel as their 'command post', in their lingo. The Americans were polite but demanding. As one Irish journalist put it, 'the intense activity at the Gresham Hotel is reaching its climax.' Great attention was on Ireland's dysfunctional telephone system, only recently described by a member of the Dáil as 'utter chaos'. Communication experts had worked around the clock to fix and modernise the system. Reliable telephone lines were absolutely critical. Open lines were necessary to Washington, day and night, as well as to London, Paris, Bonn and Milan. There would be no room for failures, even snags.

There was great excitement around the Gresham Hotel as people gathered outside and tried to peek in. Presidential advance staff hurried in and out. The ballroom was being converted into a press centre: there were thirty telephone kiosks on one balcony, with typewriters and teleprompters. Journalists would have their own telephone exchange and 125 tables on the ballroom floor at their disposal. Meanwhile, American Secret Service agents were swarming around poking here and there, asking endless questions.

Before everyone's eyes, Dublin was being transformed into the news centre of the world. Salinger and his senior staff had one concern above all others: the route President Kennedy would be taking. Every yard would need to be secured. On paper, it seemed simple enough: from Dublin Airport into the city, down O'Connell Street, along the quays, to the

American ambassador's residence in the Phoenix Park. But it would travel past innumerable windows, rooftops, side-streets and alleys. Everything had to go perfectly according to script.

But in the United States there was suddenly an unexpected problem – one that could threaten the visit to Ireland.

There was a serious racial incident in the South, at the University of Alabama, where the first efforts were being made to enrol black students. The state's governor and senior officials defiantly resisted integration, fuelling the racism of segregationists. On 12 June, Medgar Evers, a black civil rights leader who had been trying to facilitate integration, was shot dead by a white supremacist. It was now turning into a national crisis, and Kennedy said he was 'appalled by the barbarity' of the act. Some of his closest aides were encouraging him to cancel his trip in order to deal with the emergency.

The visit was suddenly placed on hold. Yet organisers could hardly halt their preparations. They would forge on and hope things cooled down.

By 19 June things took a positive turn. An American plane touched down at Dublin Airport. Eighteen communications experts were on board, under the command of Lieutenant-Colonel Doyle Hastie, whose job it was to maintain radio contact with Kennedy with an emergency set built into the plane.

———

For the next few days the President of the United States would have to share coverage in Irish newspapers with another man: the new Pope.

On 19 June the election was now under way at the Vatican, and the Irish people were following the drama. It was narrowed down to six cardinals, and there was great speculation throughout the Catholic world about which one had the best chance of being made the Pontiff.

More than 100,000 people crowded St Peter's Square. Heads were cocked upwards in expectation, awaiting the sign. Among the faithful were hundreds of Irish priests, nuns, brothers and laypeople. Irish newspapers had their Vatican reporters on the scene.

By 20 June no smoke had yet arisen. The suspense grew.

———

At Rathfarnham Courthouse in Co. Dublin there was suspense of a rather different sort. Two men, sitting in silence, were the centre of attention. Both were refusing to talk, much to the displeasure of Detective-Inspector John P. McMahon, who was growing increasingly impatient with their act. Before him sat David Richard Smith of London and Denis Bond of no fixed address. They were charged with 'stopping the Collinstown mail van with the intent to rob, and with conspiracy and the larceny of a car.' Upon his arrest, Bond had given the false name of 'Sissons'. And he hadn't been truthful about much else either, giving nonsensical answers or saying that he didn't remember. Sometimes he replied, 'I won't say.' His companion was not much better.

Looking at the two men straight on, McMahon advised them that they should tell the truth. Sensing an opportunity, he focused his attention on Smith, eye to eye. He told the defendant he should 'consider his own family, particularly his mother and father.' McMahon must have touched a point of vulnerability, because Smith became distressed and cried.

Yet he still refused to co-operate.

––––––

Meanwhile, newspapers devoted their sports pages to the Irish Derby, featuring the French horse now being referred to as the 'amazing Relko'. This sounded rather like a magician, which is how many of the horse's admirers viewed him: he had the ability to suddenly spring from the pack and break into the lead. Bred by his renowned owner, François Dupré, he was described as a 'strong, compact, perfectly balanced' bay horse. His superb reputation was well earned. Already in 1963 he was off to a spectacular start in the spring months, winning the Poule d'Essai Poulains at Longchamp and the Prix de Guiche at Chantilly. His most impressive victory was in the Epsom Derby, where 'three furlongs from the finish he pulled away from the rest of the field to easily win by six lengths.'[86]

Spectators were thrilled to see the mighty Relko turn on his bewildering speed. Now Irish race-goers would have their chance to witness his greatness at the Irish Derby. In pubs, talk of the race was lively. The *Irish Independent* was hyping it as the 'million-pound race'. M. V. Cogley wrote of it as a world sporting event on Irish turf:

The eyes and ears of the racing world will be focused on the Curragh, where the second running of the Irish Derby will be staged. Apart from its being one of the richest races in the world – a million pounds and more hangs on it – the result of the great race will be the news of the day.[87]

So impressive had Relko been in his recent races that some sports writers had anointed him the winner before he even bolted from the gate. Cogley wrote that:

all indications, of course, point to another victory … Relko's runaway in the Epsom Derby makes him an automatic favourite.

Sometimes, however, unexpected things were known to happen at a racecourse.

––––

At 11:20 a.m., Irish time, the massive crowd cheered in jubilation, 'standing tip-toed, shouting, "Bianco! Bianco!"' as the chimney of the Sistine Chapel began giving off smoke. Then the newly elected Pontiff, Cardinal Giovanni Battista Montini, appeared on the balcony of the Vatican Palace. Bells throughout Rome rang out. In Ireland people were elated. Described as a 'dynamic progressive', Montini took the name Paul VI.

Irish people were delighted to learn of the new Pope's ties to Ireland. The *Irish Independent* wasted no time in revealing that the Pope 'was twice in Ireland'. A humble humanitarian who had great affinity for the poor and the working class, the new Pope possessed traits that endeared him to the Irish people.

––––

With President Kennedy's visit now only five days away, Dublin's housing authorities, as well as its people, were growing nervous about the possibility of another tenement collapse, especially one with a loss of life. The Corporation announced that it had now evacuated a remarkable 485 families from 147 dangerous tenements in order to reduce the chances of another tragedy. Some of the ejected families were setting up primitive tents or camps from canvas, cardboard and plywood on the footpahts. By any measure, it was a shocking sight.

Nonetheless, most of Dublin was suffused with great gaiety and excitement about President Kennedy's visit. It was an infectious spirit shared by people of all social classes. The Olympia Theatre sought to do its part in the festivity by presenting *Stars and Stripes*, billed as an all-star American extravaganza. The countdown had begun: only seventy-two hours.

Chapter 10 ✑

HOMECOMING: JITTERS AND JUBILATION

From the day President Kennedy's four-day visit to Ireland was confirmed, plans began to be made at every level. While formal ceremonies were being organised, CIE, RTÉ, the Gardaí, newspaper editors and other organisations had to prepare their own strategies. Everyone could share in the mounting excitement. Una Shaw, who still lives in Rutland Street in Dublin, only a few streets from where she saw the presidential motorcade, recalls the joy of it all, beginning well before June 1963:

> When he ran for President we prayed and prayed with all our might that he'd get in – and then, sure, it was prayers that *did* get him in! That the President of the United States was an Irishman – an Irish *Catholic* president. We were thrilled! Oh, it was like he was ours – he was our *own*!
>
> And now he was coming back home.

Garda Séamus McPhillips was on duty that historic day, as he vividly recollects:

> My attitude, and the attitude of a lot of my countrymen, was 'That guy is "*us*" … *from* us, we are *of him*! There's the success!' You could feel it. Everyone had a sense of achievement and unity … nationhood. Just magic!

With all the jubilation came plenty of jitters. For those in charge of planning the event it was like a small military operation. Gardaí were required from throughout the country 'in accordance with strict security precautions'. This meant that many hundreds of gardaí would have to be transported from stations outside Dublin to line the long presidential route. It was announced that special buses would collect gardaí from as far away as Clifden. In Dublin alone more than three thousand gardaí would be needed.

CIE would have to rush into service entire fleets of buses for transporting gardaí to and from Dublin, Wexford, Cork, Limerick, Galway and Shannon Airport.

Weeks before Kennedy's arrival, American Secret Service agents had been despatched to Dublin to co-ordinate their security plans with the Gardaí. Meetings stretched over hours and days. The American agents bombarded the Gardaí with seemingly endless questions about features of the route. Garda brass were not accustomed to feeling interrogated themselves, and their patience would wear thin. But to the American agents they were anything but inconsequential questions. Garda Ray Campion, who would be part of the Irish security detail, recalls it today with some amusement:

It was a *huge* security problem for the Garda Síochána, so these meetings were held with the Secret Service. But the Garda side were getting annoyed at the silly details the Secret Service were putting forward – asking about the number of manhole covers along the route!

For their part, the American agents were not entirely happy either. Some answers were too brief, or too vague. Some were outright worrying, as when the Gardaí 'could not guarantee that a break-through from the crowd would not occur at some point.' The Irish people, it was explained, were sometimes so exuberant that their excitement was difficult to contain. But the Gardaí assured the agents that the street would be lined with guards holding the crowds back – as well as possible. And how would this be accomplished? By cordons – and gardaí linking their arms.

The spectre of a massive crowd suddenly breaking through, swarming freely into the street and enveloping the presidential limousine was a nightmare for those agents responsible for protecting Kennedy's life, at any cost.

At RTÉ, Burt Budin, a producer for Teilifís Éireann, faced his own challenges. It would be, he told his staff and the press, the most ambitious project ever undertaken by RTÉ. It was made all the more daunting by limitations of time, equipment and technical personnel. Yet everyone at the station was eager to take it on. It demanded an army of technicians, camera operators and commentators, all of whom had to be set up at strategic sites and tapping into power stations. Their sprawling network of cables would be an ever-present danger to stumblers. And they would be competing for space and vantage points with America's huge news networks NBC, CBS and ABC – not to mention the BBC and other foreign broadcasters. Ulster TV was also planning on documenting Kennedy's visit, devoting much coverage to his trips to Wexford and New Ross.

This brought the realisation that Teilifís Éireann would need help from outside television companies. It would mean arranging for some twenty-five vehicles to cross the border carrying equipment from the BBC, UTV and Welsh stations. Budin was immensely grateful for the help.

On 21 June a plane arrived in Dublin with a party of 125 American journalists. They called it a 'proving flight', to make certain all was satisfactory to them. It was at about this time that the American Secret Service commanders presented to Budin and newspaper editors some rules and regulations regarding the coverage of Kennedy's visit. The most simple, rigidly enforced one was to keep a respectable distance from Kennedy at all times. It was important to stress this, because some Irish journalists were accustomed to wriggling their way forward to stick a microphone or camera lens in a subject's face. The American agents could not allow this to happen. Any person, regardless of rank, who failed to keep a respectful distance would be sharply reminded – at once.

––––

Unknown to Gardaí, on the night of 19 June a small but dedicated group of men met at Moran's Hotel in Dublin to go over some final plans. They were a protest group against the partition of Ireland, under the leadership of Liam Ferguson. Their plan was to carry out a 'unity march' in O'Connell Street. They welcomed Kennedy's visit and saw it as an opportunity to grab the attention of hundreds of journalists from all over the world.

They informed officials of their intentions, telling them they expected a large number of supporters from the North to join them. They would carry banners and be headed by several small bands. The Gardaí expected no problems but would keep its eye on the march well after Kennedy had passed by.

Irish politicians wanted everything to go smoothly when they greeted Kennedy. They expected a flurry of handshaking, smiles and welcoming words, along with a few quips.

In May the Lord Mayor of Dublin, J. J. O'Keeffe, had met Kennedy in the White House. They got on famously, immensely enjoying each other's company. But before they could shake hands again in Dublin, a hitch arose. On 26 June, when Kennedy stepped off his plane, he would be facing a new Lord Mayor. Newspapers called it 'an unfortunate coincidence' of dates. The mayoral successor did not have to assume office until 1 July. A postponement could easily allow O'Keeffe to remain in office for a few days in order to greet his 'old friend' President Kennedy. In an editorial entitled 'A courtly gesture', the *Irish Independent* explained that a simple act of generosity on the part of the new Lord Mayor, Seán Moore, could easily resolve the sticky problem.

If, that is, Moore agreed to it.

————

Nowhere was there more commotion than in Ireland's newspaper offices, where editors and reporters were energised by the challenges they were facing. The big newspapers knew they would be in competition to cover the story in its entirety. There would be at least three hundred Irish and visiting newspaper reporters covering the event.

Never had Irish newspaper editors required such elaborate arrangements. All staff members would be working extra hours, some nearly around the clock, for four days, and without complaint. A few days before Kennedy's arrival, the *Irish Independent* made a pledge to its readers that its coverage would be of the highest standard:

> Ireland will be the centre of world news interest during the four days of President Kennedy's visit. Our coverage of the event will be worthy of this great occasion … every aspect of the historic event.[88]

Thick in sentiment and nostalgia, Kennedy's visit would be treated in the Irish press as his 'homecoming'.

Burt Budin might well have been speaking for everyone involved in the event when he said:

The Irish Press

That Wonderful Whiskey!
'GREEN SPOT'
J. J. 10 YEARS OLD
Mitchell & Son
21 KILDARE STREET, DUBLIN.

SPECTACLE FRAMES
17'6
repaired while you wait
DUBLIN PHARMACY
POWNES ST. (off Dame St.)

DO CUM SLOIRE DE AGUS ONORA NA h-EIREANN   The Truth in the News

Vol. XXXII. No. 310   MONDAY, DECEMBER 31, 1962   PRICE 3d.

CITY⁴

PLEASANT RELIEF FROM COLDS WITH
WINTER EASERS
THE FAMOUS THROAT SWEET BY Oatfield

Main roads blocked, power fails, air services disrupted

BLIZZARD LASHES COUNTRY

Huge wave sweeps girl to her death

THE raging blizzard which swept the whole country yesterday cut off the Co. Dublin villages of Glencullen and Bohernabreena. Huge drifts blocked the main roads out of the city and all flights from Dublin Airport were cancelled. Power failures occurred in many areas and E.S.B. repair gangs were standing by all night to answer calls.

Storm claims five lives in England

The South County was severely hit and glassy mountain roads made farmers unable to reach their sheep. In the city a freeze-up was expected after a day of binding snow and Corporation workers toiled all night putting sand on dangerous roads.

At Dalkey, Co. Dublin, a 31-year-old shorthand typist was swept to her death by a huge wave which crashed over the sea wall as she stood watching the heavy seas.

A PRESTON schoolteacher poking through a 12-foot snow...

The first days of 1963 were met with ferocious blizzards, snowdrifts and arctic cold. (*Courtesy of the National Library of Ireland*)

SUNDAY INDEPENDENT
Incorporating the "Irish Weekly Independent"

VOL. 58. No. 2.   D   DUBLIN, SUNDAY, JANUARY 13, 1963.   PRICE FIVEPENCE

Everyone's eating TAYTO crisps

B-R-R! THE DAY THE LIFFEY FROZE

Buses, cars skid on ice

DUBLINERS will remember it as Skid Saturday. Fire Brigade ambulances, supplemented by private cars, operated a shuttle casualty service to Dublin hospitals yesterday when over 100 people were treated for head injuries, sprains, broken arms, legs and wrists following falls on the icy roads and pavements.

Cardinal Spellman and the forgotten bishop

The 'Day the Liffey Froze': Dublin's streets were coated with layers of ice which caused accidents across the city. (*Courtesy of the National Library of Ireland*)

Villages were cut off and isolated, and road passengers marooned, facing cold and hunger – a Siberian world. (*Courtesy of the National Library of Ireland*)

Airlifts parachuted much-needed parcels of food to those stranded in rural areas. (*Courtesy of the National Library of Ireland*)

Situation 'desperate' in Wicklow: emergency in Tipperary

BLIZZARD BATTLE GOES ON

Doctors fear for patients in mountains

HUNDREDS of families are still isolated, desperately short of food, and rescue teams are fighting tirelessly to relieve villages and lonely mountain farmhouses banked-in by snowdrifts as the worst blizzard since 1947 tightens its

He fought through drifts to bring food to 35 families

IRISH PRESS REPORTER

I JOINED yesterday a party of men and women in the Wicklow Mountains who are fighting to bring much-needed food and fuel supplies to families cut off from the outside world by Sunday's snow, described locally as worse than the 1947 blizzard.

Isolated amid the snow-carpeted mountains, many of the families had not received any food nor had they any contact with the outside world until volunteer food-carriers, from the newly-set-up supply line,

When we joined him yesterday, on the last desperate stage over five miles of treacherous icy mountain, he was leg-weary, bearded and frost-bitten, but still fighting on.

"I walked from my home in Oldcourt, where I ran out of food for 35 families who are my customers. I got my supplies in Dublin, and took them by bus to Crookstown. Then, when the bus could go no farther, I had to get a lift in a lorry. Eventually that had to stop and I travelled by tractor for a few miles."

Must reach baby

A second do-or-die effort was that made by Seamus Boylan and Maureen Fitzpatrick, of Valleymount, who passed through Blessington yesterday in an effort to reach their home from which they have been cut off since late last week.

Against warnings from gardaí

of foxes playing havoc in the district. They just attack and kill the sheep which are half covered with the snow. There must be hundreds of sheep drowned and smothered as well."

And for Mrs. Louis Byrne, proprietress of the Devonshire Arms Hotel, in Blessington, the snow has a special meaning; her husband and her mother-in-law, Mrs. Elizabeth Hand, are isolated in a mountain cottage about five miles from the town. "I have been talking to them by phone and their greatest worry

Too late now for talk, UN tells Tshombe

AS a strong Irish and Indian United Nations force reached the outskirts of Jadotville yesterday, U.N. Secretary-General, U Thant repulsed a cease-fire proposal by Mr. Moise Tshombe and reinforced his ultimatum to the Katangan leader. The time for negotiation is over, he said. It is too late for talk. It is time for action in the reconciliation of the Congo.

'Land armies' of rescuers fought against 15 to 20-foot snowdrifts blocking roads. (*Courtesy of the National Library of Ireland*)

CARDINAL IS MOURNED

Death of the beloved Primate shocks nation

THE nation is in mourning at the passing of its great and beloved spiritual leader, John Cardinal D'Alton, D.D., Archbishop of Armagh and Primate of All Ireland, who died peacefully in his sleep in St. Vincent's Nursing Home, Dublin, early yesterday morning. He was aged 80.

THE Cardinal's body lay on a simple wooden bed in a ground floor room of St. Vincent's Private Nursing Home last night as people filed slowly in and out to pray at the bedside.

He was laid out in ceremonial violet Mass vestments in Gothic design, surmounted by a white mitre. On a table at the bedside was the Red Biretta of his exalted office. Below his pectoral cross his violet-gloved hands were joined. On another table stood a crucifix between two lighted candles.

The distinguished callers at the Nursing Home during the day included President de Valera and members of the Diplomatic Corps.

A native of Claremorris, Co. Mayo, Cardinal D'Alton succeeded to the Primatial See in 1946. He was elevated to the Sacred College on January 12, 1953.

At noon today Church and State will unite in paying tribute to His Eminence when the remains will leave the hospital for St. Patrick's Cathedral, Armagh, where they will lie in state until Wednesday. The funeral will take place on Wednesday, after Solemn Pontifical Mass to the Cathedral grounds where a special grave is being prepared.

At 11.45 a.m., before the removal of the remains from the hospital, the last prayers will be recited by the Archbishop of Dublin, Most Rev. Dr. McQuaid.

ACTIVE TO THE END

Although he had been in failing health for the past year, Cardinal D'Alton continued to lead an active life to the end. Despite his infirmity and the bitter weather he insisted on making the long journey to London to attend the funeral of Cardinal Godfrey, Archbishop of Westminster, last Tuesday. It was to be his last public duty.

He returned to Dublin by plane on Tuesday evening, accompanied by his secretary, Rev. F. Lenny, and stayed with his niece, Miss Maura Ryan, at Sutton, Co.

TWO DUBLIN BOYS DROWN IN CANAL AS ICE BREAKS

The sudden, unexpected death of Cardinal D'Alton shocked many people around the country. (*Courtesy of the National Library of Ireland*)

It was a shock when the beloved, historic Olympia Theatre was put up for sale – possibly for conversion to a gaudy dance hall or office complex. (*Courtesy of the Olympia Theatre*)

The dramatic news of UCD students missing on the snow-packed Wicklow Mountains gripped the nation. (*Courtesy of the National Library of Ireland*)

The discovery of students' bodies on the Wicklow Mountains confirmed the tragic news and left the country in mourning. (*Courtesy of the National Library of Ireland*)

CITY SPECIAL

Irish Independent

VOL. 72. No. 56. (INCORPORATING THE 'FREEMAN'S JOURNAL')   WEDNESDAY, MARCH 6, 1963   PRICE 3d.

International combine to set up in Ireland soon, N.F.A. president reveals

BIG SUPERMARKET PLAN

Mr. R. Deasy, N.F.A. president

24 branches will cost £2,000,000

"Irish Independent" Reporter

A CHAIN of 24 supermarkets is to be built in Ireland at a cost of £2,000,000, the N.F.A. president, Mr. R. Deasy, told the association's Dublin county executive in Malahide yesterday.

Questioned last night, he said the group to which he had referred was an international concern. He understood it was connected with groups already operating in Ireland.

He declined to name it.

He added: "It is our intention to have a full discussion with the people concerned, to see that their development is beneficial to the Irish farmers as far as possible.

"We hope that, in this way, Irish farmers will be assured of an outlet for their produce through the group's chain in Britain and elsewhere."

At the Malahide meeting, Mr. Deasy urged farmers to prepare now for the supermarket era. The time to plan was before they were built, he said.

The N.F.A. was aware of many proposals by outside interests to develop this form of merchandising in Ireland and the £2,000,000 plan was only one of several.

Pre-packaging and self-service could give farmers outlets for their produce. Packaging and distribution costs accounted for 40 to 55 per cent. of the retail price of many commodities. If farmers failed to organise themselves to supply these new types of market it would be their own loss, he continued.

FARMER CO-OPS.

"We have all watched with interest and hope your efforts to get a big co-operative vegetable packing and grading station going in this area," said Mr. Deasy. "Your local organising committee deserves the greatest credit and support for its efforts.

"I am convinced that the advantages to you of such a development — stabilised markets, increased outlets and improved prices—would be a rich reward to members of your proposed co-operative.

"In addition, it offers you the possibility of extending the co-operative's activities into new forms of enterprise, which could be of still further benefit to farm income in this district."

This was one form of organising enterprise which for too long had been delayed in Ireland. It was essential to have a far more rapid growth in economic co-

BRENTANO TO PICK DR. ADENAUER'S SUCCESSOR

DR. HEINRICH VON BRENTANO, former West German Foreign Minister, was given the job of finding a successor to Chancellor Adenauer.

A meeting of the Christian Democratic Parliament group decided unanimously that he should propose a successor for their approval after sounding out party opinion.

A spokesman for the group, of which Dr. von Brentano is chairman, said the group gave him a mandate to negotiate with party bodies to find the preferred candidate.

NO DEADLINE

The spokesman said no deadline had been set for Dr. von Brentano to submit his proposal. But deputies had expressed their hope that it would be done as soon as possible.

Both Dr. Adenauer, the 87-year-old Chancellor, and Professor Ludwig Erhard, his Vice-Chancellor and Economics Minister, attended yesterday's two-hour meeting.

It followed a new dispute between the two men. After the group's executive met on

MILK IS HIT BY FALLOUT OF N-TESTS

LEVELS of strontium-90 in milk rose in all areas of Britain in late spring and early summer last year, reflecting fall-out from the 1961 nuclear tests, stated the British Agricultural Research Council said yesterday.

In "Interim Report on Radio-activity in Milk," by the Council's radio biological laboratory, the average level for the year up to September, 1962, is put at about 60 p.c. higher than the average for 1961, but slightly below that observed in September 1959 after the previous year's weapons

Mr. Philby

'I am not worried' says his wife

Mrs. Eleanor Philby, the wife of Mr. H. A. R. Philby, the British journalist, who vanished from their Beirut home on January 23, said yesterday she knows he is on an assignment and has not been kidnapped. "I am still not worried about him in spite of all that has been said or published," Mrs. Philby said in a statement to the Press.

Despite this, however, the Foreign Office in London is continuing its inquiries about Mr. Philby. A Foreign Office spokesman said yesterday that inquiries, so far as he knew, were confined to the United Arab Republic and the Lebanon.

DAIL WILL DISCUSS VOTE ON ACCOUNT TODAY

"Irish Independent" Political Correspondent

THE debate on the Vote on Account will be opened in the Dail this afternoon, when Dr. Ryan will ask the House for about one-third of the £167,000,000 odd Estimate to enable the various Departments and services to carry on until the actual Votes are passed later in the year.

The Vote on Account is usually the occasion for a full-dress debate on Government fiscal and general policy.

At Question Time today the Taoiseach will be replying to the Leader of the Opposition, Mr. Dillon, and other Deputies for more information on the forthcoming visit of himself and Mr. Aiken to London.

FARM PRODUCE

Mr. Dillon is to ask the Taoiseach whether it is proposed to review the terms of trade between the two countries with special reference to an expansion of Irish agricultural exports on terms more closely integrating with the British price structure.

The N.P.D. deputies, Dr. Browne and Mr. McQuillan, want to know whether the talks are to take place at our initiative or that of Britain, and whether it is proposed to ask for a reconsideration of the Partition problem in the new trading and political arrangements.

The Dail will sit tomorrow at 10.30 a.m.

BRITAIN TOLD ABOUT BIDAULT, SAY FRENCH

A FRENCH FOREIGN MINISTRY spokesman said yesterday Britain had not replied to a French Note some two months ago, saying M. Georges Bidault, and other anti-Gaullists, were in Britain.

But the spokesman denied that his Government had protested to the British Government about the BBC screening of a filmed interview with the former French Prime Minister —now head of the anti-Gaullist National Council of Resistance and a "wanted" man in France.

Most French commentators were convinced that the British Government had a hand in the broadcast which was seen in Paris as an example of delayed bad temper following the break-down of the Common Market talks.

"ILLEGAL" ENTRY

M. Bidault got into Britain illegally, the Home Secretary, Mr. H. Brooke, told the Commons yesterday. Police efforts to trace him had had no result so far, but there were no grounds for thinking he was still in Britain.

Mr. Brooke added that some months ago the French Government furnished the names of certain people, including M. Bidault, who, they said, were engaged in activities against the French State. "We took note of that information," said the Home Secretary.

The BBC disclosed yesterday that it was sending copies of the filmed interview to the Canadian Broadcasting Corporation and National Broadcasting Corporation of the U.S., New Zealand and Australia. Copies were also being sent, at their request, to Switzerland, Denmark and Sweden, and Holland and Belgium had made inquiries for the film.

THREE APPEAL

Defence counsel for three men condemned to death in Paris for their part in last August's assassination attempt against General de Gaulle yesterday appealed to the President for mercy.

Air Force engineer Lieutenant-Colonel Jean-Marie

Germans in the market for Irish land

REPORTS from several parts of the country indicate that bids are being made by Germans for seaside, agricultural and, to a lesser extent, industrial land.

It was disclosed this week that West German industrialists may buy properties costing almost £100,000 in Co. Donegal.

Already four wealthy Germans have flown to Ireland and inspected land in the county. They are interested in residential holdings and farms, some of them costing up to £20,000.

IN DONEGAL

A Donegal auctioneer, Mr. James Watters, of Milford, who is negotiating with the Germans, agreed that they were very interested in buying properties in the county and had now gone back home to think about it. Land in Donegal has never been selling so well, he said.

In Dublin Mr. James T. Deegan, M.I.A.A., Chairman of the Trade and Commerce Committee of the Dublin Junior Chamber of Commerce, said that with the large-scale buying of land by foreigners there was an inherent danger that the small farmer would be swept aside. It was of paramount importance that he should be protected.

£4,315 FOR YOU AT AGE 55

Dublin's 'amazing bingo craze' even made use of some major cinemas in which to hold events. (*Courtesy of the Irish Photo Archive*)

THE IRISH TIMES

Price 5d. No. 33,549   DUBLIN, SATURDAY, MAY 4, 1963   LATE CITY EDITION

MASKED GANG ROB DUBLIN MAIL VAN

Daring hold-up near airport

A POST OFFICE mail van was held up early this morning on its way from Dublin Airport into the centre of the city. The robbery was discovered when an Army officer, driving to the airport, was waved down by the driver of the van, who had been left lying, bound and gagged, beside the road from Ballymun to the airport.

The police immediately began a widespread search of the city and suburbs in an effort to track down the gang, said to be masked, who carried out one of the most dramatic robberies ever to take place in this country. The abandoned mail van was later found in a farmyard at Ballymun with its contents removed.

The van had gone to the airport to collect mail brought in on the last flight of the night from London for delivery in this country. It left the airport and had gone a little more than half-a-mile down the road towards the city when it was flagged down.

It is believed that one of the hold-up gang was wearing a uniform

A Dublin mail van heist was pulled off as dramatically as a Hollywood thriller. (*Courtesy of the National Library of Ireland*)

EVENING HERALD

Incorporating the "Evening Telegraph"

Vol. 72. No. 106.   DUBLIN, SATURDAY, MAY 4, 1963   PRICE THREEPENCE

'MAC' THE MASK IN HOLD-UP

'MAC THE MASK'—Postman Mark Feery holding the Macmillan Mask used by one of the raiders.

Frightening rubber mask worn by one of the thieves. (*Courtesy of the National Library of Ireland*)

During Dublin's prolonged bus strike, army lorries provided transportation for many stranded passengers. (*Courtesy of the Irish Photo Archive*)

EVENING HERALD

(Incorporating the "Evening Telegraph")

Vol. 72. No. 84   DUBLIN, MONDAY, APRIL 8, 1963   PRICE THREEPENCE

FINAL

FOR SATISFACTION COOK WITH JACKSON

WEDDING PRESENTS
Barometers, Cameras, Field Glasses, Opera Glasses, etc.
HEMPENSTALL
111 Lr. Grafton St., Dublin 4

● The country is now faced with two crippling disputes—one affecting road passenger transport and the other paralysing the deep sea end of the Dublin port. Although only 39 crane men are directly involved in the port dispute, more than 2,000 other employes refused to pass the pickets. More than 5,500 C.I.E. busmen are out.

FOOTSORE DUBLIN

Long trek to work by many thousands

Herald Staff Reporter

A NATION ON THE MARCH—THAT WAS IRELAND TO-DAY WITHOUT ITS MASSIVE FLEET OF BUSES, IMMOBILISED BECAUSE OF THE COMPLETE STRIKE BY 5,500 C.I.E. DRIVERS AND CONDUCTORS.

DOCK STRIKE MAY PARALYSE PORT

THE COUNTRY HAS BEEN HIT BY ANOTHER STRIKE WHICH NOW THREATENS TO PARALYSE THE ENTIRE PORT OF DUBLIN.

To-day 39 Dublin Port and Docks cranemen went on strike and put pickets on the deep-sea end of the port. More than 2,000 dockers refused to pass the pickets and twenty cargo ships are tied up in Alexandra Basin.

The cross-Channel section of the Port is not, so far, affected and ships are being worked normally. The R. and

All premises

To-day the cranemen placed pickets on all the Port and Docks premises, including the Ballast Office, the Customs House and Alexandra Basin as well as the

expired on Saturday. They are seeking an increase of 5/4 per hour for handling coal cargoes by mechanical grabs. The Board had offered them an incentive bonus based on tonnage rates.

the Irish Oak of Irish Shipping which arrived from the U.S. yesterday with general cargo. She had been tied up in America for a while because of a strike there.

Efforts by the Labour Court to arrange a conciliation conference over the week-end failed.

There was a special meeting of Dublin Port and Docks Board to-day to discuss the strike. Tradesmen, also, refused to pass the pickets. These in-

Nationwide bus strike crippled normal life for passengers, leaving them forced to walk miles. (*Courtesy of the National Library of Ireland*)

EVENING HERALD

(Incorporating the "Evening Telegraph")

Vol. 72. No. 112   DUBLIN, SATURDAY, MAY 11, 1963   PRICE THREEPENCE

HOPE FOR THE FOOT-WEARY

It could all end at 11 p.m.

Herald Staff Reporter

THOUSANDS OF FOOT-WEARY PEOPLE WERE TO-DAY KEEPING THEIR FINGERS CROSSED IN ANXIOUS EXPECTATION OF THE RESULT OF THE VITAL BALLOT BY THE 4,700 BUSMEN ON THE PROPOSALS FOR A SETTLEMENT OF THE

As this Army lorry swung into Aston Quay this morning, its passengers and crew wondered if it might be the last run in view of the busmen's ballot, the result of which could mean buses to-morrow.

As the weeks passed by, patience wore thin and frustrations rose as the bus strike continued. (*Courtesy of the National Library of Ireland*)

Army soldiers and local garda enjoyed assisting stranded bus passengers into lorries –
'great fun' for many. (*Courtesy of the Irish Photo Archive*)

EVENING HERALD

(Incorporating the "Evening Telegraph")

Vol. 72. No. 138

DUBLIN, TUESDAY, JUNE 11, 1963

PRICE THREEPENCE

DUBLIN HIT BY THUNDERSTORM

Flooding at Merrion to-day.

Flooding in many areas

DUBLIN WAS STRUCK TO-DAY BY A VIOLENT THUNDERSTORM WHICH BROUGHT SUDDEN FLOODING TO MANY AREAS—PARTICULARLY ON THE SOUTH SIDE.

Dun Laoghaire, thronged by holiday crowds, was one of the worst hit areas with flooding of many houses and streets reported.

For more than an hour the city reverberated to crashing peals of thunder accompanied by vivid flashes of lightning.

Fire Brigade units from Dun Laoghaire, as well as Corporation waterworks personnel, were "run off their feet" with distress calls, many of which came from invalids and other people confined to their homes.

The cloudburst which was punctuated by heavy claps of thunder, caught holidaymakers and workers in light summer attire, and sent them scurrying for shelter.

Severe impact

As well as Dun Laoghaire, all surrounding areas, principally Killiney, Dalkey and Kill o' the Grange, suffered the most severe impact of the cloudburst.

Pressure of the flood water in many cases forced manholes out of position and roads became rapidly submerged with drains unable to cope with the sudden deluge.

Hailstones in Mount Merrion

Residents in the Mount Merrion area experienced what could be described as a tropical storm. One resident said they had four inches of rain in the garden and this was the general picture in the area. Thunder and lightning was very bad—with raps and flashes every five seconds.

Hailstones with the rain made this a freak thunderstorm.

thunder and lightning continued to alarm people.

The storm in Galway, which lasted about two hours, brought thunder, lightning and torrential rain to interrupt one of the best summer spells for years. There had been no rain in the area for over 17 days.

Ballinasloe, too, was struck by a violent thunderstorm. Vivid flashes of lightning were accompanied by torrential rain. Telephonic communications were disrupted and E.S.B. current was put out of commission for a short period.

Sandbags

The storm also hit Banagher and lasted for over an hour yesterday. Telephone and electric services were interrupted and in the downpour everyone made for shelter. Some houses in Lower Main Street were hurriedly sandbagged to keep out water, and television aerials were bent.

Blistering

It was another blistering day over most of Ireland to-day, and in many inland places temperatures soared again into the mid-seventies.

The "long-distance" forecast, according to weathermen, remains cheerful with no immediate break expected. Apart from occasional thunderstorms here and there in the southern half of the country the long

Amazing scenes as floods halt traffic

Herald Staff Reporter

LINES of cars edged slowly through the floods at Booterstown, Blackrock and Merrion. Torrential rain, the rapid flashes of lightning and the continuous roll of thunder formed an awesome background to the drama.

Car after car stalled and

were transformed into swirling rivers and many motorists parked along roadsides that resembled river beds because of the downpour. In one road the force of the water lifted the huge iron grate and the force of water against this sent tall jets of water several feet into the air.

Householders along Merrion Road and Rock Road battled in-

BRIGADE IS SWAMPED WITH CALLS

DUBLIN FIRE BRIGADE was inundated with calls to the flooded districts of Dundrum and Roebuck, Clonskeagh. From 1.30 onwards hundreds of calls were being received by the Central Fire Station at Tara Street, and at one stage the calls were being received every few seconds.

Water reached car's roof

Many motorists found themselves stopped in floods and cars had to be abandoned. In side. As he watched the water rose almost to the level of the roof.

An explosive thunderstorm hit Dublin with torrential rains, terrifying lightning and hail, paralysing the capital city. (*Courtesy of the National Library of Ireland*)

Cars and passengers trapped in flooded streets. (*Courtesy of the National Library of Ireland*)

The search for two trapped children under the heaps of rubble evoked great national sympathy. (*Courtesy of the National Library of Ireland*)

BELL'S SCOTCH WHISKY

THE IRISH TIMES

Price 5d. No. 33,583   DUBLIN, THURSDAY, JUNE 13, 1963   CITY EDITION

OLD TIME IRISH COARSE CUT MARMALADE

TWO GIRLS KILLED AS HOUSES TOPPLE

Buried by tons of debris on way to buy sweets

Irish Times Reporters

TWO children, on their way to buy sweets, were killed by tons of rubble when two four-storey houses collapsed in Fenian street, Dublin, yesterday, shortly before 4 p.m. The 17 occupants of the two tenements escaped injury although some of them were in one of the buildings at the time.

The two children killed were : Linda Byrne (8), of 24 Holles street, and her inseparable school friend, Marie Vardy (9), of 11 Holles street. Firemen working in relays and helped by Corporation workmen, found their bodies on the pavement after three hours of non-stop digging through the rubble.

Their parents were among the hundreds of people who watched from both ends of the cordoned-off street as the efforts to find the children continued during the afternoon. Within 15 minutes of the collapse, police had ascertained that all the occupants of neighbouring houses as well as those of the collapsed buildings, were accounted for, with the exception of the two children.

The fact that they were missing and that they habitually bought sweets from a shop on the ground floor of No. 7, started intensive rescue operations by the teams of firemen and workmen.

The two landlords, Mr. George Perry, who owned a barber's shop on the ground floor of Nos. 4, and Mr. John Maher, who owned the general stores on the ground floor of No. 3, were among the people who escaped.

In Nos. 3, Mr. John Hanlon, aged 76, the stage manager of the Royal Irish Academy of Music, had warned the other people in the building about an hour before the houses collapsed. They all had left.

However, next door, in No. 4, although some of the residents had left when they heard cracking noises, others stayed on. All of them succeeded in escaping through the rear windows of the building to safety.

The two victims were known and liked by most of the people in the area. They constantly frequented

The two children who were killed: Marie Vardy (above)

Claims for flood damage

SCORES of claims from householders and motorists for damage caused by Tuesday's floods in Dublin were received by the insurance companies yesterday. The total involved may mount up to £1,000,000 or more. (Full report in Business and Finance, page 12.)

300 houses still flooded in Dublin

The tragic Fenian Street tenement collapse killed two young girls, shocked the country and terrified other tenement dwellers. (*Courtesy of the National Library of Ireland*)

CLARKS SERENITY

GRIFFITHS
Wicklow St. and Talbot St., Dublin   65/-

EVENING HERALD

(Incorporating the "Evening Telegraph.")

Vol. 72. No. 140   DUBLIN, THURSDAY, JUNE 13, 1963   PRICE THREEPENCE

KONICA 8 mm. ZOOM CINE CAMERA
available £49-19-6
HEMPENSTALL
155 Lr. Grafton St., Dublin 2

TV?
MURDOCHS
Dun Laoghaire, Bray. City Branches

STUNNED PEOPLE OF FENIAN ST.

Marie Vardy

Linda Byrne
More Pictures on Page 5.

Mothers, children in protest march

Public inquiry called

Herald Staff Reporter

THERE WAS AN AIR OF STUNNED SHOCK AND SILENCE IN FENIAN ST., DUBLIN, TO-DAY. ITS RESIDENTS ARE GRIPPED BY A DEEP SENSE OF TRAGEDY AS THE FULL IMPACT OF THE DISASTER IN THE STREET WHICH TOOK TWO YOUNG LIVES MAKES ITSELF FULLY FELT.

Dublin Corporation has called a special meeting next Monday to consider this and other recent house collapses in Dublin. The Minister for Local Government (Mr. Blaney) is to arrange for a public inquiry.

MEANTIME, THE WHOLE CITY IS APPALLED BY

One of the cars which was buried in the collapse.

BOY DIES WHEN HIT BY LORRY

CHRISTOPHER FRANCIS DARKER, aged 12, of 33, Innisfallen Parade, N.C. Rd., was killed this morning when, while cycling, he was struck by a cattle lorry and trailer near the Mater Hospital.

The boy was dead on admission to the hospital.

Birthday gift

The dead boy was a pupil of St. Canice's C.B.S. and had received the bicycle he was riding as a birthday present.

His father, Mr. Christopher Darker, is a driver employed by a city firm.

Christopher had been living with his aunt, Mrs. B. McCann, Innisfallen Parade, since his mother died some years ago. A number of his school friends saw the accident.

Rev. F. McQuaid, S.D.B., Ballinakill, Co. Laois, who was travelling in a car behind the lorry, gave absolution to Christopher

Photos of the two young victims across national front pages upset many readers. (*Courtesy of the National Library of Ireland*)

FUNERAL OF VICTIMS HIGHLIGHTS TRAGEDY

Families in grip of fear

Herald Staff Reporter

ALL-DUBLIN SEEMED TO MOURN TO-DAY AS THE FUNERAL OF THE TWO LITTLE CHILD VICTIMS OF THE FENIAN STREET HOUSING COLLAPSE WENDED ITS WAY FROM ST. ANDREW'S CHURCH, WESTLAND ROW, TO DEAN'S GRANGE CEMETERY.

But amid the sorrowing, anger and fear tightened their grip on Dublin's tenement areas again to-day as fresh rumours of

Children from the neighbourhood with wreaths at St. Andrew's Church, Westland Row, to-day.
(More pictures on Page 3)

Sad scene as cortege passes Fenian St.

Herald Staff Reporter

A MID mourning throngs.

THE OLD LADY

Mrs. Kane (85), of Fenian St., spent last night in the open.

Dundrum child is drowned

Herald Staff Reporter

AN inquest is to be held on three-year-old Judith Hogan, daughter of Mr. and Mrs. Thomas P. Hogan, Churchview House, Dundrum, who was drowned yesterday at Mosney Co. Meath.

Mrs. Hogan was visiting Mosney with her four children, who decided they would like to go in for a bathe in the indoor swimming pool. While Mrs. Hogan was helping the other children to get into their togs, Judith, who had been got ready first, wandered off unnoticed by the others.

It is believed that Judith must have gone too near the edge of the water and have fallen in. She was seen in the water by two life-guards, John Hart, from Nenagh, Co. Tipperary, and Brian O'Hara, from Dun Laoghaire. They immediately took her out and

Funeral of small tenement collapse victims drew huge crowds and tears from men as well as women. (*Courtesy of the National Library of Ireland*)

Firemen removing bodies of two small girls at Fenian Street tenement collapse. (*Courtesy of the Eamonn Fitzpatrick*)

The tragic scene of Fenian Street tenement collapse where two young girls were killed under the rubble. (*Courtesy of the Irish Photo Archive*)

The search for victims in the tenement ruins had to be delicately carried out by hand for fear of further collapses. (*Courtesy of the Irish Photo Archive*)

Two tenement collapses at Bolton Street and Fenian Street terrorised the thousands of tenement dwellers in Dublin. (*Courtesy of the Irish Photo Archive*)

'Welcome Home': President Kennedy's arrival truly felt like his homecoming for many. (*Courtesy of the National Library of Ireland*)

The nation regarded Kennedy as one of their own – as indeed he was. (*Courtesy of the National Library of Ireland*)

President Kennedy's 'homecoming' four-day visit to Ireland drew a crowd of one million ecstatic citizens – for many the most exciting moment of their lives. (*Independent News and Media/Getty Images*)

The most poignant moments of Kennedy's homecoming occurred in Dunganstown, Co. Wexford, his ancestral home. (*Courtesy of the National Library of Ireland*)

The announcement at the Irish Derby that hot favourite wonder-horse Relko would not compete shocked racegoers. (*Courtesy of the National Library of Ireland*)

Scenes of helpless, homeless tenement families on Dublin's streets appalled many foreign summer visitors. (*Courtesy of the National Library of Ireland*)

The grisly murder of 16-year-old Hazel Mullen horrified the public, who followed the story day to day. (*Courtesy of the National Library of Ireland*)

In 1963 canal barges and pleasure boats were connected to the River Shannon and west of Ireland. (*Courtesy of the Dublin City Archives*)

Corporation plans to fill in both Grand Canal and Royal Canal to accommodate the car boom ignited an impassioned battle with outraged locals and preservationists. (*Courtesy of the Dublin City Archives*)

Dublin's canals provided escape and serenity for residents of congested city life. (*Courtesy of Dublin City Archives*)

The Irish show jumping team's victory, winning the coveted Aga Khan Cup, was a thrilling moment for the country. (*Courtesy of the National Library of Ireland*)

Thousands of Dublin housewives marched in protest against the new turnover tax that would affect the household budget. (*Courtesy of the National Library of Ireland*)

Fans greet Beatles at airport

Herald Staff Reporter

LOOKING nothing at all like four young men who earn between £650 and £1,000 per night, the famed Liverpool Beatles strode nonchalantly into the V.I.P. room at Dublin Airport shortly after mid-day to-day.

At a glance journalists detected the world acclaimed hair styles; their casual, though colourful attire and their likeable approach to show business in general.

Certainly they were "flabbergasted by their success during the past 10 months, but we feel we are appealing to the masses and the type of stuff we are giving them at present is near to their hearts."

But their very appearance will more than please the 3,500 admirers who will pack Dublin's Adelphi Cinema to-night, and the many thousands more who will mob them in Belfast to-morrow.

In Drumcondra

Lead guitarist George Harrison (20), whose mother flew into Dublin airport on an earlier flight, admitted that his grandparents were from Ireland.

"I was here before, you know, when I was about eight years of age. I think I stayed in Drumcondra, but I'm told I have dozens of relatives in Dun Laoghaire and other parts of the country."

With Harrison was the Beatles' leader, John Lennon (23) and the remaining two

"I hope we're not trampled on in the crowd."

who go to make up the four-man group, Paul McCartney (21) and Ringo Starr (23).

While they chatted with reporters at least 40 screaming 'teenagers clamoured to gain admittance. They were held back however by Airport police and special gardaí who had been drafted from the city in case of incidents.

In demand

At the airport also was Beatles' promoter, Arthur Howes, who said the boys were learning to live with their phenomenal success. He did not think the notoriety which had attached itself to them over the past 11 months had changed them in the slightest.

It was a fact, he said, that the Beatles were in tremendous demand all over the world and at the moment he was having difficulty in pleasing would-be promoters as far away as New Zealand, Australia and South Africa.

After meeting journalists, the Beatles left the building and were hustled away by gardaí. They did have time, however, to sign autographs. Members of the Beatles' fan club who were present included Lena McDevitt, Coastguard Terrace, Dun Laoghaire; Kaye Ryan, Tivoli Terrace, South, Dun Laoghaire; Rita Hempenstall, Thomas St. and Evelyn Healy, 163 James's Street.

Said the girls, whose ages ranged between 14 and 16—"We think they're the most. We haven't got tickets for the show to-night, but we expect to be in Abbey St. to lend them moral support."

Three other young girls who were approached for their names declined to give them. "We are on the bounce," they said, meaning they were giving school a miss for the day.

Danced 'fling'

Having earlier danced an unscheduled "fling" for photographers on the tarmac, the Beatles were unprepared to stage a repeat performance for the 40 odd screaming teenagers who had gathered outside the door of the V.I.P. lounge.

One of them stuck his head through the half-open door and the crowd surged forward, forcing the gardaí into the lounge. However, order was soon restored, and the four boys were smuggled through a back door, and whisked away from the airport by car.

While in Dublin the Beatles will stay at the Gresham Hotel.

---

away

The last of the eleven, Bernhard Wolter, came up at 1.19 p.m. The last stage of the rescue operation had taken 57 minutes.

The men had been down the mine a fortnight almost to the minute.

Youngest

At 1.42, 20-year-old electrician Adolf Herbst, youngest of the 11, reached the surface. Six feet tall and thin, he was carried from the rescue platform to the tent. His right leg was heavily bandaged from an injury caused by falling rock. Waiting for him was his fiancée, 20-year-old Dagmar Waletzko.

Six minutes later, Johannes Sitter, an explosives expert, became the fifth man to get out. He was lifted from the escape capsule on to a stretcher.

It took between six and nine minutes for each man to reach the surface.

The capsule had been turned around so they would not face directly into the sun. Their first experience of life above earth for nearly two weeks was the stiff north wind which swept the rescue area.

Sitter came up at 12.47 followed six minutes later by Helmut Webranitz, 28.

stunned when she saw her husband's face covered by a thick beard. Then she broke into tears.

The last

Both the miner volunteers who went down to the underground cavity to help the miners into the rescue capsule returned safely to the surface.

The rescue was carried live over West Germany's television network. Millions were able to follow the drama on their screens throughout the country.

At the site, all eyes were on the engineer directing the lifting and lowering of the capsule. He gave directions by waving his helmet to the machine operator.

MORE LAND SOLD

Following closely on the news that 15 acres of land have been sold in Swords, to be used, it is thought for a site for a new industry, comes the news that more land in the locality has changed hands.

This time the site, at Rockbeale Road, measures 16 acres, and the purchaser is Dublin Co. Council, which intends to build houses there under the Small Dwellings Act.

The rescue capsule which was used in to-day's operation.

They will really throw a party!

When the ambulances—one for each miner—were lined up to start their trip to hospital, the men who had participated in the rescue ran up and down the convoy shaking hands with the rescue men. Each man's wife or nearest relative was in the ambulance with him.

Other miners who had participated in the rescue shouted to their colleagues: "When you're out of hospital, we will really throw a party."

Baby for Shirley

Shirley Bassey, the singer, gave birth to a daughter at London Clinic, to-day. The baby weighed 6 lb. 10 ounces. Both mother and daughter were reported to be doing well. Shirley Bassey is the wife of film director Kenneth Hume.

Weather

A south-westerly airstream covers the country. Forecast—Bright periods and occasional showers. Light south-west winds. Average temperature. Outlook — Fog patches, clearing to-morrow morning. Otherwise little change.

Dixon Heinpenstall, 111 Grafton St. Dublin 2—Barometers. (Advt.)

The Beatles at Dublin Airport this afternoon
Another picture on Page Five

The Beatles arriving at Dublin Airport, where they would soon face 'Beatlemania' Irish style. (*Courtesy of the National Library of Ireland*)

THE BEATLES TAKEN TO SAFETY
IN EVENING HERALD VAN

Like champagne, this Beatle stuff goes to your head.

Secret operation carried out in three minutes

By LIAM KELLY

WITH the precision of a commando operation and within ten musical beats of their closing number—"Twist and Shout"—the Beatles were whisked to the safety of their hotel in an Evening Herald delivery van last night.

And "Rescue Beatles Operation," of which I was a part, was planned in top-secrecy an hour before the final curtain, only took three minutes to carry out.

Knowledge of the "dangerous mission" was confined to a mere handful. Not even the Gardaí knew.

First blueprint of the operation was "hatched" in the Beatle-rocking Adelphi Cinema. Armed with the knowledge of what an after-show siege on the Beatles is like, the group's manager consulted the cinema manager and an S.O.S. was sent to the Herald, whose premises adjoin the Adelphi.

The management of Independent Newspapers Ltd., willingly put a van and driver at the disposal of the operation planners.

Inconspicuous

For 30 minutes before the rescue began the van, with driver garage foreman Mr. Jack Flanagan, was parked in the shadows outside the stage door. In the intervening period several groups of curious teenagers 'nosed' around the area.

But what could be more inconspicuous than a newspaper van parked near its despatch department, waiting, as everyone thought for the first editions to come off the presses? It was a first rate camouflage and was vital to the success of the plan.

As unruly fans raved and ranted inside and outside the cinema, assistant manager of the group, Ron King gave the driver the signal to start the engine. As the engine purred quietly and with no lights switched on to attract attention the curtain came down inside and seconds later the four grey-suited Beatles raced to the safety of the van, still covered in make-up.

Slammed doors

Manager King slammed the doors shut, and the van eased out of Princes Street where the overflow of the Abbey Street crowd had gathered.

With photographer Jack Murphy I sat, as they did, on old newspapers, in the back of the unlit van and chaperoned them to the hotel—with fingers crossed for the entire journey.

It was an ironic situation driving through the crowds with thousands of heads turned in the opposite direction shouting the now-famed "war cry", "We Want the Beatles." They had been fooled.

Quenching their thirst with minerals—they don't drink—they chatted amiably all the time commenting on the ingenuity of their "escape."

Their reaction to the Dublin reception—"It was fantastic. We did not expect anything like it. We will be back," they

the way I had arrived. And outside I was mobbed by fans who pleaded with me to go back inside and get "A tie, a lock of hair or anything from THEM."

What a crazy world we live in!

For these three girls it was one long scream at the Adelphi last night.

Three of the Beatles (from left): Ringo Starr, John Lennon and George Harrison, in the Evening Herald van in which they were driven from the Adelphi to the Gresham Hotel.

Mr. Jack Flanagan, who drove the Beatles in an Evening Herald van from the Adelphi Cinema to the back door of the Gresham Hotel.

Fine show—if one could only hear it

By TEMPO

BECAUSE of the noise, which apparently goes hand in hand with the Beatles' stage shows, many were last night inclined to gloss over the entertainment value of the Adelphi show altogether.

It can be said, however, that of its type, this was one of the best stage productions to come to our shores for some time. The incessant screaming, clapping and feet-stomping inside the theatre however resulted in it being impossible to hear but snatches of the artists.

Despite condemnation in the past, this type of thing continues and I expect there is little that can be done in order to allow everybody to hear everything that goes on.

Sang well

The Beatles were just as I had expected. They sang their numbers with rare enthusiasm, their colourful appearance

adding immensely to the overall presentation.

But not far behind in the honours list was Peter Jay and his Jaywalkers who sported a variety of guitars and injected the atmosphere with a sound rarely heard on these shores.

First-rate

The other artists too turned in first-rate performances. The Vernon Girls, coming early in the programme, before much of the noise began to take its effect, proved to be a delightful group; the two voices of the Brook Brothers were often inaudible but most of the passages that did come across were pleasing; the Kestrels, who we have heard before, came just before the Beatles and by this time the audience was buoyed to such a level of enthusiasm that I doubt if they took much notice of this quartet at all.

The Rhythm and Blues Quartet were competent soloists and accompanists. Master of ceremonies was Frank Berry.

KYLEMORE BAKERY LTD.

American rock 'n' roll sensation Chubby Checker appeared in Dublin to show off his twist dance – sometimes to perplexed viewers. (*Courtesy of* RTÉ)

The Irish Press

Vol. XXXIII. No. 304   MONDAY, DECEMBER 23, 1963   PRICE 3d.   The Truth in the News

SHIPS RACE TO RESCUE OF 20,238-TON CRUISE VESSEL

LINER ABLAZE IN ATLANTIC

950 ON BOARD ABANDON SHIP

THE Greek cruise ship, Lakonia, was ablaze in the Atlantic north of Madeira this morning, and radio messages said that all aboard were abandoning ship. A spokesman for the line said in London that the Lakonia was carrying about 650 passengers, most of them from Britain. She has more than 300 crew.

A message received at The Hague said: "S.O.S. from the Lakonia last time. I cannot stay any more in the wireless station. We are leaving the ship. Please immediate assistance. Please help."

The Lakonia (20,238 tons) left Southampton on December 19 on a cruise. Formerly Dutch-owned, her present owners are the Grimos Shipping Co., Ltd., of London.

A number of ships radioed that they had changed course and were heading towards the position of the Lakonia. The Argentine liner, Salta, was expected to arrive there about 3 a.m. The U.S. ship Independence also signalled that she was

Fateful day for Common Market issue

The Common Market's whole future will be decided to-day when ministers of the six member states meet for the last time this year to see whether they can reach final agreement on a package deal on important farm and trade

Canoes reach rallying point

END OF ICY SPELL

Irish Press reporter

MOTORISTS had their first respite from the hazards of the cold spell yesterday. But last night temperatures along the East coast and in the North West again hovered around freezing point and some roads were as bad as ever.

In the West and South, however, temperatures yesterday averaged 45 degrees F, and the Meteorological Office forecast last night that milder weather would spread to the whole country gradually, giving better weather than for the past week. The weather is expected to be milder over Christmas and there is likely to be rain in some places.

Cork had one of its coldest nights of the year on Saturday night but yesterday was fine and sunny, although mild. It began freezing hard again last evening and there was heavy fog in

Rescuers rushed to the sinking *Lakonia* liner with 950 passengers on board, who were forced to abandon ship in the middle of the night. (*Courtesy of the National Library of Ireland*)

EVENING HERALD

Incorporating the "Evening Telegraph"

Vol. 72. No. 305   DUBLIN, MONDAY, DECEMBER 23, 1963   PRICE THREEPENCE

DUBLIN FAMILIES ON BLAZING LINER

Babies thrown to rescuers

The Lakonia

MANY IRISH PEOPLE—INCLUDING A DUBLIN FAMILY OF SEVEN— WERE AMONG THE PASSENGERS WHO HAD TO ABANDON THE BLAZING 20,238-TON GREEK LINER, LAKONIA, IN THE ATLANTIC EARLY TO-DAY. ABOUT 100 PEOPLE WERE REPORTED THIS AFTERNOON TO BE STILL ABOARD THE LINER, WHICH WAS BEING RAKED BY EXPLOSIONS.

The liner, with more than 1,000 passengers and crew on a sunshine cruise for the Christmas holidays, was on its way to Madeira. Her position was given as 100 miles north of Madeira.

The Dublin family of seven on the vessel were Mr. Tim Hynes and his wife, Molly, Strand Road, Merrion, who were travelling with their four children, Ena, Tom, John and Iverna, and the children's nurse, Miss Molly Walsh.

Rescue ships and British and American aircraft were to-day making a dramatic bid to save the Lakonia's passengers and crew. More than 300 were known to have been picked up by two ships early in the operation, and more and more lifeboats were being spotted by the rescue armada.

Boat drill

Thirty Irish citizens were on the *Lakonia* during Christmas week when it went ablaze and started to sink. (*Courtesy of the National Library of Ireland*)

The *Lakonia* liner with 950 passengers on board, including at least thirty Irish citizens, afire and sinking during Christmas week. (*Courtesy of Topfoto*)

At Christmas, there were still hundreds of passengers missing at sea as worry increased for survivors. (*Courtesy of the National Library of Ireland*)

Irish doctor James Riordan, who was on board the *Lakonia*, gave his life to save others, and was hailed as a hero in national newspapers. (*Courtesy of the National Library of Ireland*)

Muckross House, a national treasure, was threatened by developers who wanted to convert it into a luxury hotel for the elite. (*Courtesy of Alamy*)

It was very exciting ... just an amazing buzz, we were working ludicrous hours. It was superb, unsurpassed ... Everyone stood a foot taller.[89]

Home television sets assumed a new, important role, since Budin and his team would be covering the event in detail. But only a minority of families owned one. Feeling left out, many decided that it was a good time to purchase one. Nearly everyone else had a radio on which to follow the proceedings.

Hundreds of thousands of people preferred to participate in person, out on the streets. Dubliners were fortunate to be able to witness it all conveniently. Those from other counties had to make plans to reach Dublin. Days before Kennedy's arrival people began flowing in to Dublin from outside; roads feeding into the city had traffic backed up for miles. Traffic heading down from the North was also extremely heavy, with hundreds of cars crossing the border every hour.

CIE put on special fleets of buses to carry crowds to and from Dublin. Additional trains were put into service, many of which had to run during the night to accommodate the crowds.

For many visitors real problems faced them upon arrival. Those who had anticipated it had booked accommodation well in advance. Many people showed up only to find that hotels and guesthouses in the city, and for miles around, were booked out. Some private homes began opening their doors to take in guests.

Behind all the excitement was a nagging worry about weather, which had been a spoilsport on every major occasion so far that year.

Meanwhile, the newspapers tried to keep people informed of any news leading up to the 26th. It was confirmed that Jacqueline Kennedy could not accompany her husband, since she was expecting a child. Instead, Kennedy's sister Eunice Kennedy Shriver would accompany him.

The White House was predicting that Kennedy would probably see as much of Ireland during his brief stay 'as a tourist would in many weeks', since he would be flown around by helicopter. Hearing this, many towns and villages began extending invitations for him to drop in for a visit.

The *Irish Independent*, bolstering its own hype, decided to offer a word of advice to its readers. Confident of an 'unprecedented demand' for copies of the paper, it suggested that readers, 'to avoid disappointment', should 'place an order with your newsagent *now*!' And thousands did just that.

Much newspaper coverage was devoted early on to Kennedy's plans to head south to Wexford and New Ross and on to Dunganstown to visit his cousins and ancestral home. There were many members of his extended family still scattered around.

At eighty years of age, Noel Hughes of Coleraine Street in Dublin recalls with a slight smile how many people liked to say that they were one of Kennedy's cousins. He heard it wherever he went. 'They were *all* claiming, "Oh, *I'm* a cousin!" – they were *all* a cousin of Kennedy's!'

———

No challenge for the Dublin Corporation was more conspicuous than the need for tidying up the city. Journalists who had written about the world spotlight being on the city were not using hyperbole. In the 1950s and early 60s Dublin had the reputation of being one of the most despoiled cities in Europe. Streets were littered, buildings were defaced, shopfronts were gaudy.

A joint effort of Corporation authorities and property-owners was required. It meant not simply scouring the roads and pavements but also cleaning and repainting façades and shopfronts, removing graffiti and other stains, and cleaning windows and polishing brass fixtures.

One of the most glaring problems was how to disguise the large signs and advertisements on buildings that stood out before cameras. In some cases it was decided that the only solution was to hang huge *Welcome, Mr President!* banners, or giant American and Irish flags, over them.

At peak effort, this meant a Corporation 'staff of 250, with the help of another 100 men from the Lighting Department', who worked tirelessly to 'put up over 1,000 flags along the route'.

As O'Connell Street was being made fit for presentation to the world, the process of refining and embroidering began. This meant bringing in lorry-loads of fresh plants and flowers and hanging bunting from one end of the street to the other. Businesses sometimes competed in doing up their premises. Along Dorset Street and other streets the same preparations were under way. Even the most humble shops and houses could be made festive. The *Irish Independent* wrote:

> With lavish displays of flags, flowers and bunting, Dublin will wear its gayest festive garb for the visit.[90]

O'Connell Street was being transformed before the eyes of astonished Dubliners. With flags fluttering in the wind, the street took on a lively character. Floodlights were installed to illuminate the most attractive buildings and banners. At night, after the traffic diminished, people from around Dublin began ambling about the streets to marvel at the transformation.

Appearances were also important for the more than three thousand uniformed gardaí who were to be lined all along the route and placed on duty elsewhere. An order was passed down from the Commissioner that their appearance was to be flawless. Bill Herlihy was then a sergeant stationed at Store Street. Now well into his eighties, he recalls the seriousness of the order:

> Kennedy's visit was a rare phenomenon – and it *had* to be done properly … Everybody had to wear their best uniform, be properly cleaned, be shaved, haircut. 'Look well' – there were no two ways about it!

A few gardaí were selected for special duty to accompany President Kennedy at close range and act as security, in conjunction with the American agents. Among them was Garda Paddy Farrell. He was born in 1929 and was from a farming family in Co. Meath:

> I was more or less settled in to be a farmer. I was the eldest, of three girls and my brother, so I would have got the land.
>
> But through a fluke, when I was in a forge one day getting a horse shod, the blacksmith said to me, 'Why don't you try out for the guards?' Just like that!

It had never occurred to him to be a guard, but he joined up and was stationed in Store Street. Then, in 1960, he was sent to the Traffic Department to become part of the motorcycle escort squad. The duty was enjoyable, if routine. That is, until June 1963.

Having an outstanding record, he was rewarded with an important public assignment. He and his squad of six motorcycle escorts would lead the way for the presidential motorcade from the airport into the city and then on to Áras an Uachtaráin and the American ambassador's residence. They would co-ordinate their escort with that of the army motorcyclists. Farrell, however, learnt that his position was to be special:

I was at the *very front* of the motorcycles – the spearhead, if you like. I was the lead – just up in front of his car.

Today, reflecting on his role, he stresses that Kennedy was travelling all the way in an open limousine, even standing up from time to time to wave to the crowd. It was an eight-mile route, with his car moving slowly all the way to the Phoenix Park.

——

On the evening of the 25th, when canny politicians knew that the attention of the nation was on the events of the following day, they met to advance the turnover tax one step further. 'Shortly after 8 p.m., every seat in the public gallery was occupied.' The tension was palpable. With unexpected brevity, the Government 'carried the Second Stage of the Finance Bill – by *one vote*, 72 to 71':

> To the surprise of many, the debate ended rather tamely ... On the positive motion the bill will be given a second reading. To the crowded gallery the result was quite disappointing ... [and was met with] cheers, boos and cat-calls.[91]

But, for the moment, nasty politics would have to be put aside to allow for the unfolding of glorious history.

Chapter 11 ∽

HOMECOMING: RAPTURE

Wednesday 26 June

Garda Paddy Farrell was awake early. As were, most likely, the five other members of the motorcycle escort. Though President Kennedy was not due to arrive at Dublin until eight that evening, Farrell had plenty to keep him occupied during that long day. Nothing was more important than checking his motorcycle for the umpteenth time. Assuming the 'spearhead' position for the presidential escort placed him centre stage for the historic spectacle. He had no margin for error. His motorcycle had been tuned as finely as a watch so that it would hum through the streets.

Most Dubliners were up and out of bed with unusual zest that morning. After months of growing anticipation the day had finally arrived. Thousands were planning to take off early so they could book their spot on the pavement or at a window to get the best view. This would mean standing *in situ* for up to five hours. But, as Garda Terry Brady recalls, everyone was charged with extra energy:

> When it was announced that President Kennedy intended to visit Ireland a great buzz of excitement enveloped the country. When the day actually *arrived*, everyone was in a euphoric mood.

Newspapers extended headline welcomes, one reading 'Céad míle fáilte'. The *Irish Press* emphasised the significance of the event:

> Today, the great wheel of history swings round to complete the circle. In the ceremonial confrontation of the two Presidents a whole relationship stretching across the broad Atlantic for centuries reaches a new climax … [with] a firm handclasp on Irish soil.[92]

To the young firefighter Jim Fitzpatrick 'it was like the long, lost son coming home ... like in the Bible!' In every newspaper and on the streets it was simply being called a 'homecoming'.

Throughout the city, people began their daily routine – though the day was far from normal: Dublin was suffused with a state of happy anxiety. Along Moore Street the traders Lizzy Byrne and May Mooney set up their stalls as usual, as did Nanny Farrell and Margaret O'Connell over in the Daisy Market. Hardly a word would be heard all day from the city's storied street traders and their regular customers that did not pertain in some way to President Kennedy.

People were hoping fervently for good weather. They knew that Kennedy planned to travel the entire route in an open limousine, even standing often to wave at the crowd. Rain could be a terrible spoiler, for it would mean that the top on the limousine would have to be closed.

At about noon the workaday mood in the city began to change. To Garda McPhillips, who would soon be taking up his position outside Dublin Airport to await Kennedy's arrival, the very pulse of Dublin changed discernibly. 'We could *feel* the excitement that was building up in the city!'

RTÉ and other broadcasters were checking their elevated platforms along O'Connell Street. Along the route, thousands of gardaí were being assigned their posts. American agents carried out their own surveillance, paying special attention to windows and roofs.

―――

By mid-afternoon, crowds began gathering in and around Dublin Airport, securing coveted spots on the balcony. Some Government and diplomatic authorities were having their own rehearsals for when President Kennedy emerged from his aircraft. There was a convention for these procedures, and some dignitaries would get considerably more attention than others.

Throughout the day there was occurring what the *Irish Independent* called 'one of the biggest ever invasions from the Six Counties' as cars were travelling almost bumper to bumper, hour after hour. Customs officials were forced to cut the formalities in order to keep a decent flow going. The all-night trains had been disgorging thousands of drowsy passengers. By the time many emerged into the morning sunlight they were groggy and giddy with the thrill of it all. Now they faced having to stand for hours along the pavement.

For the vast crowds who would gather along O'Connell Street for up to five hours the prolonged wait was strenuous, both for body and for patience. Any diversion was welcomed – a joke, a buffoon, colourful characters, a trouble-maker being removed.

Kennedy's sister Jean Kennedy Smith was already in the city. She had slipped in the day before, undetected, to visit her good friend Dorothy Tubridy. Throughout the day on the 26th they strolled through Grafton Street and Dawson Street.

In the latter part of the afternoon, gardaí began shutting down traffic, cordoning off sections of streets and getting ready to secure O'Connell Street for the pageantry.

Yet there existed, only a few streets away, a shocking juxtaposition. Here were decayed and crumbling tenements, and evacuated families sitting and sleeping on the cold ground. The only interest the Government had in them on that day was that they not draw attention to themselves and 'embarrass' the nation.

Protocol was on the minds of Dublin's elite. There had been much discussion about what type of welcoming ceremony would best suit President Kennedy. Some favoured a resplendent greeting; others a subtle, dignified one. As Ryan Tubridy writes, it was decided that 'a solemn affair', yet one exuding warmth and grace, would be best.[93] And it was thought, quite correctly, that this would be more pleasing to President de Valera. Of course, there would still be the artillery salute and an army band.

Of course, the Lord Mayor of Dublin would formally welcome the President of the United States to the city. But *which* mayor? The newly elected Lord Mayor, Seán Moore, had decided to take on his new role and greet President Kennedy himself. J. J. O'Keeffe, who preceded him as Lord Mayor, would greet Kennedy as a private citizen in a friendly exchange.

By 7 p.m. everyone who had needed to do so had staked out their vantage point. Tens of thousands of anxious, happy spectators all along the route had planted themselves in prime position. Gardaí had orders to weed out any trouble-makers well in advance, leading to a few scuffles here and there.

Most gardaí had been in their positions for at least two or three hours. Garda Herlihy was posted at the junction of O'Connell Bridge and O'Connell Street; Garda McPhillips stood on one of the lower approaches to Dublin Airport, where Kennedy would directly pass by; and the young garda Tony Ruane was positioned in Westmoreland Street. They had the same orders:

to keep their eyes fixed on the crowd, with their backs to the motorcade as Kennedy passed. This applied to all three thousand uniformed gardaí placed along the route. It sounded easy – till the motorcade actually came along.

The newspapers had their senior journalists posted in prime positions. The *Irish Times* gave Dermot Mullane a coveted assignment. He would first cover Kennedy's arrival at the airport, then follow the motorcade all the way to Áras an Uachtaráin and the US ambassador's residence.

At 7:30 p.m. dignitaries stood in their places at the airport, close to where the plane would come to a halt. That is, every person except *one* – the most dignified of all. It was recalled by Garda McPhillips, who remembers it with a smile. As he stood along the edge of the road, just below the airport entrance, there was a sudden 'surge of excitement when we saw President de Valera *speeding out* in his old Rolls-Royce as Kennedy's plane was approaching – he was running a bit late.'

At about 7:45 thousands of heads were craned upwards into a cloudy sky in hopes of catching a first glimpse of the plane as it descended. An *Irish Press* journalist described the scene:

The huge blue and white Boeing jet crossed the Irish coast ... as rain clouds cleared away to blue skies. In the sunshine below his jetliner circled the city where he could see the thronged streets ... as the jet dropped down for its historic landing.[94]

At 7:55, when it was announced that Kennedy's plane was now circling, a 'great shout of expectancy went up through the throng'. It touched down just before eight. Kennedy appeared 'framed in the doorway ... with a wave of his hand as he stepped down the gangway.' When Kennedy was seen 'smiling broadly' a 'mighty roar of welcome' arose from the packed balcony:

With hand outstretched, President Kennedy walked down the ramp. First to greet him was President de Valera who shook him firmly by the hand. Both Presidents smiled warmly.[95]

According to protocol, the American national anthem was played by the Army No. 1 Band, and a 21-gun salute was fired by an artillery battery. After being greeted by the Taoiseach, Seán Lemass, Kennedy proceeded along the reception line. However, the full 'Kennedy effect' would not be felt until he was free of the confines of the airport. Once he was in his limousine, on the roads, 'the love affair between Ireland and Kennedy would begin'.[96]

_____

Outside, crowds were amassed along the road. Everyone realised that their sight of Kennedy would be fleeting. They would be happy enough with that, since the motorcade moved at a slow pace. John Howard of the *Irish Times* observed that 'security surrounds the American President to a fantastic degree.'

Some in the crowd held transistor radios in order to hear the commentary as they waited for the motorcade. In fact, this was more than the gardaí posted all along the route had at their disposal. As Garda Terry Brady, assigned to Swords Road, explains, the 'communication system', as he sardonically puts it, available to the guards along the route was somewhat lacking:

> At that time we had no mobile phones or personal radios, so communications were practically nil. We depended on motorcycle gardaí occasionally coming from the airport to keep us in the picture. So there was huge excitement – and expectation. Rumours flying around the crowd, 'He's *coming* in a few minutes!'

Finally, Brady got word that Kennedy was coming within sight:

> The entourage was on its way! Suddenly, in the distance, we could hear the cheering and clapping, and this developed into a type of 'Mexican wave' – until at last the President's car was upon us. Cheering and clapping! And the brief view that people had seemed to satisfy them.

The motorcade rolled slowly towards the city centre. At Santry the crowds thickened. By Larkhill and Whitehall it had become a sea of humanity, people climbing trees and lampposts. At Drumcondra people began building towards the kerb and worrying gardaí that they might break through into the street.

Garda Farrell was leading the motorcycle escort squad. If there was any trouble in the road he would be the first to spot it. Kennedy's agents kept their eyes unflinchingly on the crowd for anything suspicious. Irish reporters were impressed by their absolute dedication to Kennedy's welfare. In the *Irish Times* Dermot Mullane depicted the American agents as 'crew-cut, limber young men riding the running boards just behind the President.' Another journalist noted their 'granite expression'. Michael Foy of the *Irish Times* referred to them as 'the square-jawed members of the President's bodyguard'.

Along sections of Dorset Street the gardaí began to worry about the crowd density as people surged forward. Gardaí hurried to link arms to try and hold them back. This surging had been a concern of the American agents. They understood the dangers of stampeding, even among well-meaning spectators.

At 8:50 the motorcade approached Parnell Square. Suddenly, ticker tape, looking 'like a shower of confetti', was released from the windows above. As he passed by Parnell Square, Kennedy must have noticed a few banners saying *An undivided Ireland welcomes you* and *Welcome from the united Ireland.* He probably got the message. Ahead of him the cinemas had replaced their billings with a simple *Welcome, President Kennedy.*

Una Shaw and her husband, Tom, had walked from Rutland Street hours earlier to stake out a prime position. It was well worth it for the thrill of a lifetime:

> Tom and I had a great vantage point standing by the Parnell monument. And when [Kennedy] came down from Dorset Street we got a terrific view of him. He was so happy, relaxed, standing up in the car, with de Valera sitting next to him … and the cheering was *deafening.* Everybody was happy. Everybody was laughing. Oh, sure, we were in rapture over him!

When Kennedy entered O'Connell Street the excitement and cheering went ballistic, making television platforms quiver. Having waited impatiently for hours, people finally let loose, as the *Irish Independent* described:

> The din of cheering erupted into an emotional crescendo as the cavalcade entered the broad sweep of O'Connell Street. The moment of fulfilment, a close-up look at the most dynamic leader in the world … It brought tears to the eyes of many.[97]

As an *Irish Press* reporter observed, it was at this ground level that the real connection between Kennedy and the Irish people was made.

There were now thirty garda and army motorcycle escorts guiding Kennedy's limousine, which was moving at a snail's pace. Superintendent Thomas Culhane and Superintendent John Coakley were in charge of crowd control. At certain points heavy ropes had to be used. Above, RTÉ television platforms vibrated from being knocked.

Kennedy had a joyful but calm demeanour, as noted by an *Irish Independent* reporter:

> I think never a welcome made him so relaxed and happy … One could almost see him unconsciously shedding the cares of statesmanship, forgetting the world crises and basking in the warmth of a real Irish welcome.[98]

Before the big day arrived, some people had staked out what they thought was a perfect perch on Nelson's Pillar. But their plans were quickly thwarted by the Gardaí, who had closed it off as dangerous. Even those who wanted to climb onto its base were driven away. Nelson was strictly off limits!

Journalists vied with one another in trying to describe the emotions of the crowd. The *Irish Times* emphasised that the Irish people embraced Kennedy 'in a more affectionate way' than they had any other leader, including the Pope, who had visited a few years before. With the Pope it was a reverential love; with Kennedy it was an unbridled love of a familial type. 'One of us!' as so many exulted in saying.

Among the crowd was Noel Hughes, who remembers the emotions of the day half a century later:

> He won the *hearts* of people … they let loose. People idolised him! It was 'He's one of our *own!*'

The motorcade finally reached O'Connell Bridge, where Sergeant Bill Herlihy was on duty. While all gardaí were supposed to face the crowd, he could not resist turning to take a good look:

We'd seen him in photographs – but *now* he was driving by, quite slowly.
And he waved to everybody. I remember seeing him quite clearly – he
had that certain charisma!

Above Dublin, the sky was growing ominous. A blanket of dark clouds
was moving in. Photographers grumbled that their good light was fading.
The main worry, however, was that Kennedy's limousine top would be
drawn up if there was rain.

In Westmoreland Street stood Garda Tony Ruane. After several hours
he became bored and fidgety, gazing around for any welcome distractions:

> I was distracted by a shop window and wandered over to have a look. I
> saw a pair of fawn-coloured suede desert boots, on sale … and promised
> myself that I would make that purchase on my next payday.
>
> Then I was roused from my daydreams by the heavy hand of an
> inspector on my shoulder. He spun me around and, in justifiably
> furious tones, hissed at me, '*Do you realise* that the President of the
> United States is about to pass this way at *any* moment – and you are
> f***ing well *window-shopping*!'

Repentant, he assumed his position and stood steadfastly. But when the
motorcade finally approached, pandemonium erupted. He was not about
to be the only one to miss the once-in-a-lifetime spectacle. The inspector
was nowhere in sight. Once again, he defied orders:

> I was transfixed when I set my eyes on Kennedy, in all his splendour.
> He was only *feet* away … and I felt as though I had seen something
> supernatural!

Above the street level, and understandably feeling more detached from
the excitement of the moment, James Downey, who would become one
of Ireland's most distinguished journalists, was on duty at the *Irish Times*.
He was stuck up in an office as Kennedy was passing, following it on the
radio. In 2014, at the request of the author, he shared some memories. One
esoteric recollection came to his mind, even after so many years:

I was in a junior position on the late shift. But Kevin O'Kelly was on the radio covering Kennedy's motorcade. And he said he was *refusing* to use the neologism 'motorcade' – and would call the thing a 'procession'. I thought, What *pedantic nonsense!* Doesn't he know that a procession is on *foot!*

Shortly after 9 p.m. the motorcade had rounded the Bank of Ireland and passed into College Green and Dame Street. People had remained long after work to see Kennedy pass by. A reporter spotted some Trinity students taking chances for a good view:

> High on the roof of Trinity College a few hardy men jockeyed on the tiles … as girls in jeans had equally chancy footing on railings and window sills.[99]

It was at this point that the weather turned. The sun, now slanting, was frustrating photographers. Then more clouds moved overhead and a shower broke out, which could only have increased the danger for the students on the roof.

At the junction of George's Street hundreds of schoolchildren had their own welcome for Kennedy. Clustered together, they waved flags and hoisted banners reading *Fáilte, a Sheáinín* and *Dia duit, a Uachtaráin*. To their delight he spotted them and gave a special wave as he passed by.

The north quays presented quite a different environment, as noted by the reporter Andrew Hamilton:

> Even the drab riverfront of the North Quays took on a new appearance. Thousands of flags fluttered from small cafés and warehouses … and from the bridges straddling the Liffey the Stars and Stripes and Tricolours hung. The people in the area gave him a true 'Céad Míle Fáilte', wore lapel badges and waved miniature flags.[100]

The pride of people in working-class areas struck Kennedy as they welcomed him. As his limousine crept along, he saw the faces of the labourers, street-dealers and factory workers. The reporter Michael Foy witnessed it all:

Here was the welcome from the people of York Street and Cook Street and from the other working-class areas near the city centre, and it could not have been more sincere.[101]

Years later, most journalists and historians would write that it was Kennedy's appearance before the Dáil and at Arbour Hill that were the highlights of his visit. But those closest to him would verify that it was the ordinary people in the streets who had been most meaningful to him and touched him most. This was a sentiment with which the *Irish Press* agreed:

It was the *people* who waited long hours and crowded the streets, who poured out their hearts in welcome and obviously touched the young leader with their warmth and open-heartedness.[102]

Upon his return to America, when sharing the experience with his wife, it was his feeling for the people that he would express most fervently – a memory she would often share as the years passed.

———

As the motorcade reached the Phoenix Park the army motorcyclists peeled off and returned to their barracks. This left Garda Paddy Farrell and his escort in charge. Only a short time earlier the gathering clouds had sent down a torrent of rain. It passed quickly, leaving the lawns fresh and green and the air crystal clear. Entering through the gates, they found a world of serenity as they proceeded to Áras an Uachtaráin:

The quiet around Áras an Uachtaráin was broken by the purr of well-tuned engines … The two Presidents had arrived at the first oasis of quietness after their triumphant drive from the airport.[103]

Everyone in the motorcade immediately felt more relaxed. The reporter John Howard called it a 'quiet haven after a storm of people'.

It was only seconds, however, before they heard another roar of cheering and saw a throng waiting in Phoenix Park. Garda Terry Brady had got there before them. He and his fellow-gardaí had been hurriedly sent over to the Park well ahead of Kennedy's entourage. He was positioned about a hundred yards from the American ambassador's residence:

The crowds gathered in the Phoenix Park were *unbelievable* ... tens of thousands. At around 9:30 we once again heard the cheering and clapping in the distance. The presidential car came into view, slowly, and stopped at a point *directly* in front of where I was standing – much to my and my colleagues' disbelief!

Then there was a massive surge from the crowd and great difficulty was experienced by us trying to contain the situation ... people hoping to shake hands with the President. He shook hands with as many people as he could, and all the time with the most winning smile.

When the presidential party reached Áras an Uachtaráin, Kennedy went in for the customary visit for a head of state. Afterwards he climbed back into the limousine for the short hop across the road to the American ambassador's residence.

By now, visibility was poor. Garda Campion, another member of the six-man motorcycle escort, recalls the next surprise they encountered:

At the ambassador's residence there was *another* vast crowd! And we had to work hard to clear the way for the convoy. The six of us got off our bikes when we noticed that the President's car had stopped outside the gate. And he *got out* of the car – and was being surrounded by the crowd ... in a good-natured way.

Neither the gardaí nor the American agents had been prepared for this last hurrah of the day. Dipping into his own reserve of energy, Kennedy unexpectedly got out to shake a few more hands, throwing all his security men into something of a dither, as reported by the *Irish Press*:

The President was visibly impressed by the warmth of his reception ... About 15 yards from the gates he alighted from his car. As he got out, the crowd surged forward to meet him.

Hundreds of hands were outstretched to him as he shook as many as he could. His security guards were *appalled* by this turn of events, *rushed forward* and pushed the crowds back.[104]

It was late in the day; everyone was weary and patience was being tested. Gardaí and American agents were now working together to establish order and free Kennedy from surging bodies and outstretched hands. They struggled to get him the last few yards through the doors of the ambassador's residence.

They didn't have that far to go. It was at this moment that Garda Paddy Farrell was suddenly struck with fear: Kennedy was inching his way slowly forwards to walk through the gates, and he and the American agents all had their eyes fixed on the crowd around him.

But Farrell's eyes were cast downwards. It had just rained, and the cattle grids at the entrance were wet and extremely slippery. Stepping on them unawares could be dangerous. Farrell recounted his thoughts to the author in 2012:

> I immediately got off the bike and ran back a few yards. Just ran – and grabbed him! Put my arms around him from the side and warned him of where he was standing. He wouldn't have seen that … at night time! I actually held him [back] – said something like, 'Be careful, Mr President, you're standing near a cattle grid!' He was in a very vulnerable situation.
>
> I was afraid that the Secret Service would be edgy … [wondering] 'Is this fella an impostor?' Because I must say that anyone who would have touched the President when he was here would have been eaten alive! And I actually held him. It must have been a nightmare for the Secret Service.

The danger was quickly recognised, and Farrell was thanked for his quick thinking and bold action. In reflection, Farrell added, 'For the record, I have to say that it was a wonderful moment … to get that close to him.'

As Kennedy stepped through the doorway of the American ambassador's residence for the night, all those in the presidential convoy could finally relax and head home themselves.

————

In Dublin the streets were still alive with spectators enjoying the afterglow of the day's experience. Gardaí were still on hand in considerable numbers to get the crowds off the streets and to clear the way for traffic. College Green was especially charged with excitement. The gardaí, however, had put in long hours and were visibly weary.

The *Irish Times* reporter Andrew Hamilton hung around, doing a bit of interviewing among the spectators. All were still in high spirits. Then he spotted one exception: a large, tough-looking garda from Co. Mayo. He wore a dour expression. He had been on duty the entire day and gave Hamilton a scowling reply:

I will not be sorry when the Kennedy visit is over. There is nothing so hateful as having to stand here doing *nothing*, all day long![105]

The visit, however, was far from over.

Chapter 12 ∿

HOMECOMING: FAMILY GATHERING AND GARDEN PARTY

On the morning of 27 June, President Kennedy was rested and eager to depart for his 'homecoming' in Co. Wexford, where he could truly 'cut loose and enjoy himself'.[106] As Ryan Tubridy puts it, it was the moment when the 'Famine generation of the 1840s met the generation of the 1960s' – one having departed in tatters on coffin ships, the other returning in bespoke suits, limousines and helicopters.

Long before President Kennedy had been served his breakfast at the American ambassador's residence, Garda Séamus McPhillips and hundreds of other gardaí had been roused from their sleep in the middle of the night to begin their long day of duty. Yet they were all excited and honoured to be a part of it, he recalls:

> Our orders for 3 a.m. that morning were to go to Westland Row Station, for Wexford. Five hundred of us uniformed guards. I thought, This is great! You know, that we were *part* of it. It was an adrenaline flow!

Arriving in Co. Wexford, they were sent into town and to the GAA field, where they were brought sandwiches. Then they began waiting for Kennedy's helicopter to land. There was plenty of time to consider what the day might hold for them. The *Irish Press* was already describing the previous night's chaos in the Phoenix Park as 'a real Donnybrook'.[107] It was hoped that crowd control in Co. Wexford would be far easier.

Meanwhile, CIE was conducting a massive operation to take more people, equipment and supplies to Kennedy's various destinations. From Dublin the early-morning trains took hundreds of gardaí to Wexford and later on to Limerick and Cork. At Kingsbridge Station gardaí began to board the trains at 5:30 a.m. CIE also provided a fleet of buses to take gardaí on to New Ross from Wexford. This all required ten coaches, two mini-coaches, thirty-five limousines and sedans, and six baggage lorries. There were also two lorries with raised platforms for TV crews.

In New Ross, Judge McDonagh was doing his part, issuing an exemption order allowing publicans to open their premises in the morning from 8:50 to 10:30 during Kennedy's visit. The rationale for this was never fully explained, but no-one questioned it. By the 26th, some fifty thousand people had converged on the town, creating a carnival atmosphere, with dancers and singers giving open-air concerts.

The town's transformation was quite astonishing. All the shops and streets had been cleaned up and gaily decorated. Everyone was in high spirits. With so many visitors, any notions the Gardaí had of simply having to manage a local crowd fast dissolved. Another hectic day lay ahead.

Out at the GAA field things were not quite as spirited as in town. Finally, soon after eleven, the first flutter of helicopter blades was heard. Everyone watched it descend, and after a few minutes the door opened and Kennedy appeared. The Artane Boys' Band struck up 'The Boys of Wexford', known to be one of Kennedy's favourites. He beamed with delight.

The gardaí flashed to attention. According to McPhillips:

> his helicopter landed and he was with Minister [Frank] Aiken, and as he was passing us by he said, 'Hi, guys!' I was as close to him as I am to you [about five feet].

After the orderly greetings and formalities, Kennedy walked over to and *into* the crowd, shaking hands, exchanging comments. This predictably created a surge towards him. Within a few minutes, wrote the *Irish Press*, it resulted in some 'wild scenes ... fantastic scenes'.[108] Gardaí thrust themselves forward to try and exert control. Kennedy's security closed around him and grimaced slightly.

When Kennedy reached the podium from which he was to address the crowd, he first flashed his famous smile, which ignited roaring and cheering. The introductions by officials proceeded well enough. There was a fault with the amplification system, but his powerful voice projected throughout the crowd. His short speech there became one of his most enduring. He told of how his great-grandfather had left his cottage in Ireland to become a cooper in Boston, carrying with him only his 'strong faith and a desire for freedom', which his descendants had emulated. The crowd loved it. Then, true to form, he climbed down from the podium and again stepped into the crowd to shake more hands.

Kennedy then enjoyed the short journey to Dunganstown in his open limousine, travelling along the country roads. Along the way, people stood along the narrow roads and sat on walls, sometimes so close that they could have jumped into his car. This was unfamiliar terrain for the befuddled American agents.

President Kennedy was nearing his ancestral home – for a genuine family gathering. His limousine and entourage pulled up in front of the house, where he was greeted by some of those relatives he said were 'left behind' or 'stayed behind' in Ireland. This was the moment so many had waited for, according to the *Irish Times*:

> The highlight of President Kennedy's sentimental journey came when he crossed the threshold of his family's ancestral home in Dunganstown.

Just outside the gate of his great-grandfather's home, a group of shy schoolgirls lined up to greet him. He went over to shake their hands and talk to them in 'a kindly, fatherly way'. At once, 'their shyness melted away' with his easy, warm words.

From that moment on, everything seemed comfortable and casual, 'like a neighbour dropping in for a cup of tea', as one reporter with the *Irish Independent* wrote. It was a 'heart-warming welcome from his own people':

> When he entered the neat little Ryan home he lightly kissed his third cousin, Mrs Mary Ryan, on the cheek warmly, shook hands with her daughters Josie and Mary Ann, sat down at the open fire and blew the bellows. It was the spontaneous action of a man who felt he was truly among his own people.
>
> With a boyish gesture, he drank another cup of tea and said, 'To all the Kennedys who went away, and to all who stayed home.'[109]

Mary Ryan, who had been described as anxious before he arrived, became quite at ease upon meeting him in her own home. At the little party they sat together sipping tea and chatting easily. He called everyone by their first name, mingled naturally, joked and teased and 'won their hearts'. There was plenty of laughing and giggling when Kennedy asked if the salmon had been poached. There was not an awkward or clumsy moment noticed by anyone.

It all had the feeling of a genuine family reunion. By the time the cake was brought out, everyone felt as if they knew one another. While Kennedy's attention was on his host, Mrs Ryan, he engaged fondly in conversation with her daughters. During the meal, Mrs Ryan and her daughters received an invitation to visit the White House. As Josie told a reporter, 'he told us that he would be delighted if we could come ... next year, or in the near future.'

None of them had imagined that it would be so much simple fun. It could have gone on all day. But only half an hour after he arrived, Kennedy put his arm around Mrs Ryan and said, 'I've got to go. Thanks a lot, dear. I'll be back.'

After he bid everyone else farewell, there was one person left: Margaret Whitty, at eighty-six the eldest of the Kennedy cousins. As he clasped her hands to say goodbye, she 'wished himself and his family all the best ... that they would have a long and happy life'.[110]

Kennedy's whirlwind visit to New Ross, Wexford and Dunganstown had lasted 165 minutes, journalists calculated. His schedule for the remainder of the day was filled till near midnight. Every day would be the same: one important event after another. Journalists were astonished at his hectic pace.

Mercifully, a leisurely garden party was planned for that afternoon at Áras an Uachtaráin, as a restful interlude. Though it was the least important of all the events, Kennedy said he was looking forward to the relaxed afternoon.

After his splendorous welcome the evening before, the newspapers were filled with praise for his dynamism – what journalists were calling his 'charisma' and 'mystique'. Readers wanted every detail of his visit.

Naturally, everybody wanted to see him in person if at all possible, even if it meant driving from Dingle to Dublin for a ten-second sighting. For most people, their dream was fulfilled if they caught a good view of him passing by in his open limousine.

Many who were prominent in society regarded themselves as important enough to be entitled to meet Kennedy. They expected an introduction, a handshake and an exchange of pleasantries – possibly even a bit of congenial chat and a photograph. Their best chance to achieve this was at the garden party, since it was to be *the* social event of his visit. Only 1,500 VIPs had been invited, 700 of whom were of exalted position – privileged. Dignified social luminaries who doubtless felt entitled to a personal introduction to the dashing President.

The success of any garden party of course depends upon favourable weather. By the afternoon it was overcast and a bit chilly – not ideal, but there was no immediate threat of rain. After being seated at their tables, people were free to stroll about the gardens and socialise as they pleased.

Every newspaper had their 'women's reporter' on the scene to cover the fashions, do a bit of interviewing and pick up a few quips. The reporter for the *Irish Independent* set out to gather material for her article, intended to be titled 'Gay dresses were garden party feature'. But she saw that everyone on the lawns had the same obsession: meeting President Kennedy in person. As she would write, Kennedy:

> seems to have the irresistible attraction of a Pied Piper, for the crowds at the garden party followed him wherever he went.

Her term 'followed' was a euphemism: in truth, he was *hounded* relentlessly. Order and civility were forgotten. As one *Irish Press* reporter exclaimed, 'protocol was swept aside – when the crowd surged forward.' The *Irish Times* reporter Tom McCaughren admitted to being shocked by what he was witnessing:

> There was pandemonium on the lawns … as a crushing, pushing crowd of guests literally mobbed President Kennedy … The elegantly dressed women wanted to shake hands. In the middle of the melee an obviously distraught Mr de Valera motioned the crowd back with his hand and appealed, 'Move back, move back, *please!*'

It was at this point that the weather worsened. A persistent drizzle began making the lawn soggy, soaking tables and chairs, ruining expensive outfits.

Worse, it became apparent that Kennedy would be moved indoors. This set off a rush to at least get a handshake before he was withdrawn. As David McCullagh wrote in the *Irish Independent*, 'it soon got wild ... push, shove, heave!' 'A rugby scrum,' according to one British reporter, or, as another journalist put it, '*mania* reigned!'

Daniel Costigan, the Garda Commissioner, ordered members of the Special Branch to 'try and preserve some order – but the guests were too many for them.' Tables and chairs were knocked over, fancy hats were knocked off, toes were trampled, and shoes lost, and guests were knocked off balance, a few toppling to the muddy earth. A bishop had his cape torn and ripped. One reporter wrote candidly that the:

> over-exuberant guests crowded into an uncontrollable mass ... One woman fainted ... photographic equipment was lost ... dignitaries were caught up in the rush ... security men *tried.*[111]

'I have never seen anything like this', wrote one American journalist. 'I had expected a relaxed social occasion.' So had everyone else. What most appalled observers was the shocking manner in which the elderly President de Valera was treated, how disrespectfully he was jostled and nearly pushed to the ground. Irish journalists did not hesitate to express consternation in their articles. It was a shameful incident that marred what should have been a perfectly lovely social occasion.

The most unlikely person on the grounds in fact ended up getting probably the most personal attention from Kennedy. It occurred when Kennedy and de Valera slipped out for a brief tree-planting ceremony. Only about twenty people were in attendance. Outside, with a shovel in his hands, was the Áras gardener Patrick Buggy, who had worked there for fifty-nine years. Kennedy, smiling, asked his name and congratulated him on his remarkably long and dedicated service, then shook his hand with real sincerity.

The next morning, those 'distinguished' guests who awoke feeling disappointed, ignored or snubbed at the garden party would read of the considerable attention received by Mr Buggy.

Kennedy had escaped the garden party unruffled, but his day was far from over. It was to stretch past midnight, as it was for Garda Farrell and the other motorcycle escorts. At 7:45 p.m. Kennedy's limousine arrived at Iveagh House at St Stephen's Green for a state dinner given by the Taoiseach, Seán Lemass and his wife. Outside was a crowd shouting, 'We want Jack!' He stepped out of his car looking remarkably fresh, smiling and waving to the crowd.

During the dinner and speeches, there was a three-hour recital of Irish and American airs on the bandstand in the Green by the children's choir of Loreto Convent. By the end of the dinner, many guests still had not made their personal contact with Kennedy. He graciously extended the evening to make certain that everyone left happy. All this time, American agents, gardaí and limousine-drivers waited patiently outside, twiddling their thumbs.

Finally, well past midnight, Garda Campion saw a flurry of activity around the entrance, and everyone scrambled into place. Kennedy emerged to find another screaming crowd. What happened next caught his own security men and the gardaí off guard – once again. As Campion describes:

I was still on motorcycle duty when the dinner was over, about 12:30. He came out and stood on the steps waving to the crowd on the far side of the road. They were standing on post boxes, hanging off lampposts and out of trees, standing on each other's shoulders.

Suddenly, he ran down the steps – completely ignoring his own security people, across the road and *into* the crowd. His security and the gardaí were taken completely by surprise!

My function was to stay beside the President's car. But suddenly he ran past me. And I got off my bike and followed him. And I had to *tear* through the crowd to try and get him back safely to the car … because everybody was so friendly, clapping him on the back, shaking hands. And pulling and dragging him! Not in a malicious way … but the fear was there that he might be injured by accident. Eventually assistance arrived and we got him back into the car safely, and back to the ambassador's residence.

The absolute nightmare for American and Irish security – Kennedy being surrounded by an ecstatic crowd, slapped on the back and 'pulled and dragged' by admirers – was finally over.

———

The next day, 28 June, Kennedy would create history with his appearances in Dáil Éireann and at Arbour Hill. But the morning of the 28th began with another helicopter trip, this one to Cork, where he wanted to pay tribute to his ancestors on the Fitzgerald side of the family. Cork residents turned out *en masse* to see him and listen to his brief speech. The entire journey lasted about ninety minutes.

He was then rushed back to Dublin for a luncheon given in honour of President de Valera at the American embassy. And this time there was a surprise awaiting Kennedy – a most delightful one. Kennedy's press secretary, Pierre Salinger, and the US ambassador, Matthew McCloskey, had conspired to pull it off secretly. They felt it was just what Kennedy needed at that point in his demanding schedule. They were right.

Clandestinely, eight Bunratty Castle singers had been whisked to Dublin in one of the President's helicopters to entertain the two Presidents. 'The eight girls', wrote the *Irish Times*, 'dressed in their 15th-century gowns' presented 'a somewhat incongruous picture' as they boarded the '20th-century helicopter' at Shannon. When they climbed out, on the ambassador's lawn, Kennedy beamed. After they dazzled everyone with a number of Irish verses, Kennedy had a personal request: would they sing 'Danny Boy' for him? As Kennedy joined in, Salinger and McCloskey, sitting close by, knew that they had pleased him.

Afterwards, Kennedy signed autographs for the singers and gave them flowers that McCloskey had provided. In contrast to the garden party fiasco, this had come off flawlessly.

At Arbour Hill – the sacred ground of Irish independence – the solemnity was felt by all in attendance. Standing before the graves of the leaders of the 1916 Rising, executed for their heroic role, Kennedy was sombre. In a short, dignified ceremony he laid a wreath on their graves, after which he paused to examine the memorial.

Shortly after departing Arbour Hill for Leinster House he got yet another pleasant surprise. As he was passing the Mater Hospital he encountered two hundred nurses forming a guard of honour, all waving Irish and American flags. In appreciation, he gave them a special wave. Doctors and patients on their feet were also there, and others watched from the windows. It was quite a sight.

President Kennedy's appearance before Dáil Éireann was an incomparable moment in Irish history. And in his own. He spoke before 144 TDs and 50 senators for twenty-six minutes. His eloquence held the audience spellbound. It was suffused with symbolism and poetry, linking the Irish and American people together in poignant phrases. In his speech 'there was a fierce pride and glowing joy in his Irish descent.' Kennedy himself appeared moved.

Before he left Ireland, Kennedy managed to squeeze in short visits to Limerick and Galway, where he had the same thrilling effect on all who saw and heard him. In Eyre Square in Galway, a harpist, Ruth Bradley, had the honour of performing before him. Half a century later, at the age of sixty-six, she recalls the effect on her of Kennedy's presence:

> The charisma just oozed from the man ... and it wasn't just the women that were getting hot and bothered. It was everyone. He just had an aura ... I never saw such euphoria in my life.[112]

On his last night in Dublin it was time for President Kennedy to say goodbye to Garda Paddy Farrell, who had jumped to keep him from injury, and to the other motorcycle escort gardaí who had been at his side from the beginning. They had gone beyond the call of duty to protect him. Some fifty-two years later Farrell quietly told the author about that goodbye:

> That last evening we had with him, he got out of his car and it was a sort of misty rain, but he came over to thank us. I don't think any other head of state would do that – but *he* did!
>
> We were lined up, standing off our bikes. He came right up to us, which I thought was a very nice gesture ... and I thought to myself, This man, he's different! And he gave each of us a little tie pin, which is the boat he was on during the war – a replica of that.
>
> We all felt honoured by his presence here ... He was a wonderful man.

On the morning of Saturday 29 June it was time for Kennedy to bid farewell. At the airport, with 'a warm, fond handshake' for President de Valera and 'an affectionate kiss' for Sinéad de Valera, he said 'goodbye to Dublin'. President de Valera's parting words for the young American president were: 'We wish you long life, health and happiness.'

As he climbed the steps of his helicopter, for Shannon Airport, he turned and gave a last broad smile and wave to the crowd, which was cheering, 'Hurry home here again!'

At Shannon Airport, as he boarded the plane for his final departure, his emotions caught up with him, as told by a senior official at the American embassy to an *Irish Independent* reporter:

> I was in close touch with Mr Kennedy throughout his stay ... it was obvious that the man was affected by it all. Before boarding his jet aircraft at Shannon, he was so filled with emotion that he could scarcely say goodbye.
>
> I was one of the last he was with at Shannon ... and I assure you he was full to the throat with emotion.[113]

Responding to the crowd's shouts of 'Return soon', he got his last words out: 'I will be back again!'

————

Everyone was left with their own memories of what it meant to them and to the Irish nation. Gerry Creighton, then nineteen, doubtless spoke for many young people:

> To us teenagers here, President Kennedy was a real-life hero. Suddenly, politics became very interesting for teenagers. President de Valera was an old man ... and so it seemed was the rest of the Government ... sombre, dull.
>
> [Kennedy's] visit, to teenagers, showed us that *anything* was possible – he gave a great moral boost to the country.

In 2013, marking Kennedy's visit a half a century earlier, the Taoiseach, Enda Kenny, seemed to concur when he expressed his view that President

Kennedy's visit 'has come to represent a genuinely pivotal moment in our collective experience.'[114]

Garda Séamus McPhillips, on escort duty during Kennedy's visit, today sees it in national terms:

> Everyone had a sense of unity ... *nationhood*. The positivity of it ... The country was uplifted! And there was the warmth of the after-glow.

Similarly, Dermot Keogh views it in a transcendent light:

> There was an indelible 'mystique' to the man and his visit. His visit electrified the country ... his charismatic personality.
> They were three magical days.[115]

Chapter 13 ~

RELKO'S RIDDLE, BINGO CRAZE AND OLYMPIA'S JEOPARDY

The Irish people had been on a high for the previous three days. A natural let-down seemed inevitable.

However, only hours after President Kennedy's departure, two captivating events helped to ameliorate people's spirits after this sudden absence from the country: the Irish Derby, featuring the 'amazing' Relko'; and the coronation of the new Pope, to be broadcast live on television. Both events had been highly anticipated for weeks. They were certain to capture the attention of most people over the weekend of 29–30 June.

Horseracing enthusiasts had anxiously awaited the Irish Derby, especially since journalists had written that it was 'attracting world-wide interest'. There had even been a hope that President Kennedy might be able to prolong his visit for a few hours in order to witness the spectacle.

The hype about the race had mounted daily, and by the afternoon of Saturday, the 29th, racing fans were wound tight with expectation. They had followed Relko's impressive wins at other European races during the spring season. It was this type of thrilling race that Irish race fans hoped to see.

Spectators and sports writers fully expected a Relko victory, and an exciting one. Relko's experienced French jockey, Yves Saint-Martin, was confident as well. He knew he was astride a champion – a rare steed, in his opinion. Knowing that all eyes would be on his horse, he exuded pride. When the horses appeared, spectators began sizing them up, impressed by Relko's powerful physique and his natural gait. In appearance he met all the requirements of a 'wonder horse'.

As the crowd at the Curragh Racecourse reached 40,000, race time neared. When the horses began moving towards the starting-gates the tension was palpable, and people leaned forward or stood up. Many had brought their binoculars. Would Relko bolt out in front to have a clear path, or hang back until the right moment, when his jockey would turn him loose? Even with a great horse, strategy was important.

When the horses were ready to take their positions, a puzzled expression appeared on Saint-Martin's face. He even seemed worried. He motioned stewards over to converse with him. Few in the crowd could see what was taking place. The other jockeys were left perplexed by the delay, and their horses were getting fidgety. Fans were squinting through their binoculars. Race aficionados knew that horses, especially top breeds, could be temperamental just before the start, so perhaps there was nothing to be concerned about.

Then came word from the announcer's box: the race would be delayed for a few minutes. This was followed by a hubbub among those inside the box. Spectators saw Saint-Martin 'gesticulating wildly' as the horses nervously 'walked around the starting port'.[116] There seemed to be some communication problems. The starter was seen in conversation with the jockey, who then dismounted. He was put into telephone contact with the grandstand, evidently to consult the horse's trainer, François Mathet. By this time, the spectators, as well as the television audience, knew that something was amiss – but *what*?

Saint-Martin was clearly exasperated – even angry. Then everyone saw the jockey, dismayed, take off his helmet and fling it to the ground. This was followed by a shocking announcement from the box above. It was later reported that:

> the crowd of 40,000 at the Curragh this afternoon gasped in amazement just before the start of the Derby when the announcement came … that the hot favourite, Relko, had been found to be lame and had been withdrawn with the agreement of the stewards.[117]

The crowd was stunned into silence. Then there was a wave of chatter. Puzzled and disappointed expressions were written on their faces. People were riddled with questions. How could a great racehorse so suddenly seem to go lame – only *seconds* before the start of a big derby?

As the minutes passed, Relko's jockey, trainer and owners were in consultation with track authorities, all showing frustration. The crowd stood wondering what had really happened. Britain was then rife with horse-doping scandals. Could there be any connection?

After a delay of about fifteen minutes orders were given for the race to commence – without the star of the show. It was now a derby featuring Irish horses as the favourites. The winner turned out to be Ragusa, trained by Paddy Prendergast and owned by J. R. Mullion. Sports writers were left to cover the derby with whatever enthusiasm they still possessed:

> It was a great day for Ireland as the Irish-trained horses took the first two places. But, of course, some of the gilt was taken off the victories by the sensational withdrawal of Relko.[118]

This was quite an understatement, considering that nearly everyone had expected Relko to be the *whole* show.

At day's end, fans filed out of the Curragh, not with enthusiastic chatter about the winner, but with talk of the Relko 'mystery'. These suspicions would grow as journalists kept the story alive and investigators were brought in to try and resolve the matter.

It would become a great riddle to be debated in pubs for some time to come.

———

Relko and his handlers were not the only ones to have had bad luck over the derby weekend. Andrew Gardiner, a farm labourer from Loughrea, Co. Galway, had toiled on other people's land since the age of fourteen to save up enough money to buy his own small plot. It was his life's dream. In June he finally spotted a notice for a modest piece of land he could afford. He withdrew his savings of £2,300 and stuffed the cash into his hip pocket. Then he climbed on his bicycle and pedalled off to buy his dream.

When he was half way there he discovered that the money was missing. In a panic, he swung his bicycle round to retrace his route. Along the way, his eyes darted back and forth on the road, expecting to spot it at any second. No sign. Distraught, he reported it to the Gardaí.

A newspaper, hearing of his misfortune, shared it with readers in hopes that a Good Samaritan had found the money and would return it to him. This gave Gardiner a glimmer of hope that he might still buy his little farm. All he could do was wait – and pray.

———

On Sunday 30 June, Catholics around the world focused their attention on the Vatican for the coronation of the newly elected Pontiff. Through the miracle of the Eurovision link, established in 1954 to co-ordinate European television networks, countless millions could follow the glorious pageantry.

There were few viewers more enthusiastic than the Irish people. Upon the Pope's election ten days earlier it was revealed that he had meaningful connections to Ireland. History was now being made, and ordinary Irish people could watch it on their television sets – if they were among the fortunate owners of one. According to the *Irish Independent:*

> the course of history flows on remorselessly. A Pope died and the world mourns him … and a new Pope is crowned and the world greets him with expectancy.[119]

Newspapers gave lavish attention to the new Pope, emphasising his humility, kindness and humanity. Irish readers were especially receptive to his empathy for the poor and downtrodden. One small example of the new Pope's generosity especially resonated with Irish viewers. It was a gift given by the Pope, 'at his own expense', it was stressed, to all of Rome's prisoners – all 2,635 of them. It was a special meal to be served on his coronation day:

> Ham and salami with pickles, boiled meat, spaghetti, green beans, a quarter of chicken with fried potatoes, two peaches, a quarter-litre of wine, coffee, ice cream. And five cigarettes.

Viewers crowded close to their sets. The first two hours held their rapt attention. Then, just as the crucial point was reached and the coronation was to take place – their screens went blank! In exasperation, people jumped up to bring it back to life. To no avail.

This distressing surprise was quickly explained: the Eurovision link 'unfortunately' could not be maintained a minute past 8:30 p.m., for contractual reasons. However, a recording of the ceremony was made, and it would be shown later that night.

Both of the weekend's long-awaited events had been marred by surprise and disappointment.

———

On the first day of July meteorological data for the month of June was released. Because of the torrential rainstorms, flash floods and lightning, there was far more interest than usual in the report. Statistics verified that, during the sudden and enduring thunderstorm of 11 June, rain was indeed falling at a rate of over an inch per hour in many places. At the rain gauge in Ballsbridge 3.85 inches was recorded. At Mount Merrion the rainfall amounted to an astonishing 7.25 inches – 'greater than any previously recorded amount in such a short span of time', the Meteorological Office reported.

Thunder and lightning could not be measured in so precise a manner. But older people confirmed that it was the worst in living memory.

Ireland's weather experts could not promise that the violent weather was over for the remainder of the summer. In fact, climatic conditions were still somewhat unstable and therefore unpredictable. There were still accounts of sporadic abnormal lightning activity. Everyone could only hope that July and August would have pleasant and safe weather for all the coming outdoor events.

———

On 2 July, Relko was back in the news. Reporters had been digging deeper into the puzzling case. The *Evening Herald* published an article entitled 'Signs of strange ailment'. The horse's trainer, François Mathet, had been asked point blank for an explanation. He was the one who had called it a strange ailment – which revealed nothing to the press. Such a vague answer was not satisfactory to journalists. Had the horse been examined by a veterinarian? Had his urine been tested? Was there any history of such ailments?

Well, Mathet replied, everything appeared perfectly normal. Only minutes before the race, the horse was 'in very good shape' in the paddock, and his canter was excellent. But then 'things rapidly went wrong'. While he was trotting 'he went lame … then became worse'. By the time he reached the starting-post 'he literally could no longer trot, his left rear leg was stiff … and there was no way of knowing why.' Yes, his urine was normal, Mathet answered, implying that it had been tested.

Mathet then told reporters that, only a few hours later, 'by Saturday evening', Relko no longer limped.

That's all he knew: he was a horse-trainer, not a scientist. He was as puzzled as anyone. He summed up by saying that there was 'no indication of *why* the horse suddenly went lame.' After which statement Mathet 'could not be reached for further comment.'

By now, many people saw the sudden 'ailment' – and miraculous recovery – as so suspicious that they believed something nefarious had to be afoot. A conclusive report by the Turf Club, the sport's governing body, was promised in a few days. It would present the medical findings of the case. Such evidence would hopefully identify what was behind it all – and solve the 'Relko riddle' once and for all.

————

On Wednesday brilliant sunshine brought out Dublin's shoppers and pedestrians in droves. It was also the perfect day for ten thousand small grocers and other traders to march through the city to demonstrate their opposition to the new turnover tax and the invasion of British supermarkets. They came from every county, closing up their shops. In some towns, including Mullingar, Ballinasloe, Navan, Tipperary and Portarlington, other traders shut down their shops in support. Business almost came to a standstill. Their demonstration was nearly a mile long. The *Irish Times* called it 'one of the largest protests staged in Dublin in recent years.' Public sentiment was torn: while they wanted to support their local small grocer, they also wanted to aid their families with the economic advantages offered by supermarkets.

Under the energetic leadership of Leo Keogh, secretary of RGDATA, the traders condemned the tax on the grounds that it impinged on their rights and was 'unjust and unfair!' They promised rebellion, carrying placards reading *We are traders, not tax collectors* and *Traders of Ireland, unite – Oppose unfair turnover tax*. They marched to the Department of the Taoiseach, where they delivered heaped baskets of protest notes.

Their most evocative slogan was *Turnover tax sounds the death knell of small traders*. As they saw it, they faced extinction.

While they received much local support and sympathy, they knew the odds were stacked against them in defeating the Government. It did not help their cause when, only a few days later, the highly influential *Irish Banking Review* wrote that it favoured the turnover tax on the grounds that 'a new method of indirect taxation' was necessary for the health of the national economy.

——

Only a few days into July another threat alarmed the general public. It began with a small notice placed obscurely at the bottom of a page in the *Irish Independent*. It was titled 'Well-known theatre to be sold'. Since business properties in Dublin changed hands all the time, it is likely that most readers skimming the page didn't even take it in. However, those who took the time to read it more carefully were struck when they saw the name of the theatre: the venerable Olympia Theatre in Dame Street:

> One of the best-known theatres in these islands … it will go up for public auction in the autumn, if not sold in the meantime.[120]

Reporters converged upon the theatre to ask Leo McCabe, joint manager with Stanley Illsley, why the Olympia was being sold. He had no comments to make. They then asked the question on the minds of avid theatre-goers, who were highly distressed by the unexpected news. When sold, would it still be a theatre?

He could not say.

It had been only a year since the grand old Theatre Royal in Hawkins Street had been shockingly demolished before the eyes of all who loved it, to make way for an office block. Now the Olympia could become a similar target for profiteering developers.

'Hands off the Olympia!' quickly became people's cry.

Every newspaper reacted with strong opposition to any plan to harm the Olympia. All cited its long and illustrious history. The *Irish Times* declared that the desecration or destruction of the theatre would constitute a moral violation:

> For over 80 years (since 1880) this great theatre, where many famous actors and actresses have appeared, has played an important role in Ireland's theatrical life … and its site has been associated with entertainment since before 1800.[121]

Unfortunately, records of the earliest theatrical days on the site had been destroyed in the fire at the Four Courts in 1922. But it was known that in 1834 the Widow Quinlan's Free and Easy had been on the spot. Over time it had changed hands and names but always continued as a place of entertainment. McCabe and Illsley became directors in 1951. It was renovated in 1957 at the considerable cost of £45,000. When newspapers began revealing its star-studded history, one filled with world-famous names – including Noel Coward, Dame Sybil Thorndike, Sir John Gielgud, Margaret Rutherford, Sir Alec Guinness, Tyrone Power, Paul Scofield, Noel Purcell, Robert Morley, Arthur Rubenstein, Beatrice Lilly, Peter O'Toole, Charlie Chaplin and Laurel and Hardy – the public were more determined than ever to protect it.

The battle to save the Olympia was under way.

––––

Throughout the first week of July violent weather erupted again, injuring people and taking lives. Lightning bolts were flashing, forking and striking throughout the country. On 1 July a ten-year-old boy, Noel McCluskey, had been visiting his grandparents when the sky flashed and frightened them. He sheltered under a tree with his brother and two cousins but was struck by a lightning bolt and killed. His brother, badly burnt, later described it as a blinding flash. It was part of a sustained thunderstorm.

In the coming days more reports came in about people being struck or nearly struck. Lightning was striking with an abnormally high frequency. To calm people's fears, the *Irish Independent* stated that 'the chances of a person being killed by lightning in this country are reckoned as millions to one.' Yet there would be *four* people killed by lightning in the first five days of July.

This startling figure was given a personal dimension when the newspapers attached names and stories to them. Gerard Murtagh, a fifteen-year-old, was cycling near his home in Cork when he was struck and killed. Timothy Hyde, thirteen, of Macroom, Co. Cork, was killed when lightning struck his father's house, where he had been sheltering.

But it was the case of James Scanlon that received the most graphic treatment. A twenty-year-old from Co. Mayo, he had been standing in a field with other men when he was struck. His friend Anthony Ruddy, who had been with him, related what had happened. When heavy rain began falling, the friends all put on their oilskin coats and sat on the boggy land waiting for the storm to pass. Then they saw Scanlon stand up. Ruddy then 'heard a crack and was stunned for about five minutes … When I recovered I saw him lying on the ground, his clothes ripped to pieces.' His rubber boots were torn, and portions of his clothing were scattered in the field some thirty yards away.

By the middle of July there was a growing feeling that in the summer of 1963 there was something amiss in the sky. It was serious enough that, as the skies continued to crackle with electricity, gardaí, ESB technicians and other outdoor workers were asked to keep a record of lightning strikes in their area. Garda Sergeant K. Derrane of Belmullet, Co. Mayo, jotted down that he was on duty in Muingmore when he saw a flash of lightning 'remain on the top of an ESB pole for five seconds', as if dancing wildly. It so unnerved him that he decided to return to his station.

Newspapers and safety authorities reiterated the standard warnings: stay away from such high points as trees, steeples, aerials, chimneys, corrugated roofs, wire fences – and keep out of ponds and rivers. But Dr McNulty, a coroner with experience in lightning deaths, also warned about safety *indoors*:

> Keep away from telephones, water taps, stoves, chimneys or other large masses of metal. Radio and television should be earthed … and water should be avoided.[122]

If people were at such risk in their own homes, where *were* they safe?

To these fears J. A. Culliton of the Defective and Dangerous Buildings Department added another. The explosive thunderclaps so often accompanying lightning had caused many decrepit and brittle brick buildings to tremble and weaken further. New cracks and loosened mortar could cause some to topple.

To many, the summer of 1963 would be remembered as an electrified summer.

———

Pigeon-breeders and racers also became victims of the summer's stormy weather along the east coast. In early July they had sent out their most valuable birds for a race from Saint-Malo in north-western France back home to their lofts in Ireland. When severe weather arose off the Irish coast many of their prize pigeons became disoriented and got lost. It was a big-money race, as the prize amounted to £5,000. Worse, they were to lose some of their most valuable animals:

> Racing pigeon fanciers all over Ireland stand to lose thousands of valuable birds believed lost in a storm while racing to lofts all over the country in exceptionally bad weather.[123]

For days thereafter the skies were anxiously scanned for signs of returning survivors. Indeed, a few valiant birds did drop to their lofts, but so emaciated that they were barely recognisable.

———

Finally, on 6 July, there was an official explanation of the controversy surrounding the racehorse Relko, in the form of a report by the Turf Club. Everyone was hoping that their medical findings would solve the mystery. Their conclusion, released to the newspapers, was brief:

> Relko was not doped. This was revealed beyond all doubt by the laboratory where the samples taken from Relko were analyzed. It is positive that Relko's withdrawal was the result of some natural cause … Some suspect a liver complaint.[124]

Contrary to their assertion, it did *not* remove all doubt. Many continued to suspect foul play, with good reason. What 'natural cause' could appear so suddenly, at the starting-post, and then completely vanish a few hours later, with no treatment? What extraordinary timing! expressed sceptics. To most, it would remain the unsolved 'Relko riddle'.

In his article 'Relko: chances of a parallel remote', the journalist Tom McCormack offered a few last words on the subject. 'That the Relko incident will go down in history there can be no doubt.'[125] Half a century later, his prophetic words ring true.[126]

———

The public awaited further word on the fate of the Olympia Theatre. Everyone knew that business transactions in Dublin could take place clandestinely, the news released only after the deal was sealed. Even if the building survived, the *Irish Times* stated, 'it is a matter of conjecture as to whether or not it will continue' as a theatre under new owners. If not, it would be a serious blow to Dublin's cultural life.

On 7 July the *Sunday Independent* pitched in, noting that 'news of the sale has shocked the Dublin theatrical world and fears have been expressed that its future may not be as a theatre.' Yet, Stanley Illsley insisted:

> I cannot see any reason why the Olympia will not continue as a theatre – it will be a tragedy if it doesn't.[127]

When queried again about *why* he was selling the property he danced around the question, vehemently denying that the theatre was not a 'commercial success'. This made people all the more curious about why he and Leo McCabe would want to sell it.

Wrapping up the interview with reporters, Illsley let slip a worrying comment that the auctioneers had already received enquiries about the sale from 'cross-channel' interests. This bit of news greatly heightened apprehension. Such buyers could not have the same sense of attachment to the theatre.

People flooded the newspapers with letters, expressing grief and anger, and there were some love letters to the theatre, filled with poignant memories. One person surely spoke for many when they lamented that nothing was done to 'save the good old "Royal". We, the public, just let it go down – and *cried afterwards!*' The writer asked, 'Is the same thing going to happen with the Olympia?'

What was needed, however, were pounds, not pleas. In the early 1960s there were many business people and developers profiting from the economic boom. Yet they did not help in rescuing the theatre.

On 11 July the *Evening Herald* in its editorial 'Crisis in Dame Street' considered the challenges of raising rescue funds. It was not an optimistic outlook, but several good ideas were proffered:

> We wonder if the Olympia can be saved. We suggest an influential group calling themselves 'Friends of the Olympia' might be formed. Bord Fáilte, too, could be asked for help. Could the Olympia not be

bought by Radio Éireann as a concert hall, hired out for plays? Every avenue should be explored.[128]

Even if vigorous rescue groups were formed, time was not on their side.

———

By July the game of bingo had reached the status of a craze. Its astonishing expansion in Dublin, Cork, Limerick and elsewhere was a significant social development for many people, especially women, who began making it a weekly habit to head out with a few pals to play. It freed them from the shackles of housework, slaving away while their husbands enjoyed their 'entitlement' to the pub, gambling and sports matches. Many men did not approve of the new women's night out. Men hypocritically condemned bingo as 'gambling' or 'gaming' – not suitable for decent women. However, priests who had at first preached against bingo when it appeared were now coming to welcome it into their parish halls when they learnt of the money it brought in to them.

Coinciding with the rising popularity of bingo was the decline of 'men only' pubs. It was a social transformation. After bingo sessions, some women found that they enjoyed a stop for a drink on the way home. This, of course, further irritated many husbands. But there was no turning back the tide of social change in the sixties.

To fully appreciate the significance of this social and cultural transformation, one must view it in historical perspective. Pubs had always been men's sanctuaries. As they saw it, it was an escape from cramped quarters or domestic stress. As James Higgins, a regular at O'Dowd's in Stoneybatter, put it:

> a pub is a man's domain … A working man deserves his relaxation – it's his safety valve! It was almost unknown for a woman to go into a pub; it was *verboten*! She would be looked down upon by her neighbours.

May Hanaphy, born in 1908 in the Liberties, agrees:

> It was a man's world then. The pub was a way of life for them. The old pubs, they weren't fit for women, they weren't nice. Oh, a woman would be *murdered* if she was caught in a pub. It was a disgrace for a woman!

The only exceptions were for elderly women and tough street dealers who would ensconce themselves in a little snug and drink without disturbance. Máirín Johnston, now eighty-five, grew up in the Liberties of the 1930s and remembers that:

> grannies could go in because they were beyond sin! But they wouldn't be served a pint: they'd drink a bottle or get their baby Power's [whiskey] … have a little jar in the snug.

This segregated world of the pubs survived largely unchallenged until the 1950s, when there was a slight change in attitudes, but at a glacial pace. In the liberated atmosphere of the 1960s, however, change was dramatically accelerated. Frank Fell, executive director of the Licensed Vintners' Association, explains that the:

> changes in pubs came very quickly in the beginning of the 1960s when more liberal views began to take over. One of the first things to go was the 'men only' pub.

By 1963 the chauvinistic havens were falling like dominoes. There were still, however, those stubborn publicans and their regulars who refused to open their holy ground. Some of these pubs were picketed by women. It was a challenge to men who were protective of what they saw as their last bastion of independence. Bingo-playing women would not be served.

The last men-only pub to hold out in Dublin was probably Walsh's in Stoneybatter. As late at 1988, Tom Ryan, head barman for fifty years, still groused that:

> it's a *male* preserve. Men prefer to be on their own. I know this from experience! Women just wouldn't fit in.

A year later the owner ordered that women be served. Ryan retired soon afterwards.

The social transformation of pubs meant improving interior features. They were made cleaner and more comfortable, women's toilets were installed, and there was to be better carpeting, lighting and ventilation. Pubs were made to meet modern standards of safety and sanitation. By drawing in women, and even tourists, the traditional pub culture was inevitably changed. In many cases the old regulars who had been unwilling to change their ways found to their surprise that they could still enjoy camaraderie with their mates.

———

In July at least one tradition was surviving, though it was hardly a controversial one. In fact, it was barely noticed by many people.

The annual ritual known as the 'blessing of the buses' was still being carried out by CIE. This year's ceremony was held at Merchants' Quay, with the Rev. Killian Mattimore officiating. CIE officials watched reverently as if it were a procession of schoolchildren making their First Holy Communion. The parade of buses, washed and cleaned for service, rolled past.

Though the *Irish Independent* sent a reporter and photographer, the event was given only scant notice in the paper. While some might have mocked it as anachronistic in the 1960s, it nonetheless had a certain charm of bygone days.

If this ceremony was civil and serene, however, duty on board the buses was quite the opposite. For some it could be nightmarish. During the summer months of 1963 the beleaguered drivers and conductors feared being attacked by gangs of teenage hooligans who would barge onto a bus and terrorise crew and passengers. By mid-July several conductors had been beaten, kicked and stabbed. Passengers had been cursed at, knocked about and intimidated. Because this behaviour was regularly reported on in the newspapers, people were growing fearful of using buses late at night, especially on weekends.

CIE officials faced a crisis. Some of their drivers and conductors were suffering from bad nerves and insomnia – even heart problems. Finally, Dublin's most famous garda, Jim 'Lugs' Branigan, and his imposing squad had to be called in to quell the threats and violence. This sometimes meant that Branigan himself would board the bus and take a seat at the top to await any teenagers intending to bully others. Spotting Branigan, and fearing his tactics for dealing with hooligans, they fell as meek as lambs.[129]

The city's motorists, meanwhile, were enduring their own form of stress. In the third week of July, after due forewarning, the Garda Commissioner announced that the dreaded parking meters were being installed on some streets in the city centre. And the gardaí intended to strictly enforce them.

This marked a drastic break with tradition. Motorists had previously parked their vehicles almost anywhere they wished – and for as long as they liked. Sometimes for days. Now the Government was 'interfering' with this right. O'Connell Street was logically chosen as the test area, as there was already a supposed two-hour parking limit along the middle of the street. This was little better than a joke to many, especially to big shots with connections to Garda brass. Now, with the installation of expensive parking meters similar to those in London and New York, restrictions were a more serious matter. How were shoppers, business people and entertainment-goers supposed to carry out their affairs hampered by a ticking meter?

———

On the 17th, bingo was front-page news as it made the giant leap from small local halls to large venues. The first such venue was a cinema theatre with a capacity of more than a thousand. The prize money skyrocketed.

It began when G. Kearns, manager of the Apollo Cinema in Sundrive Road, decided to experiment by devoting Friday nights to bingo sessions. The city's other cinema-owners watched with great interest. When 'bingomania', as it was now being called, took off, other cinemas were sure to follow. Kearns noted that already in Britain 'a lot of suburban cinemas have regular bingo sessions'.

Critics complained that a cinema was meant to be a *cinema*! Unapologetically, Kearns replied that 'we are in the *entertainment* business: whatever people want we will give it to them.' He added that cinemas could provide comfortable seating, good lighting and a warm setting in winter.

Bingo was about to hit the stratosphere.

———

While women were flocking to bingo sessions in record numbers, men preferred their sporting events. On 28 July a large, enthusiastic crowd gathered in Co. Meath to watch a highly anticipated hurling match. It promised to be a spirited clash between Killyon and Kildalkey in the intermediate hurling final.

It began with intensity and some rough contact. When fouls were called against both teams, some players protested. Some vociferous fans shouted their protests, further igniting the emotions of the players. Tempers really flared when some intentional illegal contact began.

An *Irish Times* reporter watched with dismay as traditional fair play and civility disintegrated. The referee's demand for a halt to fouls was ignored as the fray spread among both teams. Then the players 'attacked one another viciously with their hurleys'. Some fell to the ground injured and bloodied. To stunned spectators it looked more like a brawl than a match.

The brave referee made an effort to halt the violence – but suffered cuts and bruises himself in the act. Play was called off and the Gardaí called in. By the time the fighting ceased, ten players had been injured, some seriously enough to require treatment in hospital. The referee shouted, 'They acted like *savages!*' He swore that he would never referee again.

The disorder made the front pages of the newspapers. GAA officials were outraged and ashamed. Patrick Conway, former chairman of the Meath Hurling Board, called it the 'most disgraceful incident' ever to have taken place in a Meath GAA contest. Patrick Everard, the chairman, told reporters that it made one 'ashamed to be associated with the GAA'. In his opinion, the 'worst feature' of the incident was that the players struck one another with their hurleys – and not their fists!

———

A more significant fight was meanwhile developing in Dublin, and there was a likelihood that it would be prolonged. It was to capture the headlines: 'Publicans will fight Guinness's'.

A formidable battle was emerging between the mighty brewer and the legion of powerful Dublin publicans – a struggle over the fabulously profitable ownership of the city's pubs.

It stemmed from an announcement by Guinness that it had purchased three pubs in Cork. It intended to buy more licensed premises in Dublin. Rumours were rife that it was intent on grabbing all the pubs it could get its hands on in the city. Publicans cited evidence to verify this fear. The Publicans' Association and the Licensed Grocers' and Vintners' Association responded sharply:

> Any attempt by Guinness to break into the retail trade will be resisted by the licensed trade in Dublin. Our members must see that the trade they have built up will be protected.[130]

Publicans quickly reminded Guinness that they formed a solid force of over 300 members ready to do battle if necessary. In recent years they had worried about Guinness trying to invade their trade by putting the squeeze on the 'little men', then working their way up, aiming to monopolise it. In July 1963 they sent a clear message to Guinness: publicans were not to be bullied. If necessary the dispute could be nasty and protracted. The bad press could be extremely harmful to Guinness's sterling reputation – and to its brand.

———

On the evening of the 29th Dubliners enjoyed a performance of grace and beauty. The arrival of the Bolshoi Ballet from Russia had long been a fantasy for many. The Bolshoi had never appeared in Dublin, so to see them upon the Irish stage would be a rare thrill.

On the opening night, patrons of the Gaiety Theatre began arriving early to share the excitement with others. From the moment the music was heard and the dancers appeared, the audience fell awestruck, as described by the *Irish Press*:

> Immediately one was struck by the musical sensitiveness of all the dancers and their absorption in the matter at hand, whether in classical or traditional dancing. Everyone on the stage in the Khachaturian number danced brilliantly, and in the long and moving Adagio from 'Swan Lake' seemed to *live* the experience ... danced with sensitivity and elegance.[131]

Another critic agreed that they had just seen something truly fantastic:

> The 14 leading dancers of the famed company made history, and their performance far surpassed anything previously staged here.[132]

———

During the last three days of July, Dublin authorities experienced a midsummer's nightmare. The *Irish Times* announced it on its front page: 'Evicted tenants sleep in the street'. Seventy-eight tenement-dwellers from Jervis Street and Wolfe Tone Street had been evicted and dumped onto the pavement. There was no offer of alternative housing from the Government.

Reporters wrote that they found 'beds, chairs, sofas piled up beside the street-side railings ... including 18 children ... Women sat with their babies' in conspicuous despair. They had tried to set up shelters and cook on open fires.

Front-page photographs portrayed the scene of the dispossessed with ragged clothing, blankets, mattresses, boxes and pots and pans strewn about the street. To many it evoked historical images of cruel landlords and poor tenant-farmers.

The juxtaposition, on the front pages, of their plight and the Dublin Horse Show at the RDS was soul-stirring. Compelling articles about people who had been evicted drew widespread sympathy.

The following morning there was a large protest through the main streets of Dublin, comprising people who had been evicted and of sympathisers who were appalled by what had happened. They sought to capitalise on the timing of the incident, during peak tourist season, and expose the Government's treatment of the poor and homeless. Although every newspaper covered the march, the *Evening Herald* had an especially evocative headline: 'Protest in our streets ... and the pity of it all'.

As it happened, that day Ireland was having its first real heatwave of the summer. A meteorologist, dispensing with technical terms, described the weather as 'smashing'. The *Irish Independent* exulted in the fact that:

> it was sun all day for a change ... The whole of Ireland enjoyed brilliant sunshine and thousands left their homes for the seaside, parks and countryside.

Everyone was in high spirits, delighting in the prospect of August holidays just ahead.

Taking advantage of the weather, many tourists trekked off the main streets to explore the city. Some were curious to find the poorer areas that were being written about in the newspapers. One reporter, accompanying some of the tourists, recorded their impressions:

> Many of the city's visitors, astounded by these scenes, and the spectacle of families sleeping in the open, have been photographing these sights and commenting on what to them appears to be an amazing state of affairs.[133]

How could such conditions exist in Ireland in 1963?

Those who had been evicted had made large placards, one reading *Christian country.* Another likened the housing authorities to 'Boss Capone', referring to the American gangster. Cameras clicked away.

Just when it looked like things couldn't get worse for Irish authorities, they did. In a most unconventional editorial decision, the *Evening Herald* published on its front page some damning photos taken by American tourists. They showed the piteous expressions of the evicted families and their children living on the open streets. The photographs were proof of moral injustice and a national disgrace.

Chapter 14 ～

JUMPING FOR JOY

The August holidays were greeted with a sumptuous heatwave. In Dublin, the warmest place in the country, temperatures of 26 degrees were recorded as crowds headed for the beaches by bus and train. Shopkeepers depressed by weeks of wet weather 'felt a new hope as cash registers jingled merrily'. With temperatures high throughout most of the country, farmers were up at cock-crow to catch up on the backlog of work.

Summer holiday season meant the Dublin Horse Show, festivals, parties, sporting events, travel – and tourists. Motorists were warned by the AA to drive carefully and be aware that recently tarred roads were nearly melting in the piercing sun. Those enjoying the seaside were reminded not to take any chances while swimming and to be cautious about sunburn. Within days there would be an influx of tourists from Britain, Europe and America. Travel agencies were reporting record bookings as hotels and bed and breakfasts were filling up fast. No-one stood to profit more than publicans from the warm spell and the tourist invasion.

In the summer of 1963 the most enthusiastic attention was on the Dublin Horse Show, where the highly touted international showjumping competition promised to be exceptionally exciting. The *Irish Times* predicted that the Irish team was the best ever and stood an excellent chance of winning.

With everyone in high spirits, August seemed off to a positive start. Everyone, that is, except Dublin's fraternity of barmen. With the insufferable temperature and stale air behind the counter, theirs could be a hellish job. All the while they were working in a choking cloud of smoke. They longed for a few gasps of fresh air from the open doorway.

Publicans profited handsomely from this labour. Barmen had to subsist on paltry wages, working gruelling hours. In the summer of 1963, Dublin's 2,600 barmen worked a 45-hour week, with senior barmen earning an average of only £15 per week. Overworked and underpaid, they were ready to demand more. It seemed the perfect time to confront their bosses.

On 1 August, newspapers reported that barmen were demanding a more humane forty-hour week, a night off in six, and an agreement to negotiate a fair pay increase. The publicans, and their patrons, saw the writing on the wall – a perfectly timed pressure tactic, the threat of a strike never overtly mentioned.

Publicans grimaced and drinkers began fretting. The prospect of a strike at such a time was too distressing to contemplate. Nonetheless, most publicans at first stood firm in their opposition to the demands. One prominent licensed vintner vowed to 'fight this tooth and nail'.

Behind the tough talk was a memory of July 1955, when barmen did indeed go out on a costly five-week crippling strike in similar stifling weather. Now, patrons were nervous once again, though many were sympathetic to the plight of the workers. With the economic boom of the sixties, much of society was receiving higher incomes. Barmen were feeling left behind.

———

Meanwhile, Dublin Corporation was facing its own problems. After President Kennedy's visit, for which streets in the city had been tidied up, people had reverted to their old habits of littering. After only four weeks the city looked filthy once again. Around the time of the Dublin Horse Show city authorities always tidied up major streets and placed down colourful planters. But it was never enough to hide the fact that, once again, Dubliners were soiling their own nest during the summer months.

This prompted Bord Fáilte to conduct a survey among tourists, asking some 14,000 to give their impressions. According to the survey, 'the main stream of critical comment was directed against the untidiness in streets, accommodations and public toilets.'

Environmentally conscious Irish people wrote blunt letters to the newspapers lamenting the condition of the city:

I stood on O'Connell Bridge at 8:30 a.m. and along O'Connell Street I could see paper six inches high. A sad story. Unswept during the night or early morning. It is pitiful to look at.

On Henry Street even the biggest shops sweep out their premises right on to the road around 9 a.m. It's *appalling* … discarded lunch bags, cigarette packets …

It makes one weep.[134]

In the early 1960s Irish people were more than ever before able to travel abroad, many for the first time. Some confessed that they had never realised how *abnormal* Irish cities were in their untidiness. During the first week of August, J. Hennessy sent a letter to the *Evening Herald*:

I am amazed at the dirt of our fair city, and why something isn't done to eliminate such. I have just returned from holidays in several countries and nowhere have I seen such a dirty city. O'Connell Street is disgraceful. It is a pity such a lovely city is so dirty … I wonder what our visitors think of it all.[135]

This was easily enough answered. In greater numbers than ever before, tourists were complaining to Bord Fáilte and writing letters to newspapers. They wondered why Ireland seemed to lack an environmental consciousness. One wrote:

I am one of a party of Canadians visiting Ireland on a holiday. We all agree that hospitality is tops and your scenery beautiful. The *one* thing with which we did find fault was your appalling amount of litter on the streets of your cities and towns.

Dublin must be one of the most litter-strewn capitals in the world. Even main streets are strewn with newspapers, ice cream wrappers, cigarette packs … Oh, your country is too nice to be disfigured by litter. Bring out a law against the throwing of litter on your streets.[136]

It was a plea as much as a criticism. Visitors understandably assumed that there was no law against littering when they saw people so casually tossing it on the pavement – right in front of gardaí who paid no attention to it. To set this matter straight, the *Evening Herald* wrote a candid editorial, 'Keeping Dublin tidy':

Far too many people use our streets as litter receptacles and they are made unsightly by a litter of papers, cartons and other waste. Those who are so careless are liable to prosecution, but it is a long time since we have heard of anybody appearing in court for such an offence.[137]

And therein lay the problem: in 1963 the litter laws were never enforced, so no-one took them seriously. Did this mean that the Gardaí and the courts were really the culpable ones?

As a result, Dublin Corporation undertook a 'Hurry Up and Clean Up' campaign to give Dublin its holiday tidying. A better job was done of sweeping the streets. It would look jolly for August, even if it was not as sanitary as it could be.

To divert attention from Dublin's disgraceful homeless problem, authorities promised a new, luxurious Hilton Hotel in Santry. Efforts were made to interest would-be visitors in the £800,000 ultra-modern hotel. In the end, it would never be built, but promoters boasted that it would 'satisfy the requirements of the highest international standards'.

Henry Brennard of North King Street, who was unlikely ever to stay at such a hotel, wanted to make certain in early August that tourists were aware of some of the other parts of Dublin. He submitted a poem to the newspapers entitled 'The Homeless on the Streets':

Upon the streets the lonely lie
In grim determination;
Victims of modern Pompeii,
Caused by the Corporation.
The storm that lashed our city
Was made to bear the blame
For houses so neglected;
Their existence causes shame.[138]

———

There was one feature of the city that didn't lend itself to a superficial improvement: the filth and stench in the River Liffey as people crossed O'Connell Bridge or walked along the quays was all too evident. The same was true of parts of the city's canals. In some parts of the waterways the smell was nauseating. During the night – and sometimes boldly during daylight hours – people dumped every imaginable type of rubbish into the water: old tyres, mattresses, broken furniture, oil, car parts, chemicals – even dead dogs and cats.

Some parts had become contaminated. People complained, pleading with authorities to halt the abuse and clean up the water. Environmentalists never stopped appealing for help.

Parts of Dublin's rivers and canals had become so putrid that they were now health hazards. Nonetheless, children often couldn't resist them on a sweltering summer's day. During the first week of August a distressed mother wrote a letter regarding the condition of the River Tolka. She was primarily concerned about a tar-like substance in the water that stuck to the skin of her children when they tried to swim there. Parents had to scrape the substance off their children's bodies, she wrote, adding that some had surely got it in their lungs as well. When it was reported to the Corporation a spokesperson told them that it would investigate the matter. This was often followed by a statement that funds were not available at the present time for taking action.

––––

On 7 August other Dublin workers decided to follow the example of the protesting barmen. Some four hundred workers in the wholesale tea and wine trade, including porters, packers and lorry-drivers, announced that they too were seeking a forty-hour, five-day week. Their present agreement was an 85-hour fortnight with rotational Saturday-morning work.

Like the barmen, they were not explicitly using the term 'strike'. Yet.

The spectre of a joint strike in the midst of the holiday season was more than a little worrying: customers left without their pints and their tea?

––––

As the holiday crowds grew in early August, Dublin Zoo enjoyed huge attendance. This was also due to the zoo's exotic new attraction, just arrived, which the zoo superintendent, Dr Terry Murphy, called 'exceptionally rare'. He described it as a 'prehistoric' reptile, an almost extinct creature, to be seen wild in only a few parts of the world. Some zookeepers were referring to it as a 'living fossil'.

This was the tuatara, the sole surviving member of an order of creatures known to have been in existence 200 million years ago. It grows to about two feet long, with soft spines down its back. It certainly looked prehistoric – and quite frightening to many. It had been presented as a gift by the New Zealand Department of Internal Affairs.

It was an instant attraction for adults and children alike. On 5 August the zoo had the biggest day in its history, with nine thousand visitors. The 'prehistoric creature', as many people liked to call it, was suddenly the pride of Dublin Zoo.

———

Above all else in August, the Dublin Horse Show at the RDS reigned supreme. This was more true in 1963 than ever. 'The biggest and best yet!' acclaimed the newspapers. It was the most spectacular show since its first one some ninety-nine years before. Even the cautious *Irish Times* dared to predict victory for the talented Irish riding team, despite the superb teams from Switzerland and Germany that would also be competing. Within the RDS grounds excitement was percolating. The *Irish Independent* captured the mood:

> At the moment we are involved in a highly contagious social epidemic of international proportions called, in brief, the Dublin Horse Show. The epicentre is Ballsbridge ... and you will see horses and people from all over the world. All the world is here.[139]

The showgrounds in Ballsbridge had been finely combed. A chewing-gum wrapper indiscreetly dropped was quickly spotted and snatched up. Everything was smelling fresh and looking lovely. In the long rows of stables the leatherwork was being given a final polish.

That year there were 1,486 entries, for all events, a thousand more than were received for the first show in 1864. And people were awed by the variety of exhibitions accompanying the show.

Then there was the galaxy of social events surrounding the main event. It was a whirlwind of grand balls. Everyone had good reason to celebrate. As the 'Tatler' put it in his column in the *Irish Independent*:

> if I was to list all the functions that are going on in this city we would have to leave out all the news, advertisements and sporting.

While party-goers were having their fun, serious attention was on the international showjumping competition. Never had confidence in the Irish team been greater. Such confidence was founded on the fact that, for the first time, the team was to consist of both military and civilian members, each of whom was superbly talented. In the public's eyes they were unbeatable. This gave rise to boasting – before the jumping had even begun. Even the *Irish Times* was guilty of being brash:

> This is Ireland's year. Everybody knows that the re-cast Irish team is certain to win. Only the experts have reservations – and they are out-numbered by at least ten thousand to one.[140]

While such audacious predictions might have emboldened the public, they surely placed a great burden of expectation on the Irish team.

Whether the highly talented Swiss, German and British competitors read the Irish newspapers is not known. They were tough, talented and disciplined – accustomed to winning. On a good day any one of them could emerge victorious. Yet there existed a spirit of hope for the Irish team – one in which there was no place for failure. In an editorial the *Irish Independent* was prompted to wax poetic:

> The Dublin Horse Show is the Wagnerian climax of an equine symphony which opens with the crescendo of the Galway Races and the andante of Tuam. Then comes the largo of Leopardstown, the intermezzo of Mallow and Mullingar. Today the new and final movement begins, swift, colourful, with variety of theme.
>
> Our new jumping team gives the week an extra excitement as Dublin lives again the hours of glory it knows every year. Perhaps the Horse Show with its fantastically cosmopolitan attendance is the greatest of them all … The streets are a Babel of languages and East meets West in the wonder that is Dublin in Horse Show week.
>
> And all because the horse is king.[141]

The dream was winning the coveted Aga Khan Cup, the ultimate in showjumping prestige. And it had not rested in Irish hands since the 1940s. The *Irish Times* made it all the more suspenseful with their repeated predictions on the front page:

This year's Horse Show will be unique … For the first time in history Ireland's colours will be carried by a mixed military-civilian team in the Aga Khan Cup competition.

And none of the cautious predictions of the experts has diluted the growing optimism of the less expert.[142]

After which was repeated the prophecy that 'this is Ireland's year'. Any heretical doubters dared not state their view in polite company. The stars were aligned.

———

Not far from the stables was a social world in full swing. Some Ballsbridge residents waited all year for this festive week of parties and galas. To them, this was when the *real* social events of the year were held. But it would be only the elite socialites who would make the society pages. And, to certain of them, this was as important as winning the Aga Khan Cup – and no less competitive.

To appear in the society pages of the *Irish Times* was always a coup, which meant that the social columnist, Irene ffrench, was in greater demand than anyone else at social functions during the week. She wrote lively, flattering descriptions that delighted those lucky enough to be mentioned. She was attentive to social sensibilities, always endeavouring to give a fair amount of coverage where it was due. There was an art to her task, as she explained:

Racing at Leopardstown was one of the outings marked on many Horse Show visitors' engagement lists and it was followed by the customary cocktail parties. Some of the invitations clashed and there was something of a 'round' carried out by a number of people who were determined not to disappoint hosts and hostesses.[143]

Ah, the price of popularity during Horse Show week.

ffrench attended the 18th Cavalry Ball at the Gresham Hotel, featuring the Trinidad Steel Drum Band, with their fifty-gallon oil drums. One of the most exclusive social functions was the reception in Ailesbury Road held by the Swiss ambassador, Julien Rossat, and his wife. At such events ffrench was highly attentive to what one wore, especially women. Readers learnt that Lady Charlemont 'wore a charming pale apricot floral hat with multi-coloured floral dress and fur stole.' Later, as she proceeded on her rounds, ffrench wrote that at the 'delightful home of Prince Fernando d'Ardia Carraciolo there was an elegant party'. Princess Carraciolo received guests with her husband, she looking 'charming in a black slubbed silk dress with an almost U-shaped neckline adorned with pearls.'

Among that year's bashes ffrench found that, for sheer fun and frolics, the Kildare Hunt Cotton Ball at the Shelbourne Hotel took the prize. Its outlandish theme was that it was supposed to be a pyjama party. Guests were asked to toss aside conventional party dress – and even behaviour – and join in 'appropriately'. Journalists delighted in the silliness of the evening, one writing, seemingly aghast, that 'I spotted Lord Oxmantown in slacks and a jacket, cowboy-style.' While Lord Petersham, Lady Jane Stanhope and Lady Abena Stanhope were actually 'seen dancing the "twist"!' The *Irish Times* described the scene:

> It was an evening out where almost anything went. I saw a striped curtain worn as an elegant sari, a dish cloth used as an apron over black slacks, large gold-coloured curtain rings as ear rings. Gingham and denim made satin and brocade look over-dressed.[144]

For this event, creativity and humour were most in fashion.

———

Dublin's weather suddenly turned chilly and gloomy. Swirling winds at the RDS showgrounds made it seem even cooler. But Ladies' Day went ahead as planned, with some last-minute changes of outfits.

Elsewhere in Dublin, people enjoying the holidays were not troubled by the bit of chilly weather. Many flocked to the two blockbuster films that were showing. At the Metropole there was *Lawrence of Arabia,* starring Peter O'Toole; and at the Adelphi there was Audrey Hepburn in *Breakfast at Tiffany's.*

On 9 August competition for the coveted Aga Khan Cup got under way. The British, French, Swiss and German teams appeared unruffled by the bold predictions for an Irish victory, and their practice rounds were superb.

The competition began promisingly for the Irish team with Séamus

Hayes on Goodbye taking a clear first round. Then, early in the competition, the 'redoubtable partnership of Wade and "Dundrum" gave an impeccable performance'. This drew a flood of applause that filled the showgrounds and spilled out into Ballsbridge. Hopes were raised to a new high.

Then, however, came some 'outstanding performances by other teams', particularly the disciplined Germans and Swiss.

Irish nerves held steady. Tommy Brennan followed with a flawless ride – until 'he knocked down two fences before completing the course.' Some gasps were heard. At this point, spectators knew that it was going to be highly competitive.

The Germans and Swiss jumpers didn't flinch. The crowd now held their breath for every ride. Several European jumpers were unnervingly talented, and by the end of the first round Switzerland had 'pushed to the fore'.

In the second round, wrote one reporter, 'the thrills came quickly, as fences were toppled – or nearly toppled.' There was no doubt that Irish nerves were rattled. But the team toughened, gained composure and finally showed their mastery: at the end of the competition Ireland had five faultless rounds and a total of four faults, against Germany's eight faults. Germany was the runner-up. The *Irish Times* captured the moment:

> The roar that had been repressed by the Irish for 14 years broke over the crowded stands, as President de Valera stepped down from his box to hand the gleaming trophy to Colonel James Newlon, Chef d'Equipe of the team. The coveted Cup stays at home for the first time since 1949.
>
> The competition was everything we could have hoped for. The roars of applause that greeted this success testify to the delight the large crowd felt. The win was tonic for everyone.[145]

Had the competition not been so tight and dramatic, the win would not have been so thrilling – and so sweet. That evening the victorious Irish team celebrated at the Grand Hunt Ball at the International Hotel in Ballsbridge.

The next morning the *Irish Independent* gave full credit to the 'gallant Switzerland and German teams who battled so bravely throughout.' They had indeed made it breathtakingly close.

With the trophy won, the Irish team-members could finally relax. The editors of the *Irish Times* must have made a deep sigh of relief as well, having so audaciously predicted a certain win. Their great athletes got them off the hook. On the morning of 10 August the paper could hang out the huge headline 'Ireland wins the Aga Khan trophy'.

Hail the conquering heroes!

Chapter 15

A MACABRE MURDER MYSTERY

After Ireland's success at the Dublin Horse Show, everyone was basking in the glow of its success. Among them was the sixteen-year-old Hazel Mullen of Shankill, Co. Dublin. She had been able to earn some extra money by modelling at the Horse Show. It had been an exciting atmosphere in which she received attention and met new friends. It left her in high spirits, and she told her friends that she looked forward to modelling there again the following year.

A bright and reliable young woman who was said to 'look a bit beyond her years', Hazel had a good job at the Bank of Ireland in College Green. She worked five days a week and half a day on Saturday mornings. She was from a family of eight whose father, a sexton, had died a few years previously. Hazel's steady income helped her mother provide for everyone. Her siblings were close and very protective of one another. Her eighteen-year-old brother, Desmond, always took great care in looking after Hazel, of whom he was particularly fond.

She enjoyed picking up modelling work here and there, accepting only prestigious jobs. During the Horse Show, the highly respected Charles Ward Mills Agency employed a number of models to display fashionable clothes for some of Dublin's finer shops. Hazel fit perfectly the image they were seeking. She had a natural flair and was delighted when offered the job.

On Saturday 17 August she left the Bank of Ireland at 12:30 p.m. at the end of her working day. She told colleagues that she was going to have lunch with her boyfriend in Harcourt Street. As she walked towards Grafton Street she cheerfully waved goodbye to some of them. A few minutes later an apprentice printer at the bank, Karl Cowser, saw her going towards St Stephen's Green. He reported that she was walking quickly.

By Saturday evening Hazel had failed to return home. Or to phone her mother, which was most unusual. Her mother, Bridget, was always made aware of her movements, and her daughter was highly responsible. She decided to phone Hazel's boyfriend, Shan Mohangi, a student from South Africa. He told her that Hazel hadn't shown up for their lunch appointment. He too thought it was quite unlike her. They agreed to keep in contact.

As the hours passed and it neared midnight her family grew alarmed. They understood that it was a new decade, with a greater degree of freedom, and it was not that unusual for a teenager to go missing for a night. But such behaviour was so contrary to Hazel's character as to strain credibility. And she couldn't possibly have run away, since she was so happy with life and was devoted to her family. Something had happened.

For hours on Saturday night her brother Desmond, along with two of her sisters and some of her friends, had been out searching for her in the most likely places. There was no sign of her. Late that night her boyfriend, Mohangi, came over and joined the Mullen family to help and comfort them. He agreed to stay overnight and go looking for her again first thing on Sunday morning.

When the Mullen children returned with no word of Hazel, Mrs Mullen became frantic and decided to contact the Gardaí, who had become quite accustomed to reports of missing teenagers in 1963, especially on Saturday nights. They took down the information, filed a report, and promised to keep a lookout for her.

An odd incident that occurred on Saturday afternoon would soon be brought to the attention of the Gardaí. At first it seemed to have no connection with Hazel's case. In the middle of the afternoon a husband and wife had been walking past the Green Tureen restaurant in Harcourt Street when they noticed smoke coming from the basement. They immediately knocked on the door to alert those inside. The young man who opened the door seemed unconcerned, saying that it was only a smouldering rag on a burner. He was insistent in telling them not to notify the fire brigade. As the couple were speaking to him in the doorway, they detected a curious smell – a sickly odour.

He closed the door and the couple left. But they had both found his demeanour strange, so they decided to notify the fire brigade anyway. Firefighters showed up to find the man naked to the waist and sweating profusely. He told them that there had been a minor fire that he had put out. Pushing past him, they quickly made a check of the premises, finding the smells sickening but not suspicious.

At dawn on Sunday the Mullen family were up and in contact with the Gardaí. There was no news of Hazel yet. Bridget Mullen stayed home as her son Desmond and several others went out searching again. Later that morning a few inspectors came to the house to get more details about Hazel and her friends so that they could begin their background check. When they contacted those who knew her and worked with her a profile emerged of a kind, respectful, honest and hard-working young woman. A neighbour, Mrs C. de Vries, who had known the Mullen family for years, couldn't praise her enough, saying she was 'a *very* nice girl, light-hearted and high-spirited'. Eric Dillon, her office supervisor, told gardaí much the same, mentioning her maturity and reliability. 'We were all very fond of Hazel.'

When inspectors learnt that she had worked in a chemist's at St Stephen's Green before her job in the bank they had a talk with the proprietor, a Mr Brown. He told them that Hazel had worked there for eight months as a cosmetician, was very competent and was most pleasing to have around. She had informed him that she was leaving the job to 'better her position in life'. Though sorry to see her go, he quite understood.

Inspectors finally got around to asking Bridget Mullen about her daughter's boyfriend, Shan Mohangi. Well, she told them, she had not known him for very long and didn't really know much about him. In fact, she hadn't approved of him at first, mostly because of their difference in age: he was twenty-three – quite a disparity. But he seemed nice enough. It was the fact that he was a student at the Royal College of Surgeons that convinced her that he must be a decent young man. Gradually, she came around to accepting him. She further told them that he seemed to have a good work ethic, as he had taken on a job to help pay for his tuition. And where did he work? a garda asked. At the Green Tureen restaurant in Harcourt Street.

She added that there was one other fact that might be of some interest to them: Mohangi had an intense jealous streak.

————

On Sunday, Mohangi stayed at the Mullen house to console family members and join in the search parties for Hazel. He appeared to be fitting in with the family, ready to help in any way possible. He did, however, seem a bit nervous in the presence of gardaí at the house.

By the end of the day, gardaí determined that Hazel had last been seen between 12:30 and 12:45 p.m. in Grafton Street and St Stephen's Green, according to Hazel heading towards Harcourt Street and the Green Tureen to meet Mohangi for lunch.

On Monday morning Cecil Frew, proprietor of the Green Tureen, who liked to get to work early, arrived at 6 a.m. He was widely known in Ireland as the chairman of the Irish Boxing Board of Control and as a former university heavyweight champion. He was not easily shaken or frightened. Upon entering his restaurant he immediately detected a fetid odour and began trying to trace it. In the basement he was struck by a stench coming from the drains. Within minutes a discovery was made. The sight he came upon caused him to bolt out of the restaurant and run to Harcourt Terrace Garda Station to report it.[146]

Gardaí swarmed back to the restaurant and began to cordon off the scene as a number of detectives rushed inside. Detective-Superintendent Bernard McShane and Superintendent Thomas Culhane soon arrived to take charge. By 7 a.m. things were moving swiftly. Technical Branch experts were ordered to take control of the basement while the state pathologist, Dr Maurice Hickey, was called from Co. Donegal to perform a *post mortem* examination.

Meanwhile, gardaí were questioning Frew. When he told them that Shan Mohangi lived in a flat upstairs, several detectives hot-footed it up the stairs to talk to him. Knocking repeatedly without receiving an answer, they decided to force the door open. Mohangi was found on the floor unconscious, seemingly from gas poisoning. He was immediately removed to St Vincent's Hospital.

By now, reporters had got wind of the discovery and showed up outside seeking information. Anxious to get the name of the victim, they asked gardaí who were coming and going – but they were under orders to remain silent. One simply said they were 'having a hard time' with a positive identification.

Bridget Mullen was about to be struck a cruel blow. Shortly after 8 a.m. gardaí were on their way to her house to inform her of Hazel's murder. By an unfortunate coincidence, at the moment when her son Desmond was opening the front door to let them in, Mrs Mullen was in another room listening to the radio as news of Hazel's death was reported on the air. The family at once fell into shock. As gardaí comforted her, they refrained from giving her any of the grisly details of the discovery. She would learn soon enough.

By about 10 a.m. Mohangi had recovered consciousness and was taken to Harcourt Terrace Garda Station for interrogation. He was dressed in pyjamas and an overcoat. Nearby, at the Green Tureen, a crowd had gathered and rumours were flying. None of them yet knew the facts of the discovery. Chief Superintendent Leo Maher was assigned to take charge of the investigation. A highly respected and experienced officer, he had dealt with grim murder cases before – but never one so savage as this.

In the afternoon, Dr Hickey was apprised of all the details known at that early stage. He too had never faced such an unpleasant task.

Having sufficiently gathered their composure, Mrs Mullen and her son, as well as several other family members, were being gently questioned at home by several inspectors, who hoped to elicit helpful information. Many of the questions were about Hazel's boyfriend. Later that afternoon Desmond visited the Garda station to make statements.

One statement of Mrs Mullen's had particularly struck the garda questioning her. After telling them that she had known Mohangi for about ten months, she added that Hazel had recently mentioned to her that she was thinking of ending the relationship. And soon, apparently. Her mother didn't know exactly why. But there had been a few hints that she had met a boy she might like better.

Meanwhile, interrogators were finding Mohangi co-operative but nervous. He was telling them how much he cared for Hazel. Then the questioning shifted to his job. What was his position at the Green Tureen? Cook. Did it require some skill with sharp cutlery? Yes. What type of utensils did he use? Knives and cleavers. Saws? Sometimes. What were the knives and cleavers used for, specifically? Slicing and dicing meat.

Upon learning these details, interrogators informed the gardaí combing the restaurant to expand their search to include nooks and crannies.

On Tuesday the story broke. Most shocking was the front-page headline in the *Evening Herald*. 'Missing girl found murdered: dismembered body in café basement'. Such gruesome murders rarely occurred in Ireland. They were the stuff of horror films from America.

———

Later on Tuesday, Chief Superintendent Maher expanded his search
by sending a team of investigators to the dump in Ringsend. They were
equipped with digging gear. Corporation workers were also despatched to
the site to cordon off the area and assist the gardaí.

In the latter part of the afternoon came a startling revelation. A
spokesperson for the Royal College of Surgeons came forward to announce
what he believed was an important fact: 'Shan Mohangi was not a student
at the College – and *never had been*.'[147]

At eight o'clock on Tuesday evening Mohangi, a raincoat thrown over
his head, was driven from Harcourt Terrace Garda Station to the rear of
the Bridewell Garda Station. He was then taken through the underground
passage to Court No. 2 in the Four Courts, to face Judge O'Grady of the
District Court.

Mohangi took his seat. His hair was dishevelled, and during most of
the ten-minute hearing his eyes were downcast or closed. His arms were
crossed in front of him. At times he trembled noticeably. To observers, he
'remained slumped in the dock during the proceeding.'[148]

Evidence was given by the arresting garda. Earlier in the evening
Superintendent McShane had informed Mohangi of the murder charge he
faced. He was asked if he understood the charge, and he nodded his head.
Sergeant Doherty then asked him if he wished to reply. He stood by his
statement, which he had previously given to Doherty. Judge O'Grady asked
Superintendent Culhane to read the statement aloud.

'I want it all over quickly.'

At the end of the proceeding the accused was remanded in custody until
the following Tuesday.

On Wednesday morning the *Irish Independent* confirmed suspicions:
'Student on murder charge'. Except that it was now known to the Gardaí
that he had not really been a student at all.

———

With a pause in the case until Mohangi's next court appearance, newspapers
turned their attention to other matters. With the spell of warm weather
during the August holidays, motorists seemed to be driving faster and more
recklessly than ever. This was confirmed by the bloody statistics on road
injuries and deaths. The *Irish Independent* called the third week of August

a 'black week on Irish roads': twenty-four people killed and more than fifty injured. It was noted that, in two days alone, *nine* people lost their lives.

E. M. Deale, secretary of the Safety First Association, lamented, 'I cannot recall anything as bad!' Motorists were seen driving fast and furiously, cutting over the median line, swerving sharply, braking too hard and too quickly, failing to signal – and crashing. Many called it a 'massacre'. One alarmed reader wrote to the *Evening Herald* that:

> it is *appalling*! Behaviour on the roads is nothing short of a menace. The standard of driving is deplorable. And I am amazed at the indifference shown by the Gardaí to infringements.[149]

Laws were still lax, even for drink-drivers. And motorists were still not required to undertake training in order to qualify for a licence. As so many visitors simply put it, the Irish people just didn't know how to drive!

Nor did many know how to swim, even into adulthood. Unnecessary drownings continued in August. One person drowned in the Royal Canal within only feet of the bank. Off the coast of Sutton a dinghy capsized, which was a common enough incident. But, as the *Irish Times* wrote, it left a twenty-year-old man clinging to the upturned boat while having to 'watch helplessly as his father drowned' before his eyes. With every new drowning, the advocates of mandatory swimming lessons pleaded their case more strongly.

———

During the third week of August, Shan Mohangi awaited his appearance in court, on the 27th. Investigations continued at the Green Tureen restaurant and out at the dump in Ringsend. As a result, one newspaper printed the headline 'Gardaí switch murder search: clues may be in city dump', which spawned repulsive speculation. Gardaí assigned to the task were seen wading into the rubbish 'wearing overboots and old clothes' as they picked carefully through the mounds.

On the 22nd it was announced that there was a 'new turn in the murder case'. Garda authorities revealed that their investigations were not complete: 'it is now considered possible that further arrests may be pending.'[150] Did this mean that Mohangi might have had an accomplice? Gardaí would say no more.

Later that afternoon, a garda spokesperson updated reporters:

> The police had found in the floors above the Green Tureen restaurant
> other parts of the body. Gardaí continued their search at Ringsend
> for internal organs of the dead girl. The body was so completely
> dismembered that the State Pathologist had a difficult job in piecing it
> together.[151]

Owing to the growing complexity of the murder scenes, about fifty
detectives and Technical Bureau experts were now working on what was
being called an increasingly puzzling case. Readers who were riveted to the
mystery followed every step of the investigation, as if they were amateur
sleuths.

All the while, Mohangi's family, who lived in Natal, South Africa, knew
nothing of the murder charge against their son. No-one had bothered to
inform them. A garda spokesperson said it was not their duty to tell the
parents, unless specifically requested to do so. The South African embassy
in London said they had not been officially informed, and the honorary
consul for South Africa in Dublin, N. P. McEvoy, stated that 'he had no
information on the matter'.

Mohangi's father was a wealthy sugar farmer. His parents regarded their
son highly, praising him for studying at the Royal College of Surgeons. At
least, that's what he had told them. All his relatives were proud that he was
such a success in faraway Ireland.

But on 22 August all that changed. His parents were informed of the
charges, probably by Mohangi's solicitor in Mountjoy Prison, Herman
Good. The news greatly shocked the family. An aunt, Leela Mohangi, stated,
'He is a well-behaved boy, and very intelligent.'

The following day the Gardaí retracted their suggestion that there might
be further arrests. No accomplices were sought: they were confident they
had caught the lone murderer.

Dr Hickey had completed his examination and was able to determine
the cause of death: strangulation. Hazel's remains were removed to Crinken
Church, on the Bray Road.

Word came that Mohangi's parents and several other family members
were making plans to fly to Dublin to visit him in Mountjoy.

By the 23rd, investigators were completing their search for evidence. The Green Tureen had been swept clean. Some evidence had been found in the most unlikely hidden pockets. Out at Ringsend work was halted when it was determined that any remaining human fragments had probably 'been destroyed by vermin'. On that hideous note, the investigation was concluded.

———

Hazel Mullen's funeral took place on 24 August at Deansgrange Cemetery following a church service at 10:30 a.m. The chief mourners were her widowed mother and her brothers and sisters. The Rev. J. C. Coombe conducted the funeral service and officiated at the graveside, where he reminded those gathered that Hazel had been a 'nice, quiet girl' of whom everyone was fond. Her life had been cut short. She would be profoundly missed.

Shan Mohangi spent the day in his cell at Mountjoy awaiting his appearance in court.

On Tuesday 27 August, Mohangi left the cells and entered the dock, moving slowly, head bowed. Gardaí scrutinised everyone. No cameras were allowed. In a four-minute appearance at the District Court, before Judge O'Hagan, gardaí re-swore their depositions. Superintendent Culhane repeated what Mohangi had told him: 'I want it all over quickly.' His statement seemed to crown all the evidence compiled. Judge O'Hagan then announced that a trial would be required.

Mohangi's trial would play out over several days in the courts – and in the newspapers. The macabre details would test the sensibilities of those in court and of newspaper readers. Some details were more grisly than many had imagined.

———

On the day of the murder, 16 August, a Saturday afternoon, Hazel Mullen met her boyfriend, Shan Mohangi, for lunch at the Green Tureen. He let her in. But before they ate she wanted to talk to him about something. She was nervous as he listened. According to Mohangi, she expressed to him her wish to break off their relationship. Compelled by honesty, she discreetly revealed that she had an interest in another boy. She mentioned that she had already been intimate with him. Early in her relationship with Mohangi he had fallen into a rage when she told him she had once kissed another boy – before she had even met Mohangi. And he had been physically abusive in their relationship.

In court, under intense questioning, Mohangi confessed that hearing her words had triggered a jealous rage that consumed him. In his mind, she had betrayed him. He described lunging for her throat uncontrollably, squeezing it and keeping the pressure on until she went limp, then lifeless. He had lost his senses, he said, and hadn't meant to kill her.

He realised that there was no way he could dispose of her body without being seen. To avoid detection, he would have to dismember it. Remains would be hidden in different parts of the building. Some remains were collected with the refuse and taken to Ringsend or burnt on the premises.

His task complete, Mohangi felt satisfied that it had been accomplished cleanly and efficiently and that he would not be discovered.

He left the basement of the restaurant and climbed the stairs to his flat. And there he sat thinking. Then worrying. Only part of his plan had been carried out. Now there would be questions. He intended to tell Gardaí and Hazel's mother that she had failed to show up for their lunch appointment. Then he would feign worry, go to the Mullen home and help them with the search. That should cover him. Or so he thought on Saturday.

By Sunday, his confidence in the plan had weakened. He was growing increasingly fearful. Under a battery of questions from the Gardaí, how could he remain composed? Surely he would slip up and trigger suspicions. He began to feel trapped.

Early on Monday morning, feeling that there was no way out, he decided to end it all. Not long thereafter the Gardaí showed up and broke down his door.

It all came out in the courtroom during the trial. It would be deemed one of the most heinous crimes in modern Irish history.

Mohangi was found guilty and sentenced to death, but his conviction was immediately appealed. In January 1965 he was found guilty of manslaughter and sentenced to seven years' imprisonment. After serving only four years he was deported to South Africa.

The story hardly ended there. In fact, what occurred on his return home is one of its most extraordinary aspects. He immediately changed his name to Narentuk Jumuna. Still only in his twenties, he embarked upon a career as a successful businessman. Before long, he was enjoying a life of respect, wealth and comfort. Back in Ireland, Hazel's family had no knowledge of this remarkable transformation.

Next he decided to enter politics, serving as an MP for the ruling National Party until 1996. He lived not only in high style but with power and prestige. In 2009, forty-six years after his crime, he was nearing seventy years of age. In good health, he decided to run for election for the Independent Democrats.

But now it was an age when anyone could use the internet to uncover past history and events in seconds – and in detail. One of his political opponents decided to run a background check on Narentuk Jumuna – and then on Shan Mohangi. Suddenly he was exposed. On being confronted, he abandoned his election campaign and resigned from the party.[152]

Chapter 16 ~

UFOS, UNISEX, SHARKS AND A PRINCESS

In contrast to the tragedy of the Hazel Mullen murder that had been preoccupying the newspapers, there was some happy news on the front pages: the coming visit to Ireland by Princess Grace and Prince Rainier of Monaco. It would be a cheerful diversion. The visits of Grace Kelly always created an aura of glamour and excitement. Only a few years earlier she had been proclaimed the number 1 Hollywood film star and the 'most beautiful woman in the world'. Now she was a princess – one of Irish ancestry.

There was great excitement at Dublin Airport. More than five thousand admirers gathered to welcome Princess Grace and her family. When the door of the aircraft opened, the first person out was an energetic, smiling boy. The five-year-old Prince Albert was led down the steps by an Aer Lingus official. After shaking hands with Lord Killanin, the honorary consul-general, the boy looked around 'rather anxiously' for his mother.

When Princess Grace appeared, wearing a turban and a light-pink woollen coat, great cheers went up. Despite the cloudy weather she wore tinted glasses. She smiled and waved to the crowd. A reporter welcomed Princess Grace back to Ireland and apologised for the poor weather. 'It's great to be here anyway', she replied, smiling.

Prince Rainier soon arrived in a separate plane with his seven-year-old daughter, Princess Caroline. Right away, she 'took the limelight from her father … as most eyes were on the pretty little Princess in the halo hat.' From that moment, every 'women's reporter' would be attentive to mother and daughter's every outfit. The reporter for the *Irish Independent* described Princess Caroline, her hair in two neat pigtails, as 'trim as a posey'; she possessed every bit of her mother's charm. Clutching her favourite doll, she went 'skipping into the airport'. Quite accustomed to such attention, mother and daughter took it all in good humour.

More than seventy gardaí were on duty to cope with the airport crowds and with thousands more lining the route of their twenty-mile drive to Carton House at Maynooth, Co. Kildare, the home of Lord Brocket. It would be the royal family's base while on their three-week holiday. At the entrance to Carton House another cheering crowd of two hundred people met them.

From the outset, Prince Rainier and Princess Grace wanted to make it clear to reporters that they were in Ireland for a private holiday – no official business of any sort. It was to consist of sightseeing, visiting friends, horseriding, fishing and a bit of shopping. The press promised to be respectful. In return, the family assured them that they would pass along any items of interest.

The next morning Princess Grace awoke in high spirits, and she spoke to the press for a few minutes. Looking 'absolutely radiant', she exclaimed, 'I *love* Carton House already.' Young Prince Albert was already exploring what he called 'secret passages' in the great house in hopes that he might find hidden treasure.

The big story of the day for the hungry press was that the 'adventurous Prince almost fell into one of the ornamental ponds' on the grounds. Even the *Irish Times* would make certain that their readers heard of that newsworthy episode.

————

On the afternoon of 1 September, hurling fans were wildly excited about a huge match in Croke Park. It was the all-Ireland senior final, to be played before a crowd of 72,123. Kilkenny were facing Waterford, and everyone expected a fiercely competitive contest. Princess Grace and Prince Rainier, sports enthusiasts in their own right, were told all about the excitement for the final. Friends encouraged them to attend if possible, promising them that it would be an experience they would never forget.

As the Prince and Princess were escorted into Croke Park they were quickly spotted, prompting a great cheer. What a wonderful welcome, both said. Then they sat down to enjoy the 'pageant-like preliminaries': a colourful display featuring the Artane Boys' Band.

From the start, the game was a top-flight display of hurling. The royal couple were clearly enjoying it, even if they had to try hard to keep up with its pace.

At half time there was a surprise: the Artane Boys' Band broke into a lively rendition of 'I'm Off to Philadelphia in the Morning', a tribute to the Princess and her home town. She beamed and clapped.

The match lived up to expectations, so everyone said. Kilkenny won decisively, 4-17 to 6-8. One sports writer described it as being as 'exciting a final as ever has been played between two counties' – a perfect day for the royal couple to have been in the stands. Asked how she had liked the match, Princess Grace, who understood the fundamentals of the sport, replied that it was 'so fast … almost too exciting … It's marvellous.' Her husband was most impressed by the 'speed, skill and stamina' of the players.

Speaking candidly, Princess Grace told the gathered reporters that what she had enjoyed most was the performance by the Artane Boys' Band. 'They are *wonderful*! I have never seen a nicer band.'

——

September, normally a benign month, following the hectic holiday season, began with talk of a possible extra-terrestrial invasion of Ireland. 'Odd things are happening on the Hill of Howth', one newspaper stated ominously. These seemed to be strange, other-worldly occurrences.

The year 1963 had already had a spate of UFO 'sightings' around the world, particularly in North America, Australia, South America and parts of Europe. Some American films depicted an alien invasion in which 'Earthlings' were subdued or carried off. It was a hot topic in the early sixties.

Ireland, with its climate, was hardly prime UFO-spotting country. However, on the night of 2 September, shortly after nine, Brian Hipwell was driving through Clontarf when he spotted an 'unusual light' hovering over Sutton and Howth. It was so captivating that he stopped to observe it carefully. He later described it to a reporter.

> The sky was cloudy and I had just glanced over the sea in the Howth-Sutton direction when I saw a pale orange light. Rather elliptical in shape, and long. I stopped the car immediately in the lay-by and watched the light. I never saw anything like it before.
>
> The light was stationary for five minutes. As I watched, it seemed to move away quickly, upwards in an easterly direction. And then it disappeared in about *five seconds*![153]

The next day, news of the inexplicable sighting appeared in newspapers, generating speculation. However, a spokesperson at Dunsink Observatory declared, in a rather dismissive tone, that it was probably only 'the light of a cloud or some smoke illuminated by the sodium lights. Or a low-level cloud reflected by light.' To Hipwell, who had been precise in his account, this was a flimsy explanation. As he told the *Irish Press,* 'the night was windy and smoke or a cloud would drift – this light was *stationary!*'

The sighting stirred some lively discussion among the public, especially in pubs. Some believed it could have had unearthly origins. It was noted that the United States and the Soviet Union were already involved in space exploration, with plans for landing a craft on the moon. Perhaps they had provoked some response from those 'out there' in space. One journalist wrote mockingly, 'Could it be the "little people" from Mars?'

Hipwell preferred to just forget about it.

––––––

Throughout the summer months there had been rumours of an invasion of Ireland – of quite a different sort. It was to be carried out not by Martians but by Beatles. All four of them. It was sure to create a craze.

By early September, newspapers were lending credibility to the possibility of the Fab Four appearing on a Dublin stage some time in the autumn. Since the mid-fifties, when the rock-and-roll era began, young people in Ireland had fantasised about the big stars from America and Britain coming to Ireland – not merely on a cinema screen but in person. Inevitably, it was also rumoured from time to time that the 'King' himself, Elvis Presley, was to appear.

After all, President Kennedy had come, after much speculation and many denials. Once the papers printed a few titbits about the possibility of the Beatles coming, many young people began to believe it was legitimate. 'They're *coming*. It's a *fact*! Some time … *Soon!*'

––––––

The day after the report of Brian Hipwell's mysterious sighting had been met with contemptuous doubters, Niamh Moran of Sutton decided to step forward in support of his account. She too had witnessed the phenomenon at exactly the same time. She was out walking in Sutton when she clearly saw 'an eerie, pale light'. She stopped in her tracks. Her description perfectly matched Hipwell's, and she found the light just as mysterious as he had, and somewhat unsettling. She was certain that the Dunsink Observatory's claim that it was merely 'a cloud or some smoke illuminated' was flat-out wrong. She verified that it had remained perfectly stationary, before vanishing in seconds.

Neither Hipwell nor Moran were frightened, just mystified. They left the speculation to others.

———

Meanwhile, a new phenomenon was causing both controversy and complaints. Some newfangled concept called 'unisex' was taking over in some places. In America and Britain it had already invaded the barber's – and Irishmen had better beware. Male customers were being lured into mixed barber's, where men and women sat together to have their hair cut – and 'styled'.

It really became a brouhaha when the *Evening Herald* published an article with the headline 'Women employed as barbers?' It was the disbelieving question mark that really lit the fuse of debate in Dublin among its barbers.

Those who took the time to read the articles about the appearance of women barbers on what was seen as men's turf would learn that it was not merely a fad: there was an economic rationale behind it. Like their counterparts in America and Britain, Irish barbers by 1963 were finding it increasingly hard to draw young apprentices into their trade. Many young men found that barbering paid poorly and offered a dull life, stuck in a stuffy shop in the one spot all day. With the economy booming, almost every other decent job paid better wages. Hiring women barbers to fill the gap was a logical solution. Nonetheless, it involved a social transformation, especially for older men. To them the local barber's was much like the local pub: an escape where they found companionship and good conversation.

Throwing fuel on the fire, journalists began conducting their own informal interviews with men in order to get their opinion of the phenomenon. Opponents all gave the same arguments: the barber's was for 'men's talk', with their trusted barber. If you had women there, men would clam up. A terrible idea altogether.

One reporter decided to put the question to barbers themselves, concluding that 'in nine cases out of ten the answer was negative'. Peter Comiskey was one of the longest-serving barbers of the twentieth century.

Born in 1915, he rose through the ranks to eventually own the famous Waldorf barber's in Westmoreland Street. No barber in the city was better known or more respected. His regular customers included Jimmy O'Dea, Patrick Kavanagh, Brendan Behan and Ronnie Drew, as well as chief justices, sports stars and other luminaries.

In the 1990s, and still working at eighty-one, Comiskey sat down with the author to relate his memories. Asked about the unisex 'revolution' in the early sixties, he said he had an open mind on the subject, recognising the practical need for taking on women barbers. Yet he empathised with those older men who were upset by the change because it threatened their open expression:

> They tell you *personal* things, because they trust you – trust you and want to get something off their mind, to ease their mind. *Very* personal matters, I'll say that!

It was, he explained, a trust built up over decades, in which the barber became a sort of psychologist-confessor for certain customers. He understood that the introduction of women might intimidate some men. There were those who felt too shy to have a woman cut their hair. 'What would I say? What would I talk about?' they worried.

In 1963 Comiskey saw Ireland's traditional barber culture changing slowly. Yet he had the vision to see the future – that, before long, the presence of women would be accepted as a refreshing change.

It was one of the more peaceful social revolutions in Dublin during the early 1960s.

———

With Princess Grace and Prince Rainier settled comfortably in Carton House for their visit, people went on the usual 'Princess watch' in hopes of catching a glimpse of her – or even of encountering her in Dublin when she went for one of her frequent strolls. Whenever she stayed in Dublin for several days she resided at either the Shelbourne Hotel or the Gresham Hotel.

Ireland's love affair with Grace Kelly began long before she became royalty in Monaco. It actually began when she was Hollywood royalty – a spirited Irish-American woman from Philadelphia whose beauty and talent carried her to the zenith of stardom. Born in 1929 to an Irish-American family, Grace Kelly was forever reminded of her Irish roots by her father, John 'Jack' Kelly. He was a champion sculler who won three Olympic gold medals. Though well-to-do, the Kellys lived modestly, visited Ireland often and valued education and hard work. At first, Grace's father didn't favour her going into acting and not furthering her education. But once she arrived in Hollywood her ascent was meteoric.

By the mid-1950s she was starring in films with some of the biggest male actors of the day. In 1955 she won an Academy Award for her role in *The Country Girl*, playing alongside Bing Crosby. She carved out her own niche in Hollywood, where she was the epitome of beauty, elegance and refinement.

When she married Prince Rainier of Monaco her life changed for ever. Gone were the freedoms she had known. Her new life was regal and opulent but very confined. Visits to Ireland became a great escape for her. Here she was adored and people respected her privacy, so she could relax as nowhere else.

Whether at her hotel or out in the streets, she liked being among ordinary people for a change. Jimmy Dixon started as a page at the Shelbourne Hotel in 1946 at the age fourteen, rising to concierge during his fifty years there. Over the years, he had to deal with plenty of people who demanded a lot of pomp and ceremony when they arrived, but Princess Grace was always different:

> The dearest one we had here was Princess Grace. She was the *most charming* person I've ever dealt with in my life. She was really something! People would be waiting in the hall to have a look at her – and she would come down and say hello to them.
>
> I remember when she was going to Grafton Street and she wouldn't take the chauffeur-driven car – she *walked* down. She'd walk ... and meet people! She was the most beautiful lady ...

At the Gresham Hotel, Paddy Fogarty, the concierge, was just as fond of her, and for the same reasons. She had a warm, gracious and unpretentious manner. '*Every* famous person and film star stayed here ... but no-one as dear as Princess Grace', he says.

———

During the first week of September there was some grim reading in the newspapers when the statistics for road deaths in August were released. As predicted, it had been a black month, with a record forty-two deaths, well over one per day. As if that were not appalling enough, the first week of September alone added *eleven* road deaths. In a distinct understatement, the *Irish Independent* called it 'a bad start for September'.

A national epidemic of speeding, as some were calling it, was determined to be the principal cause of the deaths. Letters from distressed readers continued to flow in to newspapers, and some proposed ideas for improving road conditions. These ranged from common sense to the more unusual. The *Evening Herald* printed one letter, intended quite seriously, that was sure to be entertaining, if not enlightening:

> At the moment, the chances of being caught [speeding] are about 10,000 to one. Up to now, few Irish drivers looked down at their speedometers. If we *must* have a speed limit, then why not a differential one? Every different make of car is capable of a speed which is still safe. For instance, it is safer for a 30-year-old man to drive a Jaguar at 50 mph than for an 80-year-old man to drive a Mini at 25 mph. Therefore, why not set a limit for each make of car?
>
> Finally, taking driving tests – they are of little value. Or *no* value. Anyone who passes feels he can do anything with a car, and becomes careless. Secondly, no standard can be set for each individual who has his own opinion of what is a good driver ... and there is no proof that a speed limit prevents accidents. – 'Speed Merchant'[154]

If his ideas made some readers chuckle, they surely made others shudder.

Foreign visitors were becoming wary, if not fearful, of Irish motorists. Some American travel agents were warning their clients about the risks on Irish roads. The statistics spoke for themselves. Drink-drivers in Ireland were a menace. Many visiting motorists described Irish driving as a 'chaotic situation'.

P. Pennisk, an Irish driver, was also frustrated about road safety and public health. His contention was that Ireland's fleets of *buses* were perhaps even a greater threat to one's health: 'they rattle, vibrate and screech to a halt in a cloud of poisonous diesel fumes.' Inhaling such clouds regularly, he felt, was a greater hazard than the cars.

As with deaths on the roads, drownings continued at an alarming rate. In the first ten days of September five lives were lost in Irish waters. All were close to shore and probably preventable by elementary swimming ability. In one case an upturned boat on a mud bank led to the discovery of the bodies of James Sullivan and his nine-year-old son. The Sullivans' two dogs, which had swum to safety, were found standing on top of the boat.

———

The American swimmer Mary Margaret Revell, who had been in Ireland in April to make preparatory checks for her swimming challenge in Galway Bay, was one of the most accomplished long-distance swimmers in the world. In her challenge it was sharks that worried her most. They were always an unpredictable element. She consulted members of the Galway Bay Anglers' Club, who told her that the local shark population had been higher than usual, and 'now, with the water growing colder, sharks were more dangerous because they could not get their normal food.'[155]

In late July a Belfast man, Jack McClelland, had become the first man to swim across Galway Bay – the same twelve-mile course that Revell was to swim. It had not been without its risks and close calls. Indeed, during his swim 'a school of huge sharks came alongside the official's boat'. Without hesitation, McClelland's wife tried to persuade her husband to leave the water. Though he was himself worried, he forged ahead to finish.

For her swim, Revell would have the Anglers' Club launch, the 45-foot *Sea Angler,* with officials and reporters on board, following her closely along the way and keeping a watch for sharks.

While waiting for the right conditions for her attempt, she remained in Galway, where she was much liked, giving lectures to local groups. When she was informed of Ireland's drowning rate, she took up the cause of water safety and gave talks on the necessity of swimming lessons at an early age.

———

On 7 September the weather in Dublin felt positively tropical. At least, so it seemed at Dublin Zoo, where the Royal Zoological Society of Ireland was holding its first Carnival Night and Ball to raise funds for a new reptile house. The publicity generated by the zoo's present from New Zealand of the reptile tuatara meant that a far better reptile house was required.

Promotions had promised guests of the ball that they would feel as if they were in the Caribbean. There was to be lively calypso music in a 'tropical setting'.

When the big night arrived, some 1,500 guests were met at the main entrance of the zoo by chartered buses and driven to the marquee, where Donal Nugent's band and a calypso group, the Trinidad Steel Drum Band, performed. People danced and swayed to the tropical rhythms. Everyone seemed to love it. To show their appreciation, guests were generous in their donations. And, of course, everyone hoped that the exotic affair would become an annual event.

———

The following morning the weather in Galway interfered with Mary Margaret Revell's plans. The *Irish Independent* reported 'gale gusts and high seas', which 'foiled the 25-year-old American champion in her attempt.' She was disappointed, as were the reporters on the scene. She could postpone it for a day or two, but no longer, because she was scheduled to swim the English Channel the following week. She would be on stand-by, she promised, and would jump at the first opportunity.

The next morning, 9 September, Revell and her crew were up early and ready to go. There was finally a good forecast that favoured the swimmer. Word spread quickly in Galway: the American swimmer was going for it!

After being transported to her starting-point at Black Head she consulted Noel Hickey, skipper of the launch that would accompany her. He assured her that he was carrying a shotgun, which he would have in hand at all times during the twelve-mile crossing. Dr J. Haskins would be ready to treat her if anything went wrong. A last check confirmed that the weather and tide conditions were very good.

After a final few good wishes, she slipped into the sea. Slowly and then steadily she began to swim at 2½ miles per hour. All appeared to be going perfectly according to plan.

Revell was the first to spot the sharks. She had had encounters with many species of shark over the years, enough to know that sharks of any species drawn by flapping on the surface of the water were to be taken seriously. Their unpredictability was one of their most fearsome traits. Even sharks usually harmless to people could betray their reputation. And certain varieties of shark can appear in waters not normally part of their territory.

The blue shark, which can be dangerous to humans, had not been seen on the coast for more than a century, but in the previous two months 'two large specimens' had been caught in Galway Bay.[156] Revell had been informed of this anomaly only shortly before her swim.

At the speed at which she was swimming she could arrive safely at Salthill in about five more hours. Her first sighting of sharks had not halted her swim, but it had caused her to watch with more caution. Anything within fifteen feet she considered perilously close. Everyone on board the launch could confirm that the sharks being sighted were definitely not basking sharks, which pay no attention to humans.

It was only when the unknown type of shark 'moved directly towards her' that she first felt alarm. She would later say that the 'shark that approached looked like a tiger shark', which could be dangerous in waters where they could not get their normal food. Nonetheless, she continued her swim.

Twenty minutes later a very large shark came too near. She was completely vulnerable. After a few minutes she motioned to the launch that she wanted to be hoisted out of the water – and fast.

Reporters on board several boats were keeping a close eye on developments. Their stories would claim that blue sharks had showed up. The *Irish Independent* described:

> a dramatic ending to the attempt of a woman to swim Galway Bay. Revell was forced to abandon her attempt when Blue Sharks began to circle her.
>
> Miss Revell was pulled out of the water in a shocked condition and taken to Galway where she was given sedatives at the dockside by Dr J. Haskins.[157]

The following morning she confidently told friends and reporters that she 'would be back to swim Galway Bay next year' but that she would bring 'a team of US Navy frogmen with her,' adding that 'they would be equipped with spear guns and would rotate around her as she swam.'

Then she packed her bags, bade farewell, and headed for the English Channel.

———

As Galway Bay was fading from the news, Dublin Bay grabbed the headlines. Dock workers were on strike again. The dispute was over one ship, the Swedish vessel *Neva*, tied up at Alexandra Basin. The Dublin Master Stevedores' Association claimed that two gangs of eight men should unload the cargo, but the Marine, Port and General Workers' Union insisted that each of the gangs should be composed of twelve men. For the second time in two months, all work at the deep-sea end of the port was halted.

Meanwhile, a new export business was developing. It involved the simple collecting and selling of bags of stones. The idea was floated in early September when the Mayor of Limerick, Frances Condell, shared with the press a letter she had recently received from an American organisation. They were 'looking for Irish stones'. The letter she received went on:

> Several weeks ago one of our friends picked up 25 stones near the airport and gave them to us. We put the stones on sale and found that there is a demand for *real* stones from 'Old Ireland'.[158]

The head of this organisation requested stones of about three-quarters of an inch to an inch and 'rather smooth', such as could be found 'at the beach or in a stream bed'. The letter ended by assuring Condell that they would of course 'come to an understanding as to the payment for the stones.'

Was it American ingenuity – or absurdity? A new opportunity for the Irish export trade? When Condell was asked by a reporter what she thought of the proposition, she replied, 'What's next!'

———

By September, bingo had really taken off. Large cinemas were filled with 'bingomaniacs' enjoying the fun of the game and the socialising that went with it. Great profits were being made by organisers and proprietors. It was becoming part of Dublin's culture, changing family life and social patterns. Men were flummoxed by the new freedoms women were enjoying and by their absence from home in the evenings. Some men declared bingo to be a 'menace' and beseeched the Church and the Government to put a stop to it. On 25 September the *Evening Herald* published a letter of condemnation, titled 'The bingo menace', from an angry husband:

Why does the Government allow this bingo stunt? Of all the gambling systems known over the past 40 years, bingo is the worst menace we have here, more so as it is women who go for it.

In Britain, we are told by visitors who come here, the game of bingo has been the cause of more broken homes than any other form of gambling … It is not an uncommon sight to see women crying outside of bingo halls after losing the household money. Stop it here, before it is too late.[159]

Women dismissed such grumblings as no more than pure hypocrisy. As one woman plainly put it:

most men spend more money on drink, cigarettes and gambling every night of the week, while the 'little woman' of the house works a long day, looking after the house and needs of the family. And she will come home after bingo and a drink with her senses, and maybe with a little profit for her night out – instead of a growl and abuse [from her husband].

Elizabeth McGovern, a teacher, noted that, after the bingo sessions, 'mothers could go to the pub and *enjoy* themselves, even if tomorrow they had to face their troubles again!'

————

In Dublin on 16 September there was the sound of several thousand dockers' boots marching in protest, accompanied by five trade union bands. Jimmy Dunne, general secretary of the MPGWU, who led the march, gave a forceful speech.

Thirty ships were now immobilised, a number of them carrying cargoes of perishable fruit. A fortune was being lost. In an impassioned editorial the *Irish Independent* conceded that both the union and the employers 'have some cogent points' to make, but the livelihood of thousands was at stake:

The union leaders are not wild men, and the employers are not out to grind the oppressed. But something is wrong at the root – and it is time it was diagnosed and cured.[160]

If emotions among the dockers were running high it was not solely because of the new strike: a far more significant and threatening change was looming. As new technology modernised work at the docks, they foresaw their own demise. Throughout Ireland many of the old crafts and trades were being rendered obsolete almost overnight. Workers saw it happening at Guinness when the new metal casks, known as 'iron lungs' or 'depth charges', were introduced, dealing a death blow to coopers. Shoemakers, saddlers, stonemasons, sign-writers and others were being replaced with new technology. Everything, it seemed, was becoming mechanised.

By 1963 this was a fearful spectre for dockers – among the proudest occupations in Ireland. Martin Mitten was one of the protesting dockers. Born in the 1920s, he became a fourth-generation docker at the age of fourteen. It was in his blood, he liked to say. But he foresaw that his was the last generation – the one to witness the death of his occupation:

> The docks, it was full of *life* … a terrible interesting life. Oh, but the writing was on the wall! It was 'containerisation' – the idea of roll-on and roll-off ships. That was the beginning of the end. I used to see two thousand of us doing the work – and then only 150 dockers. Just *imagine*! Oh, some men were kicking up murder – they wanted to stop it!

Others saw that such tactics were doomed to failure. You couldn't hold off modern technology: it was progress.

Most dockers were realists who recognised that their day was gone: a new era was upon them. But realising their fate and *accepting* it were two different things. Willie Murphy, who went to work at the age of fourteen in the 1920s, knew his destiny. It was heart-breaking, as he recalled in the 1980s:

> The docks in my younger days … it was *magic*! Fantastic activity! Never a dull moment. I saw the end coming, first about 1961 with palletising cargo, then the forklift trucks … then containers coming in. 'Too many men on the docks!' Dockers started realising what was happening to them.
>
> Now it's gone. It's terrible sad. It was part of history. I go over there and, now, to me, it's a graveyard.

———

On Sunday 22 September there was unbridled excitement in Dublin for the all-Ireland football final. For weeks, supporters had had their expectations heightened by journalists who assured them that this would be one of the greatest matches of the century. Two superb teams, Dublin and Galway, were seemingly evenly matched. The sports pages were filled with analyses and prognoses – down to the minutiae.

The day before the great clash Stanley Bergin, a much-respected cricketer and sports writer for the *Evening Herald*, presented his final thoughts on the much-ballyhooed contest:

> Many thousands of words on every aspect of the two teams has been analyzed … interviews on fitness, winning margins and the like. It was over-kill. Forecasters appear to be divided among themselves, an indication of just how open the match really is.[161]

No wonder the tension was so high. Bergin dared a prediction: 'I am prepared to cast my vote in favour of Dublin.' His wisdom was about to be tested.

———

Naturally, everyone had encouraged Prince Rainier and Princess Grace to extend their Irish visit by only one day to see the colossal event. Regrettably, they couldn't make it.

At the airport on Saturday, Princess Grace effusively praised the Irish people for their kindness and warmth. 'The *whole* holiday was marvellous, the peace and quiet, and chance to see the countryside. Really, it could *not* have been nicer!'

Then she extended special thanks to her driver, Maurice Power of Ballyfermot, for his skilled driving. With him at the wheel on Ireland's narrow, twisting roads, she had always felt safe. She was known as an advocate of road safety. In recognition of Power's companionship, she gave him 'a small gift and told him that it was for his newborn son'. Power felt it was 'a very nice gesture'.

Then the royal family departed for Monaco, taking with them two presents they had received, a toy poodle and a small pony named Trixie.

———

On Sunday afternoon, before 87,106 delirious spectators, the Dublin and Galway teams finally confronted one another. As predicted, the players exhibited a level of skill and determination seldom seen. It was close and tense, and the roar of the crowd spilt out of the stadium.

At the end of the match the 'continuous din of cheering ... erupted into a mighty crescendo as the final whistle saw Dublin win their 17th title'. It was a close win, 1-9 to 0-10. Within seconds, the vast sea of blue and white that had dominated the stands burst forth to carry their winners shoulder high to the Hogan Stand, where the Sam Maguire Cup was presented to the captain, Des Foley.

Sports writers agreed that it had been a match of unparalleled thrills and sportsmanship. Long after the crowds had left Croke Park, Dublin supporters 'thronging the streets continued to vent their jubilation well into the night.'

For a while, all went well as people cheered and danced in the streets. The majority were ordinary fans simply enjoying the fun of the victory. Residents told of their 'having a nice, quiet celebration'.

But between 8 and 9 p.m., wrote the *Irish Independent*, the 'celebrations got out of hand'. In some parts of the city hooliganism broke out, fuelled by drink, and there was an intent to do damage. Fighting erupted, windows were smashed and cars were overturned. Hooligans roamed about looking for trouble as gardaí and firefighters were called in. The emergency services were met with verbal abuse and tossed stones and bottles.

The most serious trouble occurred where large bonfires had been lit and had flared out of control, threatening homes and shops. Between nine and midnight 'bonfires blazed as the Brigade answered at least 40 calls.' Where their efforts were thwarted by the hooligans, gardaí were called in to give assistance. Finally, the guards were given an order: they drew their truncheons.

In at least one street a disaster was barely averted:

A woman had a quantity of paraffin in her yard which was quite near the fire. She had pleaded with those responsible not to throw a cabinet into the flames because of the oil nearby. A woman who lived nearby ran screaming to a member of the Brigade and warned that the bonfire should be quenched immediately.[162]

It took until well after midnight for the Gardaí and the fire brigade to restore order, and 'a number of people were treated in city hospitals for injuries'.

During the height of the hooliganism in parts of the city, the victorious Dublin football team were enjoying a sumptuous dinner at the South County Hotel in Stillorgan. The Lord Mayor, Seán Moore, rose to congratulate the team, saying that they had 'played with gentlemanship and sportsmanship' and that 'their qualities could well be emulated in the ordinary life of the city'.

After dinner, 'to wind up a perfect day', wrote one reporter, 'the team went to trip the light fantastic' at the Laurel Park Ballroom in Bray. Team members still had enough energy to dance the night away.

———

After lengthy negotiations at the Mansion House, the dockers' strike ended at 8 a.m. on 24 September. The following morning, 'reads' resumed as usual. With the strike over, fruit-and-vegetable merchants flew into action to try and save their produce from further spoiling. While some merchants threw away over-ripe produce, others gave it to charities. Generous carters volunteered their services in distributing the fruit and vegetables to the needy.

Along North William Street in Dublin were rows of small houses dating back generations, with a convent school at one end. It was a tightly knit community of working-class residents, in which everyone knew one another and helped neighbours during illnesses and crises. Ellen Preston was a typical resident. She was a fruit-and-vegetable dealer in Henry Street. The occupation went back nearly 150 years in her family. Every day she pushed her rickety pram to the market. She is proud to say that she raised her twelve children 'out of my pram'.

One day towards the end of September a six-ton lorry rumbled down the narrow street, moving slowly. People were curious. The driver must be lost.

Then they noticed that it was heaped with a mountain of perfect, just-ripe bananas. The lorry halted near the entrance of the convent school, and two men got out and knocked on the door. After a few minutes of conversation with a nun the men returned to the lorry and began unloading mounds of bananas.

By this time, many people were standing outside their houses trying to see exactly what was going on. Some began drifting down the street to see what it was all about. It was quite a spectacle: boxes of fruit being stacked up along the kerb as if they were being delivered to the Dublin Fruit Market. Their aroma was heavenly. Surely, many people thought, there must be some mistake.

But there was none: it was simply a charitable act by a 'silent giver'. The banana bonanza was for everyone: nuns and the orphaned schoolchildren who were their wards, and *all* the occupants of the street.

A reporter quickly got wind – and scent – of the 'great banana mystery' and showed up to investigate. However, the nun at the convent, which looked after sixty children, said she had no idea who the benefactors were.

Chapter 17 ∼

THEATRE DRAMA, AND DRIVERS, BEWARE!

On the first day of October nine young people, aged thirteen to fifteen, were hauled into court in Dublin for playing a game. It was a 'cool' new game they had learnt about from American films. It was easily adapted to Ireland. It wasn't a party board game but a type of gambling – for real daredevils. Gambling with one's life, actually. It was called 'playing chicken'.

It sounded innocuous: anyone could play. The goal was simply to run from one side of the street to the other – and make it safely to the other side. It was thrilling to play. And winners were proclaimed the most daring.

To adults it was pure insanity, for it meant running through, and dodging, speeding vehicles on busy roads. This caused motorists to swerve or jam on their breaks, putting drivers at serious risk as well. In America playing chicken had caught on among teenagers as being the ultimate in thrills. And several deaths had resulted.

The nine young Dubliners had been brought before the judge before for playing chicken on the busy dual carriageway on the Clondalkin Road. But they had ignored his warning. The judge, now angry, delivered a stern lecture, after which he fined them ten shillings. Then, eyeing them directly, he vowed that he would 'send them to Marlborough House for a month' if he saw them in court again.

Authorities were determined to crack down on this incredibly dangerous fad, since it could easily catch on among younger children, who were impressionable. Opponents of American films, music and television, who disapproved of their corrupting influence on Irish culture and society, saw this problem as a prime example. In 1963 such films and programmes were flooding into Ireland. The Church and parents were growing increasingly alarmed by their harmful effect on impressionable young people.

The booming pop music scene, originating in America and Britain, was especially disturbing to adults. Called the 'pop craze' by journalists, it drove children to act wildly, twisting, gyrating and convulsing as if they were in some sort of trance. Girls screamed, cried and fainted. Some pop idols elicited unrestrained behaviour. Irish reporters were giving increased coverage to the country's 'teen scene', which they now saw as here to stay.

It had all begun in the mid-fifties with Bill Haley, Elvis Presley and a host of American and British rock-and-rollers. In the early sixties a new pop group, the Beatles, burst onto the scene. Newspapers in Britain, Germany and elsewhere reported that audiences went mad with excitement.

By early October 1963 it had been confirmed that the Beatles were to appear on stage in Dublin in November. The dates and the venue were being pinned down. While young people waited for details, adults grew apprehensive about what they were reading in the papers.

The reputation of the Beatles certainly preceded them. They not only roused their audiences to a frenzy of excitement but also commonly triggered disruption in the streets. It was called 'Beatlemania', and for good reason: Irish Beatlemaniacs were already showing signs of heightened tension in anticipation of actually *seeing* them. The *Irish Press* expressed its concern about the phenomenon. 'There were dangers behind the mass hysteria of young teenagers over the pop singing group.'[163] It was a type of hysteria, they felt, that ought to be taken seriously by Dublin authorities and the Garda brass.

———

A big story splashed on the front of newspapers in early autumn was what the *Irish Press* lauded as 'the city's first skyscraper … thrusting upwards.' For developers, politicians and other city authorities it symbolised modern development in the old city of Dublin. They imagined the gleaming Liberty Hall as the centrepiece of a new Dublin skyline, with similar skyscrapers mushrooming all over the city centre. They would loom over the drab Georgian architecture – which so many felt needed to be demolished – to make way for more skyscrapers. In this they would be emulating progressive European and American cities.

Standing in admiration of Liberty Hall, their heads tilted upwards at its towering form, those in awe of the achievement smiled and congratulated one another. This was just the beginning! For them, this skyscraper truly marked Ireland's arrival in the modern, progressive era.

Not all Dubliners, however, admired Liberty Hall. Some, in fact, detested it, calling it an abomination or a monstrosity, dominating what had been a charming traditional cityscape on a small, intimate scale. This was a city of buildings of three and four storeys that did not blot out the sky. To those who objected, the skyscraper craze sweeping other countries was a disease that would transform Dublin into a hotchpotch of towering glass, steel and concrete – a soulless environment. To them, the fact that Dublin had lagged so far behind other countries in architectural modernisation had, in fact, resulted in the preservation of the city's historic houses and buildings. In fact, that was something other countries were even starting to *envy*.

But there was a fear that 1963 might mark the beginning of the onslaught against Dublin's venerable streetscapes. The battle lines were drawn.

———

If Liberty Hall stood out – grandly or grotesquely – as a sign of transformation, there were subtler symbols that told of a city still rooted in the past. In 1963 Ireland was still firmly in the pre-computer age. Communication and business were dependent on typewriters, calculators, business machines and clunky home phones. Some still served their users faithfully, providing, of course, that they were well maintained and regularly serviced.

So in the first week of October, when ninety typewriter and business-machine technicians and mechanics employed by the six largest companies in Dublin went on strike, it was no mere inconvenience: it was a crisis. All large companies – as well as government offices, universities and newspapers – depended on a regular cycle of maintenance, sending machines in periodically in lots, and in rotation. With the strike the servicing rotation came to a halt.

The workers demanded a five-day, forty-hour week. Pickets were placed. Those businesses most dependent on such machines would not be long in feeling the effects of the strike. Their reliable use was something taken for granted in the city.

Without realising it, the typewriter and business-machine technicians, who had seen themselves as indispensable, were soon to face extinction themselves, along with the dockers, coopers and workers in other trades and occupations. Perhaps a visionary few had had a hint of the 'computer age' looming just ahead.

And 1963 tottered between the past and the future.

Most people could never have imagined the swiftness with which the venerable mechanical inventions that had advanced civilisation would vanish from offices and work-places. Alas, even the old, ornate cash registers on wooden counters in shops that had gone back generations would be ignominiously yanked off their perches and dumped into antiques shops. And their companions, the vintage typewriters, with their comforting *clack, clack, clack,* would soon join them.[164]

Dublin was never a city to quickly embrace technological change, and many small shops either couldn't afford computers or didn't know how to operate them. This meant that they held on to their ancient cash registers, typewriters and business instruments for a while longer.

––––

On the other hand, some social changes in Ireland were long overdue. The Commission on Driving While under the Influence of Drink or a Drug finally published its much-anticipated report on 3 October. It was predicted that it would hold great significance for society. It was advised that *everyone* read it.

Filled with medical and scientific terms, it was difficult for the average person to wade through. Newspapers endeavoured to interpret the report for the public. The commission's central, 'unanimous declaration' was that the 'consumption of alcohol tends to affect for the worse a person's ability to drive'. The more alcohol consumed, 'the more detrimental the effect'. This was hardly a revelation.

But behind this finding was scientific evidence that would be useful to the Gardaí and the courts. It was hoped that this would be accepted by drivers as proof of the need to crack down on drink-driving. In an editorial the *Irish Press* took up the cause, encouraging people to examine the report and to support it on moral and rational grounds:

> Drunk driving is a scandal – yet it is one which our courts find hard to deal with effectively under current law.
>
> The moral case for change is so strong that it hardly needs stating. It is hoped that it will have the backing of public opinion.[165]

The *Irish Independent* made the greatest effort to distil the report's findings. It declared drink-driving to be indisputably the principal cause of road accidents in Ireland. This raised the pressing question: *when* did a person reach the stage of too much drink for driving safely? The newspapers reduced this to a formula:

> The weight of scientific opinion is in favour of the view that most persons will be unfit to drive when the blood-alcohol level reached the range of 100–150 milligrams.

This, of course, required further explanation in order to be useful to the ordinary reader:

> As a very general guide, a man of 11 stone would be unlikely to exceed a blood-alcohol level of 125 milligrams *unless* he *drank more* than six small whiskeys or gins in a period of approximately two hours. Or more than four pints of stout or beer in the same period.[166]

Readers were required to do a quick bit of mental arithmetic. For some, the figures didn't come out very favourably. Everyone knew that a person's size and health had a lot to do with their drinking capacity. Clearly there could not be a set number of drinks applicable to everyone. The only solution was to measure a person's blood-alcohol level. This meant that a *test* would have to be administered.

Herein lay one of the most controversial aspects of the commission's report. For many, the concept of testing seemed too personal, too invasive. While conceding that the report was far from perfect, the *Independent* championed the use of blood tests:

> The traditional methods of establishing whether a person is too drunk to drive have been of limited use in courts of law. In coming down in favour of an objective blood *test*, the results of which could be used as *prima facie* evidence, the Commission has taken the bit between its teeth.
>
> It is clear and reasonable … of utmost importance in civil and criminal proceedings, for it would provide solid scientific and medical evidence.[167]

The rationale for the test seemed irrefutable. Predictably, however, there were those who argued that it was a violation of individual rights.

While people were poring over the drink-driving report, another horrific road accident occurred, dramatically reaffirming the importance of its findings. On a Saturday night, the 17th, a seventeen-year-old girl and her three friends – one of whom had been making final preparations for his wedding in a week's time – all died in a head-on collision just before midnight along a straight stretch of the main Dublin to Belfast road. Weather was not a factor.

––––––

Earlier in the month a disquieting report of a different sort was released to the press. It was a notification that the venerable Olympia Theatre would be put on the auction block on 10 October.

For months there had been speculation about the future of the theatre, but few were prepared for the suddenness of the news. Patrons and friends of the Olympia had commiserated with each other but failed to come up with a definitive plan for saving it. Now their fears were being realised: the historic theatre truly seemed doomed.

The distressing news spread quickly while people talked of a last-minute rescue. On the Monday of auction week, Dick Condon, an ardent supporter of the theatre, formed an emergency committee. They needed to raise £80,000 from individual contributions in the final forty-eight hours. They believed it could be done.

They contacted reporters and others in the media in order to reach the public as quickly as possible. Their pitch was simple: they needed four thousand contributors to donate £20 each, without delay. In return, contributors would be entitled to a number of prime seats in the following ten years. A good investment.

As the hours passed, Condon told the press that he hoped some companies in the city might buy blocks of seats to award to their best customers. And perhaps banks, stockbrokers, insurance companies and car dealerships could get in on the act as well. Of course, there was always the possibility of a lone rescuer appearing with £80,000 in hand to save the day. After all, with Dublin's economy booming, there were enough newly minted millionaires.

At least the hope flickered.

––––––

As people delved into the report on drink-driving, the controversial question of 'penalties for conviction' arose. If drink-drivers did not feel the lash of the courts, it meant that tests and convictions were meaningless – a mere sham. And there would be little incentive for gardaí to enforce the laws. Depending on the severity of the offence, recommendations ranged from fines and a loss of driving rights to prison sentences. Judges would have great discretion in handing down punishment.

Among the public there were those who favoured mandatory prison time for *all* drink-drivers, to teach them a lesson. But some women would plead with judges not to put their husbands behind bars, since it would mean the loss of his wages. A vexing decision indeed.

——

It had been a quixotic idea to save the Olympia at the last moment. A smattering of generous contributors had indeed come to the theatre to hand in their £20 in cash. But, alas, far too few.

On 10 October a crowd of people wearing anxious expressions filed into the Shelbourne Hotel. All headed for the auction room. Reporters had already claimed their seats. Present also were staff members of Illsley-McCabe Productions, along with some of the actors, singers and comedians who had graced the stage over the years. Among them sat the bidders, perhaps feeling like villains in the unfolding drama.

As the room filled, people sat nervously, murmuring to one another. To some, it was like witnessing the final moments of an old friend. Only the bidders knew their intentions for the theatre if it fell into their hands. Would it be demolition, office space, a garish dance hall? Yet there was always the possibility that a new owner would retain the Olympia as the unique theatre it had always been.

The auctioneer took his rostrum and scanned the crowd. He then announced that, since the property could be turned into a very profitable business premises, he felt that £50,000 was 'a reasonable sum to start the bidding'. This apparently threw some prospective bidders off, as they had not been prepared for such a high initial bid. If necessary, bidders would need to quickly revise their strategy.

When bidding was opened, a solicitor, apparently ignoring the statement – or calling the auctioneer's bluff – made a paltry bid of £15,000.

Undaunted, the auctioneer declined the bid and repeated, '*Fifty thousand. Will anyone open at that figure?*'

Silence. Receiving no reply, he repeated the figure a number of times. No-one was prepared to make such an offer, perhaps believing that the auctioneer would have to lower the figure.

He waited. And then waited a little longer, the bidders now looking at one another rather uncomfortably. Then he calmly closed the sale, saying, 'I am only an auctioneer, not a magician. I cannot sell if I get no bid.'

The Olympia had won a reprieve.

Sighs of relief were audible. It was clearly not an outcome anyone had expected, least of all the surprised reporters, who had been prepared to write the full story of the Olympia's sale. The reporter for the *Evening Herald* dashed back to his office with the news. That afternoon's front-page headline captured the story in startling brevity: 'Not sold'.

The following morning, another headline blared: 'Show goes on at the Olympia'. Readers throughout the country could rejoice in the good news. 'Saved from the auctioneer's hammer yesterday, Dublin's Olympia Theatre relaxed somewhat today'. The theatre welcomed actors for fresh rehearsals of Robert Bolt's play *A Man for All Seasons*. This was to be followed with a performance by the Irish National Ballet.

However, the euphoria over the theatre's salvation was to be short lived. A spokesperson for Illsley-McCabe Productions issued a candid declaration: 'Although the theatre was withdrawn from the auction, it is still open for private sale.' Assuming they received a 'good offer … we will sell.'

The Olympia was cast again into limbo. Already there were rumours of British investors expressing an interest in the theatre. 'Hands off the Olympia!' was the public cry.

Also in financial crisis were many of Dublin's cinema theatres. The culprit was easily identified. 'Bingo: and bang go the cinema crowds', one headline read.

As the bingo craze took hold throughout the city and in surrounding areas, more and more cinema proprietors wanted to get in on the action. They began devoting one or two nights a week, often on weekends, to the game. Cinemas offering the best prizes drew the majority of bingomaniacs. This left many cinemas now nearly empty and suffering financial loss. At a meeting of cinema executives, one noted, 'They are playing it *everywhere!*

And it is cutting out our attendances.' For Dublin's cinema-owners, bingo could mean either boom or bust.

———

As people continued to page through the report on drink-driving they discovered a surprising revelation. It might have struck them as humorous if the statistics did not attest to its seriousness. The report prominently identified drunken *cyclists* as a major road hazard and cause of injury and deaths.

It was the conclusion of the commission's members that cyclists guilty of 'drink-pedalling' should be treated more seriously than in the past. Their tottering, weaving act, swerving through the streets, imperilled drivers and pedestrians. Sublimely oblivious to the havoc they were creating, they forced motorists to react dangerously. In mist, fog or heavy rain they could become nearly invisible hazards.

The commission's statistics verified that, of the total number of road accidents caused by a drink-driver in the years 1958–60, 'almost 25 percent were cases in which the "driver" was a pedal cyclist.' This was a figure most people would never have imagined. In short, drunken cyclists were a menace on the roads and should be punished accordingly. Therefore, 'to emphasise the seriousness of the offence', a maximum punishment was recommended of a fine of £50, three months' imprisonment or both.

The commission's message was clear: cyclists, beware!

———

While the Olympia's fate was hanging in the balance, new attention was drawn to the city's threatened canals. On this topic, letters of protest were especially heartfelt, as is evident from the following, sent by J. D. Hanna to the *Irish Independent.*

> The recent announcement that the Dublin Corporation are considering closing a major portion of the Grand Canal must have come as a great shock to many people. How can a normally intelligent gathering of legislators possibly defend such a suggestion?
>
> May I add one more voice to the thousands who would plead with our City Fathers to allow the Grand Canal to be used for the purpose for which it was built – and leave this age-old waterway in peace?[168]

Such pleading was commendable – but would it precipitate change?

On 19 October the *Evening Herald* published a blunt editorial that was critical of the people of Dublin themselves. Titled 'Apathy in the city', it stated that, in the face of threats to the city's treasured amenities and historic buildings, people had been 'strangely uninterested ... so strangely silent' in the streets, where protest was needed. People were caught up in the 'humdrum, day-to-day affairs' of their own lives. There was 'little public stir' or sense of a *fight* for the good causes – before it was too late. Most Dubliners, it said, were guilty of appalling apathy:

> Historic and beautiful buildings have been desecrated or allowed to disappear with only a few voices raised in protest ... and now part of the Grand Canal. And yet, there is no outcry.
>
> If this form of apathy continues too long, it could be a sleep of death.[169]

Where were Dublin's *activists?*

There were those dedicated to architectural preservation who were combating the destruction of Georgian buildings, many of whom were university students. But among the masses a comfortable apathy prevailed. In each case of a threat to Dublin's irreplaceable amenities, the clock was ticking.

————

A few days before Halloween, residents near the docks in Dublin heard strange sounds. A repetitive *pop, pop*, like fireworks. People looked out their windows but couldn't see anything. Finally the Gardaí were called in to investigate.

This was a mystery quickly solved. During the strike at the docks, mountains of crates in warehouses stored fruit that had become over-ripe and rotting. It was a harvest for pigeons, which converged on the bounty. As they feasted they contaminated the area, so much so that it was declared a health hazard. The pigeon population had to be drastically reduced, but their extermination needed to be conducted safely and humanely.

It was decided that the best method was for them to be shot by sharp-shooters. Acting on orders from the Dublin Port and Docks Board, members of a Dublin gun club were asked to carry out the extermination over several days along Alexandra Basin. Every precaution would be taken to avoid unnecessary pain to the birds. Some pigeon-fanciers expressed sadness that any birds had to be shot to death. But had they stuck their heads inside some of the warehouses they would have readily understood the problem.

———

As October neared its end, people began to look forward to Halloween, which still retained much of its fun and sense of innocent wonder, for children and adults alike. Its true spirit had not yet been ruined by commercialism and the influence of gory films. As the *Irish Independent* wrote of Halloween in the year 1963:

> the old ways still linger in most homes ... Children duck for apples in basins of water. Shop windows display a cornucopia of enticing fruit displays of ripe, polished fruit and nuts. Hotels are booked for parties and dances.
>
> Halloween is by no means on the wane.[170]

Children wore home-made costumes and magically became ghosts and witches. They were thrilled to be given an apple, an orange, a few nuts or a piece of barmbrack. They scampered from door to door, where they were greeted with warm smiles.

Adults accompanying the little ones enjoyed the experience every bit as much, the *Irish Press* reported:

> It's a wonderful night for children ... a great night for grown-ups who gather to seek warmth and gay companionship ... The elusive Stardust of wonder will shimmer when we open the door to the little figures ... the hopeful look in those bright eyes.[171]

How wonderful, parents and grandparents said, that Halloween was still a magical time for children.

Chapter 18 ～

BEATLEMANIA!

To adults, November's calendar looked fairly uneventful: a period of calm after what had been an exciting and tumultuous year. It was a few weeks of tranquillity before the joys of Christmas ahead.

For young people the month would be the pinnacle of their pop music fantasies. On the 7th the Beatles would be performing twice at the Adelphi Cinema in Abbey Street. 'Beatlemania' had swept into other countries – and now it was heading for Dublin.

The madness really struck when Beatles fans first heard on the radio that tickets were actually on sale for the two performances. Since the Adelphi had a capacity of 2,300 it meant that only twice that number would be able to see their idols on stage, despite their massive following in Ireland. Those with money in hand rushed to snatch up their tickets.

Then there were the scores of enthusiastic fans, like Bridie Colgan and her two pals, who were mad to see the Beatles but didn't have the money. She and her friends were at work in the Two Owls sewing factory in St Augustine Street when Bridie:

> heard on the radio that the Beatles were coming! We *wanted* to go – but we didn't have the money. So we were thinking of ways to raise it.

Like so many others in their predicament, they could scrimp and scrounge, beg and borrow. Some of the more desperate teenagers confessed to a bit of pilfering at home. After all, it was a once-in-a-lifetime chance – and, anyway, they'd make up for it.

Bridie and her friends conspired in a plan to obtain money for the tickets. They knew time was against them: there wouldn't be enough time to get another little job for extra cash. Just as they were getting discouraged, one of Bridie's friends, Margaret Devlin, had an idea. Her brother Thomas was employed at Guinness's brewery, and she knew that he had just received a tidy little bonus. Maybe – *possibly* – 'he might lend us the money!'

Approaching him nervously, they explained their predicament. They were in luck: Thomas 'kindly lent us the money from his bonus – and we *got* the tickets!' But they had to act with haste:

> The demand for tickets was *intense*, so we took a half day off work to queue at the ticket office to buy them. We got tickets for the second show, which began at nine. The first show took place at 6:30.

They were over the moon, counting the days and hours till they saw the Fab Four – Paul, John, George and Ringo – before their very eyes.

They were among the lucky ones – and the much-envied. Multitudes of others would never hold the precious tickets in their hands. However, that wouldn't stop them showing up in Abbey Street that night and maybe getting a glimpse of their idols.

In the weeks before the Beatles arrived, young people were filled with excitement and anticipation. Even journalists were enjoying writing lively, sometimes provocative articles about 'another British invasion', as they dubbed it. Irish teenagers sought to adopt a real Beatles 'look' from head to toe: dress, hair, mannerisms, lingo. Beatlemania was in full bloom by the first week of November.

For true Beatles fans there were two musts: a Beatles haircut and Beatles boots. Everything in between could be improvised. The result was that Dublin's barbers and shoe shops felt under siege as young people pushed their way in. Since most Dublin barbers were traditionalists trained in the 'short on sides, long on top' style, suddenly being asked for Beatle bangs was a challenge. And, to many, an annoyance. Some barbers put out signs saying *NO Beatle cuts!* Others gladly advertised *Beatle cuts here!* as they rang up their profits. Regular customers were either perturbed or amused.

Even the august *Irish Times* got in on the fun. They despatched a reporter to a number of barber's to gather impressions. The article assured readers that 'Beatlemania is well established in Dublin – barbers have their hands full.' As one barber told the reporter, 'our prices have to be increased – too much trouble involved'. This was because teenagers wanted their bangs cut 'just right'.

At the classy Waldorf barber's in Westmoreland Street, an authentic 'gentleman's hairdresser', the barber Peter Comiskey politely indulged Beatlemaniacs. They could strut out feeling just like Paul or Ringo.

Beatles boots, the other essential component of the look, were all the rage. And they were big money-makers for the shoe shops, which were competing for the business. They were swamped with urgent requests for the *real* Beatles boots. Several newspapers had entire pages filled with advertisements for 'huge new shipments' of the boots. While profits rolled in, the sales staff were in a state of near-frenzy trying to keep up with fitting customers. The reporter Marie Farrell of the *Evening Herald* made the rounds of the city's shoe shops to find out exactly what made the Beatle boot unique.

One patient manager explained that they were 'neat, flexible, ankle-hugging boots that measure about eight inches from the ground.' They were light, with flexible toes and elegant points. Imitations were easily identifiable. Though the real ones weren't cheap, some shops sold out large shipments in a single day. One Dublin shop drew in teenagers with its catchy phrase 'Jump and *shout*, the news is *out*: Beatles boots are *in*!'

While young people were perfecting the Beatles look and adopting their mannerisms, many adults detested the phenomenon. The long hair was 'girlish', and the boots were 'silly-looking'. They thought it foolish that teenagers aped everything about their idols. It caused friction at home.

Gerry Creighton, then nineteen, worked at Dublin Zoo. His father strongly disliked the Beatles, not only for their appearance but also because they were from England. Creighton recalls that the Church condemned them as well:

> At the time, the Catholic Church had complete control over our lives ... Archbishop McQuaid's control. The Beatles were seen as wild, immoral boys from a pagan country! As teenagers we were trying to struggle and break free of parental control. I was there [at the Adelphi] with three of my friends, but for me to see an *English* group was frowned upon by fathers and mothers ...

For weeks before the appearance of the Beatles in Dublin, newspapers printed letters about them. There was a fascinating back-and-forth between young people and older contributors. The letters were evidence of an emerging generation gap. Readers enjoyed following the lively dialogue. They could occasionally be sweet and innocent, like the poem sent in by the teenager Nuala Maloney:

Those gorgeous hunks with their crazy smile,
Their crazy suits in such fabulous style;
And their hair in that unusual cut,
If you don't like them you're just a nut.

Other contributors were not so keen:

This Beatles craze is getting me.
Beatles for breakfast, dinner, tea.
I should get some DDT, a hefty dose and lethal.
And wait there in Abbey Street,
And when the Beatles I did meet,
Just spray them all from head to feet
And suffocate each Beatle.

If this was a bit of ribbing intended to provoke teenage replies, it worked. There was an avalanche of letters from offended fans:

Have the grown-ups in Ireland got no intelligence, that they cannot recognise good music and talent when they hear it. People who condemn them are just jealous of the younger generation.

Some teenagers with a sense of history took adults to task for their hypocritical reasoning:

I think the people who moan about teenagers screaming at the Beatles are just plain jealous. I'm sure the same thing happened when Rudolph Valentino appeared in public.

One disgruntled writer, signing themselves 'J. B. (a square)', submitted 'An Ode to the Beatles', published only two days before their arrival:

I'd love to have a Beatle drive,
It would be lots of fun,
I'd chase them all down Abbey Street,
I'd have them on the run.
They'd gallop down O'Connell Street,

I wonder would they sing
A banshee's wail as they rushed past
The thing we call 'The Thing'.
And when they'd run down Eden Quay
They'd never sing a note,
I'd pelt them here, I'd pelt them there,
Until they reached the boat.
I wouldn't let them take a break,
To you I may seem cruel,
And I'd be happy when they'd board
The boat to Liverpool.[172]

Teenagers tended to view such writers as stuffy old curmudgeons rather than mean-spirited adults. After a flurry of letters about Beatles bangs, one mother decided to jump in with a revelation:

My teenage daughter won't believe me when I tell her that the 'Beatle cut' that all the teenagers are now raving about is nothing new – I saw it 20 years ago! Didn't one of the great entertainers, Moe Howard of the Three Stooges, always wear his hair in the style now called the 'Beatle Cut'!?[173]

An indisputable fact.

To most people 'Beatlemania' was merely an amusing name, but it also conveyed something of the hyperactivity and disorderly behaviour well documented at Beatles performances. Some reporters simply dubbed this 'rioting'. The *Irish Press* warned of the 'dangers behind the mass hysteria' aroused in teenagers at their concerts.

On 5 November the Beatles put on a terrific performance at the Prince of Wales Theatre in London. Among the audience were Queen Elizabeth, the Queen Mother and Princess Margaret, who enjoyed the show. Outside, however, the scene was tense. The police, knowing that there would be a huge crowd of fans jamming the streets, had prepared accordingly. More than five hundred constables were called in to control the crowd of about three thousand, and streets had been cordoned off well in advance. There was a crush when the crowd tried to get closer to the theatre. However, because of the high level of organisation among the police, the crowd was kept under control. There was no rioting and only a few minor injuries.

Following their success in London, the Beatles prepared to head over to Dublin for a similar performance. Dublin newspapers heralded their arrival and gave the impression that the Gardaí were well prepared for any problems that might arise.

Irish Times: 'Dublin is braced for the Beatles'.

Evening Herald: 'Gardaí prepare for "Operation Beatles".'

Another newspaper, however, suggested that the Gardaí might be rather naïve in their planning:

> Tomorrow the Liverpudlian Beatles hit Dublin and if they do not have the same effect as an exploding bomb the Gardaí will be profoundly grateful. They will provide a 'headache' for authorities.[174]

In response, the Gardaí assured people that 'there would be dozens of gardaí on duty.' *Dozens!*

On 7 November there was intriguing news: 'us to probe Moon landing sites'. It was thrilling to imagine what had always sounded like science fiction. Space exploration was in its infancy and was capturing the imagination of the world.

For young people in Ireland, however, the exhilarating landing that day was at Dublin Airport, where the otherworldly Beatles had arrived. As the *Irish Times* acknowledged:

> this morning four young men from Liverpool will try to enter Dublin unobtrusively, spend 24 hours in the capital, and just as unobtrusively leave.
>
> Their efforts, however, will be a waste of their valuable time. Everywhere they have appeared in recent months they have been mobbed by their fans, inside and outside the theatres.[175]

The Gardaí announced that additional ushers were being drafted in for the Adelphi Cinema, and 'at least 30–50 guards would be on duty at Middle Abbey Street.' They were confident that they were ready to handle any disorder by fans.

Garda Sergeant Bill Herlihy and Garda Séamus McPhillips experienced the Beatles 'invasion' first-hand. Fifty years later they vividly recalled 'Operation Beatles' as a sham. As Herlihy puts it:

> some of the superintendents, they thought this was just kind of a non-event, a few fellas with long hair coming over from Liverpool to sing at the Adelphi. Our orders were just to be there.

To Herlihy the Gardaí were in a haze of unreality about performances by the Beatles elsewhere and the disorderly behaviour and rioting of their fans.

Garda McPhillips is blunter in his recollection. Then twenty-one, he was stationed in Blackrock, Co. Dublin, but he had to be rushed to Abbey Street when things got out of hand:

> What happened here was that the officers in charge didn't really understand the *extent* of the hysteria that would come with the Beatles. And they miscalculated … The officers from the age of forty to sixty-five were totally stuck in their old mind-set. Some of the older officers were caught in a time-warp. They weren't properly prepared for it; they didn't properly research it.
>
> They didn't have enough men on the ground – and then they started calling in more and more. And the next thing, we were *all* pushed into Middle Abbey Street, and all the people were screaming!

Caught by surprise, the Gardaí would be unprepared and unprofessional. Because they had no plan for controlling the frenetic crowd, the result would be absolute chaos.

———

Shortly after arriving at Dublin Airport, the Beatles strode nonchalantly over to the reporters, telling them that they were 'flabbergasted' at their success in the past ten months. George Harrison, then twenty, was accompanied by his mother, who told the press that the Harrisons had 'dozens of relatives in Dún Laoghaire and other parts' of the country.

Outside, a crowd of teenagers, mostly girls between the ages of fourteen and sixteen, were giddily hoping for an autograph. When asked by reporters, they declined to give their names, one girl admitting, 'We're on the bounce [mitching]!'

At the Gresham Hotel the concierge, Paddy Fogarty, and the rest of the staff were preparing to welcome the Beatles. Used to accommodating the rich and famous, they were confident that they could handle the four lads.

Later that afternoon, at the Adelphi Cinema, the Beatles mixed congenially with journalists. Their answers to questions were not always profound. One reporter, hoping to secure a juicy revelation for his newspaper, asked Ringo what he liked most in life. The reply: 'Girls, drums and cars.' Hardly the seeds for an interesting article. Yet the reporters seemed to be enjoying the relaxed press session, finding the Beatles to be polite and modest, even shy.

By 5 p.m. gardaí were walking along Middle Abbey Street warning shop-owners that they might want to shutter their windows in case a few boisterous teenagers became a bit rowdy that night. Some motorists were advised not to park in nearby streets. Some took the advice, others not.

The first performance was to begin at 6:30. But quite a crowd had already amassed by 5:30, including those without tickets. In high spirits, they were singing Beatles songs and dancing. The thirty or so gardaí on duty stood in twos and threes chatting and enjoying the scene. All the while, more Beatlemaniacs steadily streamed in from streets all around.

Josie Sheehan was one of those fans who couldn't afford a ticket but just wanted to be there for the fabulous night:

> I was twenty-four years old, married, and had three children at the time. Struggling, working for my kids … and I hadn't got a lot of money. And you hadn't got much excitement in those days – and so the Beatles were a *great* thing!
>
> So, I went down. I wanted to see all the excitement that was going on – 'cause we were all liberated by the Beatles! Oh, it was unbelievable. Everyone screaming … and it was fun! Oh, you would have loved to have been *in* the cinema … but I just hadn't got the money.

One garda, Tony Ruane, who had not been despatched there, decided to show up anyway. Then twenty-two, he also happened to be a big Beatles fan and wanted to share in the excitement. He was without a ticket, but he had a little scheme that might get him in anyway:

I was not detailed for that mission, but I snuck in! – put on my uniform and jumped on the 15A bus and headed for town. I wanted to see these guys!

When I got to the scene I was confronted by a sergeant who asked, 'What the f**k are you doing here? Okay,' he said, 'take up a position somewhere.' When his back was turned I made a bee line for the stage door, hoping to see my idols. There were young women screaming and collapsing all over the place – but I was on a mission!

By six, the ecstatic crowd were celebrating the most exciting thing that had ever happened in Dublin, as they put it. Then the doors opened to take in ticket-holders for the first concert. This triggered the first scenes of pandemonium of the night, as thousands began pushing and shoving. Ticket-holders were in a panic to gain entrance and secure their seats. People without tickets were trying to squeeze in without being detected. Young people were fighting with one another to reach the doors, and ushers were placed on alert for gatecrashers.

Within minutes, the gardaí on duty realised what they were facing. Twenty more gardaí were called in.

In an absurdly futile effort, the gardaí belatedly cordoned off streets and the area in front of the Adelphi to keep the crowd back, supposedly to allow only ticket-holders to gain entry. They linked arms against the waves of pushing, shoving and fighting fans. Somehow, by 6:30, the gardaí and the ushers had regained just enough control to allow the Beatles to take the stage.

When they appeared on stage the 2,300 fans inside went wild, exploding into screaming, yelling and crying. There was a deafening noise that made it nearly impossible for anyone to hear the music. The ushers and the dozen or so gardaí inside the theatre appeared to be dumbfounded by the sudden eruption of noise. Some fans bolted into the aisles in an attempt to reach the stage – and the band.

Paul McCartney, clearly annoyed, appealed for quiet so that the band could be heard. Even Ringo's drums were being drowned out by the continuous screaming. McCartney had first politely asked for 'hush' – but he eventually shouted, 'Shut up!' To no avail. Frantic ushers had to keep fans out of the aisles and off the stage.

The audience eventually lowered their noise level to a point where some singing could be faintly heard. But it was the commotion *outside* the theatre that worried gardaí as they prepared for the second performance of the night.

Between 6:30 and 9 the crowd outside would treble. Teddy Boys showed up in their drainpipe trousers and flashy shirts. Some carried knives and razors. Their presence was menacing, to the gardaí as well as to the fans.

Ticket-holders for the second performance were kept away from the doors by the tightly packed crowd in front of them. They were becoming frantic in their fight to the entrance, knowing that some of those without tickets intended to barge past ushers and take their seats.

The *Irish Times* reporters Cathal O'Shannon and Tony Kelly were on the scene as tensions rose. Then the powder keg exploded. The trouble began after the Beatles' first show ended, at 8:30. Thousands of people leaving the theatre 'mingled with those going in for the second show.'[176]

It was more of a collision than a 'mingling'. As a reporter for the *Irish Independent* wrote, 'amazing scenes were witnessed after the first show'. Fighting frantically to get in, fans pushed, clawed, elbowed and knocked down those in their way. Journalists watched in horror as 'young girls, some only 13 and 14, were knocked down and trampled upon and injured.' Members of the St John Ambulance Brigade tried to reach them. Garda Paddy Farrell was:

> outside the cinema and, oh, it was *wild*! The force of the crowd was like a stampede – and we weren't used to that. Some got overcome. The worst thing was seeing that youngsters were trampled.

The situation was exacerbated by the fact that not all fans from the first performance were actually trying to leave the theatre. They were sticking around in their seats in hopes of seeing the Beatles perform a second time. This meant that incoming fans would have to drag them out of their seats. Gerry Creighton and his pals, valid tickets in hand, managed to squirm their way towards the doors:

> The atmosphere was *electric* – girls just totally screaming their heads off! They were going mad! Police arrived as crowds were being thrown

out and people trying to get in. Chaos … complete chaos. Some police overreacted and pulled their batons.

The gardaí were never ordered to use their truncheons on the fans, many of whom were children. In fact, as Garda McPhillips verifies, they never had *any* specific orders regarding tactics:

My orders were to go down to Middle Abbey Street and 'control the crowd'. Young people there and great excitement – and at the same time an anxiety among the officers: they didn't know *how* to control it! And there were guys asking, 'Is there going to be a baton charge?' 'A baton for *what*?'

Groups of teenagers seemed to go berserk and surged forward, breaking through the garda lines with ease. As 'police battled the crowds, fights broke out', reporters witnessed. Violence erupted when fireworks were thrown at the gardaí, followed by stones and bottles. Bollards were pushed over, windows broken and cars turned over. Ambulance crews carried out bloodied victims. It was a scene of young people gone haywire and of guards over-powered. Garda authorities kept ordering more reinforcements to the scene. Garda Pat Malone was sent into the fray:

I was picked up in a patrol car at Terenure Station and taken in [to Middle Abbey Street]. This was the first time this sort of mass hysteria was witnessed in Ireland for pop stars. It was a new phenomenon, as far as we were concerned … a large number of teenagers who were *hysterical.*

Reporters on the scene were shocked as well. The *Irish Press,* calling it a 'battlefield' condition, described the scene:

About 250 gardaí grappled four hours with an unruly mob … In the stampede more than 50 boys and girls fainted. Abbey Street was 'walled off' by a double line of gardaí as frenzied rioters swept along O'Connell Street.[177]

Bridie Colgan and her pals from the sewing factory had struggled with all their might to gain entry, then had to fight to secure their seats:

> We found ourselves in the middle of mass hysteria. The crowd were waiting to go *into* the show, but people were refusing to leave the theatre. The ushers were practically having to drag them from their seats, kicking and screaming!

More gardaí were ordered to go inside and help the besieged ushers. Garda Herlihy, who had been controlling the crowd outside, was ordered in. 'We went in, and to have a gawk at these long-haired fellas ... but then it was a matter of trying to keep a lid on things.' As Bridie and her friends found, the 'euphoria was so enveloping ... [but] we found ourselves in this bedlam!'

Then the curtain was drawn and the band jumped on stage. Sam Bolger was in the audience for the second performance:

> That was a wild one! When the four guys arrived on the stage it was mayhem – people jumping up and down ... There was *hysteria* ... You'd see them fainting and all. Packed! And the constant noise. The ushers couldn't handle it.

As the *Irish Times* put it, Beatlemaniacs were 'ecstatic, hysteric, demented ... danced, shouted, yelled, jumped and roared and fell on the floor.' When the rushing to the aisles and the stage got completely out of hand the gardaí had to step in, as McPhillips explains:

> We were brought in because the ushers were totally terrified. A whole row of us were lined along the back of the theatre. But there was chaos ... oh, girls swooning and fainting. And our officer said, 'Use no more force than is necessary.'

At one point, reported the *Irish Press*, there was a 'flying wedge of cinema ushers' to try and keep the 'maniacs' from climbing onto the stage. One ambulance-driver exclaimed, 'This is shocking – they've gone *mad*.'

Throughout the second performance the ushers and the gardaí co-ordinated their efforts. Outside, the scene was explosive. By 10 p.m. there were 250 gardaí, twenty patrol cars, several ambulances and three fire engines. The firefighters were instructed that all they were allowed to do in order to 'help break up the crowds was to have their fire engines ringing their bells'.

It finally occurred to the Adelphi management and the Gardaí that a plan had to be quickly hatched for getting the four Beatles safely off the stage and to the Gresham Hotel. No-one had previously thought of this.

When the Beatles were about half an hour from the end of the second concert, the Adelphi management had a brainwave. The manager sent an urgent message to the *Evening Herald* office adjoining the cinema. Could they immediately put one of their delivery vans at the Adelphi's disposal? Jack Flanagan, the garage foreman, approved the plan and even volunteered to drive it.

The van unobtrusively pulled in to the alley near the side door. 'We had to smuggle them out the door', explains Herlihy, 'because they would have been mobbed. And hurt.'

When the Beatles began their last song, 'Twist and Shout', which induced a general frenzy, the crowd sensed that the show might be ending. But they didn't know how many curtain calls there would be. So they would wait … and wait. Once the band had disappeared from the stage for the last time, the escape plan sprang into action:

> The curtain was dropped altogether and the safety curtain was brought down as a precaution. Then the Beatles *ran down* the steps to the stage door to the open doors of the van.[178]

They leapt inside, speaking not a word.

Meanwhile, when the crowd realised that there were no more curtain calls, they ran towards the stage, the *Irish Independent* reported, 'as attendants were powerless and were crushed.'

When the crowd outside realised that the performance was over, they made a mad dash to cut the band off, hoping to catch them as they left the building through one of the exits. They ran right past the van, roaring, 'We want the Beatles!'

The danger was real, and inside the van still not a word was murmured as it rolled inch by inch to safety. Only when they reached the Gresham Hotel could they relax and speak freely.

The young garda Tony Ruane came away from the night with his own minor historical footnote. Wearing his uniform, though not really on duty, he had managed to sneak around to the side door of the theatre to get a glimpse of his idols. But he did a bit better: during a brief intermission the Beatles graciously had an impromptu backstage chat with reporters. No-one noticed the young garda as he slipped in among them:

> And I did get to meet them! They were just four young boys like myself, really. And I went home singing, 'It's been a hard day's night, and I've been working like a dog ...'

The next morning, the Beatles headed north to Belfast to repeat their performances. They had been in Dublin for scarcely twenty-four hours, yet, like a hurricane passing through, they left destruction in their wake. As the *Irish Press* put it, 'it was one of the wildest nights in Dublin for many years.' Estimates of damage and injury would vary widely. According to one newspaper, 'at least 200 people were injured or fainted'.

After the second show, crowds continued to sweep through the streets, causing havoc. 'Behind the mob lay a scene of destruction and chaos,' reporters wrote. Not until the wee hours of the morning did a stillness return to the city.

Every Dublin newspaper printed headlines telling the tale:

Irish Times: 'Many arrested as city crowds riot'.
Irish Independent: 'Dublin gardaí battle Beatles fans'.
Irish Press: 'Many injured as Beatles crowds run riot in city'.

There was a collective sense of outrage. The public and press would vent harsh criticism of nearly everyone involved. There was plenty of blame to go round. Letters of criticism would stream in to newspapers for the following two months. Teenagers were called 'blackguards', 'hooligans' and 'thugs'. One wrote:

> Did we deserve black anarchy? Those who inflict their 'gutter' habits on innocent people! I think people who scream or go hysterical are mentally unstable. Our country, its culture, are sullied by this riff-raff.

Why are our Gardaí not provided with trucks to remove male and female thugs from our streets?[179]

Clearly, well-behaved fans, who formed the majority, were taking the blame for the bad behaviour of a few. Many teenagers wrote in to set the record straight:

> I strongly object to all the blame being attributed to Beatles fans. It was nothing of the sort. It was caused by Teddy Boy hooligans.

Gardaí and firefighters were criticised as well. Some of this was justified, most not. Barbs were unjustifiably directed at some of the gardaí who bravely struggled on in the midst of flying stones and bottles. One writer stated that the:

> ineptitude of the Gardaí in dealing with a few trouble-makers and a large crowd of high-spirited teenagers in Abbey Street bodes ill for the ability of the police to control any real trouble.

Similarly, firefighters came under some criticism for not turning their hoses on the crowd. Michael Ryan of the *Evening Herald* came to their defence:

> In many circles the view was aired that the Brigade's hoses should have been used. But a spokesman for the Brigade said that the hoses could not be used 'unless in case of dire emergency' – and by 'direct Government order'.[180]

Some of the most caustic criticism came from a few of Dublin's most respected journalists, who were ordinarily fair and impartial in their reporting. In relation to the Beatles, however, there seemed to be a bias. As 'An Irishman's Diary' put it:

> four hairy youngsters appeared on stage to be greeted with shrieks and whinnies … [They] walloped electric guitars amplified to the decibel limit. The words were unintelligible. A noise that could only be compared with the baying of jackals from the audience. The only impact that I got was that they were not particularly talented.

'Why don't they turn on the hoses?' 'Why don't they turn the grape-shot on?' Fair comments in my opinion, perfectly reasonable reactions to the display of moronic barbarity put on by the youthful citizens of Dublin.[181]

At the *Evening Herald* the normally fair-minded Tom Hennigan did little to conceal his contempt for the Beatles and their 'rabid' fans. While most reporters found the Beatles to be modest and polite lads, he took a dislike to them during a press meeting at which 'they stood or sat in the room, their hair down over their sunken eyes like African thatched huts.' He found their singing amateurish, even primitive. He continued:

When one has heard some of the greatest voices in Europe sing Ponchielli's 'La Gioconda' one has nothing but pity and contempt for such as the purveyors of the 'Mersey Sound'.

As if that were not enough, he asserted that:

if this is the sort of mass hysteria aroused by the Beatles, then they should be banned from this country. Strong words, but many lives were in danger. The city's youngsters let us down badly, to the level of morons.[182]

Hennigan then made a claim so preposterous that it undermined his credibility as a serious journalist. It was that the Beatles had engaged the services of 'cheerleaders'. The emotions of the audience, he claimed, were:

played upon by professional screamers who follow the Beatles everywhere and, by acting as a sort of claque, rouse the audience to hysteria when their idols appear. These imported professionals did their work well last night.[183]

For many young people who were Beatles fans in those days – the vast majority – the appearance of the Fab Four at the Adelphi would be a memory to be long savoured. When queried fifty or so years later about the year 1963, what inevitably pops into their minds is 'Oh, that was the year the Beatles came here!'

Chapter 19

IMPERILLED TREASURES

November 1963 would be beset by threats to some of the nation's most treasured amenities. In Co. Kerry attention was on Muckross Abbey. In its grounds is the magnificent Muckross House, one of the country's grandest edifices. Its beauty had enthralled visitors for generations. It was always assumed that it was at the top of the environmental protection and preservation lists.

So when the *Evening Herald* printed a startling headline in November – 'Muckross House to become a luxury hotel' – people were alarmed. Such a thing would be in contradiction to the wishes of the benefactor, who had given it to the government in 1932 in order for it to be preserved for the enjoyment of all. The news so stunned local people that the Killarney Tourism Committee called a crisis meeting. The *Irish Times* hurriedly despatched a reporter to cover the discussions. Of the committee members he wrote that their 'reaction was swift and vigorous'.

Muckross House, completed in 1843, was built for Henry Arthur Herbert and his wife on an estate of 11,000 acres. In 1910 it was bought by an American millionaire as a wedding present for his daughter, Maud Bourn, who had spent her honeymoon in Killarney. Her husband, Senator Arthur Rose Vincent, together with his parents-in-law, later gave the mansion to the Irish nation. He specified how he and his family wanted Muckross House and estate to be preserved:

> I want especially to have the young people come to Muckross to trail those mountains and to enjoy nature in all its aspects … to be a real garden of friendships and one of the greatest playgrounds in the world.[184]

For more than fifty years his wishes were honoured, and it was open to visitors from all over the world.

In 1963, however, there was a storm brewing. The house had suffered normal deterioration, and it was expensive to keep it in decent condition. In the tourist off-season the Government sometimes used the estate for other purposes, always maintaining its architectural integrity. But by November developers were eyeing the estate in hopes of making a massive commercial transformation. With a luxury hotel would surely come a demand for the required amenities: swimming-pools, a golf course, a large car park. Such a conversion would require the gutting of parts of the interior. In November the *Irish Times* made it a front-page issue. 'Vigorous protest at plans for Killarney mansion'.

———

While some said it was too awful to really happen, others cited the many abominable cases in Dublin in which splendid Georgian houses had been demolished. As Desmond Guinness, head of the Irish Georgian Society, declared, it was in 1963 that 'the rot set in'. Frank McDonald, an *Irish Times* environmental journalist, wrote in his classic work *The Destruction of Dublin* that the '"battle for Fitzwilliam Street" was the first of many bitter struggles fought out in the streets of Dublin between the forces of barbarism and civilization.'[185]

The ESB offices in Fitzwilliam Street, sixteen houses from the late eighteenth century, were targeted for demolition to make way for an office block. It was immediately opposed by preservationists and conscientious citizens. Even Princess Grace of Monaco, when she visited Dublin earlier in the year, had signed the Old Dublin Society's petition calling for the street's preservation.

By November the battle between preservationists and developers had inflamed passions on both sides. University students began occupying abandoned Georgian buildings marked for demolition. They bravely dug in their heels and remained in occupancy twenty-four hours a day, for weeks and months. No-one was more committed to the cause than the renowned preservationist Deirdre Kelly, then a student. She would become a leader in Dublin's preservation struggle. Also dedicated, and angry, was Father Paul Freeney, who lashed out at developers motivated solely by profit:

Development! Ye Gods! The word is supposed to mean growth, improvement. Is it improvement to devastate our city centre and fill it with glass and concrete monstrosities? They can go to hell!

I'm angry at the devastation of my native city. I'm angry at the featureless monstrosities arising, and for the city dwellers. Dublin is no longer a living city … I could weep.[186]

Fitzwilliam Street was doomed, but it *could* have been saved. 'And so it was', wrote Fergal Tobin, 'that the longest continuous Georgian streetscape in Europe was despoiled. It was an act of vandalism.'[187] And it was carried out with the approval of the Government.

Frank McDonald and the *Irish Times* continued to champion the cause of architectural preservation. He wrote well-documented, reasoned articles exposing the strategies of the developers. In November the *Sunday Independent* joined in, noting that 'a violent change is happening' in the city. It reported that 'there is £100,000,000 worth of new buildings and houses going up in Dublin.' These 'creep up storey by storey' without an end in sight:

Big money contractors shut the sunlight from the streets as their huge powerful matchbox-like monuments reach for the sky.

They are all over the horizon, cranes rest at crazy angles … and you can see bricklayers and welders with their winking blue torches crawling along the steel girders. Steel and cement baskets swing out over the street and the monotonous grind of the mixers drowns out even the traffic.[188]

Could anyone doubt that the future of Muckross House was now in peril as well?

———

No feature of the changing face of Dublin was more personally or deeply felt than the drastic transformation of its beloved pubs. By the early 1960s developers were demolishing them with impunity. When not being demolished they were being torn asunder in favour a fancy new appearance.

To regulars it was a desecration. All over Dublin the trend of ripping out the old and installing the new was spreading. On 17 November the *Sunday Independent* brought the crisis to the fore in an authoritative article by Maurice Gorham – 'The pub is in peril' – which grabbed the public's attention. Gorham, supported by abundant evidence, contended that Dublin's traditional pubs were fast becoming an 'endangered species'. The craze in London for pub modernisation was fast catching on throughout Ireland, especially in Dublin, with a speed not allowing for a thought to be given to what was being irretrievably lost. Gorham issued a clarion call for a halt to the destruction. He questioned the judgement of the many publicans who were seeking a 'swinging sixties' atmosphere. According to Gorham, that trend meant:

> pull the whole place down, it's too old ... put in a 'select lounge' for the upper-class people, a plushed-up room like a hotel lobby. The pity is that everything goes too far ... by tearing everything out and making a brand new interior which may not look like a pub![189]

There was no doubt that many of the neglected and musty pubs needed updating and restoration. But the retention of a pub's *authenticity* was vital to its character. Tommy Smith, today joint owner of Grogan's in South William Street, was in the sixties a young barman in several old pubs, and, with emotion, he remembers witnessing that destructive outlook:

> In the sixties, that was the Formica age! I have personally seen it where I worked at McCauley's. The finest of marble countertops and beautiful ornate counters – replaced with Formica. Oh, what a *sin*! What a *disaster*! I couldn't believe it. That was alien to me ... It was a hatred of the old.

The trade journal *Irish Licensing World* felt compelled to condemn the phenomenon in the harshest terms:

> Practically every pub in the country is being redecorated. Most of them are now just factories for drinking in. It's a great pity the way some old pubs are being gutted. A pub with atmosphere should preserve it.
>
> We'll be sorry in a few years' time that we have destroyed all the old places. Marble counters, old mirrors, mahogany ... it's a sin to throw them all out. It's *vulgarity* ... vandals as regard history.[190]

In Dublin, such elegant pubs as the Irish House and the Scotch House were smashed to smithereens. Frank O'Donnell spent most of his life as a barman at the Scotch House. In his eighties he reflected, with great sadness, on the fact that:

> developers bought it … and it's a block of offices now. It was a pity to see it go … but there was money to be made.

For lifelong regulars it was emotionally shattering, one recalling that 'it's the regulars who suffer … Like fish out of water they try to adapt themselves to a new environment – and fail.' Even the toughest of old regulars could only watch in tearful silence when the bulldozers moved in to knock down their personal history. One publican, Larry Ryan, had a pub in the Coombe in the early 1960s and in recent years expressed his sentiments about his regulars:

> I hope all the old Dublin men die before the old pubs go … replaced by modern things that are not pubs at all. Because pubs were a tradition in Dublin, a *way of life*! They weren't just a watering hole: the family's life was *built* around a pub!

––––––

The canals of Dublin were equally vulnerable. Although they had lost much of their original loveliness, as well as their functional purpose, they were not irretrievably lost. But in November 1963 word of a new form of destruction leaked out. The Corporation was boldly exposing its intentions in the newspapers. These confirmed the worst fears of all those Dubliners who had loved their canals since childhood. The plans, already drawn up, called for the canals to be filled in, for the implanting of sewage pipelines, and for the constructing of motorways on the surface. All 'in the public good', of course.

Environmentalists and preservationists leapt into action. Deirdre Kelly, already dedicated to saving Georgian buildings, joined the struggle to save the city's canals:

> The ESB thing was getting started and *then* the canal issue came up. They were going to cover in the canals and build a motorway! That caused very wide protest in the city. I think it was the first time stickers were actually used, 'Save the canals!'

On cars, shopfronts and houses all over the city these stickers proliferated. It was a very personal plea, for the canals belonged to the people. There would be no apathy in this battle.

No-one knew the Royal Canal better than Michael Lynch and his daughter Maureen. Back in the 1920s he worked for the railway and one day spotted a derelict cottage along the bank at North Strand Road. He asked CIE for permission to buy it for a pittance and restore it for his own use. This permission granted, he embarked on the task of making it habitable for his family. After a few years he had it looking charming. It was rimmed with roses, and there was a vegetable garden on the bank. The best part of it was that he could draw fresh water for drinking and fish for dinner. Fresh air streamed along the banks.

As the decades passed, the cottage became a striking anachronism in the developing city. It was a popular scenic site for all those crossing the bridge at North Strand Road. Towards the end of the century Michael, then ninety-five, still lived there with his daughter, then in her seventies. Nearly blind, he still liked to sit out beside the front door, listening to the canal water at the lock. He shared his recollections with the author:

Mister, there was *great* days here. You'd think you were living in a real country place! The missus, she used to have fifty or sixty fowl, and I had pigs. We had a garden and chickens and fresh eggs every day. Take water out of the canal there and drink it – it was *that* clean!

There were eleven barges on this canal when I came. Oh, they were carrying everything from down in the country, from the west of Ireland: corn, wheat, coal, timber, potatoes. The bargemen, oh, they were *big* men.

And pleasure boats here with the ladies from Greystones and Dalkey. They'd have electric lights and the best of clothes on the deck … and have a melodeon and a small piano. Ah, they were *great* times … when I look back on the days when I came here.

Maureen joined in to share some of her memories. Born in the little stone cottage, she had spent all her years within feet of the canal:

Ah, it was *lovely* here! We used to have rhubarb and cabbage, and a pony, Molly, and a nanny goat. And there were swans and geese in the canal. And *real* barges, the real thing – they were *history*! A different race … You'd never get their likes again.

Then you got the fancy boats, pleasure boats coming up – looked like tiny houses. Lovely curtains. Well-to-do people going down to the Shannon mostly. Some were foreigners. They'd stop and chat and we'd get a cup of tea and a biscuit. Some of them would give me a dollar – and the shops wouldn't take it. So I had to go to a bank.

There was Tyrone Power and Gene Tierney and John Huston – from Hollywood – here on one boat when they were making a film. They'd sleep on board and had engine power. Ah, a long time ago … Honest to God, they were beautiful days.

Drawing inspiration from memories such as these, canal restorers drafted their own plan to save the canals and return them to their original state. Their objectives were clear: clean up the water and the canal bed, remove decaying trees and rubbish along the banks, groom the banks, plant natural vegetation, bring in native fish, and install benches and attractive lamps. Pleasure craft could then be reintroduced.

If this sounded unrealistic, it was pointed out that many other countries had already succeeded wonderfully, and with far more ambitious reclamation projects. Why not Ireland?

Working around the clock, proponents of the plan were confident of its feasibility. Its proposed modest cost of about £20,000 was even guaranteed by several business interests and organisations. The plan was drawn up at the request of Bord Fáilte and the Irish Assurance Company.

In the second week of November the restoration group submitted a cover letter with the plan, representing some twenty cultural, commercial and statutory bodies, to the Corporation. The proposal stated that:

> graciousness and beauty should play an important part in the lives of citizens. The Grand Canal should be confirmed as one of Dublin's great amenities, and guaranteed immunity against any development which would destroy it.
>
> The preservation of scenic areas is an asset. We can bring the countryside into the city, our citizens a welcome respite of trees and grassy slopes … This is why we send you this letter.[191]

To the preservationists it could not have sounded more reasonable and appealing: to 'bring the countryside into our city'. What gift to Dubliners could possibly be more wondrous?

Believing they could now save the canals, they felt 'confident it can now enter a much happier chapter in its history.' It was hoped that the Corporation members would be similarly enlightened and approve their plan. A positive reply was expected by year's end.

————

The middle of November was seeing other forms of protest. On the afternoon of the 14th Theresa Costello led more than two thousand opponents of the turnover tax on a march through Dublin to deliver a letter to the Taoiseach, Seán Lemass, at Leinster House. Reporters wrote that thousands of people 'staged one of the city's biggest all-women protest marches'. As Mrs Costello was quick to tell them, the march was 'voluntary, organised by the women themselves – not by me.' It was a gathering of those 'who don't want this turnover tax – and we *don't* intend to pay it!' A small figure dressed in red, Mrs Costello pushed her two-year-old son in a pram at the head of the march. Behind her other women pushed prams. It was a sight no-one could miss.

Along the route, she marshalled the demonstration. 'Ladies, ladies!' she exhorted them, 'let us be *dignified* – and make them know we are the backbone of the country.' They waved banners proclaiming *Exempt food! No tax on medicine* and *Stupid men make stupid taxes!* which seemed to be a favourite with many spectators. Along the way, the marchers beseeched others to 'come join us!' And some did. Many clapped and cheered them on.

The same day, inside the Dáil chamber, one man was making his own solitary protest. With the turnover tax becoming more controversial, and more likely, Richie Ryan of Fine Gael decided to add a bit of levity to the issue while at the same time taking a few jabs at his political opponents. He had a simple – but timely – query: 'Where have all the farthings gone?'

The question, delivered quite seriously, elicited chuckles and raised a few eyebrows. There was also a slow awareness that it was, in fact, a rather interesting question.

Ryan had a reputation for pin-pricking the Government on occasion. Because the turnover tax was 2½ per cent, its effect on customers and shopkeepers should, he felt, be considered. Would it create practical monetary calculation problems? He thought it judicious to ask how *many* farthings and ha'pennies there were in circulation. Would more need to be minted?

As one newspaper put it, the Minister for Finance, Dr James Ryan, was not known for being the 'best man at handling pricks'. Retaining his composure, he shuffled his papers and consulted his assistants. Eventually, after some scrambling, he coolly replied that there were 5,641,920 farthings and 23,329,930 ha'pennies in circulation. He added that the Central Bank had adequate stocks.

It was probably the most precise answer ever given in the Dáil.

Smiling appreciatively, but still not satisfied, Richie Ryan asked quite sincerely, But where had all the 5,641,920 farthings *gone*? Shopkeepers, he noted, did not use them; schoolchildren had never *seen* them. And what about the poor tourists? he asked. Could they exchange their currency for farthings to enable them to shop in the land of the turnover tax? After which question he felt satisfied that he had made his point.

Ireland's legion of small grocers and shopkeepers, however, found no humour in the turnover tax, which complicated their lives and displeased their customers. It also placed them in the role of tax collectors, as they saw it. In addition, small grocers were being threatened by the mighty British companies establishing supermarkets capable of damaging their livelihood, if not putting them out of business altogether. By November 1963 some were already shuttering their shops in defeat.

For those fighting to survive it was difficult to close up their businesses for the day and march in the streets, though some did so. Others took to writing letters to the newspapers to explain their predicament and, they hoped, gain support and sympathy. The following is a typical example:

Being a shopkeeper, I feel that I have an axe to grind in all this controversy. Firstly, we did not want the Turnover Tax. But now we are becoming Public Enemy No. 1. Shopkeepers would not object (as much) to the tax being collected at the manufacturer's level. It would be much simpler.

It's a shame, all this political hokery-pokery going on. I would ask housewives not to be too hasty in judging us shopkeepers regarding the tax. I am a married man with a wife and seven children. I work *84 hours* a week. We are only trying to live, the same as you all.[192]

With the imposition of the new tax, they feared that their customers would buy less, further cutting their small profit margin. On top of that, they had to defend themselves from the charge of being villains for having to take extra money at the counter. To them, it was manifestly unfair.

———

By the latter part of November the most exasperated man in Ireland was possibly the letters editor of the *Evening Herald*. Much to his chagrin, weeks after the Beatles' appearance at the Adelphi Cinema, their fans and critics were *still* flooding his office with letters. It seemed as if they would never cease. Dutifully, he continued to print a few nearly every day. But the stack of letters was consuming his office. Finally, he had a solution. On a day when he generously printed twelve Beatles letters, he decided to add one more: his own. It was more of a plea, really. 'No more Beatles letters, *please*, until they descend on us again!'

It worked, and the avalanche dwindled to a fading few. His caveat, 'until they descend on us again', surely brought new hope to Beatlemaniacs, and dread to their critics.

But it was the front page of the *Evening Herald* that drew the public's attention. For those hoping to save the Olympia Theatre it was bad news – unexpected news. It stated that a man by the name of Tom Gorman, a representative of an Irish syndicate in London, had just flown in to Dublin to negotiate a deal that would mean the 'end of the Olympia Theatre, and the birth of a new city centre ballroom.'

It was exactly what preservationists had feared: money coming in to strike a back-room deal, away from the open auction room. It was further stated that Gorman had with him 'a cheque for £14,000 as a deposit' and that he hoped to 'complete negotiations for the Olympia for £75,000'. The new ballroom, already envisaged, was to have impressive restaurant facilities capable of accommodating several hundred dinner-dancers.

Many a cheerful Christmas season seemed spoiled by a reading of Gorman's intentions. But the deal was not signed yet.

The other rescuers, those working to save Dublin's canals, were hoping for positive news, thinking they might receive word by late December. It would be a reason for a happy New Year's celebration.

Quite to their surprise, they received in November a response to their proposal, within a week of submitting it. The omnipotent Corporation had already rendered a startlingly quick decision: 'Rejected'.

All the distinguished signatories of the proposal agreed that it was a 'most unfortunate decision'. Father Donal O'Sullivan, SJ, director of the Arts Council, bluntly said that he was personally 'sorry and disturbed' by the apparently rash judgement. In fact, he 'deplored it'. After all the hard work put into the scheme, and given that it had the backing of Bord Fáilte, it was clear that the Corporation bigwigs had not even given it due analysis and fair consideration. It was an insult to all preservationists trying so diligently to save the canals – and for the people of the city. Father O'Sullivan, with undisguised disgust, asserted that the 'beauty of the city should weigh more with the City Fathers than it appears to have done.'

Exacerbating the situation, the Corporation revealed that it had *already* hired a traffic consultant to work on its plan for the filled-in canals. This rubbed a lot of people up the wrong way. Dermot O'Clery of Bord Fáilte surely spoke for the majority when he said, 'If the canal were closed it would be a national tragedy.'

Perhaps as an appeasement to all those who loved the canals, CIE decided to temporarily permit the use of canoes on the canal. Though a token gesture by the Government, it was welcomed by canal proponents as an opportunity to show the value of 'watermanship in the midst of the metropolis'. Canoe clubs leapt at the chance and introduced youth groups to canoeing. People found delight in watching small groups of canoeists paddling along happily. It seemed so natural. Here was evidence of what could once again be possible.

———

On the evening of 20 November the Rev. E. F. O'Doherty, professor of logic and psychology at UCD, delivered a lecture in Dublin. Not being particularly newsworthy, it would get only a brief mention in the *Irish Independent* the following day.

Hardly a cheerful topic for the beginning of the Christmas season, his topic was 'Dark areas of human motivation and evil within man'. It drew a small but attentive audience. An 'all too common assumption', he explained, was 'that all murderers are psychopaths'. And it was difficult for humankind to accept the reality of 'evil within himself'.[193] He stressed that 'a free act is not a motiveless one'. A person can carry out a most heinous act of murder, beyond all bounds of comprehension. O'Doherty concluded that it may be 'incomprehensible for others to grasp for eternity'.

His small audience probably interpreted his argument largely in abstract terms.

Forty-eight hours later, they may have thought differently.

Chapter 20 ∾

'JOHNNY, WE HARDLY KNEW YE'

On Friday 22 November, with Christmas not far off, people in Dublin were out and about doing some early shopping and admiring the colourfully decorated streets. Throughout Dublin and the rest of Ireland a holiday mood prevailed.

The holidays always offered excellent entertainment, and the cinemas, theatres, dance halls, pubs and restaurants were sure to be packed. There were some alluring films, especially *The Birds* at the Savoy. It was billed as a 'most terrifying motion picture'. At the Metropole, Marlon Brando was starring in *The Ugly American*. For those seeking lighter fare, there was the Corinthian cinema, where *The Tender Trap* was pairing Frank Sinatra and Debbie Reynolds.

The Olympia Theatre, happily still in business as 1963 neared its end, presented a superb performance of the play *A Man for All Seasons*, drawing standing ovations and rave reviews. This prompted one reviewer to write that, 'should the Olympia ever close … I would like to remember it by this production.'

In the late afternoon and early evening most people followed their Friday-night routine, heading home for dinner or out to the pub, relaxing at week's end. Along the way, people chatted or listened to the radio. Many were content just to get home and pore over the comics in the *Evening Herald*, catching up on the antics of Mutt and Jeff, Beetle Bailey, Freddie, and Jiggs and Maggie.

Those Dubliners fortunate enough to own a black-and-white television could stay in and watch the popular 'Dick Van Dyke Show'. And most television-watchers tuned in for the evening news, with Charles Mitchel. Always incisive, he announced the day's events, great and small, with a comforting calmness. That evening, however, there didn't appear to be much of interest taking place in Ireland – or around the world, for that matter.

By the early evening Dublin's entertainment-goers were heading out for the destination of their choice. Among them were Una Shaw and her husband, Tom, of Rutland Street, not far from O'Connell Street. A couple in their thirties, they worked hard to raise their young family. They liked to get out for an evening on their own now and then, and Una's mother was always happy to watch the children for a few hours. That evening they chose to attend the comedy *Period of Adjustment* at the Bohemian. As they were heading out the door they told Una's mother they would be back by about 10 p.m. Then, with the children asleep, they would catch the late news on television.

Garda Pat Malone was at his flat in Rathgar studying his notes in preparation for his Sergeant's Promotion Examination. In a short while he would have to go for the bus, looking over his notes along the way. There would be no time that evening to tune in to the news.

Gerry Creighton had put in a hard day's work at Dublin Zoo. But that night he was going to enjoy himself. He would meet three pals and have a few pints before going to a party that would probably last into the early hours.

On night duty at Tara Street Fire Station was Tom Geraghty. It seemed to be an uneventful night, leaving him and his colleagues with plenty of time on their hands. Geraghty's colleague Éamonn Fitzpatrick was getting ready to go off duty.

Garda Séamus McPhillips was not on duty that night. He was taking a course in economics on Friday nights at UCD. He knew it would pay off later in life should he decide to switch careers.

At the newspaper offices, those on night duty had no breaking stories to cover. In fact, since the Beatles pandemonium two weeks earlier, there had been a lull *after* the storm for reporters. When major news events burst forth there was no place more exhilarating than a press room. But on a dreary night in November it could be dreadfully boring.

Everyone was dumbfounded when the news broke from America: President John F. Kennedy had been killed.

As usual, Garda McPhillips had arrived a few minutes early at UCD. After chatting with fellow-students he took his seat for the lecture. Everyone awaited the distinguished professor Garret FitzGerald. His lectures always followed an orderly sequence. Except that evening. McPhillips remembers that a porter came in and:

> slipped a note to Dr FitzGerald – and he read it in horror! And I remember him saying, 'I just *can't believe* what I've just read!' And he said, 'President Kennedy is dead.'
>
> Class dispersed then. People went off into huddled corners to talk about it. And then everybody *rushed* to see the news. We were in the barracks and just couldn't believe it. We were absolutely aghast.

Only five months earlier McPhillips had been in Co. Wexford protecting President Kennedy during his visit to Dunganstown.

————

Éamonn Fitzpatrick had finished his duty at Tara Street Fire Station and was wearily heading home:

> I was coming up Dorset Street and stopped at a shop to get a few things. And when I walked in there was a girl behind the counter *crying*! And I said, 'What's wrong?' I thought she'd been burgled. And she said, 'President Kennedy is dead!' And I said, '*What!* What are you saying?' 'He's been *shot*!' 'Oh, my God!' says I.
>
> When he was here, for the Irish people, if they could touch the hand of John Kennedy it was like touching the hand of a *saint*! The same emotions welled up in me. I just walked out … got into my car and drove straight home. One of the greatest tragedies that ever happened to Ireland.

Gerry Creighton and his friends were at the party, laughing uproariously. Suddenly there was a pounding on the door:

> We thought it was the landlord complaining about the noise. But he knocked to tell us JFK was dead. We sobered up very quickly … all shocked.

None of us went home that night. It was the first night I ever stayed out all night … comforting one another. He was *one of us,* our most precious son. That was the way we felt. Families said the Rosary … had candles burning in their windows.

Garda Tony Ruane was leaving Rathmines Garda Station for his evening break, happy to have some time to himself:

My garda cap was tucked under my left arm, and with the other hand I pressed a small transistor radio to my ear. Gerry and the Pacemakers were singing 'You'll Never Walk Alone'. Reception from the little transistor was intermittent.

Then the announcer cut across, with urgency in his voice. 'We apologise for this interruption. We now go to Dallas, Texas, for an urgent news flash!' After some static buzzing and crackling, a distressed American voice, high-pitched by hysteria, said, 'We confirm that President Kennedy has been hit!' I stood there rooted on the spot – and listened to the tragic news.

Just a few months ago most of us gardaí had been on duty and witnessed JFK majestically ride through Dublin – in an open limousine.

Concentrating on his exam, Garda Malone had heard no news:

It would have been about 7:20 p.m. I boarded the bus to the station. But as soon as I got on the bus I was informed by the bus conductor. It was a huge shock.

On arrival at the station the news of his death had just broken. *Everyone* was in shock … It was regarded as a death in our own family.

Throughout Ireland people were repeating that it felt like 'a death in our own family'. In Dunganstown, it really was.

Newspapers in Dublin didn't have to call in their staffs; they just showed up to work through the night for the sensational morning editions. With news streaming in from Dallas and Washington, the assassination would dominate the pages of newspapers for days. Suddenly there was almost too much news to cover.

Irish editors saw the full story as ranging from Dallas to Dunganstown and Kennedy's Irish relatives. *Their* loss, *their* grief had to be covered as well. But how soon, and in what manner? It was a highly sensitive matter. Yet journalism was a keenly competitive business. Getting to a story first and capturing poignant statements were at the heart of the quest.

When the news broke on Friday evening, several reporters were despatched to the Rotunda Hospital to see if they could speak to the nurse Mary Ann Ryan, Kennedy's cousin, of whom he had been so fond. Hospital officials informed them that she was home at Dunganstown for the weekend.

The next decision belonged to editors: to wait until morning or to send a reporter south immediately to knock on the cottage door. The *Irish Press* wasted no time, sending Brian Farrell. He followed his reporter's instinct, asking for directions to the cottage of Mrs Ryan, Kennedy's closest relative in Dunganstown. Within minutes, he found himself walking up the path to her door:

> Grey-haired Mrs Mary Ryan ... was grief-stricken, and almost unable to speak.
>
> She murmured, 'It's tragic' – and then she broke down completely.
>
> Her daughter, Josephine, was also crying. She was too shocked for words. There to comfort them was Rev. William Mernagh who rushed over to the farm on hearing the news.
>
> It was a poignant scene. The farmhouse which had housed the now-famous tea party in June was silent except for the sounds of two women crying. It was all so sad, so tragic.[194]

The headline was 'Wexford cousins broken by grief'. There wasn't much more to tell.

Farrell later found another heartbroken relative of Kennedy's, who agreed to give him a few words:

> Almost in tears, Mother Clement recalled the President when he stepped from his car amid surging crowds, patting and hugging little orphan pupils at the convent. 'It is so difficult to even *think* he is dead', she said.[195]

Farrell's article stressed that 'numbed minds' could not grasp the 'shocked horror of a barbarous murder'.

Most reporters concentrated on covering the Dublin scene, seeking the reactions of ordinary people, as did Wesley Boyd of the *Irish Times*:

> On buses and on trains, in pubs, in dance halls and restaurants the news was received in shocked amazement. Strangers stopped one another in the streets to ask if it was true.
>
> At first, no one wanted to believe it was true. But as the radio and television news bulletins came in, hope gave way to sorrow. In many eyes there were stinging tears of grief, and in many hearts the heaviness of the horrible futility of it all. Laughter died and gossip ceased.[196]

Those multitudes at home who were crowded around their radios and televisions were at first seized with disbelief at what they were hearing from Dallas. As the *Irish Independent* wrote:

> the heartbeat of the Irish nation faltered as the tragic news was heard in numbed silence in thousands of homes throughout the land.
>
> It was almost impossible to accept that President Kennedy, who had been so close to them during his visit in June, was dead.[197]

There was a prevailing, deep feeling of 'Johnny, we hardly knew ye'.

Throughout Friday night, people would only gradually learn the news. When Una Shaw and her husband, Tom, left the Bohemian cinema they took quiet side-streets home. They were so engaged in conversation that they didn't seem to notice the people they passed:

> We came home and it had been very cold and there had been some snow on the path. We came in laughing and joking, and my brother and mother were sitting there. And, the next thing, I looked at her and there were tears streaming down her face. And I thought something had happened to one of our kids. And I said, 'What *happened*?'
>
> And she pointed to the television – and the station was off, and they were playing this Mozart music, over and over. About half past ten. And again I said, 'What's wrong?' It was terrible, 'cause she couldn't talk, she was so upset. So my brother said, 'President Kennedy has been shot.'

And I said, 'Oh, my God!'

I'll *never* forget it! Oh, the *shock* of it. I mean, it was only a few months before that we'd seen him! We were shattered.

As night wore on, many people couldn't sleep. They sat together repeating their shock and disbelief.

On the morning of Saturday 23 November people awoke in a depressed state. Immediately they sought a newspaper. Photographs from Dallas were used, so long as they were not too graphic. Special editions were written. Papers sold out as soon as they hit the streets.

Such editorials as that in the *Irish Independent* tried to place the tragedy in an Irish context:

Nowhere more than in Ireland did last night's news taste so bitter. John Kennedy was an Irishman. He was one of us, and our pride in him was without limit … He brought honour on the ancient race from which he sprung. It was good to have lived in his day.[198]

With news continually filtering in, people remained glued to their radios and televisions. By Saturday afternoon, however, many felt the need to get outside for fresh air and time alone. As Máirín Johnston puts it, in June:

everybody was happy – and then, in a few months, everybody was sad! The drama and horror of it – that they had just *seen* him! … People were bereft, you know.

Una Shaw relates that men would 'choke when they started to talk about it … they were visibly upset by it.' To teenagers like Gerry Creighton 'he was our *hero*! To us, he was indestructible … our hope and vision.'

___

On Sunday, at Masses throughout Ireland, prayers were offered for the slain President and his family. At a memorial service in St Patrick's Cathedral muffled bells were rung for twenty minutes. The American ambassador, Matthew McCloskey, and his wife attended 9 a.m. Mass in the Church of Adam and Eve at Merchants' Quay. Mass-goers felt a comforting solidarity in their heartbreak and sorrow.

'In some Catholic churches', reported the *Irish Independent*, 'the congregation were asked to remember the assassin in their prayers.'

Later on Sunday, the Chief Rabbi of Ireland, the Very Rev. Dr Isaac Cohen, called on McCloskey and offered his condolences:

> We have been unspeakably shocked by the horror of the senseless crime that has been committed against humanity. A brilliant star has been brutally extinguished, and the people of the world are left appalled.[199]

Meanwhile, President de Valera was boarding a flight for President Kennedy's funeral in the United States. Accompanying him were twenty-six army cadets from the Military College at the Curragh. This was at the 'very special request of Mrs Kennedy', who said that her husband had been most impressed by the cadets at the wreath-laying ceremony at Arbour Hill. Their average age was only nineteen, but they seemed 'full of self-assurance and confidence' as they stood on the tarmac at Dublin Airport waiting to board the plane. Then the No. 1 Army Band struck up the American national anthem, followed by the 21-gun salute, before the 'vast crowds' who had come to see them off, many with 'tears running freely down their faces'.

Upon arrival at New York, where there was to be a brief pause before he continued on to Washington, de Valera shared a few words with reporters:

> The grief of the American people is just as deep among the people of Ireland. He was one of our own race. When the terrible news of his death came, every house in Ireland felt they had lost a personal friend.[200]

———

Behind the scenes a little-known, dramatic story was unfolding – and at a frantic pace. As dignitaries from around the world converged on Washington for the funeral, Mary Ann Ryan in Dunganstown had been asked to attend the funeral in place of her mother, who was not up to making the trip. How to get there in time was her challenge. As 'tears came to her eyes', Miss Ryan expressed her feeling to an *Irish Independent* reporter:

> I had planned to go to Washington next year, following President Kennedy's invitation to me during his Irish visit. I *never dreamt* that I

would be going under such tragic circumstances. All this has been like a terrible dream and nightmare.[201]

It began with a 'hectic 135-mile midnight dash by police car' on Sunday night from her home to Shannon Airport, where she slept in an airport chalet awaiting her early flight. At 8:50 she boarded an airliner diverted from London to take her to America. At Idlewild Airport in New York she 'immediately was escorted to a twin-engine plane which had been rented' by Pan American when it was learnt that no quick connection was available.

This emergency flight reached Washington ninety minutes later, and she was whisked into a car. With motorcycle escorts and sirens blaring she was rushed to St Matthew's Cathedral. She was escorted into the cathedral, past the solemn faces and down to where the Kennedy family sat. Here she was welcomed as the relative she was.

Irish people were quietly sitting at home watching the funeral on their televisions. Thanks to the Telstar satellite, the funeral was broadcast live for almost twenty-five minutes, with commentary by Michael O'Hehir. President de Valera could be spotted on the screen a few times, but viewers in Ireland didn't get to see the procession to Arlington Cemetery and the internment.

At the cemetery, just before the procession arrived, 'a woman jumped forward with a small Irish flag in her hand', but she was halted by guards. She shouted, 'I am Irish – and my mother knew Rose Kennedy', the President's mother.

She was permitted to place her Irish flag by the graveside. No-one else had thought to do it.

———

In Ireland, Tuesday 26 November was declared a day of mourning. More than ten thousand people had already signed the Book of Remembrance at the American embassy in Dublin. Long, silent lines of men and women still waited patiently to sign their names. It made them feel part of history.

Ireland's tribute to President Kennedy reached its peak when the normal life of the nation was suspended for several hours. This took many forms. Pubs were closed until 12:30 p.m., and restaurants and theatres would not open till 6. There were no lectures at Trinity College and UCD in the morning. At the Circuit Criminal Court in Dublin, Judge Conroy cancelled

all sittings for the day. All day, bells tolled, and American flags flew at half
mast.

While there would be eloquent tributes to the fallen President in Irish
churches and at political assemblies, the humble honoured him in their
own ways. Many small shopkeepers closed for the day. Elderly and infirm
people made their way to church to pray or light a candle. And 'thousands
of dockers stopped work and marched silently from the dockland to Mass
in Seville Place.'

Moore Street traders remembered him at a Mass in the Dominican
Church of St Saviour's. Throughout Ireland 'people knelt in the rain outside
many over-crowded churches' for long spells.

As the firefighter Éamonn Fitzpatrick recalls, 'Oh, *so* many candles
were lit that the fire brigade could have been on overtime.' One newspaper
described the day:

> Grey skies hung like a pall of mourning over the land … Crowds
> moving to the churches formed silent shrines of sorrow in the streets
> … A nation bowed its head in grief.[202]

From the moment of Kennedy's death, people throughout Ireland
began clamouring for a fitting memorial to him. A landslide of letters to
newspapers began, suggesting ideas for everything from a small plaque to
a towering monument. These were often creative and sometimes quixotic.
All had genuine heart behind them. One writer suggested that Kennedy was:

> without doubt the man of this century and the greatest Irish descendant
> of all time. I feel it is up to us to honour him by removing Nelson and
> erecting a monument in his memory.

Because Nelson hardly enjoyed much popularity, it was logical that he
would become the target of many writers. Most of them favoured removing
'old' Nelson and erecting a more modest Kennedy statue on the site. A few
felt he deserved a greater monument. One citizen felt:

> sure that even Nelson himself would have applauded in being replaced
> by the figure of John F. Kennedy if he had lived to know this great Irish-
> American.

Many people, however, rejected such ideas:

Our capital is already littered with memorials, many of which form traffic hazards. I suggest a memorial park … a little piece of Ireland all his own. A place of pilgrimage.

Predictably, there were many suggestions for renaming streets and buildings. At first, renaming streets seemed a simple task. But when this was seriously considered in Dublin some years later, a few practical problems and objections would arise. But in November and December 1963 such ideas were quite common, as one letter writer expressed:

I think it would be befitting if Westmoreland Street was to be renamed John Kennedy Avenue. Also, a suitable monument to be erected on the lawn at Leinster House where it could be seen by all, at any time.

But nearly everyone agreed on one thing: *some* memorial or monument should be established. The most appropriate place was felt to be Dublin, where multitudes had welcomed and embraced him so wholeheartedly. Government authorities, of course, stepped forward to endorse the idea. The Lord Mayor of Dublin, Seán Moore, gave it his stamp of approval. 'I can pledge every possible co-operation from the Corporation for such a project.' By acclamation, it seemed an absolute certainty.

Many were the poems sent in to editors expressing love for President Kennedy. A select few were printed. Four days after Kennedy's death, Maureen McGourty submitted her poem, 'Ireland's Love', to the editor of the *Evening Herald,* who was touched by its poignancy:

Oh, Ireland, shed a thousand tears;
Oh, Ireland, bow your sorrowing head;
For he you would have crowned your king,
And made your own, is dead.
With hearts bowed down beyond relief
We think of those June days,
When, like a ray of brilliant sun,
He beamed upon our misty land.[203]

Chapter 21 ∽

'ABLAZE AND SINKING!'

As rescue ships hove on the scene survivors waved wildly from the lifeboats ... Others swam frantically from the red hot hulk.

Irish Press, 24 DECEMBER 1963

On the first day of December, President de Valera unveiled a plaque before a gathering of dignitaries in Dublin. However, it was not in memory of President Kennedy. De Valera was at the Gate Theatre to commemorate the launching of the Irish Volunteers fifty years before, in 1913, in the Rotunda.

That same day, more than three thousand people were attending a national memorial service in London for President John F. Kennedy. In Dublin the Lord Mayor, Seán Moore, promised that a memorial in Ireland 'would be considered by the Government, and plans made accordingly.' He couldn't, however, say when.

At Christmas time Mary Dooley of Phibsborough always did her part. For years she had been sewing months before Christmas, making dolls for Dublin's orphans. That Christmas she was hoping to have seventy-two dolls for the orphanages. Asked why she did it, she replied, 'Because a little girl's eyes will light up with joy on Christmas morning.' Dubliners saw her as the embodiment of the true Christmas spirit.

Children and adults alike were thrilled on 2 December when Santa Claus arrived to switch on the 25,000 lights along Grafton Street, heralding the beginning of the Christmas season. In Henry Street the traders were selling 'cheeky charlies', 'jumping monkeys', 'creeping babies' and 'monster balloons', and doing brisk business. But that year the gardaí had orders to impose new restrictions on them: they could sell only on one side of the street, and they could no longer place their boxes on the footpath, because it impeded pedestrian traffic. The grumblings of traders were heard from one end of the street to the other.

For the trader Ellen Preston every new imposition hurt:

> I *loved* Christmas! Oh, you'd walk into Henry Street and you'd *know* it was Christmas! It was a very good time for us … selling toys and holly and mistletoe.

The traders in Moore Street were also facing new restrictions. One old Henry Street trader groused that if the Government and Gardaí didn't stop interfering, 'the day would come when there would no longer be *any* street traders' in Dublin.

To Dubliners in 1963 it was a preposterous, unimaginable thought. Surely it would never go *that* far.

One profitable new activity was booming that Christmas, and, rather than its being reined in, it appeared to know no bounds. No mere passing fancy during the spring and summer months, bingo had thrived and expanded into November and December. There was now no denying it: the game was here to stay. Entire newspaper pages were now filled with advertisements for it. From the Tivoli Cinema it had expanded *everywhere*, including the Mayfair Ballroom, the Matt Talbot Hall and St Joseph's School for the Blind in Drumcondra. A few critics condemned it as gambling during the holy season – but few paid any attention to them.

A surprise in early December was the appearance of a new game from America. The papers announced its arrival: 'Ten-pin bowling comes to Dublin'. Its huge popularity in America suggested that it might catch on in Ireland. The first ten-pin bowling facility was opened in Stillorgan and promoted as a 'family sport'. Promoters enthusiastically told reporters that 'in America almost half the population have taken to the sport'. It could be played by individuals, couples, families or teams and was ideal for the country, given its often inclement weather. Even the Church seemed to welcome it as a wholesome family activity.

On 3 December, the day after Santa lit up Grafton Street with colourful bulbs, some other Dublin streets were suddenly drawing attention. A long, torchlight demonstration made its way through the city, led by Theresa Costello and her expanding contingent of housewives still fighting to abolish the turnover tax before it crippled tight household budgets. 'Don't underestimate the power of housewives' was their new slogan. They would protest throughout Christmas, come sleet or snow.

One Dubliner wrote a letter to the *Evening Herald* to express his belief that the country would be besieged by rioting against the turnover tax were it not for two safeguards that defused people's anger:

> I drink and smoke – tax them by all means to get more revenue. But why bread and butter? There is no good reason why food and medicine should be taxed so much.
>
> Fianna Fáil can thank the *pubs* and *bingo halls* – as only for these outlets the people would run riot.

His idea that the pubs and bingo halls were safety valves for public discontent over unjust taxation was intriguing. But it was hardly likely to be tested any time soon.

Road safety campaigners knew that December usually brought the year's highest toll of deaths and injuries. This was due to the combination of deteriorating weather, slick roads and increased drinking. Drink-driving especially was a menace. The *Irish Independent* tried to warn drivers with the headline 'Beware! December has a grim record'.

Campaigners stressed that December typically accounted for a ninth of annual road deaths. However, recognising that their past warnings hadn't appealed very successfully to drivers, they would try a more explicit message that December:

> Forty people alive will *not* sit down to Christmas dinner this year because they will have been killed on the roads on one of the nights before.

The *Irish Press* declared that, as the year neared its end, the appalling rate of road deaths was not only a national 'scandal' but a 'moral case' as well. On 14 December, Dr Daniel Cohalan, Bishop of Waterford, issued an appeal on behalf of the Road Safety Campaign. It was to be read at all Masses in the diocese the following day:

> I appeal to every individual who uses the roads to take real care, lest in an unguarded moment any one of our homes and families be deprived

of its breadwinner or devoted mother. Or be plunged into grief by the tragic death of an innocent child.

Perhaps hearing driving safety preached from the pulpit might help to make it a moral issue.

———

Roads in December would be more crowded than ever with the rush of those returning from abroad for the holidays. In 1963, however, there were more people than usual who wanted to *leave* the country during the Christmas season, because it heralded the arrival of harsh winter weather. The previous year was a frightful reminder. Memories of blizzards, snowdrifts, blocked roads and stranded people were still fresh in the mind.

As a result, warm temperatures and abundant sunshine were more inviting than ever. Dublin travel agencies got an early jump on their advertising for sunshine cruises during the winter holidays. Since the autumn, travel offices had filled their windows with posters and literature advertising 'gay Christmas sunshine cruises'.

One window in particular caught the eye of Timothy Hynes. A travel agency was featuring the Greek Line's luxury liner *Lakonia,* soon departing on its 'luxury sunshine cruise' to the Canary Islands. It looked so alluring that Hynes picked up a brochure to take home and show his wife, Molly. She had founded the Universal Employment Agency in 1937, by then known as the Molly Hynes Agency, and they could well afford the luxury of the holiday.

For several years they had been talking of what they called a *real* family holiday with their four children. It had been many years since they had done so. Immediately Molly Hynes was captivated by the idea of a Christmas cruise. The gleaming white *Lakonia* indeed looked like an ideal cruise liner for them.

———

Ireland's army of postal workers, meanwhile, weren't going anywhere sunny that December. They would be happy to have had half a day off to sit down and rest. The year 1963 was setting records as the busiest in Irish postal history. Mountains of envelopes, cards and parcels were accumulating, all awaiting sorting and delivery – by Christmas!

By 16 December it was announced that the Christmas 'postal traffic is now reaching its peak', the staff 'working around the clock'. They were now certain to 'break *all* records … with up to 15,000,000 letters'. Postal workers, taking pride in their performance, understood that every item, from the smallest card to the largest parcel, was important to the person sending it.

Some were especially important – even rare. That year, one in particular was brought to the attention of an *Irish Independent* reporter who was fascinated by its uniqueness. It was a present for President de Valera – one he had definitely never received before. Its origin was traced to a dusty, forgotten attic in London.

One day in the autumn of 1963 Captain Michael Farr, chairperson of a London company making sloe gin, was rummaging in the attic above his office when he came across:

> very old papers, probably 100 years old. They included a recipe for a Christmas pudding. Curiosity overcame me and I decided to follow the instructions which, oddly, mentioned sloe gin.

He dusted off the papers and showed them to staff members and friends, who shared his delight – and his curiosity. He couldn't resist at least trying to find out what the pudding tasted like. A perfectionist, he followed the recipe to the letter. The 'first puddings we made were given to several well-known gourmets who were most impressed with the result.'[204]

Those who tasted the pudding, thought by some to possibly date back to the 1840s, raved about its unique flavour. This encouraged Captain Farr to proceed, and 'we decided to make some big ones for families and friends abroad' as Christmas presents.

Then an idea struck him. It would be 'an appropriate gesture' to send a pudding to President de Valera, 'since the ingredients included, as it were, a little bit of Ireland.' He would include a note to de Valera's personal secretary, explaining the circumstances behind the present. Farr wrote that his company depended on a huge quantity of sloes picked in Ireland every year. The present was beautifully wrapped and packed for personal delivery to Dublin.

It was verified that Captain Farr's gift of the three-pound Christmas pudding arrived in perfect condition at President de Valera's office. We don't know whether Captain Farr continued to send the President a pudding every Christmas thereafter. Regrettably, history does not always tell us such things.

We *do* know the contents of the many letters that continued to stream in to the newspapers during the Christmas season with more and more suggestions for a memorial to President Kennedy. At first, most people had favoured a statue or a plaque, but as time passed these ideas came to seem cold and lifeless to many people. Kennedy was so *alive* and vigorous that it seemed more appropriate that his memorial should reflect life. This concept generated fresh ideas from such writers as Alasdair Mac Cába:

> A memorial should take the form of a new forest in Ireland. To keep his memory green … the plantation of saplings sprouting to life from the old sod and breathing the air he loved. A welcome departure from dead stone memorials that clutter our city. Trees symbolise life and immortality.

Other ideas were equally original, such as the restoration of buildings on the Rock of Cashel.

However, as the end of the year approached, no Government authorities had yet come forward with brilliant ideas. The minds of ordinary people seemed more fertile and creative.

———

By the third week of December, people were getting more into the Christmas spirit, flocking to the shops to buy presents. The *Irish Press* reported a 'boom Christmas for city shops'. As 'huge Christmas sales rang up across the country', the manager of one of Dublin's biggest shops exulted in the fact that 'it's our biggest Christmas yet!' surpassing even the previous year's '£30 million spending spree'.

For those who could afford it, nothing promised to be more relaxing than a sunny cruise during the Christmas holidays. For weeks, Molly and Timothy Hynes had been examining their brochure about the *Lakonia's* eleven-day cruise under what were promised to be 'sun-drenched' skies. Departing from Southampton, it would visit Madeira, Tenerife, Las Palmas, Lisbon and other spots.

In its advertising, the Greek Line emphasised that the *Lakonia* had been completely refitted the year before at a cost of £300,000, meaning that the luxury liner was 'built for comfort and stability'. Below the decks, however, in the engine rooms, workers had a somewhat different assessment of the *Lakonia's* 'stability'.

The brochure showed a freshly painted and outfitted liner with a passenger capacity of 1,300, with twenty-four lifeboats of different sizes. For this Christmas cruise it would sail with 650 passengers and a crew of 300. The *Lakonia's* captain was Mathios Zarbis, one of the Greek Line's most able officers. He had been with the company since 1947 and had been a liner captain for six years. His crew were a hotchpotch of seamen, mostly Greeks and Germans, young and old, seasoned and inexperienced. All were approved by the head office.

Molly and Timothy Hynes decided in favour of booking the cruise as soon as possible, but they needed to consult their adult children to see if they wanted to join them. Their son Tom and daughter Ena both worked in the family business and were enthusiastic. Their other son, John, was a medical student and welcomed the diversion. Iverna, only eleven, could hardly wait to tell her friends. The family also wanted to include their long-time housekeeper and friend, Molly Walsh.

They booked the cruise and began preparations. The ship was to sail from Southampton on 19 December for what promised to be a grand Christmas adventure – one to be long remembered.

On the 16th Molly and Timothy Hynes, with John and Iverna, sailed for Liverpool, then travelled on to London to join the rest of the family. On the 18th they would go to Southampton.

On the day before sailing, another passenger, Mary Aylward, would sit down to write a short letter to her sister Frances O'Hara in New York. Her intention was to share a thought that was troubling her: she had 'had a premonition of death before she sailed from Southampton … that she might live only a day or two' after the ship had set sail.[205] Her 'foreboding', as her sister called it, was so strong that Mrs Aylward gave her explicit instructions on what should be done in the event that she should die. It did not, however, deter her from boarding the liner the next morning.

As always, fate can play a fickle role in human plans. William P. McDonnell, who was nearing retirement from the Department of Agriculture, had booked his cruise on the *Lakonia* the previous June. He had recently checked out of hospital and wanted something to look forward to. He thought a sunny voyage would do him good. But his tickets were sent to the wrong address, which delayed confirmation of his reservation for many weeks. By the time the matter was straightened out his original accommodation was no longer available. Then a medical complication sent him back to hospital. 'So I cancelled,' he said. He put it down to bad luck.

Conversely, Howard Baker and his wife 'joined the ship as a result of a last-minute cancellation – considering it good luck'.

John and Mabel Groom were seemingly not so lucky. Three of their four suitcases were stolen from the Southampton docks. 'We had been told about the theft, but we went aboard just before the ship sailed *hoping* the luggage would turn up', but when it didn't they cancelled at the last minute. As gleeful passengers were waving to friends on the pier, the Grooms, both seventy-six, had to disembark as the ship's horns blared for departure.

What a heart-breaking stroke of bad luck, they thought.

Of the 650 passengers on board most were British, French, German, Austrian, Irish and American. There were more than thirty Irish citizens, most of whom were well-to-do. They would delight in discovering one another in the first day or two, and several would become closer than they could ever have imagined.

Alfred Haselden, a retired businessman from Ballsbridge, his wife, Peggy, and their eleven-year-old daughter, Patricia, had eagerly signed up for the cruise. As had J. Geller of Terenure, proprietor of a successful company. A widower, he was on his own.

Henry Wilson, 'one of the best known radio operators in Ireland', his wife, Edie, and their son, James, were also on board. As were Enda Maguire, a forester from Co. Cavan, and Vera Halligan of Bray, who owned a popular hair-dressing salon. Mr and Mrs Colbert were also from Bray.

Two sisters from Cork, Josephine and Kay Reynolds, both in their mid-thirties, considered themselves seasoned sea voyagers, having gone on a world cruise two years before. It was only at the last minute that they decided to book on the *Lakonia*.

Two veterinarians and good friends, Owen Burke and Gerry McGovern of Co. Cavan, decided to get away from their practice for a while and enjoy a holiday cruise. McGovern looked forward to the voyage – though he was not fond of the water and couldn't swim.

The two most popular Irish passengers, as it would turn out, didn't have to pay a pound: they were on board *gratis*. They were on duty, actually: a doctor and a chaplain. Both were possessed of a kind and engaging personality, and their presence was most reassuring.

They were on the *Lakonia* by good fortune – and to the surprise of some of their family and friends. Well before sailing, the Greek Line head office in London had sent a request to their Dublin office for a 'Catholic Irish chaplain' to serve on board the ship. Mr J. Kelly, the Irish agent, got in touch with the Rev. T. Martin, SJ, in Gardiner Street. He knew that the Rev. Edward Andrews, SJ, who was attached to St Ignatius College, Galway, had served as chaplain on a cruise ship some years earlier and had enjoyed it. But that was when he was younger and in considerably better health. Nonetheless, Father Andrews gladly accepted.

He was a native of Dublin and was educated at Belvedere College. He was widely known and much liked and respected. He seemed a perfect fit. However, his sister questioned whether or not he should have assumed the role of ship's chaplain, as 'he walked with the aid of a stick and suffered from arthritis'. Yet Father Andrews didn't consider his limited mobility to be a problem in serving as ship's chaplain. And he never declined a request to act in his capacity as a priest. Furthermore, he felt that a cruise in a warmer climate might improve his arthritis.

Dr James Riordan had been asked if he would serve as *Lakonia's* physician. A 'popular figure in medical and sporting circles', he had practised at North Circular Road. During the Second World War he was an active member of the Red Cross.

Yet, to his relatives, his decision to accept the position came as quite a surprise. His brother, also a doctor, knew nothing of it till the *Lakonia* had actually sailed. When he learnt that his brother James was on an eleven-day sea voyage he could hardly believe it. 'I cannot *imagine* that it is my brother – the sea is absolutely foreign to his nature.' Apparently James Riordan had a fear of large, open bodies of water. Other members of his family expressed similar surprise.

Dr Riordan, like Father Andrews, was an unfailingly kind and generous man who was always willing to help people. They would soon meet one another – and become immediate and close friends.

On the morning of 19 December the passengers were boarding, getting settled in their cabins and meeting others. On the ship's manifest were thirty-four children under the age of twelve, including two infants.

Once all the luggage had been loaded, the captain of the *Lakonia*, Mathios Zarbis, needed to seek the attention of passengers. He and his senior officers needed to carry out the mandatory lifeboat drill. They demonstrated how to board the lifeboats, how to use the rope ladders and how to manoeuvre the boats in the water. Some passengers took it more seriously than others. A few questions were asked and were promptly answered to everyone's satisfaction. Everything appeared to be professional and secure.

When everything had been checked and double-cheeked, the *Lakonia's* horns blared their signal for departure from Southampton. On a Christmas cruise even the captain and crew were in cheerful spirits. Captain Zarbis promised some special activities during the cruise – as well as some surprises.

The thirty or so Irish passengers easily found their compatriots. From the outset, Father Andrews and Dr Riordan were the centre of attention, being immensely popular with everyone.

––––

Back in Ireland, the winter weather was just arriving, with much of the country experiencing frigid temperatures, snow and slick roads. However, Christmas excitement made children gleeful. Five hundred children at a Christmas party in a national school 'met Santa riding a horse and carrying a sack of presents'. Elsewhere, Santa arrived on a Dublin Fire Brigade engine. For one group of orphans, Santa parachuted from 7,000 feet over Dublin, with his red robe and white beard flowing. The Lord Mayor, Seán Moore, invited some 'little angels' to join him for the lighting of the Christmas tree and for carol singing.

But there was one sad fact for the children of Dublin during the Christmas season. The Garda Depot in the Phoenix Park was having its last passing-out parade on 20 December. And, as noted by the *Irish Independent*, it would be the city's children who would miss it the most:

> For Dublin children down through the years a visit to the Zoo included the chance that the recruits might be seen wheeling and stamping about the Depot parade ground in a practice session. But it is to be no more – and the Park will be the duller for it.

The Depot, dating from 1842, was evacuated by the RIC in 1922 and handed over to the Garda Síochána the following year. As the *Independent* wrote, it was just cause for sentimentality:

It would be churlish to deny the Dubliner his sentiments, and the Dublin child his regrets. For him, the Depot was a place of pageantry. Its day is done ... and we can be generous in our memories.

During the Christmas season in Dublin there was excellent entertainment on offer. Apart from the variety of fine films, the Gaiety and the Olympia were presenting Christmas favourites. At the Gaiety, Jimmy O'Dea and Maureen Potter were starring in *Goldilocks and the Three Bears* before packed audiences for every showing. At the Olympia, critics lauded Jack Cruise in *Cinderella*.

It was the Olympia at its finest. 'The pantomime swings along, full of traditional sentiments of rollicking fun, colour, music and romance.' Best of all, the venerable theatre was still in business. Only a few weeks earlier it had appeared doomed. Plans for it to be converted into a glitzy dance hall had failed to materialise, for some inexplicable reason.

Now there were new rumours of the theatre's being saved. New plans were supposedly being formulated to rescue it. The robust applause at the conclusion of every Christmas performance was as much for the theatre itself as for the cast. That was the *real* Christmas spirit.

———

In contrast with all the Christmas gaiety, one man, Michael McGregor, was fuming – at the Government and its failure to keep its promise to honour President Kennedy. With the year 1963 within only days of ending, and with no action yet taken, his exasperation was boiling over. He wrote to the newspapers that a:

> month has lapsed since the death of President Kennedy. People in Dublin have cried out in grief and sorrow ... pleaded for a lasting monument of him to be erected.
>
> To date, *nothing* has been *done*! Our representatives twiddle their thumbs – doing nothing. Bound and gagged with red tape. It is a sad state of affairs.

His sentiments reflected those of many other Dubliners, who were voicing their displeasure in a variety of ways. It seemed that, every day, people had to read about yet another city or country honouring Kennedy in some meaningful and lasting way. Honouring *their* Irish-American President.

For scores of Dubliners, the joyful mood of Christmas was rudely violated by the Dublin Corporation. The people of the city were exposed to a brain-shattering racket – an incessant, insufferable noise.

In a classic case of bad timing and poor judgement, the Corporation decided that 19–24 December was the ideal moment to finally attack and obliterate the 'Thing' on O'Connell Bridge. As part of a scheme to promote tourism to Ireland in the 1950s, many sculptures had been erected throughout the city. Intended to be permanent, the Bowl of Light on O'Connell Bridge was a large copper bowl containing imitation flames, to which flowers were later added. For a decade, the structure had been regarded as a blot on the cityscape. Many people wanted it gone, and it was constantly vandalised.

Having long procrastinated, the Corporation decided that the time had come. The *Evening Herald* described the sculpture as 'the big flower bed ... that has been an "unwanted child".' It was a kind description. People had called it every name imaginable, and it eventually became known simply as the Thing. Now its end was near.

The Corporation despatched 'a demolition gang of twenty men with eight pneumatic drills' to eradicate it – once and for all. But within minutes of firing up their drills, they found that the 'unwanted child' didn't want to leave. 'It's hard as a bullet,' one veteran demolitionist complained. 'We'll be here for *days!*'

People all the way from O'Connell Street to the top of Grafton Street were suddenly victims of the chorus of eight pneumatic drills. All along the way, office windows and shop doors had to be shut. Seagulls sought quieter havens. It was loud enough to waken the dead.

The spewing dust was whipped up into the air and carried far beyond the drilling site. People complained that it ruined the joys of Christmas window-shopping.

After days of endurance, the 'unwanted child' disappeared from sight, to become part of Dublin folklore. For those who experienced it, it was just one more bizarre event of 1963 to remember.

Aboard the *Lakonia* on Sunday night, 22 December, the much-anticipated Tramps' Ball was to be held, always one of the most popular activities of the entire cruise. The passengers were told they could be up till the wee hours. Away from home, they may have been more uninhibited, perhaps drinking more than usual.

Most of the passengers wanted to attend the ball for at least the first few hours of the evening. By eleven they began to peel away to retire for the night. Others stayed up, as the music and merriment remained lively. Among the Irish contingent a few cliques had formed. Dr James Riordan, Gerry McGovern, Enda Maguire, Father Andrews and Owen Burke enjoyed one another's company and were amiably chatting away. Father Andrews enjoyed the socialising but bid his companions good night and wearily headed for his cabin.

At 11:40 p.m., when a good many passengers were already asleep, one person in the cabin section had reported smoke. The crew quickly investigated. A few minutes later the alarm was raised.

Some passengers seemed unfazed; others either hurriedly got out of bed and dressed or headed towards their cabins from the ballroom. Nobody appeared panicked.

Without delay, Owen Burke went to his cabin to get his life jacket. It is likely that Iverna Hynes was already asleep in her cabin when the rest of her family rushed to join her. No-one had been enjoying the merriment of the Tramp's Ball more than the Hynes family.

Father Andrews was in his cabin but not yet asleep. He suddenly heard the corridors become 'quite noisy' and wondered what the hubbub was all about. Seconds later he too smelt smoke. Thinking quickly, but slowed by his arthritis, 'I slipped a dressing gown over my pyjamas, put my lifebelt on top and made my way … without slippers.'[206] It was then that he realised he had misplaced his walking-stick. The best he could do was hobble down the corridor balancing himself with one hand against the wall.

By midnight the smoke had spread, and passengers were either hurrying in and out of their cabins or moving towards the deck. As the smoke worsened, the sense of urgency increased.

Upon reaching the deck, passengers sought their numbered lifeboats. Many remained quite calm, convinced that the problem would be quickly resolved. Riordan, McGovern, Maguire and Burke had all hastened to their cabins to seize their life jackets. Other passengers were stuffing a few valuables in their pockets, just in case. Yet there was still no sense of general panic. In fact, a few people made nervous jokes about it as they scurried about.

McGovern, however, found that he couldn't reach his cabin, since it was near the barber's, where the smoke was too dense. As he turned back to join Riordan and Maguire, a crew member handed him a life jacket, for which he was very grateful, because he couldn't swim. Instructions were already being given for everyone to grab their life jackets and assemble in the dining-room, in preparation for going to their lifeboat stations. Things suddenly seemed more serious.

It was when passengers were assembled at their stations, seeing lifeboats being lowered into the black sea in the middle of the night, that the first real shiver of fear was felt. Some people began pushing their way forward without regard for others. Father Andrews was struggling along when Dr Riordan spotted him. The doctor:

> linked my arm. He was very kind to everyone. He helped me to a lifeboat and then he returned to help other passengers.

In his fifties and very fit, the good doctor concentrated solely on assisting others into their lifeboats.

Owen Burke had been among those who had resisted orders to board the lifeboats, as 'he always felt that they would put out the fire'. But now he was ready to abide by the captain's orders – and without delay. Like so many others, when he reached the lifeboat stations he was worried to see the confusion of the scene. Having been ordered to assemble beside their lifeboats, the passengers then 'got no *instructions* from the Captain or crew'. Passengers later claimed that 'they *could* have used hand-speakers – but they did *not* do so!'[207]

It was becoming apparent that many of the crew members were not adequately trained in handling such an emergency. They fumbled about in trying to free and lower lifeboats, and then in manoeuvring them properly. More shocking, some crew members began pushing passengers aside so that they could take their places in the lifeboats. In some cases, it deteriorated into a struggle for survival.

However, there were kind and generous crew members as well, as J. Geller found. He had hoped to stay on board the ship until the danger had passed. When he finally did hurry to the lifeboats he realised that he had no life jacket. A member of the crew spotted him and quickly came to his assistance. 'A Swiss hostess saw me without a life jacket. She had one on and whipped it off.' At first, he 'protested that I did not want it – but she tied it around me', telling him that she could swim.[208]

While all this was going on, the *Lakonia's* radio operator was desperately trying to carry out his critical task. The first distress calls were sent shortly before midnight. This was followed by the ship's exact location in the Atlantic. It was confirmed by the communications official in Madeira that the distress signal meant the ship was 'in flames and going down'.

By 12:20 a.m. all seemed to have deteriorated into chaos on deck. Henry Wilson and his wife would describe it as 'confusion and horror'. Gerry McGovern found himself among those left on deck watching the lifeboats leave him behind:

> The last of the lifeboats had been launched at about 12.30 a.m. and some had been burned ... and there were no seats in any of the lifeboats left![209]

Seeing that he had no choice, he assisted Dr Riordan, who had been helping the last of the passengers into lifeboats, ignoring his own safety. Owen Burke was lucky. His lifeboat, no. 6, couldn't be launched for some reason, but he 'got away in boat number 10'. Some lifeboats were burnt or tangled and stood unused. Others were occupied by crew members who had forced their way on. However, some senior crew members conscientiously remained behind to care for the elderly and for families who had found themselves split up. This included the seven members of the Hynes family and their housekeeper.

Dr Riordan assisted Father Andrews, who had been struggling all the way to his seat in the lifeboat. As Father Andrews would later recall, 'after he had taken me down to the lifeboat we shook hands and said goodbye – that was the last I saw of him.'

As passengers were desperately trying to squeeze into the last lifeboats, there was screaming and crying from parents who feared that their children might not make it in time. There would be accounts in the newspapers of mothers, in the grip of panic, 'tossing children into lifeboats ... and of parents struggling in the water to keep their children afloat.'[210]

By 12:40 a.m. the flames had spread, and those left at the deck rail could only contemplate their fate:

> Flames were leaping from the wide afterdeck where tourists had played and danced ... The ship was blackened and scarred ... ropes which had lowered lifeboats dangled over the sides, wallowing like streamers in the water ... Fire seemed to have the ship completely in its grip.[211]

Explosions now began to erupt in parts of the ship. Those trapped on deck suffered the heat of the fire and the choking smoke. With the ship ablaze and now sinking, the stranded passengers needed to get off and away from the ship. Some saw the dangling ropes as their only escape.

Dr Riordan and Gerry McGovern stood together on deck, both wearing life jackets – knowing that only one of them could swim. They gripped a rope ladder and began climbing down the side of the ship. Reaching the water, they held on in the darkness, hoping that if they could hold on till morning the vessel would still be afloat and rescue ships would have arrived.

After some time, fighting fatigue, they heard a woman's voice. McGovern heard the doctor call out to her:

> I heard him ask a lady if she could swim. Then he went into the water ... and disappeared very quickly ... and I did not see him any more.

With only his life jacket, how long could Dr Riordan survive in the water? Or did he give it to the woman?

Unable to swim, McGovern held onto the rope, bobbing like a cork. But then the ladder 'burned out and slipped into the water – with a deck chair attached to it.' He grasped the chair and held on tightly with his remaining strength, only to discover that, in the darkness, he was clinging to the chair together with an 'old lady, an ex-matron of a hospital in London.' Both held on for dear life.

Somewhere not far away, in the pitch black, the 71-year-old J. Geller, wearing the life jacket given to him by the crew member, had been forced down a rope ladder into the sea and was also clinging to a deck chair in the water, which he would miraculously grip for the next six hours.

Even those fortunate passengers who had made it into lifeboats were hardly safe. A few of the lifeboats remained up against the ship or dangerously close to it, where an explosion of the 500 tons of fuel oil would doom them. The reason they remained so close was that some incompetent crew members didn't know how to row them. According to Father Andrews:

> while waiting to board lifeboat No. 17, a steward slipped off his shoes and gave them to me. There were about 40 other persons in the lifeboat and three members of the crew – but they didn't know much about rowing. For we were going around in circles and back toward the blazing liner – so close that we could feel the heat from the flames. A couple of explosions seemed to terrify the women, but we succeeded in calming them down … then we pulled away.[212]

By about 2 a.m. all passengers had likely deserted the ship one way or another, many in the open sea. Captain Zarbis, in that most honourable tradition of the sea, was the last person off his ship.

The *Lakonia's* radio operator had continued to send out distress calls until he lost contact and was driven out by the flames. His last message was:

> Had to abandon station … We are leaving the ship … Please send immediate assistance! Please help![213]

The US Coast Guard co-ordinating centre in New York, and the commander of the US Navy forces in the Azores, confirmed receipt of the distress calls. At 02:42 the British tanker *Montcalm* reported that it was speeding towards the *Lakonia*. 'Ship now sighted about 5.5 miles from us … No survivors [spotted] yet.' The plumes of dark smoke were directing rescue vessels to the scene.

By 04:00 'a small armada of ships and rescue planes forged through the wintry Atlantic seas'. At 04:08 the *Montcalm* radioed: 'Now approaching *Lakonia*, fire is blazing amidships … Lifeboats spotted in water.' The Argentine liner *Salta* despatched a radio signal at 04:28: 'We are now rescuing people from the first lifeboats.'

By 04:52 the *Montcalm* verified that it had taken aboard twelve survivors and would 'continue searching'. The US Air Force confirmed at 06:15 that there were several aircraft on the way to the scene. The US ship *Independence* was racing to the scene. The British liner *Stratheden* was also 'heading full speed', hoping to arrive by 9 a.m.

Not all passengers were in lifeboats and easily spotted. Many were floating on their own in the vast Atlantic, some latching on to pieces of debris. Fatigued and weak, they wondered if they would be seen. Mercifully, the 'sea was moderate, with the water temperature 64 degrees Fahrenheit – warm enough to give the chance of survival.' A *chance*.

——

As rescues were under way in the early-morning light, the news was reaching Ireland. At first it was thought that there were 'some' Irish passengers on board the sinking *Lakonia*; but this had not been verified. Details would be scanty and conflicting as they filtered into news rooms. There was at least enough information for newspapers to place the *Lakonia* disaster on the front page, as did the *Irish Times:*

> The sudden shipboard fire wrecked a gay Christmas cruise. Passengers who had been disporting in the ballroom or strolling round the spacious promenade deck found themselves a few minutes later struggling for life in the waters of the Atlantic.[214]

Father Andrews had been in a lifeboat for about four hours when he was picked up, at about 6 a.m., by the *Montcalm*, three miles from the *Lakonia*. 'After I got aboard I saw people in the water'. Among them was Gerry McGovern, still clinging to the deck chair together with the elderly woman. At last, an American plane that had spotted them flew overhead and dropped a flare to help the Pakistani vessel *Mehdi* reach them quickly.

Owen Burke, who had found a seat in lifeboat no. 10 when his own boat could not be launched, was rescued by the *Salta* at dawn. J. Geller, at seventy-one, wearing the life jacket given to him by the selfless crew member, had managed to climb down a rope ladder and clutch a deck chair. 'I had blacked out and had no idea where I was, no knowledge of being picked up' at about 9 a.m.

By now the London office of the Greek Line was releasing information about the *Lakonia's* passenger manifest. Newspaper editors in Europe and North America had been waiting for the figures to come in.

In the early hours of the morning it was confirmed that there were indeed Irish citizens on board. Throughout the morning of 23 December early figures suggested that it could be quite a few Irish passengers. It was expected that the total could now reach thirty. This was sufficient for the *Evening Herald* to print a dramatic afternoon edition emblazoned with the headline 'Dublin families on blazing liner'.

Suddenly it was a national tragedy. Staff members at the Greek Line's London office 'were inundated with calls from anxious relatives' from many countries. In Ireland the Dublin agent, J. Kelly, found his phone ringing incessantly. He told frantic callers that he was a *local* travel agent only handling bookings for the Greek Line in London. He too only knew what little he had read in the newspapers. There was particular interest in the well-known Father Andrews and in Dr Riordan.

Throughout the day on the 23rd people were being rescued, and bodies recovered. Some were identified, others were nameless. By the time the information reached London it was fragmentary, confused and often unreliable. Authorities were trying to establish three categories: survivors, deceased and missing. Meanwhile, relatives and friends of the missing were heartsick with worry.

People sat around their radios and televisions, awaiting bulletins with verified names and statuses. Aerial photographs were now coming in showing the liner ablaze and listing to starboard, threatening to sink. In Dublin and elsewhere such catastrophic images heightened the fears of relatives.

By noon, reports on Irish passengers were arriving in Dublin. Mr and Mrs Colbert of Bray had definitely been rescued, as had Vera Halligan of Bray. J. Geller and his remarkable story of survival would leave readers astonished. Gerry McGovern, the non-swimmer, had his own incredible tale, but he would be far more interested in telling of the heroics of his friend Dr James Riordan. They had descended the rope ladder together in desperation, and McGovern knew that Dr Riordan had not yet been accounted for. Knowing of Dr Riordan's excellent physical condition, McGovern remained confident that he would soon be found. After all, he had been in a rowing club and played rugby. No survivors could account for the whereabouts of Enda Maguire during the last, chaotic hours of the *Lakonia*.

On the afternoon of the 23rd, Peter Knox, an enterprising reporter for United Press International, hired a pilot to fly him directly over the *Lakonia* site in a small plane at very low altitude. At 4 p.m. they swooped down to about 200 feet over the doomed ship, where they could see bodies bobbing in the sea swells. And they could see the terrified faces of survivors in lifeboats waving madly at them.

The sea was calm and visibility good, but 'we could see no sign of life on the once-proud Greek cruise ship, still belching flames and smoke.' By this time, Knox counted five large rescue vessels in the area still searching for and picking up survivors. The 'debris field' had expanded miles from the ship, meaning that some lone survivors, kept afloat by their life jackets or by clinging to debris, might have drifted far off to face another night.

The first reporters on the scene wrote of 'many people seen swimming around the vessel, still ablaze and disembowelled, listing about 15 degrees to starboard.'[215] They might have felt they had a better chance of rescue if they stuck close to the ship, whose flames cast some light on the dark sea; but one of the survivors picked up by the *Montcalm* was an engineer from the *Lakonia* who had tried to warn people that its 500 tons of fuel could explode at any time. Any survivors should keep well clear of the vessel.

As a poignant reminder that it was a Christmas tragedy, reporters noted seeing wrapped packages, toys and even 'an almost life-size doll' bobbing on the sea.

Many Irish people were having difficulty with their Christmas preparations, with such an awful tragedy unfolding. Everyone hoped for nothing but good news by Christmas Day.

By midday that afternoon, authorities in Morocco were preparing to shelter survivors at Casablanca. At the wharf, blankets, warm clothing and nourishment would be available. Hospitals were placed on alert. Meanwhile, search and rescue efforts at sea were still under way.

Some reporters were beginning to contact the families of Irish passengers whose names had been verified. Those relatives who had already received good news might have been obliging; others were distraught and declined. The family of Gerry McGovern had just received 'a cable saying he was picked up by a ship at 9 a.m. and that he was well.' His brothers and sisters were all 'immensely happy' at the news. But while his family rejoiced, McGovern agonised about the fate of Dr Riordan, still unknown.

Rosaleen McWeeney, a relative of Molly Hynes, could tell one reporter from the *Irish Independent* only that she was anxiously awaiting news from the Greek Line, which had promised to ring her 'just as soon as there was anything to report'. Reporters couldn't coax so much as a word from Owen Burke's mother; she 'was too upset to talk to our reporters'. In Cork a sister-in-law of Josephine and Kay Reynolds stated, 'We are nearly frantic with worry ... We have no news yet.'

By Christmas Eve morning the *Irish Press* was calling the disaster 'one of the great sea dramas of all time'.[216] Statistics on passengers were now being sporadically released from the London head office. There were now 24 known dead and 135 missing. Among the 30 or so Irish passengers, it was verified that '16 are safe'. The *Irish Times* described the unfolding situation as:

> one of the greatest dramas in recent sea history ... One of the most amazing sea rescue operations ever.[217]

Later in the day there was communiqué from the Admiralty in London confirming that there were still 'many bodies in the water'. Dr Riordan's family were still bewildered by his decision to go on the cruise. Mrs Aird, a close relative, could tell reporters only that his family were growing increasingly worried as the hours passed, 'waiting by their radio all day for more information'.

The wait was soon over for Frances O'Hara of New York. Before sailing, her sister Mary Aylward had sent her a letter containing a premonition of her death 'a day or two' into the cruise. It turned out to be prophetic when her body was retrieved from the sea.

The first rescue ships were now taking survivors to safe ports. The Argentine ship *Salta* was arriving at Madeira with a load of rescued passengers – and a load of the dead. Relatives from Britain and other countries had begun congregating there awaiting the excruciating moment:

> Dread and fear mingled with happiness in the waiting crowd as relatives searched out for their loved ones – or failed to find them, and feared them dead.[218]

The dread and fear was found nowhere more so than in the Hynes home, where family members and close friends had gathered. Indeed, by this time the entire nation was emotionally invested in learning the fate that had befallen the entire family of six, and their housekeeper. During the night of the 23rd the anxiety had become nearly insufferable for the family's closest relatives. They had stayed up all night long.

Then, on the morning of Christmas Eve, a telegram arrived for Molly Hynes's sister. It was the briefest she had ever received:

A telegram with just two words brought unimaginable joy into a Dublin home to-day. The message was sent to Mrs Rosaleen McWeeney …

Mrs McWeeney had spent all last night waiting by the telephone and listening to the late night radio bulletins. She said, 'The Post Office rang us to say they had received a telegram for us.' The message was: 'ALL SAFE'. It was signed, 'Ena', the eldest daughter.[219]

One receiving the news, Mrs McWeeney exclaimed, 'We are all so excited we do not know what is happening!' The *Evening Herald's* front-page headline cheered the entire nation. 'Dublin family of six saved from liner'.

As it turned out, all members of the Hynes family, and their housekeeper, had been placed in a lifeboat together, and they were rescued by the *Salta* and taken to Madeira. Throughout Ireland it would be joyfully spoken of as a Christmas miracle.

Then came some alarming news: mistakes had been made in identification. Some of the Greek Line's bulletins about survivors could not be taken as verified. Some 'mix-ups', the term used by the London office, were now being discovered; cruel errors had been made. Reported survivors were actually dead – and *vice versa*.

This news shocked families waiting for a happy reunion. How many early reports had been incorrect? Reporters were now revealing such cases. In one instance, Kenneth Robinson had been reported missing. Then his father received word that he was safe in Madeira. Elated, his parents and girlfriend rushed to London to enquire about his return. At the office 'they were shocked to be told his name was on the "death roll"'. The company said they were sorry for the mix-up.

The *Irish Independent* drew attention to the egregious blunders with their headline 'Two reported dead are alive'. In another case, Mrs C. Robinson (no relation to Kenneth), who had been listed among the deceased, 'walked off a plane in London airport' a few days later.

For waiting relatives, these stories meant that they could not be certain their loved ones were really safe until they spoke to them on the phone or saw them arrive home in person.

At dawn on Christmas Day extensive searches resumed, as there were more accounts of 'shivering and exhausted human cargoes' among the flotsam surrounding the *Lakonia*. Experts were still saying that remaining alive in the water, with the temperatures relatively warm for the Atlantic, was not impossible – though it would be exhausting.

With the good news about the Hynes family it was now believed that there were twenty-two Irish passengers safely accounted for. Notable among those listed as missing was Dr James Riordan.

Throughout Christmas Day, survivors were arriving in London, welcomed by family, friends – and eager reporters. Most Irish passengers flew straight home to an emotional welcome. Father Andrews was a prime target for the press – and he could hardly have been missed: he stepped off the plane in London sporting a rather 'ungodly' appearance. He was wearing an orange shirt, maroon socks and corduroy trousers – none of which fit him very well – and carrying his few belongings in a brown paper bag. From some observers it drew smiles.

Father Andrews was quick to explain his unconventional garb. Upon arrival at Casablanca he was wet, cold and shivering, and was glad to accept whatever clothing was available. Reporters tossed many questions at him. But what he most wanted to talk about was his 'saviour' Dr Riordan. It was the caring doctor who had taken his arm and assisted him all the way to his lifeboat.

No-one was praying harder than him that the good doctor would still be found alive. But on Christmas Day the dreaded news arrived: the body of Dr James Riordan had been found in the sea by one of the rescue ships. His family were notified. They would arrange to have his body returned to Ireland for burial.

Shortly thereafter, however, they were informed from London that another 'mix-up' had occurred. They were horrified to learn that his internment had *already* taken place – in Gibraltar. How such a mistake had been made wasn't explained. They contacted the Department of External Affairs to assist them in having the remains returned home.

Father Andrews would tell of how Dr Riordan had 'returned to help other passengers' time after time. Other passengers added their recollections of his courage. Most poignant was Gerry McGovern's account of how he and Dr Riordan had descended the rope ladder before hearing a woman's faint cry for help. Dr Riordan said goodbye and pushed away, and that was the 'last I saw of him'. The *Irish Independent* honoured the doctor's deeds with the front-page headline 'Irish doctor's heroism'.

———

In the following days there were many interviews with survivors. Predictably, there were conflicting accounts of the chaos and of the behaviour of the *Lakonia's* crew. While some passengers accused them of cowardice and negligence, others were quick to cite acts of selfless assistance. Owen Burke 'praised the crew and said he could not criticise them'. However, William Scott and his wife, Kitty, damned them, swearing that the 'crew were very panicky, got into the lifeboats *before* the passengers – they were *terrible!*' He added, 'If I had had a gun I would have *shot* the lot of them!'[220]

Readers were fascinated by J. Geller's tale of survival. On 29 December he told the press that he had made enquiries about the Swiss hostess who had given him her life jacket, and he learnt that she was safe and well in Geneva. But Geller did make one thing clear: 'I hope I'll *never* be on a ship again as long as I live – I have seen all the water I want to see!'

One interview with a survivor of the tragedy was particularly disturbing. On 28 December the crew member Kyriakos Kokkonia had a stunning revelation to make:

I *expected* this to happen. There were filthy conditions below decks – the engines were old. Discipline was shocking.[221]

With New Year's Eve just ahead, the Dublin travel agent J. Kelly had 'good news' from the Greek Line office in London to pass along to all the Irish *Lakonia* passengers. They were all 'promised a full refund'.

Chapter 22 ～

'THE MOST UNIQUE YEAR OF THE CENTURY'

1963 was a year of the greatest sensations in living memory
... Events almost beyond belief.

Irish Press, 31 DECEMBER 1963

On Christmas Day nature brought yet another surprise. In striking contrast to the previous year, when the country was besieged by an arctic blast, it was now sunny, mild and tranquil. In fact, Ireland 'enjoyed its best Christmas for years'. People went out for delightful strolls, greeting others along the way.

Meanwhile, the search for survivors of the *Lakonia* disaster was still under way. Among the missing was Enda Maguire, from Co. Cavan, who was well liked by everyone. The nation's trauma was not over.

In its annual editorial 'Life at Christmas' the *Irish Times* was notably less cheerful than in most years:

> Much has occurred during the last twelve months. We have changed ... things have shocked us. During recent months we have been faced more than once with a sharp reminder of life's transitoriness. Death has come when least expected ... Life has limped on.

Yet it had also been a time of unprecedented happiness and excitement. With New Year's Eve approaching, the *Evening Herald* wrote that 'the year that ends in a few hours will long be remembered as indeed a momentous year', from the heights of elation to the depths of shock and grief. As the 'Tatler's parade' in the *Irish Times* put it, it was 'a year of great joy and harrowing sorrow'.

The avalanche of news stories had been overwhelming. Journalists had to scratch their heads to find the right adjectives to do justice to such a year. By year's end these included 'enthralling', 'stupendous', 'exultant', 'bewildering', 'rapturous', 'mystifying' and 'cataclysmic'.

When New Year's Eve arrived, everyone celebrated the passing of 1963 and the birth of the new year. Nowhere in Ireland was the tradition more revered than at the ringing of the bells at Christ Church Cathedral in Dublin. And no person had experienced it more intimately than William Lynch, the conductor of the bell-ringers. Born in 1889, he was brought into the belfry for his apprenticeship at the age of thirteen. At seventy-four he 'had not missed a New Year's in the bell tower for sixty-one years – since 1902'. From his perch above the city, he had first gazed down on cobblestones and carriages. He had seen years of struggle and tumult, and of joy and festivity.

But *never* had there been a year so outlandish as 1963, with its unremitting emotional ups and downs. On 29 December the *Irish Independent* attempted to capture the feeling it evoked:

'It was the best of times, it was the worst of times ...' The words with which Dickens opened his 'A Tale of Two Cities'. ... Few would quarrel with them as a description of the year that is ending. It was an epoch of belief, of incredulity ... it was a season of light, a season of darkness ...

The *Independent* deemed 1963 the 'most unique year of the century'.

———

In the final minutes of the year, crowds at Christ Church sang and danced as car horns and ships' sirens wailed. Yet, the *Irish Press* reported, 'it was one of the quietest New Years we have had here in a long time.' People's spirits were not as soaring, nor were the songs sung with the same gusto. The mood was subdued, perhaps melancholy. Possibly there was some relief after a year that had been so wrenching and wearying. As Noel Hughes so plainly put it, 'an *awful* lot of things came in that one year – at *one* time!'

Looking back some fifty years later, Bill Herlihy, a former Garda Chief Superintendent who had served in the security detail for President Kennedy, muses that 'it was such an eventful year' that at the end of it 'people had had *enough!*'

In its year-end edition the *Irish Independent* best captured the essence of that most extraordinary year.

In Ireland, 1963 was a year of drama, joy, tragedy, contrasts and contradictions. It is hardly conceivable that in our time so many great and
shattering events will again fall within the span of one short year.

*   *   *   *   *   *

POSTSCRIPT

In late December 1963 Michael McGregor wrote to a Dublin newspaper lambasting the Government for 'twiddling its thumbs' in failing to have erected a fitting memorial to President John F. Kennedy. He pointed out that a number of other countries had already done so. All senior Irish political figures had fervently supported the proposal.

Many years later the 'thumb-twiddling' still continued.[222] Una Shaw, who had stood in rapture at the Parnell Monument as President Kennedy passed by in his limousine, recalled in 2015 that:

> they're still talking about a memorial of some kind. I've heard people say there's going to be one – but I've never seen any! He was really loved here!

Many older people who witnessed his visit still fume when the subject of broken promises about the memorial is raised. One 81-year-old resident of Coleraine Street in Dublin expressed his displeasure with the Government's neglect:

> It was the people who said there should be a monument or memorial to him in Dublin – and the Government reneged on that! There's none! If the Government wanted to do it, they would have done it!

In September 2015, in reply to an enquiry by the author, Dr Mary Clark, Director of Archives at the Dublin Public Library, explained the situation:

> In the aftermath of President Kennedy's tragic assassination, there were plans to erect a monument to him [in Dublin] – but this never went ahead.
>
> There was also a plan to rename Westmoreland Street 'President Kennedy Street', but the street traders [shop-owners] were opposed to it, as it would cost them money to change their letterheads – so, again, that proposal came to nothing.

Thus, despite the promises of the Government to the people of the city to erect a fitting memorial to President Kennedy – who had captured the hearts of Dubliners as had no other – the plan was thwarted by letterheads. Such is Dublin's history.

NOTES

Prologue

Christine Longford, *A Biography of Dublin* (London: Methuen, 1936); Eric Burns, *1920: The Year That Made the Decade Roar* (New York and London: Pegasus Books, 2015).

Chapter 1

2   'You squirm even as you marvel', *Irish Press*, 4 December 1962, p. 12.

3   'Irish Weather Online' for December 1962, http://www.irishweatheronline.com.

4   'Snow victim tells of night long ordeal', *Irish Press*, 2 January 1963, p. 4.

5   'Dublin gives new year a rousing welcome', *Irish Times*, 1 January 1963, p. 1.

Chapter 2

6   'Snow victim tells of night long ordeal', *Irish Press*, 2 January 1963, p. 4.

7   'Man escapes quicksands but trapped horse dies', *Irish Press, 1* January 1963, p. 1.

8   'Grim news of Wicklow hardship', *Evening Herald*, 2 January 1963, p. 5.

9   Ibid.

10   'TV engineers snowed in on Kippure', *Irish Press*, 1 January 1963, p. 1.

11   'Farmer, dogs die: inquiry ordered', *Irish Press*, 1 January 1963, p. 1.

12   'Fighting the weather', *Irish Independent*, 3 January 1963, p. 8.

13   'Aid by air to marooned families', *Evening Herald*, 2 January 1963, p. 1.

14   'This is the time of crisis', *Evening Herald*, 3 January 1963, p. 1.

15   'His only food was turnips', *Evening Herald*, 7 January 1963, p. 3.

16   'They were glad to get our parcels', *Evening Herald*, 5 January 1963, p. 5.

17   'People still cut off', *Irish Independent*, 7 January 1963, p. 9.

18   'Snow blitz brings traffic nightmares to Dublin', *Evening Herald*, 12 January 1963, p. 1.

19   'Fox up a tree', *Evening Herald*, 23 January 1963, p. 3.

20   Ibid.

21   '"Mass hysteria" in the Green' (letter), *Evening Herald*, 3 January 1963, p. 4.

22   Ibid.

23   'Shame on us!', *Evening Herald*, 15 January 1963, p. 1.

24   'Blizzards are back', *Irish Independent*, 21 January 1963, p. 1.

25   'Herald Relief Fund', *Evening Herald*, 28 January 1963, p. 6.

Chapter 3

26   'Cardinal D'Alton', *Irish Independent*, 2 February 1963. p. 14

27   'Silent crowds watch cortege pass through', *Evening Herald*, 2 February 1963, p. 1.

28　'Road safety appeal jolts public conscience', *Irish Independent*, 4 February 1963, p. 8.

29　'Road safety appeal jolts public conscience', *Irish Independent*, 4 February 1963, p. 8.

30　'Device will detect speed defaulters', *Irish Independent*, 11 January 1963, p. 13.

31　'Purchase tax is coming', *Evening Herald*, 22 February 1963, p. 1.

Chapter 4

32　'Bubbling Humour in Molly Review', *Irish Independent*, 5 March 1963, p. 11.

33　'Hands Off St Stephen's Green', *Evening Herald*, 4 March 1963, p. 4.

34　Ibid.

35　'He Faced Death for 95 Minutes', *Evening Herald*, 5 March 1963, p. 1.

36　Ibid.

37　'24 Branches Will Cost £2,000,000', *Irish Independent*, 6 March 1963, p. 1.

38　'St Stephen's Green "Must Remain Unchanged"', *Irish Independent*, 6 March 1963, p. 11.

39　'Supermarkets', *Irish Press*, 8 March 1963, p. 8.

40　'Which Type of Driver Are You', *Evening Herald*, 8 March 1963, p. 6.

41　'Don't Sneer at the Long-distance Runners – It's We Layabouts Who Are the Crackpots' by Douglas Coupar, *Evening Herald*, 11 March 1963, p. 6.

42　'Proved Their Worth – On the Road to Bray' by Tom Hennigan, *Evening Herald*, 18 March 1963, pp. 8–9.

43　'Bus Strike', *Irish Times*, 18 March 1963, p. 7.

44　'Tragic Story of Climbers' Deaths', *Evening Herald*, 27 March 1963, p. 1.

Chapter 5

45　'Says President Kennedy will visit New Ross', *Irish Independent*, 2 April 1963, p. 1.

46　'Plea to keep canal open' (letter), *Evening Herald*, 3 April 1963, p. 6.

47　'The young ladies', *Evening Herald*, 3 April 1963, p. 6.

48　'Footsore Dublin', *Evening Herald*, 8 April 1963, p. 1.

49　Ibid.

50　'Will attack purchase tax proposal', *Irish Independent*, 10 April 1963, p. 1.

51　'Busless Easter Sunday', *Sunday Independent*, 15 April 1963, p. 1.

52　'Talk of pickets' (editorial), *Evening Herald*, 30 April 1963, p. 8.

Chapter 6

53　'"Z-Car" tactics of Dublin bandits', *Evening Herald*, 4 May 1963, p. 1.

54　'Masked gang rob Dublin mail van', *Irish Times*, 4 May 1963, p. 1.

55　'Sister is charged with poisoning', *Evening Herald*, 6 May 1963, p. 5.

56　'Statements read at murder trial', *Evening Herald*, 9 May 1963, p. 9.

57　'Dublin's skyline is changing rapidly', *Irish Independent*, 4 May 1963, p. 8.

58　'Brother had affair – accused', *Evening Herald*, 8 May 1963, p. 7.

59　'Sister is charged with poisoning', *Evening Herald*, 6 May 1963, p. 5.

60　'"I will go back", says Miss Clougher', *Evening Herald*, 11 May 1963, p. 1.

Chapter 7

61   'More sunshine forecast after brilliant Whit weekend', *Irish Independent*, 3 June 1963, p. 1.

62   'Weather caused the collapse', *Irish Press*, 4 July 1963, p. 7.

63   'Pontiff slowly dying', *Irish Independent*, 1 June 1963, p. 1.

64   'Two killed as home collapses', *Irish Press*, 3 June 1963, p. 5.

65   'Pontiff slowly dying', *Irish Independent*, 1 June 1963, p. 1.

66   'World-wide tributes', *Irish Independent*, 4 June 1963, p. 13.

67   'The battle of supermarkets', *Evening Herald*, 5 June 1963, p. 9.

68   Ibid.

Chapter 8

69   'Intensity of storm explained', *Evening Herald*, 12 June 1963, p. 3.

70   'Flood havoc hits Dublin suburbs', *Irish Times*, 12 June 1963, p. 1.

71   'Thunderstorm chaos', *Irish Press*, 12 June 1963, p. 1.

72   Ibid.

73   'Flood havoc hits Dublin suburbs', *Irish Times*, 12 June 1963, p. 1.

74   'Mopping-up operations widespread', *Evening Herald*, 12 June 1963, p. 1.

75   'Flood havoc hits Dublin suburbs', *Irish Times*, 12 June 1963, p. 1.

76   'That was a day that was' (editorial), *Evening Herald*, 12 June 1963, p. 8.

Chapter 9

77   '2 houses collapse', *Evening Herald*, 12 June 1963, p. 1.

78   '2 girls die as houses fall', *Irish Press*, 13 June 1963, p. 1.

79   'Stunned people of Fenian Street', *Evening Herald*, 13 June 1963, p. 1.

80   'Lethal collapse' (editorial), *Irish Times*, 13 June 1963, p. 9.

81   'Four have died already', *Evening Herald*, 13 June 1963, p. 10.

82   'Tragedies of the tenements', *Evening Herald*, 15 June 1963, p. 6.

83   'I walk through streets of fear', *Evening Herald*, 14 June 1963, p. 10.

84   'American pianist casts a spell', *Evening Herald*, 17 June 1963, p. 7.

85   Ibid.

86   'All eyes on Irish Derby', *Evening Herald*, 17 June 1963, p. 7.

87   'Million-pound race', *Irish Independent*, 28 June 1963, p. 15.

Chapter 10

88   'Full-scale coverage of a great occasion', *Irish Independent*, 22 June 1963, p. 11.

89   'The outside broadcasters' (JFK Stories: Part 1), *Irish Independent*, 15 June 2013, p. 24.

90   'Going gay for Kennedy', *Irish Independent*, 22 June 1963. p. 11.

91   'Government wins on tax bill by one vote', *Irish Independent*, 26 June 1963, p. 1.

Chapter 11

92   'President Kennedy', *Irish Press*, 26 June 1963, p. 8

93   Ryan Tubridy, *JFK in Ireland* (London: Collins, 2010), p. 93.

94   'Dublin takes Kennedy to its heart', *Irish Press*, 27 June 1963, p. 1.

95   'Dublin's warm welcome', *Irish Independent*, 27 June 1963, p. 1.

96   Ryan Tubridy, *JFK in Ireland* (London: Collins, 2010), p. 99.

97   'Ticker tape tribute in O'Connell Street', *Irish Independent*, 27 June 1963, p. 14.

98   'Dubliners cheered along eight mile procession route', *Irish Independent*, 27 June 1963, p. 6.

99   'Nothing half-hearted about the cheers', *Irish Times*, 27 June 1963, p. 7.

100   'Oh, what a beautiful president', *Irish Times*, 27 June 1963, p. 7.

101   'Nothing half-hearted about the cheers', *Irish Times*, 27 June 1963, p. 7.

102   'Dublin takes Kennedy to its heart', *Irish Press*, 27 June 1963, p. 1.

103   'Quiet haven after a storm of people', *Irish Times*, 27 June 1963, p. 3.

104   'The capital's great welcome', *Irish Press*, 27 June 1963, p. 2.

105   'Oh, what a beautiful president', *Irish Times*, 27 June 1963, p. 7.

Chapter 12

106   Ryan Tubridy, *JFK in Ireland* (London: Collins, 2010), p. 108.

107   'The capital's great welcome', *Irish Press*, 27 June 1963, p. 3.

108   'A big family picnic', *Irish Press*, 28 June 1963, p. 3.

109   'Wexford's welcome home', *Irish Independent*, 28 June 1963, p. 1.

110   'A big family picnic', *Irish Press*, 28 June 1963, p. 1.

111   'Kennedy meets the people: President is mobbed at party', *Irish Independent*, 28 June 1963, p. 14.

112   'He just has an aura' (JFK Stories), *Irish Independent*, 15 June 2013, p. 31.

113   'Kennedy says "au revoir"', *Irish Independent*, 1 July 1963, p. 12.

114   'Green giant' (JFK Stories: Part 2), *Irish Independent*, 17 June 2013, p. 2.

115   'Deep impact' (JFK Stories: Part 1), *Irish Independent*, 15 June 2013, p. 7.

Chapter 13

116   'Derby sensation at the Curragh', *Evening Herald*, 29 June 1963, p. 1.

117   Ibid.

118   Ibid.

119   'A Pope is crowned', *Irish Independent*, 1 July 1963, p. 10.

120   'Well-known theatre to be sold', *Irish Independent*, 2 July 1963, p. 1.

121   'Olympia Theatre now up for sale', *Irish Times*, 2 July 1963, p. 1.

122   'Clothes torn from victim of lightning', *Irish Press*, 6 July 1963, p. 9.

123   'Racing pigeon fanciers lose birds', *Evening Herald*, 2 July 1963, p. 9.

124   'Relko: chances of a parallel remote', *Evening Herald*, 6 July 1963, p. 6.

125   Ibid.

126   A cloud of suspicion would long hang over Relko and the bizarre Irish Derby incident. In the following two years the horse would have a chequered record, superbly winning some races, disappointingly losing others he should have won. British newspapers, including the *Daily Express*, would assert with certainty that Relko 'failed a drug test'. Sometimes newspapers reported that 'substances detected could not be positively identified' as illegal. Drug-testing methods fifty years ago were not nearly as accurate as they are today. Therefore there will never be a definitive verdict on the Irish Derby debacle in 1963.

127   'They will tell why Olympia is up for sale', *Sunday Independent*, 7 July 1963, p. 6.

128   'Crisis in Dame Street' (editorial), *Evening Herald*, 11 July 1963, p. 6.

129   This episode is documented in detail in Kevin C. Kearns, *The Legendary 'Lugs' Branigan: Ireland's Most Famed Garda* (Dublin: Gill & Macmillan, 2015).

130   'Publicans will fight Guinness's plans for more Dublin houses', *Irish Times*, 29 July 1963, p. 1.

131   'Bolshoi Ballet's superb dancing', *Irish Times*, 30 July 1963, p. 3.

132   Ibid.

133   'Protests in our streets', *Evening Herald*, 30 July 1963, p. 1.

Chapter 14

134   'Dublin's paper strewn streets' (letter), *Evening Herald*, 16 August 1963, p. 6.

135   'Dublin's dirty streets' (letter), *Evening Herald*, 7 August 1963, p. 4.

136   Ibid.

137   'Keeping Dublin tidy' (editorial), *Evening Herald*, 9 August 1963, p. 6.

138   'The homeless on the streets', *Evening Herald*, 19 August 1963, p, 4.

139   'All the world the show!' *Irish Independent*, 7 August 1963, p. 8.

140   'This year's horse show unique', *Irish Times*, 6 August 1963, p. 1.

141   'When horse is king' (editorial), *Irish Independent*, 6 August 1963, p. 10.

142   'This year's horse show unique', *Irish Times*, 6 August 1963, p. 1.

143   'Two receptions open show's social round', *Irish Times*, 6 August 1963, p. 9.

144   Ibid.

145   'Ireland wins the Aga Khan Trophy', *Irish Times*, 10 August 1963, p. 1.

Chapter 15

146   'Missing girl's body found in Dublin', *Irish Independent*, 21 August 1963, p. 5.

147   Ibid.

148   'Student on murder charge', *Irish Independent*, 21 August 1963, p. 1.

149   'Irish road toll goes up and up', *Irish Independent*, 21 August 1963, p. 5.

150   'New turn in murder case', *Evening Herald*, 22 August 1963, p. 1.

151   'Nurse's clue in murder case', *Evening Herald*, 24 August 1963, p. 1.

152   'Shan Mohangi's Dublin past comes back to haunt him', *Irish Times*, 25 March 2009.

Chapter 16

153   'Strange light observed over Howth', *Evening Herald*, 3 September 1963, p. 5.

154   'Speed limits or tests' (letter), *Evening Herald*, 7 September 1963, p. 6.

155   'Shark threat ends Galway Bay swim', *Irish Independent*, 10 September 1963, p. 1.

156   Ibid.

157   Ibid.

158   'Stones are our latest export', *Irish Independent*, 11 September 1963, p. 1

159   'The bingo menace' (letter), *Evening Herald*, 25 September 1963, p. 8.

160   'Port of Dublin' (editorial), *Irish Independent*, 19 September 1963, p. 10.

161   'I forecast a Dublin victory', *Evening Herald*, 21 September 1963, p. 10.

162   'Disorderly scenes in Dublin', *Irish Independent*, 23 September 1963, p. 9.

Chapter 17

163   'Pop craze', *Irish Press*, 5 November 1963, p. 5.

164   In the interest of disclosure, it should be pointed out that the author of this book still (2018) uses several manual typewriters. These require a regular tune-up – a service now costing more than the original price of the typewriters themselves. And well worth it!

165   'Drunk driving' (editorial), *Irish Press*, 5 October 1963, p. 7.

166   'Main cause of accidents', *Irish Independent*, 4 October 1963, p. 10.

167   'Drink and drugs', *Irish Independent*, 7 October 1963, p. 10.

168   'Canals' (letter), *Irish Independent*, 22 October 1963, p. 13.

169   'Apathy in the city' (editorial), *Evening Herald*, 19 October 1963, p. 7.

170   'Halloween to escape tax', *Irish Independent*, 30 October 1963, p. 7.

171   'This "hallowed eve" of a glorious feast day', *Irish Press*, 31 October 1963, p. 12.

Chapter 18

172   'Ode to the Beatles' (letter), *Evening Herald*, 5 November 1963, p. 2.

173   'Moe led the way' (letter), *Evening Herald*, 7 November 1963, p. 12.

174   'Gardaí prepare for "Operation Beatles"', *Evening Herald*, 6 November 1963, p. 1.

175   'Dublin is braced for the Beatles', *Irish Times*, 7 November 1963, p. 6.

176   'Liverpool beat beaten by audience screams', *Irish Times*, 8 November 1963, p. 8.

177   'Many injured as Beatle crowds run riot in city', *Irish Press*, 8 November 1963, p. 1.

178   'The Beatles taken to safety in "Evening Herald" van', *Evening Herald*, 8 November 1963, p. 7.

179   'Irish hoodlums on the loose' (letter), *Evening Herald*, 12 November 1963, p. 6.

180   'Battle scenes for the Beatles', *Evening Herald*, 8 November 1963, p. 1.

181   'An Irishman's Diary', *Irish Times*, 9 November 1963, p. 11.

182   'Going places', *Evening Herald*, 8 November 1963, p. 15.

183   Ibid.

Chapter 19

184 'Vigorous protest at plans for Killarney mansion', *Irish Times*, 14 November 1963, p. 1.

185 Frank McDonald, *The Destruction of Dublin* (Dublin: Gill & Macmillan, 1985), p.18.

186 Father Paul Freeney, 'Dublin, how are ye!' in *Dublin: A Living City?* (Dublin: Living City Group, 1972), p. 2.

187 Fergal Tobin, *The Best of Decades: Ireland in the 1960s* (Dublin: Gill & Macmillan, 1984), p. 84.

188 'The changing face of Dublin', *Sunday Independent*, 17 November 1963, p. 12

189 'The pub is in peril', *Sunday Independent*, 17 November 1963, p. 12.

190 'Talking about pubs', *Irish Licensing World*, June 1968, p. 15.

191 '£20,000 canal plan was turned down', *Irish Times*, 13 November 1963, p. 9

192 'Turnover tax' (letter), *Evening Herald*, 12 November 1963, p. 6.

193 'Evil within is "difficult for man to accept"', *Irish Independent*, 21 November 1963, p. 14.

Chapter 20

194 'Wexford cousins broken by grief', *Irish Press*, 23 November 1963, p. 7.

195 Ibid.

196 'Ireland mourns a son', *Irish Times*, 23 November 1963, p. 8.

197 'News numbs Irish nation', *Irish Independent*, 23 November 1963, p. 16

198 'No more to give' (editorial), *Irish Independent*, 23 November 1963, p. 12.

199 'Jewish tribute', *Irish Independent*, 25 November 1963, p. 13.

200 'Grief just as deep in Ireland', *Irish Independent*, 25 November 1963, p. 17.

201 'Nurse's race to attend funeral', *Irish Independent*, 26 November 1963, p. 6

202 'A day of mourning', *Irish Independent*, 27 November 1963, p. 1.

203 'Ireland's love' (letter), *Evening Herald*, 27 November 1963, p. 6.

Chapter 21

204 'Sloe-gin pudding for President', *Irish Independent*, 21 December 1963, p. 9

205 'Liner victim's premonition', *Irish Independent*, 28 December 1963, p. 1.

206 'Irish doctor's heroism', *Irish Independent*, 25–27 December 1963, p. 1.

207 'Cavan man in sea for five hours', *Irish Independent*, 31 December 1963, p. 1.

208 Ibid.

209 Ibid.

210 'Dublin families on blazing liner', *Evening Herald*, 23 December 1963, p. 1.

211 'No sign of life on doomed liner', *Irish Press*, 24 December 1963, p. 1.

212 'Irish doctor's heroism', *Irish Independent*, 25–7 December 1963, p. 1.

213 'Dublin families on blazing liner', *Evening Herald*, 23 December 1963, p. 1.

214 '877 rescued from blazing cruise ship', *Irish Times*, 24 December 1963, p. 1.

215 Ibid.

216 'Many Irish aboard', *Irish Press*, 24 December 1963, p. 1.

217   '877 rescued from blazing cruise ship', *Irish Times*, 24 December 1963, p. 1.
218   'Rescue vessel docks at Madeira', *Evening Herald*, 24 December 1963, p. 1.
219   'Telegram brought joy news', *Evening Herald*, 24 December 1963, p. 1.
220   '"You are a widow", woman is told', *Evening Herald*, 28 December 1963, p. 5.
221   Ibid.

Postscript

222   There *is* a John F. Kennedy Memorial Park and Arboretum in New Ross, Co. Wexford.

INDEX